The Boater's *Cookbook*

450 Quick & Easy Galley-Tested Recipes

SYLVIA WILLIAMS DABNEY

Skyhorse Publishing

Skyhorse books may be purchased in bulk at special discounts for sales promotion, corporate gifts, fund-raising, or educational purposes. Special editions can also be created to specifications. For details, contact the Special Sales Department, Skyhorse Publishing, 307 West 36th Street, 11th Floor, New York, NY 10018 or info@skyhorsepublishing.com.

Skyhorse® and Skyhorse Publishing are registered trademarks of Skyhorse Publishing, Inc.®, a Delaware corporation.

Visit our website at www.skyhorsepublishing.com.

10 9 8 7 6 5 4 3 2 1

Library of Congress Cataloging-in-Publication Data is available on file.

Cover design by Tom Lau and Mona Lin
Cover photograph by iStockphoto

Hardcover ISBN: 9781944824280
Ebook ISBN: 9781944824297

Printed in China

To my father, Daniel Cyrus Williams, who raised me with affection, a zest for life, and to always seek adventure, and to my husband, Stanley, who continues to give me all of that!

Orchid Bay Resort and Marina, Abacos, Bahama Islands, taken by Steve Stresau, who along with his wife Karen, cruised throughout the Bahama Islands aboard their Tayana 42 sailboat, *Blue Lotus*.

Contents

Introduction
Where It All Started

Though I was raised on a ranch and my husband Stanley on a golf course, after we went sailing one glorious afternoon in the Caribbean, the sailing bug bit us—and bit us hard. Stanley quit his job just three days after our first sailing adventure and I quit mine three short months after that. There was no turning back from our new discovery—a life of freedom through travel. We moved into our fourth sailboat, a *Valiant 40* named *Native Sun,* in 1975 and lived aboard for fifteen years. We cruised some sixty thousand miles offshore, and still have our *Native Sun* to this day.

Stanley and I were so smitten with our newfound passion for sailing, that upon our return the following weekend from the Caribbean, we bought our first boat, a charming little *Ericson 23.* The only problem was that we knew virtually nothing about sailing, so we convinced the broker who sold us our boat to include lessons in the deal. After only four lessons he said, "You need to go out and practice and get some firsthand experience on a boat." We took his advice shortly after our last lesson, and went down to Shilshole Bay Marina in Seattle, Washington where our little *Amalie* was docked. (We named our first boat after Charlotte Amalie, the capital of the US Virgin Islands where Stanley and I first sailed.) We stopped at every boat that looked as if someone was aboard. These sailors were so kind to young dreamers like us and we will never forget their kindnesses when we simply asked if we could tour their boats. We were so starstruck by a life of sailing that it never dawned on us that these boats were these people's homes, that they could have been in the middle of dinner, or might think us rude. We were often asked to join these people for dinner or to race with them on the Wednesday night Seattle "beer can races." We never said no, and after we permanently moved aboard our own boat a few years later and met young people on the docks with the same new dreams we once had, we always asked them aboard. I smile now thinking of the wondrous prospect of living aboard and exploring the world on their faces.

Stanley and I both love to cook and in fact, we met while he was working his way through the University of Washington, cooking at a Seattle seafood restaurant. Growing up, I was sent to my parents' best friend's fishing and hunting lodge five hundred miles north of Seattle every summer. Here I earned my keep starting at twelve years old until I graduated university; hauling firewood to the cabins, cleaning cabins at the lodge, riding tractors as we brought in the hay, rounding up cattle and horses, and learning to cook from the most incredible woman

I've ever known, Millie Hamilton, at the well-known Ten-ee-ah Lodge in British Columbia, Canada. I loved every moment of my years there and Stanley and I still spend a month every year in our own cabin, on a beautiful wilderness lake just fifteen miles from Ten-ee-ah Lodge.

Even with our first small boat, we realized we could eat and prepare fabulous food aboard, but some of it, because of the lack of standing room, was prepared at home and brought aboard later. Eighteen months after we took delivery of our first boat, our new *Ericson 27* arrived. We called her *Amalie II*. It had standing room and a real gimbaled stove and oven—and that's when the real fun began. Hearty appetites can be stimulated by intense activity like sailing, so we spent weeknights poring over our favorite recipes from family, from Millie, from the restaurant Stanley had worked at, and from an already bourgeoning collection of recipes from fellow sailors who cheerfully shared hints for storing dry goods, fresh food, and what menus worked best at anchor or heeled over while crossing the Straits of Juan de Fuca. On Friday nights, we shopped, stored our goods on board, and headed off, regardless of the unpredictable Seattle weather, for a weekend of sailing (and on special occasions, a week or longer cruise up to the San Juan Islands and into Canada).

Our third boat, an *Islander 36* named *Amalie III*, was launched just eighteen months after the delivery of our *Ericson 27* and now, I had a real, total, and complete galley and I was in heaven. We realized early on that this was not a boat we wanted to possibly sail around the world, though it was a wonderful boat for our sailing adventures between Canada and Seattle. That's when we contacted Bob Perry, a man we met at a Seattle boat show where he and Nathan Rothman were putting chicken wire together and demonstrating the making of a concrete sailboat designed by Jay Benford. Concrete was not an option for us, so we put our heads together and the *Valiant 40* was born, with Stanley being the marketing manager, Nathan the president, and Bob the designer of Valiant Yachts. We had hoped to have Hull #1, but Stanley was good at his job and thus we kept getting bumped, until we finally took delivery of Hull #9. We lived aboard and cruised every free day we had and almost every weekend.

Smitten, enamored, infatuated, hooked, obsessed, fanatical, enthusiastic, and passionate are all good words to describe the last forty-plus years of our lives as boaters. We know there are others out there who have the same feelings and the same passion for cooking and good food, even while cruising or making offshore passages. As longtime sailors having sailed more than sixty thousand offshore miles, we've learned to be creative, altering traditional meals and combinations of dishes using local herbs and ingredients while enjoying both the preparing and sharing of wonderful meals with friends. We always took advantage of local markets, local food, and people's willingness everywhere we went to talk food. Most local people love to share their recipes and are happy to show you how they prepare everything from Caribbean conch to Alaskan salmon and more exotic fare the further we sailed from the continental

US. The necessity of a well-stored pantry is as essential as a well-prepared tool kit and engine spares kit. You may find that you change up your salads from arugula and romaine to cabbage and carrots depending on local availability, but you'll always eat well aboard ship if you are adventurous and well stocked.

Stanley is still involved with the boating community in manufacturing and marketing, and now for many years as a well-known and beloved broker and owner of Offshore Atlantic Yachts. I continue to write his listings and help with contracts while still holding, after thirty years, a 100 Ton US Coast Guard Master's license—both of us experimenting with food and recipes all the time. New acquaintances quickly become good friends in the sailing community, probably because of the kindred spirit that weaves itself through all of us, and because as adventurous travelers, most of us know that we'll soon be parting ways for other distant shores. Some decide to "buddy boat" for years and some reconnect in unimaginable places after years and thousands of miles of cruising. Good friends, sailing, and adventures are all part of the stories of the cruising lifestyle. Food shared with new and old friends, either aboard or offshore, are one of the most memorable times that you will talk about for years to come. It is the pure joy of sharing, laughing, and spending time together.

This book shares the story of our travels and what brought us to so many adventures in cooking aboard ship. With all the love and experience we've garnered over these years, I am passing along my best advice, cooking tips, and highly personal collection of exciting and dynamic fare and recipes to all of you who are dreaming or living the dream of living on board. I hope I will engage you with the history, lore, personal anecdotes, and stories of the boats and people who shared so many of their favorite recipes with us on our many cruising adventures. Boating puts you on a magic carpet ride with the whole world before you. For the new cruisers who are just beginning their cruising dreams with weekend cruises around saltwater bays or land-locked lakes, or the cruisers who are finally fulfilling their new lifestyle of offshore cruising to distant islands and turquoise waters, this book will prepare you with hundreds of recipes including stories and sailing lore from longtime sailors. Remember: when you're on board, you are home!

Boat Appétit!
Captain Sylvia Williams Dabney

CHAPTER 1
Bringing Provisions Aboard

Let's talk bugs. First of all, most of the bugs you find on a boat can fly, so the first and best prevention is to have screens up at every porthole, every hatch, and as cumbersome as it can be, keep a screened door or screened hatch-board in the companionway for when you're eating down below or settled in for the night or after you've gotten all your dishes and food in the cockpit and your guests have arrived for a wonderful on-deck or cockpit dinner.

We never had cockroaches, though they can be a common problem for boaters, especially in warmer climates. We were probably overcautious bringing every and anything aboard the *Native Sun*, but we learned from our dear friend and longtime sailor Captain Charlie Mead exactly where we'd find cockroaches and even scorpions in the goods we brought aboard: cockroaches live and lay their eggs in almost every type of paper or cardboard product. This fact resulted in our never bringing anything aboard in its original container and never bringing aboard paper bags, newspapers, magazines, books , mail, or anything in cardboard before first doing one very important thing: thoroughly inspecting every item. He taught us that cockroaches can live between the pages of the smallest paperback book, and that paper grocery bags can have unseen eggs in the folds of the bottom. Our fruits and vegetables, canned goods, replacement parts, even our guests' luggage went through these same vigorous checks to keep bugs at bay—but with this effort came excellent results. The only bug we ever saw on *Native Sun* was one that Stanley named Fred.

We tried to remove as much packaging as possible while we were still ashore to make the process a little less tedious at anchor. Sometimes we'd pass a plastic dishpan or large bucket to the person on the dock or dingy so that inspected gear and supplies could be loaded aboard a little easier in these containers. Once everything was on board, each item was put in the area where it belonged for stowage or sorting: laundry bags were put on the main settees until they could be emptied; mail, books, and magazines were put on the chart table until we could properly sort through them; all canned and frozen goods were put in the sink until they could be properly stowed; hard fresh fruits and vegetables such as potatoes, carrots, limes, and lemons were dunked in a small sink of fresh water with a very small amount of bleach to kill off any bugs or eggs that might have gone unseen and then dunked again in a small basin of fresh water before being laid out to dry.

One evening while Stanley and I were eating dinner down below because of an onslaught of "no see-ums," those tiny bugs that swarm and munch on you just after sunset if you happen to be anchored too close to a beach or mangrove area, we realized that we had neglected to put the screen on the forward hatch. As Stanley was going forward to secure the screen, this three-inch flying green insect came right toward me. I was waving my arms and screaming when it suddenly went through the finger hole latch of the engine room door. Stanley prepared himself, opened the engine room door, and there was this ugly insect. The first thing we said to each other was, "He can turn his head . . . he has a neck!" Stanley tried putting a cup upside down on him, but he was too big for the cup and every time we moved, so did he. For some reason, Stanley decided to give this bug a name and for half an hour, we chased "Fred" from bow to stern. Stanley never did have the chance to put the forward screen in after Fred had come aboard, and as luck would have it, Fred finally flew out from whence he came . . . the forward hatch. We never overlooked a hatch or port again when putting up our bug screens.

What Captain Charlie taught us was three-part. Remove all packing material, bags or netting, visually and manually inspect absolutely everything that comes on board, and clean fruits and vegetables as soon as they come aboard. We have always been thankful for this simple advice and the task of renewing stores aboard became as routine and normal to us as making sure the anchor was properly secured before we left *Native Sun* to go ashore. It was just simply part of our sailing life routine. Thanks, Captain Charlie.

CHAPTER 2
Galley Storage

When we made the decision to live full-time aboard our boat, I had no idea where to store all the things necessary for cruising, safety, wearing, mechanical parts, personal necessities, and especially troublesome for me, all the food and cooking gear I knew I needed to have on board. My always positive husband Stanley kept saying "the boat will talk to you," and that's exactly what happened.

When I first stocked the galley, I put things where they seemed to fit best. I soon learned that rooting through cabinets in the main saloon for items I used on a regular basis was ridiculous. It's imperative to keep a list of food items, how many of each you currently have, and where the specific location of that item is. I found it easier to keep a small recipe box with A–Z index dividers than to pull out a computer while I was cooking. For instance, canned tuna was, according to my cards, "Tuna – 6 – MSP-3." This meant that I had six cans of tuna and they were in the **M**ain **S**alon **P**ort cabinet **#3**; each cabinet had a numbered piece of tape on it starting with the smaller number most forward and ending with the larger number most toward the aft of the boat. With this system, anyone on board could find anything, from coffee to paper towels, from the good wine to the cooking wine. As soon as an item was opened, the grocery list on the inside of the pantry door was added to so that when I opened one or two of those cans of tuna, that same number of cans of tuna was written on the grocery list for our next provisioning stop. By using this system I could figure out if I really had enough tuna for a casserole I wanted to make or if I should wait until we arrived at a provisioning place before I used the last often coveted can of tuna or whatever item it was.

Grains

Flour storage was at first a real mystery to me. I kept it high in a cabinet on the starboard side, just at the same level on the boat as our very dark, steel-gray boot stripe. On one of our first, very long offshore cruises, we had been on a starboard tack for nearly a week when I decided to make bread. When I opened the flour, it was actually moving. I threw everything out, cleaned out my cupboard, and with my always present squirt bottle of bleach and water mixture I sprayed and cleaned the area where the flour had been. When we arrived at our destination, I called an old sailing friend who had worked at General Mills, and what I learned was that these little bugs' eggs are present in the wheat and survive milling and can hatch if the flour has been hanging around for too long or sitting in warm or humid conditions. I restocked all of my flour goods after that conversation, and they were then and permanently stored in a lower locker where the hull was white and not nearly as hot as behind a nearly black ten-inch boot stripe, which was most likely one inch from my flour . . . a very hot and humid location. I never had that problem again and that's when I realized that the boat may actually be talking to me.

Kitchen Junk Drawer Paraphernalia

We all have our favorite knives, serving and mixing spoons, and spatulas. We also have lots and lots of knives, but in reality, there are probably three knives that are our favorites, fit our hands the best, or slice exactly as we want them to slice. It's the same with all that "kitchen junk-drawer paraphernalia" that we've all had in our land-based homes. On our boat, I suffered from a lack of drawer space in the galley, so I found a wonderful ships carpenter in Annapolis who took the top, shallowest drawer and made special slots in that drawer for my most used knives. Actually, the drawer was so shallow, it wasn't good for much else. I still had the whole left side of the drawer available when he was finished and found that it was a perfect place for my potato peeler, knife sharpener, can opener, measuring spoons, long zester, and nesting

measuring cups. I can't stress enough the importance of stacking galley equipment such as measuring cups, and for these essential galley pieces to be stainless steel—never use aluminum in a salt water environment. For the remainder of my knives, which I really thought I could not live aboard without, including a filet knife, large cleaver, and several other odd-sized knives, I bought a beautiful teak Wüsthof Under-Cabinet Swinger Knife Block. It has eight slots and one slot for my sharpening steel. I chose to mount it under my over-the-sink cabinet and Stanley installed a small sliding lock so that when we were offshore or not using the knives, it could be locked with the handles facing the bulkhead. No chance ever of them coming out of that wonderful knife holder. A friend of ours from Texas, Hugh, opted to mount his Wüsthof Under-Cabinet Swinger Knife Block on a bulkhead side, right next to the galley sinks, which is another great option. The old-fashioned home style knife block is just too dangerous on board. It's dangerous anytime you're sailing, heeled over, or suffering the unexpected weather change that tosses your boat on its ear while you're on a weekend cruise or offshore.

Spices

My spices were stored in two separate areas. I had room over the double sinks on the bulkhead to have built and mounted a six-foot-long spice rack. Mine had a light smoky Lexan front which allowed me to see the bottles, but these bottles were always stored in alphabetical order, as it was much easier to pull out what I needed from the appropriate area rather than searching through dozens of identical bottles for a particular spice. My second spice storage space was for spices that I didn't use as often as the others, and these were stored in a series of Rubbermaid, plastic-coated spice racks that fit on the backside of my pantry door. It's very important to keep your spices as far from light and heat sources as possible and sealed tight in containers. Hugh also has the most amazing spice storage that he invented specifically for his boat. This spice cabinet cleverly hides multiple layers of spices. The ones most often used are out front on the outside shelves. The spice cabinet can then swing open to reveal the backside of the front of the cabinet containing additional spice shelves. A third layer of spices is located on the section of the spice cabinet that is bolted to the bulkhead, and a simple sliding lock keeps everything in place while at sea.

Provisions

One day while visiting our dear friends in Annapolis who were stowing their provisions for their second around-the-world cruise, I happened to notice a series of different-sized bottles and containers from palm size to five gallon containers, but all made from the same product and looking very much like they were from the same manufacturer. These were the friends who told us on their first around-the-world voyage that they had made the mistake of taking huge quantities of every type of food imaginable before they realized people everywhere ate. Stanley and I had the same moment of enlightenment a couple of years earlier, but the scale of our provisions was not nearly as grand as theirs. We also realized that many foods we were used to eating simply were not available in small little island villages so we learned to adjust our menus to items that we could find locally. Rather than eating romaine lettuce, we were able to buy or barter for cabbage—and we learned from the cabbage! We learned that it stored far longer than romaine, that it could be stored without refrigeration for quite some time, and that there were a tremendous number of salads, side dishes, and mains we could make from it. In many places, coffee is unavailable or very expensive and so we began drinking tea and interspersed it with our coffee drinking. Tea is available almost everywhere and we came to love the blends and different flavors, sometimes even using it in place of wood smoking chips while barbequing. The same thing happened with beef and pork, often not available in far off locations. Fishing while underway, diving for seafood while at anchor, and shopping for chicken and goat while ashore became a way of life and a change to our common eating habits. We of course had beef and pork and many types of ingredients in our freezer, but the longer we were offshore or away from towns or villages, the more those freezer items diminished and the more we depended on the sea.

Cooking Units

We had four cooking options onboard, the stove with oven, the BBQ, the microwave, and the one little cooking unit option which we think is essential on any boat where there will be cooking or heating of food while underway: the Forespar Mini-Galley, (there are several brands available), which is a small gimballed propane fueled, bulkhead mounted stove. We mounted the bracket for ours about waist height just in front of the sinks on the sink cabinet face. The Mini-Galley can be stowed when not in use, but in that part of our galley, it was a perfect option, not being so high that we couldn't easily see the food cooking and in a good location that would not interrupt the flow of movement through the boat. Most of our "watch crew food" was either warmed or cooked there for the night watches, including coffee, cocoa, soups, stews, and prepared meals. You do not have to be an offshore sailor to appreciate this unit. Once you've used it for hot liquids and simple meals while sailing, you'll probably never go back to leaning into a galley strap trying to clip holders on your stovetop pots and pans to hold a pot of soup or a perking coffee pot on a gimballed stove.

Macramé

To add to our storage space onboard, we used several macramé items. The first was a macramé plant hanger-holder. We secured it to the overhead in the galley, put a fairly tall, bright yellow plastic utensil pot in it, and secured the bottom with a small eye strap and tiny shock chord. This allowed minimum movement with just enough swing that the cooking utensils I stored in it wouldn't become projectiles. It also held the contents of what would have been one full drawer of cooking spatulas, spoons, and such in the galley. The second of the macramé pieces I used were two macramé "gear hammocks." Some sailors use these to stow life harnesses, etc. for easy access while offshore, and some captains, if they have crew aboard, have one of these strung up for each crewmember's personal gear. They are long, horizontal macramé hammocks with loops on the ends for tying and securing to a grab rail or bulkhead. We tied our hammocks fore and aft on the overhead, outboard, inside grab rails in the main saloon, and high over the settees. On the port side we kept fruit such as apples, oranges, lemons, limes, and sours and on the starboard side we kept hard vegetables such as cabbages, onions, potatoes, garlic, shallots, and hard squashes. In heavy seas we could bring the sides of each hammock together and clip them together if they were full so our fruit and veggies didn't come out. Also in heavy weather we secured a small bungee cord to the bottom and attached it to an overhead fastener which would keep it from swinging and banging

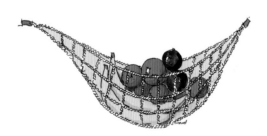

contents against the cabin. These macramé hammocks are a wonderful thing as they're inexpensive, reusable, functional, durable, and washable. On some yachts we visited, these macramé gear hammocks were strung in the lazarettes to hold ropes and lines. The best part is they stretch to fit gear and air can circulate through the macramé, thus minimizing mold on wet ropes and gear. The last piece of macramé that we had onboard were four cotton market bags. They're called "Avoska," French string bags or string market bags. These bags are perfect for grocery shopping, going to the local farmers' market, and even for hauling laundry back and forth from the laundromat. They are perfectly suited for the beach, they're reusable, washable, and pretty much "just-in-case" bags that you can use for anything you can imagine. They also come in various colors, are eco-friendly, stretch to hold an amazing amount, and fold up into a very tiny ball which you can store in your pocket.

CHAPTER 3
Galley Gadgets & Gear

- Can opener
- Chopping board
- Cooking utensils, stainless steel (large and small spoons, slotted spoons, wide and narrow spatulas)
- Corkscrew
- Fat separator
- Food processor
- Gimballed stove that can be bulkhead mounted (such as the Forespar Mini-Galley)
- Grater
- Hand mixer/beater
- Kitchen timer
- Knives
  - Paring knives (large and small)
  - Boning knife
  - Steak knife
  - Serrated bread knife
  - Slicing knife for roasts
  - 8–10-inch chef's knife for chopping
  - Santoku knife
  - Powerful kitchen shears for bone and shell cutting
- Ladles
- Macramé holders
- Measuring cups, stainless steel and glass sets
- Measuring spoons
- Meat tenderizer

- Mixing bowls (various sizes)
- Mortar and pestle
- Nalgene or other laboratory bottles
- Paper (wax, saran, towels, etc.)
- Pastry cutter/blender, sharp stainless steel (great for making egg salad, too!)
- Pet necessities (kitty litter, leash, toys, meds)
- Pizza stone
- Potato peeler
- Pressure cooker
- Re-sealable bags (various sizes)
- Rubber jar/bottle opener
- Rubber spatulas (several sizes, all heat resistant)
- Sieve (large and small mesh for straining)
- Scale (for ingredient measurements)
- Scouring pads, stainless steel (Brillo, Cooper)
- Socks for glass bottles
- Sponges (large and small assortment, Dobie pads for dishwashing)
- Stovetop espresso maker
- Thermometers (candy*, freezer, meat, baked goods, oven, refrigerator)
- Thermos (wide mouth for soups, small mouth for tea, coffee, and cocoa)
- Tongs
- Tupperware
- Turkey baster, stainless steel (won't corrode like aluminum and is easier to clean than plastic)
- Vacuum sealing machine (food saver bags, and containers for storing food)
- Wire whisks (medium and large)
- Wooden spoons (several)

---

*A candy thermometer is the perfect tool for calculating precise temperatures of water which needs to be at a particular temperature before adding your yeast when making bread—a very important part of successful bread making.

PART 2

CHAPTER 4
The Pantry

- Aluminum foil, regular and heavy duty
- Anchovies, canned or bottled
- Baking powder
- Baking soda
- BBQ sauce (see pg. 313 for homemade)
- Beans, canned* (black, kidney, lima, navy, pinto)
- Beans, dry (black, black eyed, green peas, kidney, lima, navy, pinto)

---

*Though I regularly rotated and used my pantry goods, I found that both canned tomato products and bean products were the first of all staples to go bad. Generally, this was in the form of a bulging top or leakage on a shelf. Throw anything like that out immediately! Regularly check all of your canned goods, but my experience with bad canned goods was almost always bean- or tomato-based.

- Bottled flavorings/extracts (almond, anise, banana, coconut, maple, peppermint, vanilla, etc.)
- Bouillon, crystals and/or cubes
- Bread crumbs (I prefer Progresso brand)
- Capers
- Cereals
- Cheeses (canned formats can be found online and at my old alma mater's website: cougarcheese.wsu.edu)
- Cocoa
- Coffee, instant and/or regular
- Condiments (chili sauce, hoisin, ketchup, mayonnaise, mustard, salsa, salsa verde, seafood cocktail, Worcestershire sauce)
- Cornmeal
- Cornstarch
- Crackers (saltines, graham crackers, snacking crackers)
- Flour (white, wheat, rye)
- Fruit, canned or bottled (applesauce, mandarin oranges, peaches, pears, pineapple, prunes, etc.)
- Gelatin
- Green chilies, canned
- Ham, canned
- Honey
- Hot sauces
- Jams and jellies
- Juices, canned or bottled
- Liquid smoke
- Meats, canned (bacon, beef, beef stew, chicken, chipped beef, corned beef, ham, spam, Vienna sausages, etc.)
- Molasses
- Oatmeal

- Oil (coconut, corn, hot chili, olive, peanut, sesame, walnut)
- Olives
- Pancake mix
- Paper and plastic (napkins, paper towels, saran wrap)
- Parmesan cheese, grated, canned, or bottled
- Pasta noodles
- Pasta sauces, canned or bottled (alfredo, marinara, tomato, etc.)
- Peanut butter
- Peppers
- Pesto (see pesto recipes on pgs. 293–303)
- Pet food, necessities, and supplies (kitty litter, leash, meds, pet foods, toys, treats)
- Pimientos, canned and/or bottled
- Popcorn, bottled kernels and/or microwavable packages
- Potatoes, instant flakes and/or mashed
- Pre-packaged soups for soup, seasoning, and dips
- Pre-packaged mixes (hollandaise sauce, taco mix, ranch dressing, etc.)
- Puddings and pie filling
- Raisins
- Ramen noodles
- Relish
- Rice (white Arborio, basmati, brown, sushi, wild)
- Salt (white, sea salt, Kosher)
- Sauerkraut (canned or bottled)**
- Seafood (anchovies, bottled clam juice, canned tuna, salmon, shrimp)
- Shortening (smaller cans don't become rancid as quickly as large cans)
- Soap (hand soap, hand sanitizer for heads and galley, dish soap for kitchen and cleaning bilge)
- Soups, canned

**In my opinion, refrigerated or bottled sauerkraut is far superior to canned.

- Soy sauce
- Sugars (white, brown, powdered)
- Syrup
- Tea, bags and loose leaves (diversified flavors make for more interesting drinking!)
- Tomatoes (canned, crushed, dehydrated, packed in oil, sun dried, whole)
- Tomato paste
- Tomato sauce
- Vanilla beans
- Vegetables, canned or bottled (asparagus, beans, corn, green beans, peas, potatoes, etc.)
- Vinegars (red wine, white, rice wine, balsamic, malt, apple cider)
- Yeast packets
- Re-sealable bags for storing, cooking, and freezing

CHAPTER 5
Spices

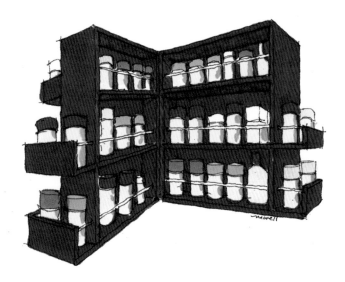

Whenever we anchored and ventured ashore during our sailing travels, Stanley and I found many wonderful herbs and spices available at local markets. We discovered rolled chocolate, fresh nutmeg still with the mace around the nut, cinnamon, mountains of mangos, and wonderful spices and herbs in St. Lucia, and literally miles of rosemary, thyme, and other savory spices growing along the paths and roads of the Bahamas. On many islands in the Bahamas and Caribbean, people grow eggplant—not to eat, but because it's pretty, so we were given bags of these wonderful veggies. Tomatoes were always abundant throughout the Bahamas and Caribbean, as were sweet and hot peppers and cabbages, both red and green. Beef and pork were unavailable in many places, but goats, chicken, seafood, and eggs were abundant everywhere we cruised. In warmer climates from Florida and throughout the Caribbean, avocados, bananas, coconuts, oranges, pineapple, lemons, limes, and sours were so abundant that we always had a constant fresh store onboard.

Of course, if you decide to pick some roadside herbs, ask a local first. The plant you pick may not be what you think it is, even when you think the "pungents" are readily obvious. Be safe, make sure you're not treading on someone's private property, ask someone along the way if you are permitted to pick, and more importantly, that what you think is rosemary . . . is actually rosemary! We spoke with the locals wherever we went and made many friends by asking questions about their islands, towns, forests, people, families, customs, and fishing. We were given access to much more than wild herbs, treated to meals in their homes, and given old, treasured family recipes. (Some of these recipes are included in this book!) We were taken to the best places to fish and dive and so often we shed tears together as we departed. We met lifelong friends from towns and villages in the Pacific Northwest, British Columbia, Alaska, Hawaii, Mexico, all up and down the eastern seaboard, the Bahamas, Bermuda, the Caribbean, and every place we dropped our anchor.

Spices

- Allspice
- Anise seeds
- Arrowroot
- Basil
- Bay leaves
- Beau monde seasoning
- Black pepper (ground, cracked, whole)
- Caraway seeds
- Cardamom (powdered)
- Cayenne
- Celery powder
- Celery salt
- Celery seeds
- Chili powder
- Cinnamon (ground and sticks)
- Cloves (ground and whole)
- Coriander
- Cream of tartar
- Curry powder
- Dill weed
- Garlic powder
- Garlic salt
- Ginger (ground and whole)*
- Italian herb seasoning
- Juniper berries
- Lemon pepper
- Marjoram
- Montreal steak seasoning (I prefer McCormick's)
- Mustard, dry
- Mustard seeds
- Nutmeg (ground and whole)
- Old Bay Seasoning (for seafood)
- Onion powder
- Onion salt
- Oregano (flakes and powdered)
- Paprika
- Parsley flakes
- Peanut butter
- Pickling spice
- Poultry seasoning
- Red pepper flakes
- Rosemary
- Salt (Kosher, sea, and white)
- Seeds (sesame, poppy, sunflower, pumpkin, etc.)
- Tarragon
- Thyme

---

*Fresh ginger can be refrigerated or stored in a very cool place in a bottle or jar filled with Sherry. Ginger-flavored Sherry is excellent in Chinese stir fry and other recipes, but remember to refill the ginger jar with more Sherry as you use it. Ginger kept like this will last for many months, but please note that the texture will be a bit different than fresh ginger.

CHAPTER 6
Appetizers

Colin's Story

The first time we visited the beautiful Windward Caribbean Island of St. Lucia, we followed our guide book's advice to anchor below the Petite Piton in a little bay named Piton Bay. The guide book said to drop a bow anchor and row a stern line to shore and tie off around one of the coconut trees on the beach. The bow was in very deep water with a significant drop-off from the shallow beach. This area was a working coconut plantation at that time owned by Colin Tennant, the owner of Tennant Stout Lager in the British Isles. At this time, he also owned the island of Mystique, but he started his coconut plantation on St. Lucia for peace and recreation.

As we were throwing out our bow anchor, a handful of young island boys came swimming toward our boat bellowing, "Rope, rope!" We didn't know what to think, nor were we comfortable with these children swimming near our propeller. We turned the engine off to protect them and then listened carefully as they tried to explain what they were saying, all the while splashing around and laughing in the beautiful turquoise-colored water. We finally understood that to make a little money to help out their families, they would swim out to each anchoring boat, grab a stern line, swim it back to shore, tie it to a coconut tree, and then wait for the owner of the boat to row ashore and pay them. The cost was minimal but the experience was priceless.

After we rowed to shore and paid the boys, they asked if we would like to buy a couple of coconuts to make popcorn. We thought, *huh*? We bought one anyway and turned our focus from the beach up toward the vast plantation hosting a magnificent Arabian-style tent with open sides, mirrors reflecting beautiful colors of reds, oranges, yellows, purples, and blues as the sun hit them—a glittering, unexpected vision that left us stunned. Suddenly, a man stood up from the tent and began motioning us toward him, so we walked up and were welcomed by plantation owner Colin Tennent who asked us to have a seat, a beer, and to talk awhile. The ground under the tent was covered with fabulous Oriental rugs and littered with giant over-stuffed pillows of every color and texture. Colin was curious about where we'd come from, where we were going, and what our plans were for the future. He literally wanted to know all about us, but we wanted to know all about him, the 3rd Baron Glenconner of Scotland, and this unusual place and the life he was living.

During the hours of our visit, we were greeted by a baby elephant standing nine feet tall at the shoulders. A baby elephant, regardless of age, is huge and powerful. Colin said her name was "Bupa." She had been orphaned in Uganda, and taken to a zoo in Dublin, Ireland where they decided they didn't really "need" her. Colin heard of this news and rescued Bupa , then shipped her to St. Lucia on his airplane to live a life of leisure and play in the water and white sands of Sugar Beach. Bupa greeted us and entertained us each time we came ashore during our weeklong visit to this beautiful island.

By the time we realized we had spent the better part of a day lunching and talking with one of the near royals of Great Britain—this gentle and friendly man, who was like the "Dr. Doolittle" of St. Lucia, having many animals and pets strolling around his vast planta-tion—we said we needed to get back onboard *Native Sun* before sunset. We shared hugs and loving words and many, many thank yous, and then I remembered the popcorn comment. I asked Colin what the boys had meant by that, and he laughed and said he'd give me the recipe.

Coconut Popcorn

YIELD: meat of 1 coconut

Ingredients:

1 coconut
oil for frying
salt

Directions:

Whack off the top of a coconut; save the coconut milk to drink chilled for a later time. Crack the coconut shell into pieces, then scrape out the coconut meat with a dull knife and cut the pieces into ½-inch cubes. Place cubes in a nonstick skillet and fry over medium-high heat until golden brown on all sides. Depending on your skillet and the oil in the coconut meat, you may need to add a bit of oil. We found that different types of coconuts needed more or less oil. Be sure to put a splatter screen on the skillet if you have one, as the coconut popcorn spits and spatters. When it's all nice and golden brown, use a slotted spoon and drain on layers of paper towels. Salt lightly. Be prepared to make this daily while you're in coconut territory—it really is that addictively good.

Pickle Juice Eggs

Eggs are just one of the most wonderful and versatile food items to have on board. They are served as appetizers, for breakfast, brunch, lunch, and dinner, and they are used in baking and cream sauces. They can be found almost anywhere you sail, can be flavored to anyone's taste, and are the perfect "on watch" snack. Eggs store well in cool, dry places and when hard-boiled and pickled, they can be refrigerated for long periods of time in a tightly sealed container. Pickled eggs are delicious sliced on salads, made into egg salad for sandwiches, and as a stand-alone yummy snack. The simplest way to pickle an egg is the pickle juice method which follows, but I've included several of our favorite pickled egg recipes shared by sailors from all over the world who invited us aboard their boats. When you've eaten all of your pickles don't toss out that wonderful spicy pickle juice! There are hundreds of ways to use pickle juice, from cleaning copper to cooking, and pickle juice can even give you relief if you dab it on a mosquito bite to help stop the itching! You can use a little in your salad dressing as a substitute for vinegar, and it's a good but unusual way to tenderize and marinate meat. If you have sunburn, you'll find some relief by dabbing pickle juice on your burned skin.

YIELD: 10–12 eggs

Ingredients:

10–12 hard-boiled eggs, shelled
1 large pickle juice jar with juice, pickles eaten

Directions:

The fastest and simplest way to pickle eggs is to first shell then chill hard-boiled eggs and place them into a jar of pickle juice, making sure eggs are covered with the juice. You may need two jars with the pickle juice evenly divided, depending on how many eggs and pickle juice you have. These eggs can be refrigerated up to one month.

Optional Pickling Method:

Heat the pickle juice in a pan until it begins to boil. You can spice it up by adding just about anything you have on hand such as powdered garlic, sliced garlic cloves, sliced onion, sliced jalapeño pepper, or cayenne pepper. Any fresh spices or herbs you have on hand will also enhance the flavor. Turn off the heat and let the spices soak into the pickle juice for a few minutes. Loosely pack boiled eggs into a warm, pre-sterilized quart jar container, then pour pickle juice over eggs. Refrigerate immediately. Don't rush the pickling process by eating them too soon. They're best if left in the pickling brine for up to six weeks.

Basic Pickled Eggs

YIELD: 10–12 eggs

Ingredients:

10–12 room temperature eggs
1 cup white vinegar
½ cup water
2 tablespoons coarse salt
2 tablespoons pickling spice
1 onion, sliced
5 black peppercorns

Directions:

Place eggs in a large pot and cover with cold water. Bring water to a boil and immediately remove from heat. Cover and let eggs stand in hot water for 10 to 12 minutes. Remove from hot water, cool, and peel. Place the eggs into 1-quart wide mouth jars. In a saucepan, combine the vinegar, water, salt, pickling spice, most of the onion (reserve a couple of slices), and black peppercorns. Bring to a rolling boil; pour over eggs in your jars. Place a couple of slices of onion on top and seal the jars. Cool to room temperature, then refrigerate for three days before serving. Keeps well in the refrigerator for at least one month in tightly sealed jar.

Dilled Pickled Eggs

YIELD: 10–12 eggs

Ingredients:

10–12 hard-boiled eggs, shelled
1½ cups white vinegar
1 cup water
¾ teaspoon dill weed
¼ teaspoon white pepper (optional, black pepper)
3 teaspoons salt
¼ teaspoon mustard seed
½ teaspoon onion, finely minced

Directions:

Bring all ingredients except eggs to a boil and reduce the heat and simmer for 5 minutes. Turn off the heat and let the spices soak into the dill brine for a few minutes. Loosely pack boiled eggs into warm, pre-sterilized quart jar containers, then pour brine over eggs. Refrigerate immediately. Don't rush the pickling process by eating them too soon. They're best if left in the pickling brine for up to six weeks.

Red Beet Pickled Eggs

YIELD: 10–12 eggs

Ingredients:

10–12 hard-boiled eggs, shelled
1 cup red beet juice from canned beets
1½ cups apple cider vinegar
1 teaspoon brown sugar
Handful red canned beets, whole or sliced

Directions:

Bring all ingredients except eggs to a boil and reduce the heat and simmer for 5 minutes. Turn off the heat and let the spices soak into the red beet brine for a few minutes. Loosely pack boiled eggs into a warm, pre-sterilized quart jar container, then pour brine over eggs. Refrigerate immediately. Don't rush the pickling process by eating them too soon. They're best if left in the pickling brine for up to six weeks.

Sweet & Sour Pickled Eggs

YIELD: 10–12 eggs

Ingredients:

1½ cups apple cider, preferably pasteurized
10–12 hard-boiled eggs, shelled
½ cup apple cider vinegar
1 (12 ounce) package red cinnamon candy
2 tablespoons salt
1 teaspoon garlic salt
1 tablespoon pickling spice

Directions:

Bring all ingredients except eggs to a boil and reduce the heat and simmer for 5 minutes. Turn off the heat and let the spices soak into the sweet and sour brine for a few minutes. Loosely pack boiled eggs into a warm, pre-sterilized quart jar container, then pour brine over eggs. Refrigerate immediately. Don't rush the pickling process by eating them too soon. They're best if left in the pickling brine for up to six weeks.

Sweet & Smoky Pickled Eggs

YIELD: 10–12 eggs

Ingredients:

10–12 hard-boiled eggs, shelled
1½ cups apple cider vinegar
½ cup water
2 teaspoons salt
2 teaspoons white sugar
1 tablespoon dark brown sugar
¼ teaspoon liquid smoke (optional, hickory
  smoke salt)
1 tablespoon pickling spice

Directions:

Bring all ingredients except eggs to a boil and reduce the heat and simmer for 5 minutes. Turn off the heat and let the spices soak into the sweet smoky brine for a few minutes. Loosely pack boiled eggs into a warm, pre-sterilized quart jar container, then pour brine over eggs. Refrigerate immediately. Don't rush the pickling process by eating them too soon. They're best if left in the pickling brine for up to six weeks.

Apple Cider Pickled Eggs

YIELD: 10–12 eggs

Ingredients:

10–12 hard-boiled eggs, shelled
1½ cups apple cider, pasteurized (optional, apple juice)
½ cup white vinegar
12 teaspoons salt
1 teaspoon pickling spice
6–8 thin slices onion
1 clove garlic, peeled

Directions:

Bring all ingredients except eggs to a boil and reduce the heat and simmer for 5 minutes. Turn off the heat and let the spices soak into the apple cider brine for a few minutes. Loosely pack boiled eggs into a warm, pre-sterilized quart jar container, then pour brine over eggs. Refrigerate immediately. Don't rush the pickling process by eating them too soon. They're best if left in the pickling brine for up to six weeks.

Pineapple Pickled Eggs

YIELD: 10–12 eggs

Ingredients:

10–12 hard-boiled eggs, shelled
1 (12 ounce) can (1½ cups) unsweetened pineapple juice
½ cups white vinegar
¼ cup sugar
1 teaspoon salt
1 teaspoon pickling spice
2 medium onions, peeled and thinly sliced

Directions:

Bring all ingredients to a boil except eggs and reduce the heat and simmer for 5 minutes. Turn off the heat and let the spices soak into the pineapple brine for a few minutes. Loosely pack boiled eggs into a warm, pre-sterilized quart jar container, then pour brine over eggs. Refrigerate immediately. Don't rush the pickling process by eating them too soon. They're best if left in the pickling brine for up to six weeks.

Almost Goat Cheese

YIELD: 1½ cups

Ingredients:

1 (8 ounce) package cream cheese, softened
2 (4 ounce) packages feta cheese, crumbled
2 teaspoons fresh parsley, minced
1 tablespoon pepper, coarsely ground
fresh parsley, basil, and thyme sprigs, to
    garnish

Directions:

Place cream cheese, feta cheese, and fresh parsley in a bowl and with an electric beater or food processor beat at medium speed until smooth. Scoop out mixture onto a long piece of plastic wrap and roll into a 10 x 2-inch shaped log. Freeze at least 15 minutes to firm up, roll in various fresh herbs to garnish, slice in discs, and serve with crackers, on toast, or in salads.

Optional: Omit the pepper and roll the log in ¼ cup chopped sun-dried tomatoes in oil.

Asparagus with Wasabi Mayonnaise Dip

YIELD: 12 servings

Ingredients:

1½ pounds thin or medium-sized asparagus,
    trimmed to the same length
½ cup mayonnaise
4 teaspoons soy sauce
1½ teaspoons sugar
2 teaspoons fresh lemon juice
2 teaspoons wasabi paste

Directions:

Blanch asparagus by placing in a large saucepan of boiling salted water for one minute. With a slotted spoon or tongs, transfer to asparagus to a bowl of water with ice chunks to stop the cooking. Drain well on paper towels and pat dry. Refrigerate asparagus while you whisk together the mayonnaise, soy sauce, sugar, lemon juice, and wasabi paste until the sugar is dissolved, then place in a small bowl. Serve asparagus on a plate with the wasabi mayonnaise dip.

Bacon Jalapeño Turkey Meatball Poppers

YIELD: 50 meatballs

Ingredients:

1 pound ground turkey (optional, ground chicken)
¼ cup cream cheese
3 slices bacon, cooked and minced
2 egg whites
3 jalapeños, stemmed, deseeded, and minced
½ cup Panko bread crumbs
4 garlic cloves, peeled, pressed, and finely minced
½ cup Mexican cheese blend
1 teaspoon chili powder
1 tablespoon dried oregano
1 teaspoon Kosher salt
½ teaspoon pepper

Directions:

Preheat oven to 350°F. Combine all ingredients in a large mixing bowl and mix until blended. With a small scoop or tablespoon, scoop meat into 1 tablespoon–sized scoops, and then with slightly wet hands, roll each into a little meatball. Bake 20 to 23 minutes until lightly browned and cooked through. Serve with toothpicks and watch them go!

Baked Brie

YIELD: 6 servings

Ingredients:

2 tablespoons butter
1 large onion, diced
1 tablespoon garlic, minced
8 ounces brie cheese, cut into large pieces, rind removed
1 (8 ounce) package cream cheese, cut into pieces
¾ cup sour cream
2 tablespoons fresh lemon juice
2 tablespoons brown sugar
1 tablespoon Worcestershire sauce
salt and pepper, to taste
paprika, to taste
1 French baguette, cut into pieces and toasted for serving
olives (optional, for serving)

Directions:

Preheat oven to 400°F. Melt butter in a heavy saucepan over medium heat. Add diced onion and garlic and sauté for 6 to 8 minutes or until onions are a light golden brown. In the meantime, place brie and cream cheese in a large microwave safe bowl and microwave on medium heat for 2 minutes or just until barely melted; keep your eye on it as every microwave is a bit different. Whisk sautéed onions and garlic with sour cream, lemon juice, brown sugar, and Worcestershire sauce. Add in melted brie and cream cheese to the onion and garlic mixture and combine. Season with salt and pepper, sprinkle with a dash of paprika, and put into an oven safe dish. Bake 20 minutes and serve with toasted baguette slices and olives on the side.

Baked Crab Rangoon

YIELD: 12 servings

Ingredients:

1 (6 ounce) can or ¾ cup crabmeat, drained and flaked
4 ounces cream cheese, softened
2–3 green onions, thinly sliced
¼ cup mayonnaise
12 wonton wrappers
12 cup mini muffin tin, sprayed lightly with cooking spray

Directions:

Preheat oven to 350°F. Mix together crabmeat, cream cheese, green onions, and mayonnaise. Place one wonton wrapper in each of the prepared muffin tin cups, extending the edges over the rim of each cup. Fill cups evenly with crabmeat mixture. Bake 18 to 20 minutes or until the edges of the cups are golden brown and the crabmeat filling is heated through. Serve hot, warm, or cooled—they're delicious any way.

Optional: For a crispier Crab Rangoon, bake wonton wrappers in muffin cups at 350°F for 5 to 7 minutes until lightly browned. Fill with crabmeat mixture and bake 6 to 8 minutes or until crabmeat mixture is heated through.

Balsamic-Glazed Meatball Poppers

YIELD: 60 poppers

Ingredients:

1 pound lean ground beef
1 cup Italian bread crumbs
½ cup milk
2 tablespoons ketchup
1 tablespoon balsamic vinegar
2 large eggs
½ teaspoon black pepper
½ teaspoon Kosher salt
1 teaspoon onion powder
½ teaspoon garlic powder
½ teaspoon nutmeg
2 tablespoons Italian seasoning
Sweet and Sour Balsamic Sauce (recipe below)

Directions:

Preheat oven to 350°F. Place beef and bread crumbs in a large bowl and pour milk over. Add ketchup, vinegar, eggs, pepper, salt, onion and garlic powder, nutmeg, and Italian seasoning. Using your hands, gently combine. When nicely blended, make 1 tablespoon-sized mini meatball poppers; keeping hands wet while forming the poppers will help make them smooth and round. Cover with the sweet and sour balsamic sauce and bake for 30 minutes on a baking sheet. Serve with toothpicks and freeze any leftovers (if you have any).

Sweet & Sour Balsamic Sauce

YIELD: 60 balsamic-glazed meatball poppers

Ingredients:

1 cup ketchup
¼ cup balsamic vinegar
¼ cup brown sugar, packed
1 cup water

Directions:

In a medium-sized bowl, combine all ingredients and whisk well to combine flavors. Coat balsamic-glazed meatball poppers (recipe above) just before cooking.

Black Bean & Corn Salsa

YIELD: 10–12 servings

Ingredients:

1 (14 ounce) can corn, drained
1 (14 ounce) can black beans, rinsed, drained
½ red bell pepper, diced (optional, green, orange, or yellow pepper)
½ red onion, diced
2–3 garlic cloves, peeled, minced
1 jalapeño pepper, destemmed, deseeded, small diced
¼ cup cilantro leaves, chopped
juice of 1 lime
3 tablespoons olive oil
salt and pepper, to taste

Directions:

In a medium bowl, mix corn, black beans, bell pepper, onion, garlic, jalapeño, and cilantro and mix well to combine. Add lime juice over and top with olive oil, salt, and pepper. Mix well, cover tightly, and refrigerate 1 to 4 hours to meld flavors. Serve with tortilla chips, crackers, or as a cool relish on the side.

Blue Cheese Spread

YIELD: 1½ cups

Ingredients:

1 cup (8 ounces) soft blue cheese at room temperature
½ cup whipping cream (optional, heavy cream)
fresh ground pepper, to taste

Directions:

Stir blue cheese, breaking up slightly, into a small bowl and gradually stir in cream and pepper to blend. Add more cream if cheese mixture is too stiff. Cover tightly and chill up to 2 days. Bring to room temperature and serve with crackers or thin crostini.

Charlie's Angels' Story

Captain Charlie Mead had two wonderful young women sailing with him over the years. Stanley and I have always called them "Captain Charlie's Angels." The first was Boshie. Captain Charlie met her while she was working at the sail loft in Seattle where he ordered all of his sails. They became friends during this long commissioning process so she simply invited herself along as the seventh member of Captain Charlie's crew, promising that she was a good cook (and had already snuck aboard squirreling away frozen stews, lasagna, and several prepared meals for the crew).

Captain Charlie was flattered that a beautiful twenty-eight-year-old woman wanted to sail with him, a seventy-two-year-old sailor, and that she also shared the passion for this lifestyle. And so it was in the middle of October when the yacht *Leo* with its seven crewmembers aboard left the docks in Seattle and started up Puget Sound toward Neah Bay and Cape Flattery, the most northwest point in the continental US and doorway to the Pacific Ocean. One seasick crewmember was dropped off there so that only six members were left onboard as the *Leo* left sight of land and headed out into the Pacific Ocean. The first days were just good cold sailing until a Pineapple Express Storm began raging and *Leo* was doing ten knots under bare poles, surfing down thirty-five-foot waves. Stern cleat warps were put out and the voyage south continued with yet another two ports of call in Oregon for exiting seasick crew.

Leo crossed into ports in Oregon, Newport, and Coos Bay with all crew on board fitted in life jackets and life harnesses—they were all at the ready. The weather was ferocious and the Coast Guard stood by those two Oregon ports, just in case there was a broaching or accident where rescue of the crew would be needed. When *Leo* sailed under the Golden Gate Bridge in San Francisco, only three remained of the original seven-person crew, with one strong, competent sailing woman among them, Boshie, now the new first mate of *Leo*.

Stanley and I first met Boshie after *Leo* had transited the Panama Canal and was at a marina in Florida where Captain Charlie asked us to visit and meet his first mate. We will always remember our first meeting. Boshie was bent over scrubbing away on a shower grate which she'd hauled onto the dock to clean. No words were exchanged, no face time was shared, and we had nothing to judge her by (which we thought we should do, just to protect our dear friend Captain Charlie and his interests), but at the same moment, Stanley and I said in unison, "she's perfect." All these years later she has remained perfect as a sailing mate and as a dear and loving friend we consider part of our family.

Boshie and Captain Charlie's sailing adventures covered a two-year span from the Pacific Northwest through the Panama Canal deep into the Caribbean and up and down the East Coast. After Boshie met Peter on the sister ship of *Leo*, the sailing vessel *Avatar*, her sailing days with Captain Charlie ended and she sailed on to the South Pacific. Some of Boshie's recipes which she prepared aboard *Leo* have become favorites of ours and are included in this book.

The second Captain Charlie's Angel was Terri, affectionately called "T." She was a friend of Captain Charlie's daughter Eva and her husband Tarry. T had been bitten by the sailing bug after sailing with Eva and Tarry one afternoon. That sailing bug bit her hard enough that she began racing on the Chesapeake and eventually became a part of an all-female racing team. One day as a twenty-six-year-old woman, T was lying on the foredeck of Captain Charlie's *Alberg 30* while trimming the spinnaker during a race, when she realized *I've finally found something I really, really love*. Eva and the other young women on the boat had been so accepting and taught her everything they knew about sailing, so T decided she was ready to take a break from her job at the FDIC in Washington D.C. Captain Charlie was looking for a new first mate and so it was we met first mate T aboard *Leo* as we all were preparing to head off to the Caribbean again. T's famous queso (pg. 81) is also included in this book. It's hot, spicy, and delicious and I'm sure with the thousands of miles that the yacht *Leo* sailed and the hundreds of people met along the way, there are others out there enjoying it as much as we do.

T continues to be a precious friend, and both her and Boshie are like family to me. Captain Charlie's Angels learned so much from Captain Charlie, as did anyone who was welcomed aboard the sailing vessel *Leo*, from wind surfing, playing cards and board games, to his secret recipes and cooking techniques.

Boshie's Ceviche

YIELD: Serves 4–8

Ingredients:

1 pound firm-fleshed, fresh fish (Mahi Mahi, red snapper, halibut, or shrimp), cut into ½-inch
  pieces
1 cup fresh-squeezed lime juice (optional, ½ cup lemon, ½ cup lime)
½ cup red onion, finely diced (optional, 5 green onions, sliced)
1 cup ripe tomatoes or more to taste, deseeded and chopped
1 jalapeño pepper, stemmed, deseeded, and finely diced
2 teaspoons salt
½ teaspoon pepper
½ teaspoon dried oregano
dash Tabasco or other hot sauce
2 stalks celery, diced
¼ cup fresh cilantro, finely chopped
Avocado slices or cubes, for serving
Mango cubes, for serving
1½ tablespoons olive oil, for serving

Directions:

Place fish in a glass or steel bowl and cover with lime juice, making sure the whole fish is covered
with juice. Tightly cover and marinate in the fridge for 1 hour. Stir occasionally to make sure the
whole fish is covered in marinade. Add all other ingredients to fish, cover, and refrigerate several
more hours. Serve in a dish on lettuce leaves or in individual small serving bowls with additional
cilantro for garnish.

Ceviche for a Crowd

This ceviche takes a lot of ingredients and some time to prep but it's well worth the praise from your guests and the wonderful taste you'll all enjoy!

YIELD: *12 servings*

Ingredients:

½ pound sea scallops
½ pound shrimp, peeled and deveined
½ cup fresh lime juice
2 tablespoons fresh orange juice
1 tablespoon grated orange zest
½ cup red onion, halved, thinly sliced
1 red bell pepper, finely chopped
1 yellow bell pepper, finely chopped
1 cup tomato, diced and deseeded
1 small serrano chili pepper, deseeded and minced
½ cup fresh cilantro, coarsely chopped
Kosher salt, to taste
⅛ teaspoon ground cumin
⅛ teaspoon cayenne pepper (optional)
1 avocado, diced
1 tablespoon olive oil for garnish

Directions:

Fill a large bowl with ice water. Boil a 1-quart saucepan ¾ full of salted water. Add scallops, reduce heat to a low simmer, and gently poach scallops until just cooked through, about 1 minute. Use a slotted spoon to transfer the scallops to a bowl of ice water to stop the cooking process. Return the water to a low simmer, add the shrimp, and poach shrimp until just cooked till they are opaque inside and have just turned pink, about 2 to 3 minutes. Remove with a slotted spoon and transfer poached shrimp to a bowl of ice water. Drain the scallops and shrimp well and pat dry. Put the scallops and shrimp in a glass bowl, pour in lime juice and orange juice, and gently mix. Cover and refrigerate for 30 minutes until nicely chilled. Pour out most of the juice, leaving just enough to leave the scallops and shrimp moist, then add orange zest, red onion, bell peppers, tomato, chili pepper, cilantro, salt, cumin, and cayenne pepper, mixing thoroughly. Refrigerate for another 30 minutes. Just before serving, gently mix in diced avocado and drizzle the ceviche with the olive oil. Serve in small serving bowls or chilled martini glasses for a fancier presentation.

Mango Grouper Ceviche

YIELD: 3–4 cups

Ingredients:

3 cups raw grouper, diced
1½ cups lime juice
½ cups grapefruit juice
1¼ cup white onion, diced
2 cups tomato, deseeded and diced
1–2 tablespoons fresh cilantro, chopped
1⅔ cups mango, peeled, deseeded, and cubed
2 avocados, peeled, deseeded, and cubed
salt and pepper, to taste
splash of tequila (optional)

Directions:

Place diced grouper in a glass bowl, pour in lime and grapefruit juice, cover, and refrigerate. In another bowl, gently mix together the onion, tomato, and cilantro. Remove grouper from the fridge, strain out the juices, and gently mix the grouper with the onion, tomato, and cilantro mixture. Add the cubed mango and avocados, then cover and refrigerate for an additional 20 to 30 minutes. Just before serving, if using tequila, splash a small amount on top and then serve in small serving bowls, or chilled martini glasses for a fancier presentation, or in one large bowl with corn chips on the side.

Bourbon & Cider Glazed Turkey Meatballs

YIELD: 18 meatballs

Meatball Ingredients:

1 pound ground turkey (optional, ground chicken)
½ tablespoon fresh rosemary, minced
½ tablespoon fresh sage, minced
⅛ teaspoon black pepper
¼ teaspoon salt
½ teaspoon garlic powder
½ tablespoon dried onion flakes

Glaze Ingredients:

1½ cups cider
¼ cup bourbon
3-inch sprig of rosemary

Directions:

Preheat oven to 375°F. Mix all of the meatball ingredients in a medium-sized bowl. Roll into 1-inch balls. Place meatballs on a very lightly oiled pan and bake in the oven for 10 minutes, or alternatively, brown the meatballs in a lightly oiled sauté pan until cooked through. In the meantime, combine the glaze ingredients in a medium saucepan and cook on high heat for 10 minutes until glaze looks shiny and has slightly thickened. Add cooked meatballs to the glaze pan and toss to coat thoroughly. Let the meatballs sit and absorb in the glaze for up to 10 minutes. Remove rosemary sprig, pour meatballs out onto a platter, and serve.

Brandied Cheese Dip

YIELD: 1½ cups

Ingredients:

½ pound (2 cups) Roquefort or blue cheese
1 (8 ounce) package cream cheese, softened
1 cup brandy

Directions:

With an electric mixer, blend cheeses and brandy together. Put in a serving bowl and serve with sliced vegetables or crackers.

Captain Charlie's Story

Our dear friend Captain Charles H. Mead USN(RET) began his sailing career in 1915 at the ripe old age of seven when he sailed in the opening day of the Pan Pacific Exposition Regatta, San Francisco's celebration marking the completion of the brand-new Panama Canal. From those exciting and early days on San Francisco Bay, "Captain Charlie" joined the US navy and served at the Battle of Midway, attaining the rank of captain by the time of his retirement. His life's work and passion was life at sea.

Most people who spend their lifetime endeavors in a pursuit as demanding as service at sea would be content to spend their golden years puttering at hobbies such as golf or tending a garden. This was not the case with Captain Charlie, who not only joined a construction supply firm in Washington D.C. after retirement, but also purchased an *Alberg 30* sailboat named *Bounty* with his son "Chico" and daughter Eva and became an active, if not renowned, very competitive member of the Annapolis sailing community.

Stanley first met Captain Charlie and his daughter Eva in 1980 while they were on an extended cruise in the Bahamas. Shortly after that cruise, then in his seventies, Captain Charlie bought and commissioned a new *Valiant 40*, taking delivery at the factory in Bellingham, Washington, and sailing once again through the Panama Canal to deliver his new "home" to the Chesapeake Bay. Until he was ninety years old, Captain Charlie lived aboard and sailed between the Caribbean, Bahamas, Bermuda, Florida, and Annapolis, often single handedly and twice on extended sailing ventures with his first mates, "Charlie's Angels," Boshie or 'T.'

Captain Charlie named this boat *Leo*. I asked Captain Charlie if that was his sign and he said no, that he'd named his new sailboat after the first vessel he ever took command of, the U.S.S. Leo (AKA-60), which was an attack cargo ship at the Battle of Midway during World War II. The U.S.S. Leo with Captain Charlie in command saw two other major actions in the Pacific, at both the invasion of Iwo Jima and the invasion of Okinawa. Captain Charlie first took command of the U.S.S. Leo in Puget Sound, only a few miles away from the birthplace of his *Valiant 40*, and he told me that the first ship he ever commanded was the U.S.S. Leo and the last ship he ever intended to command would be his beautiful yacht *Leo*.

His children have married and daughter Eva, along with her sailing husband Tarry of Annapolis, Maryland, gave Captain Charlie his first grandson, named Charlie after his grandfather. In the seagoing nature of this family, young Charlie is now at the Merchant Marine Academy—which would make Captain Charlie's heart soar with pride.

We were lucky enough to spend many years "buddy boating" with Captain Charlie from Annapolis and the Chesapeake and up and down the East Coast, sometimes in the Intracoastal Waterway and sometimes offshore to the Bahamas and the Caribbean. There were long trips to Saint Thomas, fifteen days or more offshore where Captain Charlie would single hand. By day we would close the gap so we could easily wave and signal back and forth, and by night, we would veer off enough that we were safely apart but could still see the other's running lights. We would tell Captain Charlie to go to sleep for a few hours and if need be, we'd radio him if we needed to avoid a ship or if the weather was changing. As sailors, none of us slept more than a few hours at a time, so this watch system for *Leo* worked perfectly.

If we caught fish we'd come close enough to pass either a cooked fish or a couple of newly caught tunas back and forth via a fish net on a long pole. Since we were sailing sister ships, we kept nearly identical speed on the water and since we'd sailed so many thousands of miles together, we knew just how close our boats could come to one another. (Some of our racing experiences together also taught us that lesson!)

One day when we were on a long sail in the Atlantic, a week out from St. Thomas, Captain Charlie called on the VHF radio to ask if I had a couple of oranges. I had plenty in my galley hammock, so the *Leo* came alongside with the outstretched fishing net and we tossed two oranges into the net. It was just before twilight, a time we normally veered off from one another, when Captain Charlie said he needed to come alongside again. We were a little surprised as we were pretty particular about our distances apart and the time of day. When he came alongside, the pole with the fishing net was sticking out and Captain Charlie said "Grab it". As we did, Captain Charlie started singing "Happy Birthday" and inside the net was a birthday cake for me with an orange cream frosting. I actually had forgotten it was my birthday, but that touch of love and joy and *great* food was exactly who Captain Charlie was. Many of his recipes from the yacht *Leo* are included in this book. We still cook his recipes and have the fondest memories of so many meals shared with this great man.

Captain Charlie's Beans & Cheese

YIELD: Serves a group

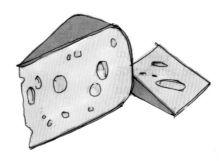

Ingredients:

1 tablespoon olive oil or bacon grease (add more if needed while sautéing onions)
5–6 onions, sliced (As Captain Charlie said, "just use a boogaloo of onions")
2 (11 ounce) cans red beans or chili beans
1 can refried beans
1 can black beans
chili powder, to taste (Captain Charlie said, "lots and lots, the more you use the hotter it is")
1 large jar hot salsa
1 pound (more is better) cheddar cheese, grated

Directions:

In large frying pan over medium heat, add olive oil or bacon grease and onions. Sauté until onions are light brown. Add red or chili beans, refried beans, black beans, chili powder, and salsa. Mix well and add grated cheddar cheese and heat until it's all mixed and melted. Serve warm with nachos or taco chips. You can freeze the leftovers (if there are any) and reheat on low. If you want beans and cheese even hotter, add a deseeded and finely diced jalapeño or Tabasco Sauce to taste.

Conch Fritters

YIELD: 8 servings

Ingredients:

oil for frying (enough to cover bottom of
    frying pot with a couple of inches of
    vegetable or canola oil)
2 medium-sized conchs skinned and diced
    (substitute lobster or squid if conch is
    unavailable)
½ onion, chopped
½ green pepper, chopped
2 stalks celery, chopped
1 jalapeño or more or less to taste, stemmed,
    deseeded, and chopped
2 cloves garlic, chopped
cayenne pepper, to taste
1½ tomatoes, diced
1 teaspoon hot sauce (optional)
½–¾ cup ketchup
¼ cup fresh thyme, chopped
2 cups flour
2 teaspoons baking powder
1 egg
1¼ cups milk
salt and pepper, to taste

Directions:

Preheat a pot with oil a few inches deep on high.
Mix all ingredients together in a large bowl
except the flour, baking powder, egg, and milk.
In a medium bowl, mix together the flour and
baking powder. In a smaller bowl, whip the egg
and milk together. Add dry ingredients to the
large bowl, then slowly add the egg and milk
mixture to the large bowl. Thoroughly combine
all ingredients. Carefully scoop tablespoons of
batter into the hot oil (fry only a few fritters at a
time, taking care not to overcrowd the pot) and
fry to a golden brown. Gently turn the fritters
and continue frying until the other side is golden
brown. When you think the fritters are done,
take one out to make sure it's cooked inside and
adjust cooking time for the remainder accord-
ingly. Drain well on layers of paper towels and
serve hot with dipping sauce. This recipe makes
a lot of fritters but this batter freezes well for
later frying.

Dipping Sauce

Throughout the Bahamas and the Caribbean Islands, we had many different types of dipping sauce, from a simple bowl of ketchup to a classic tartar sauce. The mayonnaise and ketchup-based sauce below, is one of our favorites, but experiment with what you have onboard or according to your particular taste. Besides a spicy dipping sauce, our island friends always passed the bottle of hot sauce which they liberally shook on the fritters before dipping. This additional hot sauce can make these fritters a bit too hot for unaccustomed taste buds, but add an extra layer of heat for those who enjoy the "kick" of island spicy food.

YIELD: 1 cup

Ingredients:

½ cup mayonnaise
½ cup ketchup
1 teaspoon mustard
1 teaspoon hot sauce (optional, more to taste)
2 tablespoons lime juice
salt and pepper, to taste

Directions:

Whisk all ingredients together until smooth and creamy.

Crab & Avacado Quesadillas

YIELD: 1 tortilla

Ingredients:

1 tortilla
Monterey Jack cheese, enough to cover ½ tortilla
avocado, enough to cover ½ tortilla, peeled, deseeded, and diced
crabmeat, enough to cover ½ tortilla, diced
tomato, enough to cover ½ of tortilla, diced
fresh herbs of your choice, chopped, to taste
salt and pepper, to taste

Directions:

Cover half of tortilla with all ingredients listed above. Fold tortilla in half, heat an oiled skillet over medium heat, and gently cook tortilla for 2 to 4 minutes or until lightly browned. Gently flip and heat other side until golden and cheese is melted for about 2 to 4 minutes. To serve, cut into wedges. Each tortilla serves one person.

Crab Puffs

YIELD: 60 crab puffs

Ingredients:

1 (6½ ounce) can or ¾ cup crabmeat
½ cup cheddar cheese, shredded
3 green onions, minced
1 teaspoon Worcestershire sauce
1 teaspoon dry mustard
¼ teaspoon salt
¼ teaspoon pepper
1 cup water
½ cup butter, softened
1 cup flour
4 eggs

Directions:

Preheat oven to 400°F. In a medium bowl, mix together the crabmeat, cheese, green onions, Worcestershire sauce, dry mustard, salt, and pepper. In a large saucepan, heat water and butter until boiling. Remove from heat and immediately add flour a little at a time and beat until mixture doesn't stick to the sides of the pan. Add eggs one at a time until each egg is completely mixed in, then add in to crabmeat mixture and beat. Drop 1 (1-inch) teaspoon dough onto an ungreased baking sheet. Bake 20 to 25 minutes until golden. Cool and serve immediately or freeze. To reheat puffs, place in a 325°F oven for 10 to 15 minutes.

Crab Spread

YIELD: 2 cups

Ingredients:

1 pound (2 cups) crabmeat, canned or fresh
juice and pulp of 1 lemon
3 tablespoons mayonnaise
2 tablespoons capers, coarsely chopped
salt and pepper, to taste

Directions:

Combine all ingredients. Cover and chill to meld flavors. Serve with crackers or sliced veggies.

Crazy-Easy Refrigerator Pickles

YIELD: 2 quart-sized jars

Ingredients:

3 English cucumbers, sliced
1 green pepper, sliced
2 cups onion, sliced
1 cup apple cider vinegar
2 cups white sugar
1 teaspoon celery seed
2 tablespoons salt
cold water, as needed

Directions:

Slice the veggies and put them in 2 quart-sized jars, alternating layers. Mix vinegar, sugar, celery seed, and salt into a large bowl, preferably with a pouring lip. Stir well. Evenly pour vinegar mixture over sliced veggies into each jar and add enough cold water to finish filling the jars. Place the lids on the jars and shake vigorously, then refrigerate. Shake the jars a few times over the next 24 hours to mix. The sugar will dissolve the next day after shaking. The pickles will be ready to eat after 24 hours in the refrigerator. Best if eaten in a week or two, but they'll last for months in the refrigerator. When the jars are close to empty, don't throw out the liquid. Add a few tomato wedges, sweet peppers, hot peppers, and sliced onions or experiment with any other veggies you have on hand.

Cucumbers with Smoked Salmon

YIELD: 12 or more slices

Ingredients:

8 ounces (1 cup) smoked salmon
4 ounces (½ cup) cream cheese, softened
1 tablespoon horseradish
½ teaspoon lemon juice
1 large English cucumber
salt and pepper, to taste

Directions:

In a food processor, blend smoked salmon, cream cheese, horseradish, and lemon juice. Wash cucumber, slice ends off, and slice into 1-inch rounds. With a melon baller, scoop out ¾ of each cucumber slice. Sprinkle the inside of each slice with salt and pepper. Transfer salmon blend to a medium-sized re-sealable bag with one corner cut so that you can use it as a piping bag. Fill hollowed out cucumber slices with salmon mixture and serve.

Deviled Ham

YIELD: 2½ cups

Ingredients:

1 pound smoked ham, cut into 1-inch cubes
½ cup mayonnaise
¼ cup Dijon or brown mustard
½ cup onion, chopped
2 tablespoons fresh parsley leaves, chopped
2 tablespoons hot sauce
1 tablespoon Worcestershire sauce
3 tablespoons maple syrup
2 teaspoons paprika
1 teaspoon mustard powder
salt and pepper, to taste

Directions:

Combine all ingredients in a food processor and blend until smooth. You can use a re-sealable plastic bag with one small corner cut off to squeeze onto crackers for a fancier presentation. Serve on a sandwich or on crackers as a snack.

Fast & Easy Dill Dip

YIELD: 2 cups

Ingredients:

1½ tablespoons fresh dill, chopped
1½ tablespoons fresh parsley, chopped
1 teaspoon salt
1 tablespoon onion powder (optional, dry onion flakes)
1 cup mayonnaise
1 cup sour cream

Directions:

Mix all ingredients in a small bowl, cover tightly, and refrigerate for at least 1 hour to meld flavors. Serve with cut veggies or chips.

Gorgonzola & Thyme Stuffed Green Olives

YIELD: 40 stuffed olives

Ingredients:

3 ounces gorgonzola cheese, crumbled
  (optional, blue cheese)
2 ounces cream cheese, softened
2 teaspoons fresh thyme, diced
½ teaspoon black pepper
40 whole green olives, pitted and drained well

Directions:

With an electric mixer, beat cheeses on medium speed until creamy. Add thyme and pepper and mix well. Scoop cheese mixture into a medium re-sealable plastic bag, cut a lower corner off to make a piping bag, and gently begin squeezing the bag and pipe mixture into each olive. Olives can be covered tightly and refrigerated up to 7 days. To serve, bring olives to room temperature for 1 hour.

Grilled Alaska Salmon Bites

YIELD: 36 bites

Ingredients:

½ teaspoon sesame oil
1 tablespoon olive oil
2 garlic cloves, finely chopped
1 tablespoon fresh ginger, grated
¼ cup Riesling wine
⅓ cup soy sauce
1 tablespoon orange juice
1 tablespoon honey
2 pounds fresh or frozen salmon, cut into
  2-inch squares
green onion curls or chopped cilantro, for
  garnish

Directions:

Preheat grill to medium heat. Place the sesame oil and olive oil in a large saucepan and heat over medium heat. Add garlic and ginger and sauté until soft. Add the wine, soy sauce, orange juice, and honey and simmer until liquid is reduced by half, stirring constantly. Remove from heat, cool, and add salmon pieces, marinating them for 3 to 5 minutes while turning to coat all sides. Grill salmon pieces on grill or over a grill pan, cooking just until fish is opaque throughout. Serve with green onion curls or fresh cilantro.

Grouper Fingers

YIELD: 6 servings

Ingredients:

3 large grouper fillets, cut into 2-inch strips
salt, to taste
juice of 1 lime
Hot pepper flakes, to taste
2 eggs
1 cup all-purpose flour
1 cup bread crumbs
vegetable oil for deep frying

Directions:

Place prepared grouper fingers in a flat pan and sprinkle with salt to taste. Squeeze the lime juice into a small dish, crush the hot pepper flakes into the juice, and pour over the grouper fingers. Marinate for 1 hour. Beat the eggs in a shallow dish. Spread the flour and bread crumbs in separate shallow dishes and set up a "production line." Coat the fingers completely with the flour; dip into the beaten egg, then into the bread crumbs. Place the coated fingers in the refrigerator for 10 to 15 minutes to firm up breading on grouper fingers. Pour enough oil to fry a few grouper fingers at a time into a deep pot and heat until very hot. Place the fingers into the hot oil a few at a time and fry until golden brown. Remove, drain on a wire rack, and serve hot with tartar sauce or equal parts ketchup and mayonnaise.

Homemade Boursin-Style Cheese

YIELD: 2 cups

Ingredients:

2 (8 ounce) packages cream cheese, softened
¼ cup mayonnaise
2 teaspoons Dijon style mustard
2 tablespoons chives, finely chopped
2 tablespoons dill, finely chopped
2 cloves garlic, peeled and finely minced
black pepper, to taste

Directions:

Thoroughly blend all ingredients in a large bowl. Spoon into a serving bowl, cover, and refrigerate overnight. Can also be made ahead and refrigerated up to 4 days before serving. Serve with crackers or fresh vegetables.

Honey-Fried Bananas

YIELD: 1 serving

Ingredients:

1 tablespoon honey
1 tablespoon water
olive oil, for frying
1 slightly under-ripened banana, sliced
cinnamon, to taste

Directions:

In a small bowl, whisk the honey and water together. Put a small amount of oil in a medium-sized skillet over medium heat. Place banana slices in the pan in a single layer and cook for 1 to 2 minutes, turn and cook for an additional 1 to 2 minutes on the other side. Remove pan from heat and pour the honey and water mixture over the banana slices. Cool a bit, then sprinkle with cinnamon. Serve with ice cream, over plain yogurt, or on pancakes.

Hot Artichoke Dip

YIELD: 8 servings

Ingredients:

⅔ cup Parmesan cheese, grated
⅔ cup mayonnaise
⅓ cup heavy whipping cream (don't whip)
1 (14 ounce) can artichoke hearts, drained and well chopped
2 tablespoons green onion, thinly sliced
1 tablespoon pimento peppers, chopped
1 garlic clove, peeled, chopped, and mashed (optional)

Directions:

Preheat oven to 325°F. Lightly grease a medium-sized baking dish. Blend the cheese, mayonnaise, and whipping cream together, then stir in the artichokes, green onions, pimentos, and garlic if using. Mix ingredients well and spoon into the prepared baking dish. Bake 25 minutes until lightly brown. Serve on lightly toasted sourdough bread slices or with crackers.

Hummus

YIELD: 8 or more servings

Ingredients:

2 cups canned chickpeas, drained (reserve liquid)
½ cup tahini (sesame paste) with some of its oil, optional
¼ cup extra-virgin olive oil, plus oil for drizzling
2 cloves garlic, peeled and finely diced
salt and black pepper, to taste
1 tablespoon ground cumin or paprika or to taste, plus a sprinkling for garnish
juice of 1 lemon, plus more to taste
¼ cup sour cream
fresh parsley leaves, chopped, for garnish

Directions:

Put all ingredients into a food processor and mix, adding chickpea liquid as needed to allow processor to produce a smooth purée. Taste and adjust the seasonings (I often like to add much more lemon juice). Serve in a bowl, drizzle with the olive oil, and sprinkle with a bit more cumin or paprika. Add some parsley and even pine nuts or sun dried tomato bits on top. Pita triangles, pita chips, warm chunks of torn bread, cucumbers, carrots, or just about any raw vegetable you have on hand are wonderful for dipping into this delicious hummus.

Island Conch Salad

YIELD: 4 servings

Ingredients:

1 pound (2 cups) fresh conch, cleaned, diced (optional, diced squid)
1 jalapeño pepper, stemmed, minced, and deseeded
1 tablespoon fresh cilantro leaves, chopped
½ English cucumber, peeled and minced
½ yellow bell pepper, minced
½ red bell pepper, minced
¼ red onion, minced
¼ cup fresh orange juice
2 tablespoons fresh lime juice
2 tablespoons fresh lemon juice
2 tablespoons olive oil
1 tablespoon Kosher salt
½ cup fresh tomato, diced
¼ large avocado or ½ small avocado, diced

Directions:

In a large bowl, combine all ingredients except tomato and avocado. Stir well to combine, cover, and refrigerate for at least 2 hours to meld flavors. Taste and adjust seasonings, adding hot pepper sauce for a spicier conch salad. To serve, gently fold in the tomato and avocado and serve in 4 small serving bowls or chilled martini glasses for a fancier presentation.

Jalapeño Cheese Squares

YIELD: 8–10 servings

Ingredients:

3 jalapeño peppers, stemmed, deseeded, and cut into thin rounds

1 pound bacon, cooked to crisp, drained, and crumbled

2 cups cheddar cheese, shredded

12 eggs, beaten until fluffy with electric mixer

Directions:

Preheat oven to 350°F. Spray a 9 x 11-inch casserole dish with nonstick spray. Place jalapeño slices evenly on bottom of pan and sprinkle crumbled bacon on top. Add a layer of cheddar cheese and pour beaten eggs evenly on top. Bake for 20 to 25 minutes. Cut into squares and serve upside down while still hot.

Jalapeño Deviled Eggs

YIELD: 24 stuffed eggs

Ingredients:

½ cup shredded pepper jack cheese

12 hard-boiled eggs, peeled

3 tablespoons mayonnaise

3 tablespoons cream cheese, softened

1 jalapeño, stemmed, deseeded, and finely chopped

3 tablespoons green onions, thinly sliced

salt, to taste

pepper, to taste

3 slices bacon, cooked to crisp and finely crumbled

chili powder, to garnish

Directions:

Preheat oven to 400°F. Line a baking sheet with parchment paper and place 1 tablespoon of shredded cheese on prepared parchment and pat into a 2-inch circle. Repeat with remaining cheese, allowing 2 inches between circles, as they'll spread out when baking. Bake for 7 to 8 minutes or until bubbly and lightly golden. Let stand on the baking sheet for 1 to 2 minutes until cooled but still pliable. Carefully peel cheese crisps off the parchment paper. Place cheese crisps on a wire rack and let cool completely. Once crisps are cool, break them into smaller pieces and set aside. Cut the peeled hard-boiled eggs in half, gently scoop yolks into a small-sized bowl, and mash yolks with a fork. Carefully set whites aside. Add mayonnaise, cream cheese, chopped jalapeño, and sliced green onions and mix well. Season with salt and pepper. With a small spoon, fill the egg halves with the yolk mixture and top each egg half with a little of the crispy cheese and crumbled bacon. Sprinkle with chili powder and serve immediately.

Joyce's Guacamole

We met Joyce and Gary on the jitney that ran from the ferry dock on Water Island in the harbor of St. Thomas, USVI to the Sea Cliff Hotel at the top of the island. They owned a beautiful home on the far eastern side of the island and were avid sailors, Gary often serving as our first mate when we were day chartering. Joyce was a great cook and often made appetizers for us to serve to our guests. Her guacamole was one of our favorites.

YIELD: 4 servings

Ingredients:

1 large avocado, mashed
1½ tablespoons lemon juice
2 garlic cloves, finely minced
1 tomato, diced
2 tablespoons onion, grated
2 tablespoons sour cream
cumin (optional, to taste)
salt and pepper, to taste

Directions:

Mash all ingredients together, leaving guacamole chunky. If adding cumin, start with just a small shake and add to taste. Chill and serve with tortilla chips.

Marinated Button Mushrooms

YIELD: 2 cups

Ingredients:

⅓ cup red wine vinegar
⅓ cup olive oil
½ teaspoon onion salt
¼ teaspoon celery salt
¼ teaspoon marjoram
2 tablespoons fresh parsley, chopped, or 1
    teaspoon parsley flakes
garlic salt, pepper, and dill, to taste
1 (10 ounce) can or jar of button mushrooms,
    drained

Directions:

In a medium-sized bowl, combine vinegar, oil, onion and celery salt, marjoram, parsley, and remaining spices and herbs to taste. Whisk well and add drained button mushrooms. Cover and chill for at least 4 hours or overnight. Serve as appetizer bites or on your favorite salad.

Marinated Mozzarella Slices

YIELD: 4 to 6 servings

Ingredients:

1 pound fresh mozzarella, cut into ¼-inch
    slices
3 tablespoons olive oil
1 teaspoon fresh thyme
1 teaspoon fresh rosemary, finely chopped
1 teaspoon fresh oregano, finely chopped
¼ teaspoon red pepper flakes
salt and pepper, to taste
olives, cured meats, crackers, or bread, for
    serving

Directions:

Place sliced mozzarella decoratively on a plate. Combine olive oil, herbs, red pepper flakes, salt, and pepper in a small bowl and whisk to blend. Drizzle oil and herb blend over mozzarella, cover, and let stand to meld flavors for 20 minutes up to 1 hour. Serve with olives, cured meats, crackers, or bread on the side.

Mini Cabo San Lucas Green Chili Quiches

YIELD: *24 mini quiches*

Ingredients:

½ cup butter, softened (optional, margarine)
1 (3 ounce) package cream cheese, softened
1 cup all-purpose flour
1 cup grated cheese (Monterey Jack, Pepper Jack, cheddar, Colby, or a combination)
1 (4 ounce) can green chilies, chopped
2 eggs, lightly beaten
½ cup heavy cream
¼ teaspoon salt
pepper, to taste
2 (12 cup) mini muffin tins

Directions:

Blend butter and cream cheese in a bowl until smooth. Stir in flour a little bit at a time, blending well. Form dough into a ball, wrap in wax paper, and chill 2 to 3 hours or overnight. Preheat oven to 350°F when ready to bake. Lightly grease each mini muffin pan and form dough into 24 smaller balls. Press each ball into a muffin pan to form a shell by poking it down with your finger. Sprinkle cheese and chilies in the bottom of each small pastry shell. Combine eggs, cream, salt, and pepper and pour evenly over cheese and chilies in pastry shells. Bake 30 to 35 minutes. Serve warm or cool. Leftovers can be stored in freezer, then brought to room temperature and lightly warmed in 325°F oven.

Mini Crab Cakes

YIELD: 24 mini crab cakes

Ingredients:

8 ounces cream cheese, softened to room temperature
1 cup Parmesan cheese, divided
1 large egg
¼ cup sour cream
1 teaspoon orange zest
½ teaspoon lemon zest
4 teaspoons plus 4 tablespoons chopped fresh chives, divided
¼ teaspoon Kosher salt
cayenne pepper, large pinch
6 ounces fresh lump crabmeat, picked over, patted dry, coarsely shredded
1½ cups bread crumbs
¾ cup Parmesan cheese
½ cup (1 stick) butter, melted
fresh chives cut into pieces, to garnish
1 (12 cup) mini muffin tin

Directions:

Preheat oven to 350°F. Beat cream cheese with an electric mixer in a medium bowl until smooth. Add ¼ cup Parmesan and egg and beat to blend. Beat in sour cream, orange zest, lemon zest, 4 teaspoons chopped chives, Kosher salt, and cayenne pepper. Gently fold in crabmeat. (This can be prepared one day ahead if covered tightly and refrigerated.) Spray mini muffin tin cups with nonstick spray. Mix bread crumbs, remaining Parmesan and chopped chives in a bowl. Drizzle in melted butter, tossing with a fork until evenly moistened. Press 1 rounded tablespoon of bread crumb mixture into the bottom of each muffin tin cup (make a well with your thumb), to form the crust for the crab cakes. Spoon 1 generous tablespoon crab mixture into each cup. Sprinkle more bread crumb mixture on top. Bake until golden on top, about 20 minutes. Cool in pan for 5 minutes. Gently lift each crab cake out of the pan with a fork onto a serving platter. Can be made 2 hours ahead. Rewarm in a 350°F oven for 5 to 6 minutes. Arrange crab cakes on a serving platter; sprinkle with chives.

Tapenade

Tapenade recipes originally were found in Provence, France and began showing up in the US around the sixties. They slowly made their way from restaurants to homes and are now a staple in most kitchens. Though it sounds "elegant" or hard to make, tapenades are one of the simplest dishes to make, can be used in such various ways, and lend flavor and flair to any meal or cocktail party. There are so many variations of tapenade and I've been offered so many different ways to serve it from fellow boaters that I'm including a few choice tapenades here. Go ahead and use your imagination both with the ingredients you use and how you serve your own variations of this delicious French creation. You can also use a mortar and pestle rather than a food processor to combine ingredients, just be careful not to mush it up too much as "bits and pieces" look so pretty when serving. Remember, it's always a good idea to make it a day ahead of when you plan to use it to help meld all the delicious flavors together. Tapenades keep well tightly sealed in the refrigerator for a week or in a tightly sealed container in the freezer for up to 3 months.

Try tapenades on the following:
1. Crackers or with cheese on crackers or even spread some hummus and tapenade on a cracker.
2. A topping for deviled eggs.
3. Stuffed in cherry tomatoes with a little feta.
4. In an omelet.
5. Use a dollop on broiled or grilled fish.
6. Make little slits in a chicken breast and rub tapenade into them before cooking.
7. Stuff mushrooms with a dollop of tapenade.
8. Mix with salad greens as a dressing.
9. Add to pasta with chopped tomatoes and fresh basil and a little Parmesan.
10. Roll into biscuit, gougers, pizza, or bread dough.

Tri-Olive Tapenade

YIELD: 4 cups

Ingredients:

1 cup large green olives, pitted
1 cup black olives, pitted
1 cup Kalamata olives, pitted
2 tablespoons capers, drained
5 garlic cloves
1 red bell pepper, roasted, peeled, cut into 1-inch pieces
1 tablespoon basil, chopped
1 tablespoon parsley, chopped
3 teaspoons lemon juice
5 tablespoons olive oil
3–4 anchovy fillets (optional)
crumbled feta cheese (optional)

Directions:

Put all the olives, capers, garlic, and red pepper into a food processor. Pulse at small 1-second intervals about 10 to 12 times, scraping down the sides of the bowl as necessary. Add basil, parsley, lemon juice, and olive oil and pulse another 10 to 12 times, scraping down the sides of the bowl to make a final tapenade with ⅛-inch to ¼-inch pieces of olives and other ingredients so that you can see all the colors of the olives and peppers. Place in a bowl and mix optional feta cheese in to taste just before serving.

Artichoke & Dried Tomato Tapenade

YIELD: 4 cups

Ingredients:

1½ cups pitted green olives
1 (9 ounce) package frozen artichoke hearts, thawed, coarsely chopped
2 cloves garlic, minced
1 cup drained oil-pack dried tomatoes, chopped
2 tablespoons capers, drained
2 anchovy fillets, drained (optional)
1 tablespoon Dijon mustard
1 tablespoon fresh basil, thyme, oregano, parsley, and/or rosemary, chopped
2 tablespoons lemon juice
⅓ cup olive oil

Directions:

Put the olives, artichokes, garlic, dried tomatoes, capers, anchovies, and herbs in a food processor. Pulse at small 1-second intervals about 10 to 12 times, scraping down the sides of the bowl as necessary. Add lemon juice and olive oil and pulse another 10 to 12 times, scraping down the sides of the bowl to make a final tapenade with ⅛-inch to ¼-inch pieces of olives and other ingredients so that you can see all the colors of the olives and peppers.

Almond & Orange Tapenade

YIELD: 4 cups

Ingredients:

1 cup slivered almonds, toasted
1½ cups pitted Kalamata olives
½ cup pitted black olives
2 tablespoons capers, drained
2 cloves garlic, minced
2 anchovy fillets (optional)
1 tablespoon snipped fresh basil, thyme,
    oregano, parsley, and/or rosemary
1 tablespoon Dijon mustard
⅓ cup olive oil
2 tablespoons balsamic vinegar
2 tablespoons orange juice
1 tablespoon orange peel, grated/zested
orange peel, cut into thin strips, for garnish

Directions:

Put the almonds, olives, capers, garlic, anchovies, herbs, and mustard in a food processor. Pulse at small 1-second intervals about 10 to 12 times, scraping down the sides of the bowl as necessary. Add oil, balsamic vinegar, orange juice, and orange peel and pulse another 10-12 times, scraping down the sides of the bowl to make a final tapenade with ⅛-inch to ¼-inch pieces of olives and other ingredients so that you can see all the colors of the olives and capers.

Wine, Fig & Olive Tapenade

YIELD: 4 cups

Ingredients:

1 cup dry white wine such as Sauvignon Blanc,
    Pinot Grigio, or Chardonnay
1 cup dried mission figs, stemmed and
    quartered
1 cup Kalamata olives, pitted
juice of ½ lemon
zest of 1 lemon
¼ cup extra-virgin olive oil

Directions:

Pour wine in small bowl, add the quartered figs, and soak in the wine for at least 30 minutes up to 2 hours. Drain the figs and reserve the wine and fig liquid. In a food processor, add drained figs, olives, lemon juice, ¾ lemon zest, and 1 tablespoon of the wine and pulse until blended. Add more wine up to 1 cup if the mixture is too thick to blend. Add olive oil and pulse a few seconds. Garnish with the remainder of the lemon zest.

Artichoke Tapenade

YIELD: 1½ cups

Ingredients:

1 (14 ounce) jar artichoke hearts, quartered and drained
2 tablespoons parsley, rough chopped
1 tablespoon canola oil or other mild oil
2 tablespoons olive oil
⅓ cup Parmesan cheese (freshly grated if available)
1 tablespoon lemon juice
¼ teaspoon garlic, finely grated
½ teaspoon Kosher salt or more to taste
pepper, to taste

Directions:

Pick over artichoke quarters, making sure to remove any tough outer leaves. Place all ingredients in a food processor and pulse until a coarse paste is formed. Taste and adjust flavors.

Poached Salmon Mousse with Dill Sauce

YIELD: 6 cups

Salmon Mousse Ingredients:

1 envelope gelatin, unflavored
¼ cup cold water
½ cup boiling water
½ cup mayonnaise
1 tablespoon fresh lemon juice
1 tablespoon onion, finely grated
2 drops hot sauce
¼ teaspoon paprika
2 tablespoons fresh dill, minced
1 teaspoon salt
2 cups flaked and small diced salmon
1 cup whipping cream
lemon slices, for garnish
fresh parsley, rough chopped, for garnish

Dill Sauce:

1 English cucumber, peeled,
    grated, and drained for 1 hour
1 cup sour cream
1 cup mayonnaise
1 tablespoon fresh lemon juice
1 small clove garlic, finely minced
1 teaspoon salt
⅔ cup fresh dill, finely chopped

Salmon Mousse Directions:

Lightly grease a 6-cup fish mold or serving bowl with butter or a thin layer of mayonnaise. Soften the gelatin in ¼ cup cold water. Stir well while adding ½ cup boiling water, whisking until the gelatin has dissolved, then cool to room temperature. Whisk in mayonnaise, lemon juice, onion, hot sauce, paprika, dill, and salt and mix well. Cover and refrigerate 15 minutes until mixture begins to thicken slightly. Gently fold in the salmon. In a separate bowl, whip the whipping cream until you have nice soft peaks, then gently fold the whipped cream into the salmon mixture until everything is well combined. Pour the mixture into your prepared fish mold or serving bowl and cover with plastic wrap and chill in the refrigerator for 8 hours or overnight. When ready to serve, un-mold the mousse onto a large plate. Take the lemon slices and create a "tail" on the back of the fish. Surround the mousse with parsley and serve with optional dill sauce in a small side bowl with crackers and pumpernickel bread or on finger toasts.

Dill Sauce Directions:

Combine all dill sauce ingredients in a medium-sized bowl. Cover with plastic wrap and chill for at least 1 hour.

Pub Cheese

YIELD: 3 Cups

Ingredients:

1½ cups sharp cheddar cheese, shredded
8 ounces cream cheese, softened
½ cup beer (substitute with wine, apple cider, or water)
½ teaspoon dry mustard
½ teaspoon cayenne pepper
1–3 tablespoons prepared horseradish
1 tablespoon parsley, minced
1 teaspoon salt
bacon bits (optional for garnish)
scallions, sliced (optional for garnish)

Directions:

Place all ingredients into a food processor and pulse until blended. It is okay to have some small lumps. Scoop out into a serving bowl and refrigerate for 20 to 30 minutes before serving. Top with bacon bits and scallions as a garnish. Serve with carrot or celery sticks, chips or crackers, or spread on pita chips. Garnish with green onion and parsley.

5-Ingredient Green Onion Dip

YIELD: 1½ cups

Ingredients:

¾ cup mayonnaise
¾ cup sour cream
½ cup green onions, chopped fine
1 clove garlic, finely minced
1 teaspoon Worcestershire sauce

Directions:

In a small bowl, thoroughly combine all ingredients. Cover and chill to meld flavors. Serve with sliced veggies or chips.

Baked Crab Dip

YIELD: 3–4 servings

Ingredients:

2 ounces cream cheese, softened
1 tablespoon butter, softened
1 tablespoon mayonnaise
¼ cup sour cream
¼ teaspoon seasoned salt (your preference, Mrs. Dash, Goya or any type seasoned salt)
⅛ teaspoon paprika
¼ onion, diced
¼ green pepper, finely diced
¼ cup mozzarella cheese, shredded
1 (6 ounce) can or ¾ cup crabmeat, drained and picked over
1 green onion, diced for garnish
parsley, chopped for garnish

Directions:

Preheat oven to 350°F. In a medium bowl, mix the cream cheese, butter, mayonnaise, and sour cream together until smooth. Add in salt and paprika and then stir in onions, green pepper, mozzarella cheese, and crabmeat. Scoop ingredients into a lightly greased small shallow baking dish and bake 10 to 14 minutes until nice and bubbly. Serve with bread chunks, crackers, or corn chips. Garnish with green onion and parsley.

Retro Sausages

YIELD: 10 servings

Ingredients:

1 pound Hillshire Farm Lit'l Smokies Smoked Sausage (45 sausages to a package)
1 (12 ounce) can or jar chili sauce
1 (10 ounce) jar grape jelly

Directions:

First let me say yes, Lit'l Smokies are available in many countries, and yes, people still love these wonderful little smoked sausages. They freeze well in their original packaging, so load up and freeze a few packages. Place sausages in a large pot and heat over medium heat until nice and plump. Add chili sauce and grape jelly, stir well to cover all sausages, and continue to stir until sauce is hot and thick. Serve in a bowl with toothpicks and napkins.

Retro Sausages in Bbq Sauce

YIELD: 10 servings

Ingredients:

1 pound Hillshire Farm Lit'l Smokies Smoked
    Sausage (45 sausages to a package)
BBQ sauce

Directions:

Preheat oven to 350° F. Place sausages in a backing dish, pour BBQ sauce over to cover, and bake 30 minutes. Serve in a bowl with toothpicks and napkins.

Bacon-Wrapped Retro Sausages

YIELD: 10 servings

Ingredients:

1 pound Hillshire Farm Lit'l Smokies Smoked
    Sausage (45 sausages to a package)
1 pound bacon, cut into ⅓-inch pieces
skewers, (if using wooden skewers, soak in
    water 30 minutes before using)
1 cup brown sugar

Directions:

Preheat oven to 350° F. Wrap each sausage with a piece of bacon and put several bacon-wrapped sausages on each skewer. Place sausages on a baking sheet, sprinkle them liberally with brown sugar, and bake until bacon is crisp and brown sugar is melted, about 30 to 45 minutes. Keep an eye on them, as the sugar can burn. Serve with toothpicks and napkins.

Salsa Roja

YIELD: 4 servings

Ingredients:

2 medium-sized ripe tomatoes, quartered
1 small onion, rough chopped
½ cup cilantro sprigs
2 garlic cloves, quartered
1 teaspoon garlic salt
2 teaspoons lemon juice
1 jalapeño, stemmed, deseeded, and rough
    chopped
¼ green pepper, stemmed, deseeded, and
    rough chopped

Directions:

Combine all ingredients in a food processor and pulse to desired consistency. The texture can vary depending on your use and preference, from puréed smooth to semi-chunky. Serve as a dip for tortilla chips, celery, or green pepper slices, or on bruschetta. Kick up your mac and cheese or rice, on eggs and omelets, slathered on baked or grilled chicken, in a taco wrap, on cucumber slices, on top of a bed of shredded lettuce in a crispy flour tortilla bowl, or spooned on grilled steak or shrimp as we often do. Remember that the seeds of the jalapeño are where the heat is, so if you want a hotter salsa, add a few seeds to taste and add more if desired. Be careful, those seeds heat up the salsa quickly! Store in a sealed container and refrigerate for at least 4 hours to let flavors meld together.

Salsa Verde Cruda

YIELD: 2 cups

Ingredients:

1 pound tomatillos, husks removed, rinsed, and halved

1 large ripe avocado, peeled, halved, and deseeded

¼ cup cilantro leaves and tops of stems, coarsely chopped

2 tablespoons white onion, coarsely chopped

1 jalapeño, stemmed and deseeded, (optional, chili or serrano pepper)

½ teaspoon Kosher salt (optional, coarse sea salt)

Directions:

Combine all ingredients in a food processor or blender and blend until smooth. Make ahead and refrigerate at least 2 hours or overnight to meld the flavors. Wonderful on avocado and chicken enchiladas, omelets, or as a dip with corn chips. You can use your imagination with this tasty salsa!

Sea Cliff Hotel's Simple Shrimp Ceviche for Two

YIELD: 2 small servings

Ingredients:

1 cup uncooked shrimp, shelled, deveined, and cut into bite-size chunks

½ cup tomato, finely chopped

½ cup white onion, finely chopped

1 jalapeño, stemmed, deseeded, and chopped

¼ cup fresh cilantro, chopped

juice of 3 limes

salt, to taste

1 tablespoon olive oil

Directions:

Place prepared shrimp in a glass or stainless steel bowl; add the tomato, onion, jalapeño, and cilantro. Gently stir, then cover ingredients with fresh lime juice. The lime juice should cover the entire shrimp mixture. Cover tightly and chill until shrimp is "citrus cooked," 20 to 30 minutes, stirring every 5 minutes. Remove from fridge, drain lime juice, add salt and oil, and gently combine. Serve in 2 small glasses or martini glasses, or serve in one glass bowl and serve with tortilla chips.

Smoked Salmon Dill & Goat Cheese Squares

YIELD: 25 squares

Ingredients:

1 tablespoon vegetable oil
1 cup onion, sliced into ¼-inch pieces
½ cup celery, diced into ¼-inch pieces
4 ounces cream cheese, softened at room temperature
4 ounces goat cheese
5 eggs
½ cup dry bread crumbs
¼ teaspoon salt
½ teaspoon pepper
3 tablespoons fresh dill, finely chopped
2 tablespoons capers, chopped
1 tablespoon lemon zest, finely grated
5 ounces smoked salmon, cut into ½-inch pieces

Directions:

Preheat oven to 350°F. Lightly grease an 8-inch square baking pan and line bottom and sides with parchment paper so that it hangs over the sides of the pan. In a sauté pan over medium heat, add oil, onions, and celery and sauté until onions are translucent, about 5 minutes. Remove from heat and cool. Place cream cheese and goat cheese in a food processor and pulse until smooth. With processor running, add eggs one at a time, scraping the processor often to keep ingredients all blended. Add bread crumbs, salt, pepper, dill, capers, and lemon zest and pulse to mix. Scoop mixture into a bowl and gently stir in the smoked salmon by hand. Spread salmon mixture into the prepared baking pan and bake for about 30 minutes, until the top is a light golden color. Let cool in pan, then refrigerate to chill before cutting and serving. Cut into equal size squares. Serve chilled, at room temperature, or warmed in the oven at 225°F for 10 to 12 minutes.

Spinach & Salmon Mousse

YIELD: 4½ cups

Ingredients:

1 (15 ounce) can of salmon, drained and flaked or 2 cups fresh salmon, cooked
1 (8 ounce) package cream cheese, softened
1 pound fresh spinach, cooked, drained, chopped, and cooled
⅔ cup green onions, sliced
2 tablespoons fresh parsley, chopped
2 tablespoons fresh dill, chopped or 2 teaspoons dried dill weed
½ teaspoon seasoned salt of your choice
⅛ teaspoon pepper
1 cup heavy cream, whipped

Directions:

Mix all ingredients except the whipped cream in a large bowl with electric mixer at medium speed. Fold in whipped cream and gently blend with a spoon. Place salmon spinach mixture in a bowl, cover tightly, and refrigerate at least 2 hours to meld flavors. Serve with crackers.

Optional:

Hollow out a 1-pound round loaf of bread, leaving at least a 1-inch thick shell. Place salmon spinach mixture into the bread shell, cover tightly, and refrigerate at least 2 hours to meld flavors. The reserved torn bread hunks from inside the original loaf are excellent for dipping into this mousse, and as the mousse and bread hunks are eaten, your guests can begin tearing off bread chunks from the top of the loaf until it's all gone (which is generally by the second glass of wine).

Spinach Puffs

YIELD: 6 servings

Ingredients:

1 (10 ounce) package frozen spinach, chopped and thawed
½ cup crumbled feta cheese
¼ cup onion, minced
1 tablespoon olive oil
1 teaspoon dill, chopped
1 teaspoon garlic, minced
salt (preferably Kosher)
freshly ground black pepper
2 large eggs
1 sheet frozen puff pastry, thawed, rolled out to a 12-inch square, chilled

Directions:

Puffs can be completely assembled 3 hours in advance. Just cover and chill before cooking. Preheat oven to 400°F. Have a 6-cup muffin tin ready for the puff pastry; no greasing or butter is necessary. Squeeze spinach by hand, forcing out as much water as possible until dry, as too much water will make your filling soggy. You will have about ⅔ cup of well-drained spinach. Put spinach in a medium bowl and add the feta cheese, minced onion, olive oil, dill, and garlic. Add salt and pepper to taste. Mix 1 egg with a fork and fold into spinach mixture. Cut chilled puff pastry into 3 equal strips. Reserve 1 strip for later. Cut the 2 remaining strips into 3 squares for a total of 6 pieces of puff pastry. Place a square of puff pastry in each muffin cup, pressing into the bottom and up the sides of each cup, leaving corners pointing up. Divide filling among the 6 muffin cups. Fold pastry over filling, pressing corners together to meet in the center. In a small bowl, beat the remaining egg with a fork just to blend. Brush pastry with egg wash. (I do this with all pies, as it gives the pastry a nice sheen.) Bake until pastry is golden brown and puffed, about 25 minutes. Transfer to a wire rack, leaving puffs in the tins to cool for 10 minutes. Gently run a sharp knife around pan edges to loosen and turn out puffs onto rack to cool slightly before serving.

Spinach-Stuffed Mushrooms

YIELD: 30 mushrooms

Ingredients:

1½ pounds (30) fresh mushrooms
3 boxes frozen spinach, chopped
1 cup Italian-seasoned bread crumbs
6 green onions, minced and lightly sautéed in
   butter
1 egg, slightly beaten
½ cup butter, melted
½ cup Parmesan cheese
salt, to taste

Directions:

Preheat oven to 350°F. Wash and dry mushrooms, remove stems, and reserve for another use, i.e., sliced in an omelet or as part of a homemade veggie stock. Remove the gills to give you a mushroom that holds more stuffing. Cook spinach according to package directions and drain well, then squeeze dry in paper towels. Mix all remaining ingredients, stuff the mushroom caps, and bake for 15 minutes. Serve immediately.

Shrimp-Stuffed Mushrooms

YIELD: 16 mushrooms

Ingredients:

16 medium to large mushrooms, cleaned and
   destemmed (reserve stems)
1 small onion, finely chopped
½ cup dry bread crumbs
½ cup melted butter
3 tablespoons lemon juice
1 teaspoon salt
⅛ teaspoon pepper
16 small shrimp

Directions:

Preheat oven to 325°F. Chop mushroom stems and place in a medium bowl and combine with chopped onion and bread crumbs. In a separate bowl, combine melted butter, lemon juice, salt, and pepper, then add ½ of this mixture to onion and bread crumb bowl and mix well. Fill mushroom caps with stuffing mixture and press one shrimp into each mushroom cap. Place on a lightly nonstick-sprayed baking sheet and sprinkle remaining stuffing mixture evenly over mushrooms. Bake 15 to 30 minutes until done.

Creamed Salsa Dip

YIELD: 2 cups

Ingredients:

- 1 (8 ounce) package cream cheese, softened to room temperature
- 1 cup prepared salsa (any type of salsa is great and each offers a different-tasting dip)

Directions:

Beat cream cheese until smooth and add salsa of your choice. Mix well to blend and refrigerate. Serve with tortilla chips or sliced veggies.

Sweet Pickled Peppers

YIELD: 1–2 quart glass jar

Ingredients:

- 9 ounces miniature sweet peppers, mixed yellow, red, and orange, washed, stemmed, halved, and deseeded
- 4 jalapeño peppers, stemmed, deseeded, and sliced into thin rings
- 1 cup water
- 1 cup white vinegar
- ¼ cup sugar
- 2 tablespoons pickling spices
- 1½ tablespoons salt

Directions:

Put prepared sweet peppers and jalapeños in a large heat resistant bowl. In a stainless-steel medium-sized saucepan, add remaining ingredients and cook over medium heat, stirring occasionally until sugar and salt are dissolved. Carefully pour hot vinegar mixture over peppers and let cool. When completely cooled, store in a 2-quart glass jar or divide into several smaller jars, cover tightly with lids, and refrigerate at least overnight to meld flavors. They store well refrigerated and are still delicious over a month later. Serve in small bowls as an accompaniment to meat or fish, or on a charcuterie and cheese plate with meats, cheese, pickles, olives, nuts and dried fruits, or simply poke a toothpick in a slice and enjoy.

Sweet Spiced Walnuts

YIELD: 2 cups

Ingredients:

1 egg white
1 tablespoon water
2 cups halved walnuts
¼ cup sugar
1 tablespoon ground cinnamon
½ teaspoon ground allspice

Directions:

Preheat oven to 225°F. Line a large shallow baking pan with foil. In a medium bowl, combine egg white and water and beat with an electric mixer until foamy. Add the walnuts and toss to evenly coat. Pour the walnut mixture into a strainer and let drain for 2 to 3 minutes. In a re-sealable plastic or paper bag, combine sugar, cinnamon, and allspice and shake well to mix, then add in the walnuts. Seal the bag or twist tightly if it's a paper bag and shake hard to coat the nuts evenly with spice mix. Spread the nuts in a single layer in the baking pan and bake for 1 hour on very low heat, stirring every 15 minutes. Remove from the oven and let cool completely, stirring occasionally and breaking the nuts apart if they stick together. Store in tightly covered jar.

Toasted Cheese Triangles

YIELD: 32 triangles

Ingredients:

2 cups flour
2 teaspoons baking powder
½ teaspoon salt
¼ teaspoons ground red pepper
3 tablespoons shortening
½ cup (2 ounces) sharp cheese, finely grated, plus extra for topping
¾ cup milk + 1 tablespoon

Directions:

Preheat oven to 400°F. Lightly grease 2 baking sheets and set aside. Stir flour, baking powder, salt, and red pepper in a large bowl and using a pastry blender, cut in the shortening until dough is the size of coarse crumbs. Stir in ½ cup grated sharp cheese, add ¾ cup milk, and stir just until dry ingredients are moistened. Form dough into a ball and roll on a lightly floured surface into a 10-inch (¼-inch thick) square. Brush the dough with remaining milk and sprinkle the top with grated sharp cheese for topping and lightly press cheese into dough. Cut dough into 16 (2½-inch) squares. Cut each square in half diagonally to make 32 triangles. Place triangles onto prepared baking sheets. Bake 12 to 15 minutes or until golden brown. Serve warm alone or dipped in a pesto or red pepper sauce.

T's Queso

YIELD: Serves a group

Ingredients:

½ pound hamburger, browned
½ pound ground sausage, browned
1 small onion, chopped
1 jalapeño pepper plus more to taste, stemmed, deseeded, and diced
3 pounds Velveeta cheese, cut into chunks
1 large can stewed tomatoes, cut into small pieces
1 can cream of mushroom soup, undiluted
1 teaspoon pepper
2 tablespoons Worcestershire sauce
1–2 tablespoons chili powder, to taste
½ teaspoon cayenne pepper
1 teaspoon dry mustard

Directions:

With a fork, break up hamburger and sausage and sauté in a large pan until done, making sure to continue to break up large pieces. Add onion and jalapeño and cook till soft. Remove from stove and drain off fat, put pan back on stove over very low heat. Add remaining ingredients and stir well. Cover and continue to warm until cheese is melted and all ingredients are well combined, continuing to stir every couple of minutes. Serve with tortilla chips, dipping crackers, or chips.

Tzatziki (Cucumber Sauce)

YIELD: 1½ cups

Ingredients:

1 medium English cucumber
salt for sprinkling on cucumber + ¼ teaspoon
1 cup Greek yogurt
1 garlic clove, peeled and crushed
1 tablespoon fresh dill, finely chopped
2 teaspoons white wine vinegar
2 tablespoons olive oil

Directions:

Peel cucumber, cut it in half lengthwise, and scoop out seeds with a small spoon. Grate cucumber and sprinkle with salt. Let stand 10 minutes and transfer to 2 to 3 paper towels and squeeze dry. Place cucumber in a medium bowl and stir in yogurt, garlic, dill, vinegar, oil and remaining ¼ teaspoon salt. Cover tightly and refrigerate for 1 hour up to 2 days. Serve with pita chips or on a seafood dish. It's especially good on a seafood cake sandwich and as a side with lamb.

Veggie-Seafood Skewers

YIELD: *4 servings*

Ingredients:

¼ large red onion, cut into 1½-inch chunks
½ red bell pepper, cut into 1½-inch chunks
½ green bell pepper, cut into 1½-inch chunks
½ orange bell pepper, cut into 1½-inch chunks
½ yellow bell pepper, cut into 1½-inch chunks
12 ounces fish cut into 12 (1½-inch) chunks
olive oil
salt and black pepper, to taste
1–2 lemons, halved and charred on the grill

Directions:

Preheat grill. Soak wooden skewers for 30 minutes or up to 24 hours. Water is generally used to soak but soaking skewers in beer, different types of juice, wine, or other flavored liquid is a wonderful way to impart some different flavor to the skewers. Alternate onion, several pieces of different colored peppers, and then a chunk of fish and continue until there are approximately 3 good-sized chunks of fish with 4 layers of veggies on each skewer. Brush the skewers with lots of olive oil to keep them from sticking to the grill, sprinkle with salt and pepper, and place on hot grill. Using a grill pan will help avoid losing pieces into the bottom of the BBQ. Turn skewers once during grilling and keep on the grill until the veggies have softened a little bit. You'll want a nice char for a beautiful presentation. Serve with rice, squeezing charred lemon on skewers and rice or over a bed of mixed greens.

Who Knew Pate

Who Knew Pate is a good substitute for "real" pate when time and ingredients are unavailable.

YIELD: 16–18 servings

Ingredients for the Aspic:

3 envelopes unflavored gelatin
6 tablespoons cold water
2 (10½ ounce) cans beef consommé
2 tablespoons sherry

Ingredients for the Pate:

1 (1 pound) package liverwurst
1 (8 ounce) package cream cheese, softened
2 tablespoons Worcestershire sauce
2 tablespoons sherry
1 small onion, grated

Directions for the Aspic:

Dissolve the gelatin in cold water. Heat the beef consommé and add the dissolved gelatin, then the sherry, stirring until all is blended. Remove from heat and let cool. While the gelatin is still a liquid, pour a 1-inch deep amount into an oblong or round bowl or a very lightly greased mold and put this in the refrigerator to jell. Set aside the remaining consommé mixture.

Directions for the Pate:

Place all the pate ingredients in a food processor and blend until smooth. Taste and adjust flavor, being careful not to make the mixture too thin. When the gelatin mixture in the mold is set, place the pate in the center to about 1 inch from the edge. Fill the sides of the mold, then top with the remaining consommé mixture. Chill until well set or overnight. Serve unmolded onto a chilled serving dish with crackers on the side.

CHAPTER 7
Breads

Breads

Yes you can, and yes you should make breads of all sorts aboard! There's nothing like the smell of warm bread wafting out of the galley, and nothing is as satisfying as the taste and accomplishment of serving homemade breads and biscuits of every flavor and type imaginable. Bread and biscuit making is fun, and the accolades you will get from family, friends, and crew will keep you baking as often as there are impulses for pita sandwiches, fresh pizza, bagels, English muffins, or French, dill, or any savory or sweet bread.

We generally turned our engine on once a day, even at anchor, to charge batteries and to run the compressor for the reefer/freezer holding plates. We realized early on in this routine that the interior of the boat heated up from the engine running, so we began running the engine early in the morning when the cool morning breezes were still blowing enough to cool the interior air of our boat. This was the very best time of day to begin making dough, as we learned the warm engine room was a perfect place to set nicely covered, fragrant dough to rise. When we were sailing, we put our covered dough in the warmest and safest place in the boat to rise.

Making bread is very easy but it's the time it takes to properly rise and proof (proofing most commonly refers to the second or final rise the dough undergoes) that generally causes one to shy away from making it. If you haven't made bread on board before, try the warm engine area for this step. The results will encourage you to be a regular bread maker. Sometimes the first rise can take 40 minutes to 2 hours depending on your yeast and the temperature of the area where it is rising—make sure not to rush the process or do something else while the process is taking place.

I learned something new about bread making from each of the cooks I met on boats, and though there were some common threads like good quality yeast and good flour, they each had ingredients that differed as well as their own bread baking secrets. One of the secrets I learned from a young Swedish cook is to cover the baking bread with a pan or large stainless steel ovenproof bowl for the first 10 to 15 minutes of baking, which traps naturally released steam. After 10 to 15 minutes, carefully remove the pan or bowl and continue cooking. I used this steam secret only about a quarter of the time I made bread, so my advice is to experiment and bake what gives you the most pleasure.

100-Year-Old Ginger Bread

YIELD: 10 to 12 servings

Ingredients:

½ cup shortening
½ cup brown sugar
1 egg, lightly beaten
1 cup dark molasses
2 cups flour
1 teaspoon baking soda
½ –¾ teaspoon powdered ginger or more to taste
1 teaspoon cinnamon
dash of cloves
½ teaspoon salt
1 cup boiling water
powdered sugar for sprinkling, optional

Directions:

Preheat oven to 350°F. In a medium bowl with an electric mixer, cream shortening and sugar together until well mixed and then add beaten egg and molasses. In a separate bowl, sift together flour, baking soda, ginger, cinnamon, cloves, and salt. Mix sifted dry ingredients into creamed shortening mixture until well blended. Add hot water a little at a time and continue to beat until batter is smooth. Scoop batter into a lightly greased 8 x 8-inch baking pan and bake 30 to 35 minutes until a knife inserted in the middle comes out clean. Remove from oven and let cool in pan about 10 minutes, then turn out onto a cooling rack. Sprinkle with powdered sugar, if using. Serve warm or cooled.

Banana Bread

YIELD: 10–12 servings

Ingredients:

½ cup shortening
1 cup brown sugar, firmly packed
2 eggs, lightly beaten
2 large very ripe bananas, mashed (the blacker the bananas the more intense the banana flavor)
2 cups flour
1 teaspoon soda
¼ teaspoon salt
1 cup walnuts, chopped

Directions:

Preheat oven to 350°F. In a medium bowl with an electric mixer, cream shortening and sugar together until well mixed, then add beaten eggs and bananas, continuing to mix until well blended. In a separate bowl, sift together flour, soda, and salt. Mix sifted dry ingredients into creamed shortening mixture until well blended and then gently mix in chopped walnuts. Pour batter into a lightly greased loaf pan and bake 1 hour and 10 minutes until a knife inserted in the middle comes out clean. Remove from oven and let cool in pan about 10 minutes, then turn out on a cooling rack. Serve warm or cooled.

Honey Nut Bread

YIELD: 2 medium-sized loafs

Ingredients:

1½ cups honey
1½ cups milk
¾ cup sugar
¾ cup flour
1½ teaspoons baking soda
1½ teaspoons salt
1½ cups walnuts or pecans, chopped
⅓ cup oil
2 eggs, lightly beaten
1 teaspoon vanilla

Directions:

Preheat oven to 325°F. In a medium saucepan, bring honey, milk, and sugar to a boil. Remove from heat and let cool. In the meantime, in a large bowl, sift flour, baking soda, and salt together, then add the nuts. Using an electric mixer, add oil, eggs, and vanilla to the flour mixture and mix well. Add cooled honey mixture and beat for 2 minutes more. Pour batter into 2 well-greased loaf pans. Bake for 1 hour or until a knife inserted in the middle comes out clean. Remove from oven and let cool in pans about 10 minutes, then turn out onto a cooling rack.

Individual Yorkshire Puddings

YIELD: 6 to 8 servings

Ingredients:

2 eggs
1 cup milk
1 cup all-purpose flour, sifted
½ teaspoon salt
1 tablespoon salad oil
¼ cup beef drippings

Directions:

Preheat oven to 475°F. In a medium bowl with an electric mixer, beat eggs, milk, flour, and salt for 1½ minutes. Add oil and beat ½ minute longer. Grease 6 to 8 custard cups or large muffin tins with beef drippings and then put 1 teaspoon additional beef drippings in each cup. Only fill the cups half full of batter. Place on middle rack of oven and bake for 15 minutes. Reduce heat to 350°F and bake about 25 minutes longer until browned and firm. Serve piping hot with roast beef and gravy or simply as popovers. Don't worry if they collapse—some of the best restaurants have served collapsed Yorkshire puddings!

Johnny Cake

If you haven't caught fish while crossing from Florida, then Nassau in the Bahamas is the place to find fresh fish swimming in a fish tank, fruit, vegetables and ready-to-eat delicacies. You can get your fill of cooked crack conch, conch salad, conch chowder, and Johnny Cake, all of which are considered to be staples of the Bahamian dining table. While we were in Nassau, we visited one food truck every day where more locals ate than tourists, whose specialty was Johnny Cake. The wonderful woman who owned the food truck finally just said that if we were leaving and couldn't find the best Johnny Cake on our travels, she would give us her recipe. This Johnny Cake recipe was handwritten by her on a paper napkin and proudly handed to us the day we left Nassau.

YIELD: 8–10 servings

Ingredients:

4–5 cups flour
1 heaping cup sugar or more if you like it sweeter
1 teaspoon salt
2 large eggs, lightly beaten
1 cup shortening
1 heaping tablespoon baking powder
1 cup evaporated milk

Directions:

Preheat oven to 350°F. Mix all ingredients together, starting with 4 cups of flour. Turn dough out on a lightly floured surface and knead, adding more flour if necessary to make a nice soft, smooth dough. Let dough rest about 10 minutes, then put in a 9 x 9-inch lightly greased pan. Press dough down to fill all the corners and poke the top a few times with the end of a fork. Bake 20 to 25 minutes or until a little golden around the edges. Serve warm or cooled, sliced in wedges, plain, with butter or honey, or even sprinkled with brown sugar.

Cheddar Gougères (French Cheese Puffs)

YIELD: 40 cheese puffs

Ingredients:

1 stick butter
1 cup water
½ teaspoon Kosher salt
1 cup all-purpose flour
4 large eggs
1 cup sharp cheddar, shredded, reserving 2 tablespoons
chives, thyme, or other herbs of your choice, minced

Directions:

Preheat the oven to 425°F. Have all your ingredients ready to go before you start so that your butter and water aren't boiling down while you're busy grating the cheese. Position oven racks in the upper and middle thirds of oven. Lightly butter 2 large baking sheets or line them with parchment paper. In a large saucepan, combine butter, water, and salt and bring to a boil. Remove from heat and add the flour and whisk until smooth and pulls away from the sides into a smooth ball. Let stand for 2 minutes to cool, stirring a couple of times to let the heat out. When cool enough to add eggs without "cooking" them, add them one at a time beating thoroughly between additions. Beat in all but 2 tablespoons of the cheese and chives and mix well. Scoop 1 tablespoon-sized (or smaller to your preference level) mounds of dough onto baking sheets, placing dough 1½ inches apart. Top the puffs evenly with remaining cheese, put the baking sheets into the oven, and bake for 2 minutes, then turn the oven down to 375°F. and bake for an additional 20 to 25 minutes until golden brown, switching position of pans from upper to lower and front to back if necessary. Five minutes before puffs are done, poke the sides of each puff with a sharp knife or skewer to let the steam out which will make them extra crispy, then return to oven and finish baking. Serve warm or freeze and reheat in a low 200°F oven for 5 to 10 minutes before serving. Serve plain, with a nice little piece of aged ham, or smash some nuts and camembert together or even smash some goat cheese with parsley and mashed garlic and let your guests poke some inside.

Blue Cheese Popovers

YIELD: 24 popovers

Ingredients:

2 large eggs
1 cup milk, room temperature
2 tablespoons butter, melted, plus more for
    muffin tins
1 heaping teaspoon Kosher salt
⅛ teaspoon black pepper
1 cup flour
1¼ ounces blue cheese, crumbled
1 tablespoon fresh thyme, coarsely chopped
onion marmalade for serving (optional)

Directions:

Preheat oven to 425°F. Whisk together in a large bowl the eggs, milk, melted butter, salt, and pepper. Add flour a little at a time and continue to whisk vigorously until well blended and all lumps have disappeared. Whisk in crumbled blue cheese and chopped thyme and continue to whisk until well blended. Scoop batter into an airtight container and place in refrigerator for at least 2 hours or up to 1 day. When ready to cook, place oven rack on the highest possible position and preheat oven to 425°F. Generously butter 2 small mini muffin tins and fill each cup ¾ full with the chilled popover batter. Place muffin pans in oven and bake popovers until golden brown and nicely puffed, 18 to 20 minutes. Remove from oven and serve immediately with optional onion marmalade or cool on wire cooling racks for up to 2 hours and then reheat in a 350°F. oven for 10 minutes.

Note: Don't worry if popovers collapse. I've seen them do that in the fanciest restaurants.

Onion Marmalade

YIELD: 2 cups

Ingredients:

2 tablespoons vegetable oil
2 onions, halved, thin sliced
1 cup red wine vinegar
1½ cup cabernet sauvignon (optional, pinot
    noir or merlot)
½ cup sugar

Directions

In a large sauce pan, combine oil and onions and cook over medium heat until onions are soft and translucent, not browned. Add the vinegar and continue to cook until reduced and pan is almost dry. Add the wine and sugar and again, continue to cook until reduced and pan is almost dry. Your marmalade should be very thick. Serve on hot blue cheese popovers or refrigerate in a tightly covered container for up to 2 weeks.

Christine's Beer Bread

Chris and Christine were sailing on a Valiant 40, a sister ship to our Native Sun, when I first met them at a marina cocktail party in Annapolis, Maryland. Stanley was gone that day and so I could not ask him, though it was long agreed between us that we both had to agree in order to invite some-one aboard. It was so obvious that Chris and Christine were kindred spirits to us and also that the West Coast was a very special place to all of us, that when they asked if they could come down the dock and see Native Sun I immediately said yes. I called Stanley later and told him about our meeting and evening of laughing and enjoying each other and he said he was anxious to get home and meet Chris and Christine. Our relationship has lasted thirty years and we've shared weekends of "buddy boating," chartering together in the Virgin Islands and camping in the forests of British Columbia. One night at anchor in a small cove in the Chesapeake Bay, Christine presented us with a warm loaf of beer bread. She said it was really easy to make and absolutely delicious. She was right on both counts.

YIELD: 1 loaf

Ingredients:
4 tablespoons (¼ cup) butter, divided at room temperature
4 cups pancake mix
2 tablespoons sugar
1 (12 ounce) can of beer

Directions:
Preheat oven to 375°F. Grease bottom of a loaf pan with 1 to 2 tablespoons of butter and set aside. In a large bowl, mix together pancake mix, sugar, and beer and whisk until well blended. Pour batter into prepared loaf pan, place in oven, and bake for 45 to 55 minutes until golden brown and a knife blade inserted in the middle comes out clean. Melt remaining butter on high in microwave until melted and brush over warm cooked bread. Cool about 15 minutes before slicing.

Optional:
For a change of flavor, add 5 teaspoons caraway seeds to batter and mix well before pouring into loaf pan. If you prefer biscuits to a loaf of beer bread, preheat oven to 350°F, drop mixed dough onto a greased cookie sheet, and bake for 15 to 20 minutes or until golden brown.

Fresh Mango Bread

YIELD: 2 loaves

Ingredients:

2½ cups all-purpose flour, sifted
1 teaspoon baking soda
½ teaspoon baking powder
2 tablespoons cinnamon
½ teaspoon salt
¼ cup sugar or more to taste
2 eggs, room temperature, lightly beaten
½ cup vegetable oil
¼ cup honey
½ teaspoon vanilla
½ cup chopped walnuts, lightly dusted with flour
½ cup raisins, lightly dusted with flour
2 cups fresh mango, puréed

Directions:

Preheat oven to 350°F. Sift flour, baking soda, baking powder, cinnamon, salt, and sugar into a large mixing bowl and with your hand make a well in the center. In a separate bowl, mix eggs, oil, honey, vanilla, walnuts, and raisins and then pour into the well in the dry ingredients bowl. Stir to mix thoroughly, then add mango puree. Scoop the batter into 2 loaf pans lined with wax paper, place in the oven, and cook for 1 hour or until a clean knife blade inserted in the middle of the loaves comes out clean. Cool about 10 minutes, then turn out on cooling racks. Serve warm or at room temperature. Mango bread is also delicious lightly toasted and slathered with butter as a special breakfast treat.

Glazed Lemon-Zucchini Bread

YIELD: 10 to 12 servings

Ingredients for bread:

2 cups cake flour
½ teaspoon salt
2 teaspoons baking powder
2 eggs, lightly beaten
½ cup oil
1⅓ cups sugar
2 tablespoons lemon juice
½ cup buttermilk
zest of 1 lemon
1 cup zucchini, grated

Ingredients for glaze:

1 cup powdered sugar
2 tablespoons lemon juice
1 tablespoon whole milk

Directions for bread:

Preheat oven to 350°F. In a medium bowl, mix flour, salt, and baking powder and set aside. In a large bowl, lightly beat eggs, then add oil and sugar, mixing until well blended. Add in lemon juice, buttermilk, and lemon zest, fold in grated zucchini, and mix well. Add in the dry ingredients and mix well until all ingredients are well combined. Pour batter into a lightly greased loaf pan and bake 40 to 45 minutes until a knife inserted in the middle comes out clean. Remove from oven and let cool in pan about 10 minutes, then turn out on a plate.

Directions for glaze:

While bread is still warm, combine all lemon glaze ingredients and spoon over the bread. Let the glaze set before cutting and serving.

Homemade Crackers

YIELD: 48 crackers

Ingredients:

2 cups whole wheat flour
1 teaspoon Kosher salt plus more for sprinkling
⅓ cup olive oil
1 tablespoon honey
⅔ cup water
1 tablespoon fennel, sesame, or caraway seeds

Directions:

Preheat oven to 375°F. Place flour and salt in a food processor and pulse to combine. In a separate bowl, stir oil, honey, and water until combined. Add oil mixture to dry ingredients in the food processor while the motor is running, and continue to pulse until a ball of dough forms around the blade. Turn dough onto a lightly floured work surface and divide in half using the outside edge of your hand. Cover one half with a moistened dish towel, then roll remaining half into a 15 x 10-inch rectangle. Set on a large parchment-lined baking sheet, roll out second ball of dough and set it on a second parchment-lined baking sheet. Trim ragged edges of dough with a pizza cutter or sharp paring knife so that all pieces are nicely shaped. Cut each rectangle into 24 (4 x 6-inch) pieces. Fill a spray bottle with water and mist top of dough or use pastry brush to brush water on dough. Sprinkle with seeds and more salt. With your hands, press down lightly on dough to sink seeds into the dough. Bake crackers, rotating sheets halfway through and checking for doneness frequently toward the end of baking time (they can brown very quickly, so keep an eye on them), until slightly brown and crunchy, 15 to 18 minutes. Let cool before serving—crackers will crisp up when cooled.

Marilee's Story

I was snorkeling in a small cove called Red Shank just south of George Town in the Bahama's when I met Marilee. We were both holding Hawaiian Slings and diving under a little coral ledge from opposite directions, not knowing the other was there. We each hoped to find a lobster or nice fat grouper for dinner. When we saw each other, we came to the surface and started laughing as we introduced ourselves and realized we were both out fairly early in the morning foraging in the sea for dinner as our companions slept in. She invited me over to her trawler to meet her boyfriend "Traveler" later that day and I told her I'd bring Stanley and a little lobster salad to munch on. Marilee and her boyfriend lived aboard and had been cruising on their thirty-six-foot trawler for about two years. When we came aboard, we were greeted by the smell of something wonderful baking in the oven. Marilee had made fresh English muffins, which she said were delicious with a lobster salad—and she was right! Over the next couple of weeks buddy boating and snorkeling together, wherever we dropped anchor, Marilee shared many wonderful bread recipes with me. She was an amazing bread baker and was instrumental in helping me experiment outside my routine bread recipes. She taught me how to make English muffins, bagels, salt water bread, and even pretzels. During all the time we spent together, we never knew if "Traveler" was her boyfriend's given name or a nickname, nor did we think to ask. As with most people we met while cruising, we knew first names and boat names, and most cruisers never even thought to ask last names, they just weren't relevant. It was the people, the boat, the place, and the joy of sharing wonderful experiences that we, as cruisers, all focused on.

Marilee's English Muffins

YIELD: 10–12 servings

Ingredients:

1 cup warm water heated to 110°F–115°F (measured with a candy thermometer)
1 package yeast
2 teaspoons salt
¼ cup shortening
3 cups flour
2 tablespoons cornmeal

Directions:

Sprinkle the dry yeast over the water, and then sprinkle salt over the yeast. Let liquid sit until the water has become frothy. If it doesn't froth, dump your water and start again as your yeast might not be "active." Add salt, shortening, and flour and mix until blended, then turn out on a lightly floured board and knead until smooth. Roll dough to ¼-inch thickness, adding a bit more flour to the board if necessary. Cut into 3 (½-inch) circles. Sprinkle an ungreased baking sheet with cornmeal, place circles on baking sheet, and sprinkle remaining cornmeal over them. Cover with a dish towel, place in a draft-free warm area, and let rise 1 hour. Dough is ready to bake if an indent remains when touched with the tip of your finger. Heat an ungreased griddle to 375°F, place several English muffins on griddle, and cook about 7 minutes on each side. To serve, split muffins in half and toast. You can also freeze muffins and bring to room temperature, then split and toast.

Marilee's Big Soft Pretzels

YIELD: 8–10 bagels depending on size

Ingredients:

1½ cups warm water heated to 110°F–115°F (measured with a candy thermometer)
1 package yeast
2 tablespoons light brown sugar
4½ cups all-purpose flour
1¼ tsp Kosher salt
½ stick unsalted butter, melted
10 cups water
⅔ cup baking soda
½ stick melted butter, for dipping
Kosher salt, for topping

Directions:

Sprinkle the dry yeast over the water and then sprinkle brown sugar over the yeast. Let liquid sit until the water has become frothy. If it doesn't froth, dump your water and start again as your yeast might not be "active." Add flour, salt, melted butter, and using an electric mixer, gently knead dough on low to combine all ingredients. Increase speed to medium until dough pulls away from the edges and has a smooth consistency, about 3 to 5 minutes. Place dough into a large oiled bowl, cover with plastic wrap, and place in a draft-free area. Let dough rise to double its size, from 1 to 2 hours. When dough has risen, preheat oven to 450°F. Turn dough out onto a lightly oiled board for cutting. Using a pizza cutter or sharp knife, cut dough in half, then cut each half into 4 or 5 equal portions equaling 8 to 10 pieces of dough. Take one piece of dough at a time and roll it into a skinny rope, then make a big "U" and twist the center twice into a classic-looking pretzel. Place pretzels onto oiled and parchment-lined baking sheets. In a large pot, bring water and baking soda to a boil and, taking one pretzel at a time, gently drop into the water and baking soda mixture for 30 seconds, remove with a slotted turner or large slotted spoon, and place on the baking sheet. When all pretzels have been processed, place them in the oven to bake for 10 to 12 minutes. Remove from oven, dip in melted butter, and top with salt.

Marilee's Salt Water Bread

YIELD: *2 small loaves*

Ingredients:

2 cups clean salt water (only use water from open-ocean where there are no contaminants)
  heated to 110°F–115°F (measured with a candy thermometer)
1 package yeast
1 tablespoon sugar
5 cups flour

Directions:

Sprinkle the dry yeast over the water and then sprinkle sugar over the yeast. Let liquid sit until the water has become frothy. If it doesn't froth, dump your water and start again as your yeast might not be "active." Add flour a little at a time, blend thoroughly, then turn out on a lightly floured board and knead until smooth, about 10 minutes. Place dough into a large oiled bowl, cover with plastic wrap, and place in a draft-free area. Let dough rise to double its size, from 1 to 2 hours. When dough has risen preheat oven to 375°F, punch it down, shape into 2 small loaves, and place in oiled loaf pans. Cover and let rise a second time until doubled in size, about 45 minutes to 1 hour. Place in oven and bake for 30 to 45 minutes.

Marilee's Bagels

YIELD: 12 bagels

Ingredients:

1½ cups warm water, heated to 110°F–115°F
  (measured with a candy thermometer)
4–5 cups flour, divided
3 tablespoons sugar
1 tablespoon salt
1 package yeast
water at room temperature
1 egg white, beaten
1 tablespoon cold water

Optional Toppings:

2 tablespoons poppy seeds
2 tablespoons sesame seeds
2 tablespoons dried onion flakes
1 tablespoon coarse salt

Directions:

In a large bowl, let liquid sit until the water has become frothy. Mix 1½ cups flour, sugar, and salt and sprinkle the dry yeast over the water and let sit until liquid has become frothy. If it doesn't froth, dump your water and start again as your yeast might not be "active." With an electric mixer, beat for 2 minutes at low speed. Scrape bowl down occasionally. Add ½ cup flour, beat at high speed for 2 minutes, scraping bowl. Keep adding enough additional flour or additional room temperature water, a small amount at a time as needed, to make a firm dough. Continue to scrape down the bowl during mixing. Turn dough out on a floured board and knead until smooth and elastic, about 8 to 10 minutes. Place dough in an ungreased bowl, cover, and let rise in a draft-free area until dough doubles in size, 40 minutes to 2 hours. Preheat oven to 375°F. Punch dough down, turn onto a floured board, and divide and form into 12 equal-sized balls. With your thumb, make a hole in the center of each ball, pull it open, and work the dough to make a bagel shape. Place all bagels on an ungreased baking sheet, cover with a towel, and continue to let rise for 20 minutes to 1 hour. In a large shallow pan, boil 1¾-inch water. Lower heat and add a few bagels at a time, simmering 1 to 2 minutes for each batch of bagels. Remove from water and place bagels on a towel to cool for 5 minutes. Place all 12 bagels on a very lightly greased baking sheet, brush tops with a combination of beaten egg white and 1 tablespoon cold water, dip into dishes of various optional toppings, and bake 30 to 35 minutes, rotating halfway through. I've made this recipe many times and each time my bagels come out with a different texture or density. Serve split in half and toasted with butter, cream cheese, or even with cooked egg, ham, and cheese as a breakfast bagel.

Maryanne's Whole-Wheat Banana Bread

YIELD: 1 loaf

Ingredients:

3–4 very ripe bananas
juice of 1 lemon
½ cup margarine
½ cup brown sugar
1½ cups whole wheat flour
½ cup wheat germ
½ teaspoon salt
½ teaspoon baking powder
½ teaspoon baking soda
1 cup dates, chopped
1 cup walnuts, chopped

Directions:

Preheat oven to 375°F. In a medium bowl, mash bananas and mix with lemon juice until very smooth. In a small bowl, cream margarine and sugar together, then add to the banana mix, stirring well. In a large separate bowl, mix all dry ingredients together and add this to the banana mix until well blended. Mix the dates and nuts thoroughly into the dough. The dough will be very stiff. Turn dough into a greased loaf pan and bake in the oven for 30 to 45 minutes, testing for doneness by inserting a clean knife into the loaf. If it comes out clean, the bread is done. Remove pan and let sit about 10 minutes on a rack, then gently run a dull knife around the inside of pan and invert bread onto the rack to continue cooling. I generally like to lay bread on its side to cool.

No-Knead Bread

YIELD: 1 round loaf

Ingredients:

3 cups all-purpose flour + 5 tablespoons, divided
1¼ teaspoons salt
¼ teaspoon active dry yeast
1⅔ cups warm water heated to 110°F–115°F (measured with a candy thermometer)
1 tablespoon yellow cornmeal
1 tablespoon Parmesan cheese, finely grated

Directions:

Preheat oven to 450°F just before cooking. In a large bowl, combine 3 cups flour, salt, and yeast. While stirring, add the warm water until bread mixture is evenly moistened and dough is very sticky and soft. Cover with plastic wrap or a soft cloth in a draft-free, warm place for a minimum of 4 hours or up to 24 hours. Sprinkle about 3 tablespoons of flour on a large piece of parchment paper, then turn the dough onto the floured paper. Sprinkle the dough with about ½ of the remaining flour, then with a large spatula, roll dough over onto itself. Sprinkle this side now with the remaining flour. Cover with a soft cloth and let rest about 15 minutes. Grease a 5- or 6-quart–sized Dutch oven or heavy ovenproof pot with a diameter of 8½ x 9½ inches, then sprinkle cornmeal on bottom of pan and up the sides about 2 inches. Using a large turner to help get all the dough off the parchment paper, gently scoop the dough into the prepared pan. Cover pan with a soft cloth and let dough rise 1 to 2 hours until dough has risen at least 1 inch in the pan. Cover pan with a lid or aluminum foil, place in the oven, and cook for 30 minutes. After 30 minutes, remove the lid and sprinkle with grated Parmesan cheese and continue to cook 10 to 15 minutes until top is golden brown and a knife blade inserted in the middle comes out clean. Remove from oven and immediately remove from the baking pan onto a cooling rack. Serve warm or at room temperature.

Not-Too-Sweet Corn Bread

YIELD: 8–10 servings

Ingredients:

1⅓ cups all-purpose flour
1⅓ cups cornmeal
2 tablespoons sugar
1 teaspoon Kosher salt
¾ teaspoon baking soda
1 tablespoon baking powder
3 eggs, beaten just to blend
1 cup buttermilk
½ cup whole milk
3 tablespoons butter, melted and cooled

Directions:

Preheat oven to 350°F. Butter an 8 x 8-inch baking pan or baking dish and set aside. In a large bowl, thoroughly combine and mix flour, cornmeal, sugar, salt, baking soda, and baking powder and set aside. In a medium bowl, whisk blended eggs, buttermilk, and whole milk and mix well. Whisk wet ingredients into dry ingredients, just enough to combine. You should have a lumpy mixture. Add 3 tablespoons butter and mix well into dough. Scrape batter into prepared baking dish and bake 25 to 30 minutes until the top is a golden brown and a knife stuck in center of bread comes out clean. Remove from oven and let cool, then cut into pie-shaped slices and serve. Excellent served with chili or for cornbread stuffing. If you want sweeter cornbread, you don't have to make two different recipes; simply drizzle this bread with a bit of melted butter and top with swirled honey.

Nutmeg Scones

YIELD: 8 servings

Ingredients:

2 cups all-purpose flour
⅓ cup light brown sugar
2 teaspoons baking powder
1¼ teaspoons whole nutmeg, freshly grated and divided (optional, ground nutmeg)
½ teaspoon baking soda
½ teaspoon salt
6 tablespoons (¾ stick) butter, chilled and cut into ½-inch cubes
1 cup sour cream
1 egg white, beaten, for glaze
2 teaspoons sugar, for topping

Directions:

Preheat oven to 425°F. With an electric mixer or food processor, combine flour, brown sugar, baking powder, 1 teaspoon nutmeg, baking soda, and salt and blend dry ingredients. Add butter, mixing each addition until it resembles coarse meal and all the butter has been incorporated. Add sour cream and turn mixer on and off until moist clumps form. Turn dough out onto a floured work surface and knead to form a ball. Roll dough out to an 8-inch square, ¾-inch thick. Cut square into 8 wedges. Brush with egg glaze and sprinkle with 2 teaspoons of sugar and the remaining nutmeg. Gently transfer scones to a baking sheet, leaving a 2-inch space between each scone. Place in oven and bake until tops are golden brown and a clean knife inserted into the center comes out clean, about 10 to 12 minutes. Remove from oven and gently put scones on a rack to cool a bit, then serve warm with butter, jam, or cream cheese. Scones can be rewarmed in moderate oven for 30 minutes if desired.

Perfect Pizza Dough

YIELD: 2 pizzas

Ingredients:

1 cup plus 1 tablespoon water, heated to 110°F–115°F (measured with a candy thermometer)
2¼ teaspoons (1 packet) active dry yeast
1 teaspoon granulated sugar
3 cups all-purpose flour
1 teaspoon Kosher salt
1 tablespoon olive oil

Directions:

Sprinkle the dry yeast over the water. Sprinkle 1 teaspoon of sugar over the yeast. Let liquid sit until the water has become frothy. If it doesn't froth, dump your water and start again as your yeast might not be "active." In a food processor, add the flour and salt. Pulse for a few seconds to evenly distribute the salt and then, with the food processor running, add in the oil. Add the yeast water combination to the food processor ingredients while it is still running until a dough ball forms. Spray a large bowl with a nonstick cooking spray. Put the dough ball in and cover with plastic wrap. Allow it to double in size, about 1 hour to 90 minutes. Pull the dough apart to create two dough balls for two pizza crusts. On a lightly floured surface, roll out to desired thickness and size and start adding your favorite ingredients for a fresh homemade pizza. Dough can be frozen while it is still ball shaped—just bring to room temperature before rolling into a pizza crust. Now, you can make your favorite pizza!

Pita Bread

YIELD: 12 pitas

Ingredient:

4½ cups flour, plus additional ¼ cup flour
1 package yeast
1½ teaspoons sugar
1½ teaspoons salt
1¾ cups warm water
2 tablespoons oil

Directions:

Preheat oven to 500°F. In a large mixing bowl, combine 2 cups flour, yeast, sugar, and salt and mix well. Add warm water heated to 110°F–115°F (measured with a candy thermometer) and oil and blend on low speed with an electric mixer until ingredients are moistened, then beat 3 minutes on medium speed. By hand, blend in remaining flour a little at a time to make a firm dough. Turn dough onto a floured surface and knead until smooth and elastic, about 10 minutes. Cover with plastic wrap and then cover with a towel. Let rise in a warm non-drafty place for 20 minutes or until dough doubles in size, then punch down, divide in half, and cut each half into 6 pieces, making 12 pieces total. Shape each piece into a smooth ball, cover, and let rise an additional 30 minutes. On a lightly floured surface, roll each ball to a 5-inch circle. Place 6 circles on a large cooling rack, (repeat after cooking with remaining 6 circles) then place that rack in the oven and bake at 500°F for 5 minutes until puffed and tops begin to brown. Remove from the oven and cool.

To serve, cut off top ⅓ or ½ of pita, tear into pieces, and stuff back into remaining pita; save the cut-off tops for dippers, then add scrambled bacon and eggs, sloppy joe mix, taco filling, seafood salad, or anything to your liking to the inside of each pita. You can also cut each pita into equal-sized wedges, bake them until they crisp up a little bit, and use with a multitude of dips.

Taco Filling

YIELD: 4–6 servings

Ingredients:

1 pound ground beef
½ cup onion, chopped
½ teaspoon salt
1 (8 ounce) can tomato sauce
¼ teaspoon cumin
¼ teaspoon garlic powder
¼ teaspoon cayenne
1 cup cheddar cheese, shredded
1 cup lettuce, shredded
1 cup fresh tomato, chopped
 1 onion, sliced (optional for topping)
1 avocado, diced (optional for topping)
taco sauce, green or red (optional for topping)

Directions:

In a large skillet, brown ground beef and onion and drain off fat. Add salt, tomato sauce, spices, and blend thoroughly. Reduce heat, cover, and simmer for 30 minutes to blend flavors. With a slotted spoon, remove beef mixture to a bowl and drain off all remaining fat. To serve, put some chopped lettuce into a cut pita, then add beef mixture, and top with cheese and chopped tomato. If you're using any of the additional toppings, pile them on top.

Sloppy Joe Filling

YIELD: 4–6 servings

Ingredients:

1 pound ground beef
¼–½ cup onion, chopped
¼ cup green pepper, diced
¼ cup celery, diced
¾ cup ketchup
1 teaspoon yellow mustard
½ teaspoon salt
½ teaspoon garlic powder
3 teaspoons brown sugar
1 tablespoon vinegar (optional)
1 tablespoon Worcestershire sauce (optional)
Salt and pepper

Directions:

In a large skillet, brown ground beef, onion, pepper, and celery, drain off fat. Then add ketchup, mustard, salt, garlic powder, and brown sugar, then mix and taste. Adjust seasonings and add optional ingredients if using, mix thoroughly. Reduce heat, cover and simmer for 30 minutes to blend flavors. Season with salt and pepper, to taste. To serve, spoon into a cut pita bread.

Sage Drop Biscuits

YIELD: 4–6 servings

Ingredients:

2 cups flour
2 teaspoons baking powder
½ teaspoon baking soda
1 teaspoon salt
6 tablespoons cold butter
¼ cup fresh sage, chopped
¾ cup buttermilk

Directions:

Preheat oven to 425°F. In a large bowl using an electric mixer combine flour, baking powder, baking soda, and salt. Cut 6 tablespoons of cold butter into the flour and mix until it resembles coarse meal. Stir in the sage and mix, then add the buttermilk and mix until nicely blended. With a large spoon, scoop dough into a lightly greased baking sheet.

Rosemary Bread

YIELD: 2 loaves

Ingredients:

1 cup warm water heated to 110°F–115°F
   (measured with a candy thermometer)
1 tablespoon yeast
1 tablespoon sugar
1 teaspoon salt
2 tablespoons butter, divided
2½ cups flour, divided
2 tablespoons fresh rosemary, finely chopped
   and divided

Directions:

Sprinkle the dry yeast over the water and then sprinkle sugar over the yeast. Let liquid sit until the water has become frothy. If it doesn't froth, dump your water and start again as your yeast might not be "active." Mix in salt, 1 tablespoon butter, and 2 cups of flour. Add 1 tablespoon of the fresh chopped rosemary. Knead for about 10 minutes by hand or in food processor about 5 minutes until smooth and elastic, adding more flour if necessary. Oil a large bowl, add dough, and cover with a towel, letting dough rise in a warm place for 1 hour or up to 2 hours until doubled in size. Preheat oven to 375°F. Punch down dough and divide in half. Let dough rest about 5 minutes. Spray 1 bread baking pan or cookie sheet with nonstick spray. Shape the dough into 2 small rounded oval loaves or place in bread baking pans. Sprinkle remaining rosemary over the loaves and press lightly into the surface. Let loaves rise again until doubled, about 45 minutes to 1 hour, and bake for 15 to 20 minutes until lightly browned. Carefully remove from oven, brush with remaining butter, and sprinkle with salt if desired.

Spicy Orange Nut Bread

YIELD: 1 loaf

Ingredients:

1 cup orange rind from 2–3 medium-sized oranges
½ cup water
2 tablespoons sugar
2¼ cups flour
1 cup sugar
2½ teaspoons baking powder
¾ teaspoon salt
½ teaspoon cinnamon
⅔ cup milk
3 tablespoons oil
2 eggs
¼ teaspoon vanilla
½ teaspoon orange extract
2 drops almond extract
2 drops lemon extract
¾ cup walnuts, shelled and chopped
¼ teaspoon cinnamon mixed with 2 tablespoons sugar

Directions:

Preheat oven to 350°F. Set orange rind aside. In a large saucepan, add ½ cup water and sugar and bring to a boil, then add orange rind, cover, and cook over low heat for 10 to 15 minutes until rind is tender and water has been absorbed. Remove pan from stove and let cool. In a large mixing bowl, sift all dry ingredients and then gradually add milk, oil, eggs, and extracts, beating on low speed until well mixed. Add cooled orange peel and walnuts and beat until well mixed. Pour batter into a well-greased loaf pan and evenly sprinkle cinnamon mixture on top. Place in oven and bake 55 to 60 minutes until nicely browned and a knife blade inserted in the middle comes out clean. Remove from oven, let cool 2 minutes, then slide a table knife around the edges to loosen bread and turn out onto a cooling rack. It's especially good slathered with butter while still warm, or serve cooled.

Swedish Rye & Caraway Seed Dinner Rolls

This is a great recipe when other boaters in an anchorage decide to have a potluck beach party, or you're invited to a yacht club party. The recipe can easily be converted to make half, and remember that these rolls freeze well, so even 12 or 24 rolls are really not too many.

YIELD: 48 rolls

Ingredients:

4 cups all-purpose flour
2 cups rye flour
1 tablespoon salt
1 tablespoon caraway seeds, plus extra for
    topping
2 packages active dry yeast

2 cups water
⅓ cup dark molasses
¼ cup margarine
1 egg white, slightly beaten
3 (8¼ x 1½-inch) round heat-resistant cake
    dishes for baking

Directions:

Preheat oven to 325°F just prior to baking. Lightly spoon flour into a measuring cup, level off, and combine flours in a large bowl. In a second large bowl, thoroughly blend salt, 1 tablespoon caraway seeds, and undissolved dry yeast and set aside. In a medium sauce pan over low heat, combine water, molasses, and margarine until liquids are warm. It's not important for the margarine to melt. With an electric mixer on medium speed, gradually beat liquid ingredients into bowl with dry ingredients, scraping bowl down a couple of times as needed, mixing for 2 minutes. Add ¾ cup more of original combined flours, beat on high speed for 2 minutes, and scrape down bowl occasionally. Stir in enough additional combined flour to make a soft dough and, if necessary, add additional white flour to obtain desired dough. Turn dough out onto a lightly floured board and knead until smooth and elastic, about 8 to 10 minutes. Place kneaded dough into a greased bowl and turn over to grease the top. Cover and let rise in a draft-free, warm area until doubled in size, which could be 45 minutes to 2 hours depending on weather conditions. Punch the dough down and turn out onto a lightly floured board. Divide dough into 24 equal pieces and halve rolls to make 48 pieces in all, then form each into a ball. Place 16 of the dough balls in each of 3 greased Pyrex glass cake dishes. Cover and let rise in a draft-free, warm area until doubled in size, which could be 45 minutes to 2 hours depending on weather conditions. Brush tops with slightly beaten egg white and sprinkle caraway seeds on top of each roll. Bake for 20 to 25 minutes until done. Remove from dishes and cool on cooling racks. Serve warm or at room temperature or freeze after completely cooled. They reheat nicely from the freezer—just bring rolls to room temperature and put them in a warm oven for about 10 minutes. You can bake these in batches by keeping the uncooked rolls covered and warm.

Whole Wheat Biscuits

YIELD: 12 biscuits

Ingredients:

1 cup all-purpose flour
3 teaspoons baking powder
½ teaspoon salt
1 cup whole wheat flour
¼ cup shortening
⅔ cup milk

Directions:

Preheat oven to 400°F. In a large bowl, sift the all-purpose flour, baking powder, and salt together, then add in the whole wheat flour and lightly mix. Cut shortening into flour mixture with a pastry cutter. Add the milk and mix lightly, then turn dough out onto a floured board. Roll dough out to a 1-inch thickness and cut biscuits with a biscuit cutter or an overturned cup, jar, or clean canning lid. Place biscuits on a greased baking pan or cookie sheet about 1-inch apart for crusty sides. Place in oven and bake for 12 to 15 minutes until golden brown. Immediately remove biscuits from cookie sheet and cool on a cooling rack. Serve warm.

CHAPTER 8
Breakfast & Brunch

Asparagus & Egg-Topped English Muffins

YIELD: 4 servings

Ingredients:

3 tablespoons butter
3 tablespoons all-purpose flour
1¾ cups milk
salt and pepper, to taste
¼ cup sharp cheddar cheese, grated
5 hard cooked eggs, peeled and evenly sliced
4 English muffins, halved and toasted
16 fresh asparagus spears, trimmed and lightly
    steamed
paprika for garnish

Directions:

Melt butter in a large saucepan. Add flour and whisk to blend, then add milk and cook while whisking until thickened. Season with salt and pepper, add grated cheese, and stir until blended and cheese is melted. Remove from heat. Gently fold in the sliced hardboiled eggs. To serve, place 2 English muffin halves on each plate, spoon cheese and egg mixture evenly over muffins, and arrange steamed asparagus spears on top. Sprinkle with paprika and serve hot.

BLT Ranch Wraps

YIELD: 8 servings

Ingredients:

16 bacon slices, cooked
8 (8-inch) flour tortillas at room temperature
4 cups fresh spinach or other lettuce, chopped
2 cups (3 small whole) tomatoes, chopped
2 cups (8 ounces) cheddar cheese, shredded
½ cup ranch salad dressing

Directions:

Place a tortilla on a work surface and lay two bacon strips across the center, then top with lettuce, tomatoes, and cheese. Drizzle with ranch dressing and fold bottom and sides of tortilla over filling and roll up. Continue assembling remaining tortillas in the same manner, placing remaining ingredients equally on each tortilla. Serve whole or cut in half and serve with small bowls of mixed fresh fruit or with chilled melon slices. To make ahead and store in the fridge, do not heat bacon but continue assembling remaining ingredients above, then wrap in plastic wrap and store in a tightly sealed container for 2 days.

Bacon & Egg Muffins

YIELD: 6–12 servings

Ingredients:

4 slices bacon, cut into thirds
5 eggs
2 tablespoons water
salt and pepper, to taste
1 cup all-purpose flour
½ cup yellow cornmeal
2 tablespoons sugar
2½ teaspoons baking powder
½ teaspoon salt
1 cup milk
¼ cup vegetable oil or melted butter
½ cup cheddar cheese, shredded
maple syrup, optional

Directions:

Preheat oven to 400°F. In a large skillet, cook bacon until it just begins to crisp. Remove from skillet, drain, set aside, and reserve bacon drippings. Place 2 teaspoons of drippings back into skillet. In a small bowl using an electric mixer, beat 3 eggs together with 2 tablespoons water, salt, and pepper. Over medium heat, pour egg mixture into skillet, do not stir, and gently cook until eggs begin to set around the edges, then lift eggs gently and tip pan to let uncooked eggs flow underneath. Cook until eggs are cooked but still moist. Place cooked eggs in a bowl and set aside. Brush the 12 cups of a muffin tin with remaining bacon drippings and set aside. In a medium bowl, stir flour, cornmeal, sugar, baking powder, and ½ teaspoon salt. In a separate bowl, whisk together milk, oil or butter, and remaining 2 eggs, then mix into flour mixture until well blended. Gently fold in scrambled eggs and cheese and add to muffin tins. Bake 15 to 17 minutes until lightly browned and a toothpick inserted in the middle comes out clean. Remove pan from oven, leaving egg muffins in the pan, and cool on a cooling rack for a couple of minutes. Use a table knife to run around the edges of the egg muffins to loosen and then gently remove from pans. Serve with syrup or just fresh out of the pan.

Baja Mexicali Baked Eggs & Cheese

YIELD: 4 servings

Ingredients:

6 eggs
1 cup milk
½ teaspoon salt
1 tablespoon butter
1 cup mushrooms, sliced
1 medium onion, chopped
½ cup green pepper, chopped
1 can (7½ ounces) tomato sauce
1½ teaspoons taco seasoning or chili powder
½ cup (4 ounces) Monterey Jack cheese, sliced

Directions:

Preheat oven to 325°F. With an electric mixer, beat eggs, milk, and salt until well blended. Pour into a greased 9-inch pie plate, place in oven, and bake 25 to 30 minutes or until eggs are set. In the meantime, melt butter in a medium saucepan; add mushrooms, onion, and green pepper and sauté until tender. Stir in tomato sauce and chili powder and bring to boiling, then simmer uncovered 5 minutes. Remove baked omelet from the oven, top evenly with slices of cheese, return to oven, and bake 4 to 5 minutes more or until cheese is melted. To serve, cut omelet into wedges and spoon tomato sauce on top.

Banana-Blueberry Crepes

YIELD: 6 servings

Ingredients for crepes:

3 eggs
⅛ teaspoon salt
1½ cups all-purpose flour
1½ cups milk
2 tablespoons vegetable oil

Ingredients for topping:

3½ cups (16 ounces) blueberries
2 ripe bananas, chopped
1½ cups maple syrup
powdered sugar, for topping
orange slices, for topping

Directions for crepes:

In a medium-sized mixing bowl, whisk eggs and salt and slowly add flour, alternating with milk, and beat until smooth with an electric mixer or wire whisk. Slowly add oil, stirring to blend. Batter should be the consistency of a light cream. If too thick, add 2 to 3 tablespoons milk a little bit at a time until you have the right consistency. It should not be the thick consistency of pancake batter. Cover tightly and chill in fridge 30 to 60 minutes or up to 1 day ahead. Lightly oil a griddle or round skillet and over high heat, ladle 3 to 4 tablespoons (¼ cup) of crepe batter into the center of the pan. Lift and tilt the pan and swirl the batter evenly to all sides to form a round crepe. Cook 1 to 2 minutes or until the bottom is lightly browned. With a thin spatula, gently flip the crepe and cook for 1 more minute on the other side. Transfer the cooked crepe to a large plate and repeat with the remaining batter, making 18 crepes total, making sure to oil the pan between each crepe. If desired, separate each crepe with parchment paper so they do not stick together.

Directions for topping:

In a medium size saucepan over medium to low heat, gently combine and warm blueberries, bananas, and maple syrup. To serve, place one crepe at a time on a plate, and ladle a small amount of warm blueberry mixture down center of crepe, fold the sides of the crepe over, and gently press to seal. After you have 3 filled crepes on each plate, top them all evenly with remaining warm blueberry mixture, sprinkle with powdered sugar, and garnish sides of dishes with an orange slice. Unfilled crepes will remain fresh in an airtight container in the refrigerator for 1 day or in the freezer for 1 month. Just bring frozen crepes to room temperature before filling.

Breakfast Pita

YIELD: 2 servings

Ingredients:

4 large eggs
3 tablespoons milk
nonstick cooking spray
salt and pepper, to taste
4 slices bacon, cooked and drained
2 pita breads, cut in half
2 slices Monterey Jack cheese
1 large avocado, deseeded, peeled, and sliced
    into 8 slices
1 tablespoon green onions, chopped
hot sauce, for topping,
sour cream, for topping

Directions:

In a medium bowl, combine eggs with milk and whisk until well blended. Spray a large skillet with nonstick cooking spray and heat over medium heat. When warm, pour in the beaten eggs and sprinkle with salt and pepper. Continue to stir the eggs with a spatula or wooden spoon until cooked to desired consistency. Remove from heat and set aside. Cook bacon to desired doneness, drain on paper towels, and set aside. Cut 2 pitas into 4 halves and divide scrambled eggs, bacon, cheese, avocado, and green onions evenly into each pita pocket. Shake a couple drops of hot sauce on top and scoop a bit of sour cream on top if using. Serve warm or at room temperature.

Broccoli & Feta Frittata

YIELD: 4 servings

Ingredients:

1 tablespoon butter
½ onion, finely diced
1 cup broccoli florets, chopped
salt and pepper, to taste
7 large eggs
⅔ cup (about 3 ounces) feta cheese, crumbled

Directions:

Preheat broiler to high with oven rack 4 inches from heat source when ready to bake. In an 8-inch ovenproof non-stick skillet or well-oiled ovenproof skillet, melt butter over medium heat, add onion, and stir until onion is soft and translucent for 4 minutes. Add broccoli, salt, and pepper and cook, stirring occasionally until just barely tender, for 6 more minutes; set aside. In a medium bowl, whisk eggs and season with additional salt and pepper to taste. Pour egg mixture over pan with onions and broccoli, stir to combine, then dot the surface evenly with crumbled feta. Cook on stovetop over medium heat without stirring for about 5 minutes until eggs on bottom are set. Place pan in oven and broil until top eggs are set and beginning to brown, about 2 to 3 minutes. To serve, cut into pie-shaped wedges and serve hot or at room temperature.

Caviar & Smoked Salmon with Scrambled Eggs & Potatoes

YIELD: 4 servings

Ingredients:

2 medium-sized potatoes
4 large eggs
¼ cup half-and-half or milk
Kosher salt and pepper, to taste
4 tablespoons (½ stick) butter, chopped into small pieces
2 or more ounces smoked salmon, thin sliced
green onions, chopped
2 teaspoons caviar or salmon roe, for garnish

Directions:

Preheat oven to 350°F. Clean skins of potatoes and dry well. To "bake" potatoes in the microwave, use a fork and prick each potato all over to let out steam. Rub potatoes with oil, lay them on a paper towel in the microwave oven, and cook for 8 minutes. Check doneness and cook for an additional 2 to 3 minutes if necessary. To bake potatoes in the oven, prick a couple of holes on the top surface and wrap each potato in aluminum foil. Place on a baking sheet and bake for 60 minutes. When potatoes are cooked, remove from microwave or oven and set aside. In a medium bowl, whisk together eggs, half-and-half or milk, salt, and pepper and set aside. In a large skillet over low heat, melt the butter, add the egg mixture, and cook until the eggs are cooked but still moist. Gently add the salmon slices and chopped onions to egg mixture, combine, then remove from heat. Cut each potato in half lengthwise and scoop out some of the insides (and reserve for a soup thickener if you wish). With a fork, mash down the potato left in the skins, forming a well for the eggs. Evenly scoop egg and salmon mixture into the potato shells, top with optional caviar, and serve immediately.

Baked Eggs in Creamed Spinach

YIELD: 8 servings

Ingredients:

1½ pounds baby spinach
3 tablespoons butter
2 tablespoons onion, finely chopped
2 teaspoons garlic, peeled and finely chopped
¼ cup all-purpose flour
2 cups half-and-half or milk
½ cup Parmesan cheese, finely grated plus more for topping
salt and pepper, to taste
½ teaspoon dry mustard
⅓ teaspoon fresh nutmeg, grated
pinch cayenne pepper
8 large eggs

Directions:

Have a large bowl of ice water ready. Bring a large saucepan of salted water to a boil and add spinach (you may have to work in batches), pushing down into the boiling water until it wilts, about 5 to 7 seconds. Transfer each batch of spinach into ice water to stop the cooking and then drain in a colander. It should be bright green in color. Squeeze spinach to remove liquid, roll into paper towels, and repeatedly squeeze or press down with the back of a large spoon to completely dry the spinach. Chop spinach coarsely and set aside. In a large skillet over medium-high heat, melt butter, then add the onion and garlic, whisking continuously until just tender, about 1 minute. Sprinkle flour over onion mixture, continue to whisk, and cook for 1 to 3 minutes. Don't let the flour get brown. Stirring constantly, whisk in the half-and-half or milk until well blended and bring to a boil. Reduce heat and simmer for 2 minutes until thickened and smooth. Stir in spinach, ½ cup Parmesan, salt and pepper, dry mustard, nutmeg, and cayenne pepper and mix well. With the back of a large spoon, make 8 indentations in the spinach mixture and gently break an egg into each indent. Cover skillet and cook over low heat for 12 to 15 minutes or until eggs are set, but still jiggle slightly when pan is shaken. Sprinkle evenly with Parmesan cheese and serve immediately. Baked eggs can also be refrigerated with a piece of plastic wrap pressed directly on the top and then reheated over low heat, just until bubbling.

Ham & Egg Muffins

YIELD: 12 (1-egg) servings or 6 (2-egg) servings

Ingredients:

nonstick spray for muffin tins
12 eggs
½ teaspoon seasoning salt
3 tablespoons onion, diced
1 cup cooked ham, bacon, sausage, or smoked
   salmon
black pepper, to taste
¼ teaspoon garlic powder
¼ cup mushrooms, diced and sautéed
1 cup sharp cheddar cheese, grated
½ cup baby spinach, finely shredded

Directions:

Preheat oven to 350°F. Spray a 12-cup muffin tin with nonstick spray and set aside. In a large bowl lightly beat eggs with an electric mixer until creamy, add remaining ingredients, and mix until well blended. Scoop ½ cup egg mixture into each muffin tin, place in oven, and bake 20 to 25 minutes until center of egg muffins are cooked. Serve one or two egg muffins on each plate with roasted potatoes, toast, or fruit.

Hash Brown Potato Nests with Baked Eggs

YIELD: 12 servings

Ingredients:

2 (12-cup) greased muffin tins
nonstick cooking spray
6 medium-sized russet potatoes, grated
24 large eggs
salt and pepper, to taste

Directions:

Preheat oven to 400°F. Generously spray 2 muffin tins with nonstick cooking spray and evenly scoop grated potatoes into the 24 cups, about 3 to 4 tablespoons each. Gently press the sides and bottom in each potato cup to make a "nest." You'll want the potatoes to fit lightly in the pan, not squished down. Lightly spray each potato nest with nonstick cooking spray, place in the oven, and bake for 15 to 20 minutes. If they're not browning, raise the oven temperature to 450°F but keep a sharp eye on the muffin tins. They should come out golden brown. Remove from the oven and let cool on cooling racks. Crack one egg into each potato nest, season with salt and pepper, return to the 400°F oven, and bake until whites are just set, about 15 minutes. Gently remove nests from the muffin tin with a spoon or fork and serve.

Note: Potato nests lend themselves to so many optional ingredients such as minced jalapeño, shredded cheese, cooked and chopped breakfast meats, and various herbs mixed in with the grated potatoes. You might want to experiment with what you have in your fridge and on board.

Huevos en Salsa

YIELD: 2 servings

Ingredients:

3 cups salsa
4 eggs
½ cup cheddar cheese, crumbled
fresh cilantro, chopped
tortillas, warmed (optional, for serving)

Directions:

In a large skillet over medium heat, bring salsa just to boiling and reduce heat to a simmer. Break one egg at a time into a cup and slip egg into the simmering salsa, repeating until all 4 eggs are sitting evenly in the salsa. Cover and simmer 3 to 5 minutes or until egg whites are set and yolks begin to thicken but are not hard. Remove skillet from heat, sprinkle cheese and cilantro on top, and with a large serving spoon, carefully dish up 2 eggs with plenty of salsa on each dish. Warmed tortillas make a nice side to this simple breakfast.

Joe's Special

YIELD: 4 servings

Ingredients:

1 cup onions, peeled, sliced, and chopped
2 tablespoons olive oil
1 pound ground round
1 teaspoon seasoning salt, your choice of flavors
1 cup spinach, chopped and squeezed dry
6 eggs
½ cup grated Parmesan cheese

Directions:

Sauté onions in olive oil in a large skillet over medium high heat. Add ground round and seasoning salt and cook until meat is browned, breaking up with fork as necessary. Add squeeze-dried spinach, and while stirring, add eggs and cook until ingredients are done but not dry. To serve, dish Joe's Special on 4 plates and sprinkle each plate with cheese. Joe's Special is great for breakfast or dinner.

Margaritaville French Breakfast Muffins

YIELD: 12 servings

Ingredients:

nonstick cooking spray
1 cup butter (2 sticks) room temperature
1½ cups sugar
3 eggs
4¼ cups flour
½ tablespoon salt
½ teaspoon nutmeg or more to taste
2 tablespoons half-and-half
1½ cups water
¼ butter, melted, for dipping
2 tablespoons sugar mixed with 1 tablespoon cinnamon, for topping

Directions:

Preheat oven to 350°F. Grease a 12-cup muffin tin and set aside. With an electric mixer, cream 1 cup butter, sugar, and eggs until smooth. Mix in flour, salt, and nutmeg, alternating with half-and-half and water, to blend. Thoroughly mix all ingredients and then spoon or pour into prepared muffin tin and bake 25 minutes or until cooked, testing for doneness by inserting a clean knife into a muffin. If it comes out clean, the muffins are done. To serve, remove muffins from muffin tin, dip tops quickly in melted butter, and roll in cinnamon-sugar mixture. Serve warm.

Orange French Toast with Glazed Apple Slices

YIELD: 4 servings

Ingredients for French toast:

2 eggs, beaten
½ cup orange juice
¼ teaspoon salt
8 slices day-old bread
2 tablespoons butter, divided

Ingredients for glazed apple slices:

½ cup orange juice
⅓ cup light brown sugar
⅛ teaspoon ground allspice
3 large apples, cored and thinly sliced

Directions for French toast:

In a shallow bowl or pie plate, combine beaten eggs, orange juice, and salt and mix well. Dip bread slices in egg mixture, turning to coat on both sides. In a large skillet, melt butter, add bread, and brown on both sides, repeating until all the bread is cooked. Set aside and keep heated while making glazed apple slices, or you can make the French toast at the same time the glazed apples are cooking.

Directions for glazed apple slices:

In a large skillet over low heat, combine orange juice, brown sugar, and allspice, stirring until sugar dissolves and mixture comes to a boil. Add apple slices and simmer uncovered over low heat for 8 to 10 minutes until apples are tender. Spoon orange juice and sugar mixture over apples during cooking. To serve, place 2 pieces of hot French toast on 4 plates and spoon hot glazed apples evenly over top.

Overnight Sausage & Egg Casserole

YIELD: 8–10 servings

Ingredients:

9 slices white bread, cubed
2 cups sharp cheddar cheese, grated plus extra for topping
2 pounds sausage, browned and broken into pieces
1 large jar (7 ounces) sliced mushrooms, drained
12 eggs, lightly beaten to blend
1 teaspoon dry mustard
salt, to taste
pepper, to taste
2 cups milk, divided
1 can cream of mushroom soup

Directions:

Preheat oven to 350°F when ready to cook. Lightly grease a 9 x 13-inch casserole dish and spread cubed bread evenly over the bottom. Sprinkle grated cheese evenly over top of bread and then the cooked sausage on top of the cheese. Add mushrooms. Lightly beat 12 eggs just so they are blended, add dry mustard, salt, and pepper, and 1½ cups milk and mix well to combine. Pour egg mixture over casserole, cover tightly. and refrigerate overnight. In the morning, dilute cream of mushroom soup with ½ cup milk and pour over the casserole. Top with more grated cheese and place on middle rack of oven. Bake for 1 hour or until liquid has been absorbed and the top is nicely brown and bubbling.

Classic Herb & Gruyere 2-Egg Omelet

Omelets are fast and easy to make and can be served warm, at room temperature, or chilled. They are served for breakfast, lunch, and dinner and often as hors d'oeuvres in the shape of a spiral or pinwheel rolled up jelly-roll style and sliced.

YIELD: 1 serving

Ingredients:

2 large eggs
¼ teaspoon sea salt
black pepper, to taste
2 tablespoons Gruyere cheese, grated
2 tablespoons fresh herbs, chopped
leftover meats or vegetables (optional, tomato, onion, bacon or sausage)
½ tablespoon butter
sour cream (optional for garnish)
Tabasco sauce (optional for garnish)

Directions:

In a medium bowl, gently beat the eggs with sea salt and black pepper and set aside. Prepare cheese, herbs, and any optional meats or vegetables you may be adding so that they're all ready before you start cooking. Heat an 8-inch nonstick skillet for 2 to 3 minutes, add butter, and wait for it to bubble before adding the eggs. If pan is too hot, it will dry out the eggs. Pour the egg mixture into center of the hot pan and tilt pan so eggs spread around the entire surface. As they set, gently stir with a spatula, pulling wet eggs up and allowing the liquid to spread into the pan evenly so that there are no gaps or holes in the egg mixture. Keep cooking and letting any remaining liquid spread under omelet. Cook until bottom of omelet is set but top still looks moist, about 1 to 2 minutes. Sprinkle cheese, herbs, and add in any optional leftovers. Using a rubber spatula, loosen the edges of the omelet, slide the spatula under half the omelet, tilt the pan, and let gravity help to fold the omelet in half. The eggs will continue to cook even after removed from the heat, so slightly underdone is best. Gently slide onto a plate and serve with toast, fresh fruit, or breakfast meats. A good dollop of sour cream and a few drops of Tabasco sauce can add some creamy heat to your omelet!

Supreme Pinwheel Omelet

YIELD: 8 servings

Ingredients:

½ cup (4 ounces) cream cheese, softened
¾ cup milk
¼ cup Parmesan cheese, grated plus extra for topping
2 tablespoons all-purpose flour
12 eggs
1 large green pepper, chopped
1 cup fresh mushrooms, sliced
1 small onion, diced
1 teaspoons oil
1½ cups (6 ounces) mozzarella cheese, shredded
1 plum tomato, deseeded and chopped
1¼ teaspoons Italian seasoning, divided,

Directions:

Preheat oven to 375°F. Line the bottom and sides of a greased 15 x 10 x 1-inch baking pan with parchment paper and set aside. With an electric mixer, beat cream cheese and milk together in a small bowl until smooth. Add ¼ cup Parmesan cheese and the flour and continue to beat until well blended. In a separate large bowl, beat the eggs until frothy, add the cream cheese mixture, and continue to beat until well blended. Pour the mixture into the parchment-lined pan and bake for 20 to 25 minutes until set. In the meantime, in a large fry pan sauté the pepper, mushrooms, and onion in 1 teaspoon oil until tender and slightly crisp; keep warm until ready to form the rolled omelet. When omelet is done, turn it out onto a work surface and gently peel off the parchment paper, spoon warm vegetable mixture, mozzarella cheese, chopped tomato, and 1 teaspoon Italian seasoning evenly over omelet. Carefully roll the omelet starting with the short side and place in warm oven until serving time. Cut into 8 (1-inch) thick slices. Serve alone or with fresh fruit or sliced tomatoes, or for a heartier breakfast, serve with 2 cooked link sausages and buttered toast for each serving. Top with Parmesan cheese and remaining Italian seasoning. For a dinner option, serve with beans or potato wedges, a green salad and some crusty bread.

Note: Plum tomatoes have less water content than the regular tomatoes we generally see, so if you're going to substitute the plum tomato for a regular tomato, seed, slice, chop and drain the regular tomato on a paper towel to remove some of the liquid, then use an amount equivalent to the size of a plum tomato.

Chicken & Spinach Spiral Omelet with Cheesy Mushroom Sherry Sauce

YIELD: *4 servings*

Ingredients for the omelet:

nonstick cooking spray
6 eggs, whites separated from yolks
½ teaspoon salt
2 tablespoons cornstarch
1 teaspoon dried thyme
¼ cup Parmesan cheese, shredded

Ingredients for the chicken and spinach filling:

½ cup onion, chopped
1 tablespoon cooking oil
1 cup cooked chicken, chopped
1 package (10-ounce size) frozen spinach, chopped, thawed, and well-drained
4 hard-boiled eggs, chopped
salt and pepper, to taste

Ingredients for the sherry mushroom sauce:

1 can (8 ounce) sliced mushrooms, drained, or 1½ cups fresh mushrooms, sliced
6 tablespoons butter, divided
3 tablespoons flour
½ teaspoon ground nutmeg
2 cups milk, warmed
½ cup Gruyere cheese, shredded
¼ cup sherry

Directions for the omelet:

Preheat the oven to 350°F. Evenly coat an 11 x 17-inch jellyroll pan with cooking spray. Line the pan with parchment paper and spray again. Using an electric mixer, beat egg whites in a medium-sized bowl until just stiff. Don't let dry peaks form. In a second medium-sized bowl, beat egg yolks with salt until thick and creamy and lemon colored. Pour beaten egg yolks over whites and sprinkle cornstarch and thyme on top, then gently fold mixture lightly with rubber spatula until blended. Scoop eggs out and spread evenly into the prepared pan. Evenly sprinkle ¼ cup Parmesan cheese over the top. Place in oven and bake 12 to 15 minutes until eggs are set and lightly browned. When omelet is done, gently invert omelet onto clean platter and spread spinach filling evenly on top. Roll omelet into a tight "jelly roll" shape and turn over seam-side down. Cover and keep warm. Top with the mushroom sherry sauce.

Directions for spinach filling:

In a medium skillet, sauté onion in 1 tablespoon oil over medium heat until soft. Add chicken and spinach and stir well, then stir in chopped eggs, salt, and pepper. Taste and adjust seasonings. Place spinach filling in an ovenproof bowl and keep warm until ready to spread over omelet.

Directions for sherry mushroom sauce:

In the same skillet used for the spinach filling, sauté mushrooms in 2 tablespoons butter. With a slotted spoon, remove mushrooms from the pan and drain. In the same skillet, melt remaining butter and whisk in flour and nutmeg, then gradually whisk in the milk. Continue to whisk over medium heat until sauce thickens. Remove from heat. Stir in mushrooms, cheese, and sherry, continuing to stir until cheese is melted. To serve the omelet, place the rolled omelet on a serving platter, cut into approximately 2-inch slices, and plate with sherry mushroom sauce poured evenly on top.

Poached Eggs in Tomato Sauce with Garlic & Cheese Toast

YIELD: 4 to 6 servings

Ingredients:

1½ tablespoons oil
3 garlic cloves, peeled and finely minced + 1 garlic clove cut in half
1 small onion, chopped
2 cups crushed tomatoes
1 tablespoon Worcestershire sauce
½ teaspoon cayenne pepper
½ teaspoon cumin
½ teaspoon paprika
1 large tomato, diced
8 eggs
4 slices sourdough bread or any good crusty bread
feta cheese, crumbled for garnish
mozzarella cheese (optional)
¼ cup parsley, chopped for garnish

Directions:

In a large skillet, heat oil over medium heat. Add minced garlic and onion and cook until soft and translucent. Add crushed tomatoes, Worcestershire sauce, cayenne pepper, cumin, and paprika and stir well to blend all ingredients. Add diced tomato and cook until sauce has thickened. Use the back side of a large serving spoon and make 8 wells in the tomato sauce, cracking one egg into each well. Cover and cook over medium heat for 5 to 8 minutes or until egg whites are cooked and the yolks are still a bit runny. In the meantime, preheat oven broiler to high and place bread slices on a baking sheet. Broil 1½ minutes on each side or until toasted. Rub bread with halved garlic clove, then sprinkle feta and mozzarella cheese on each bread slice and return to oven and broil 1½ minutes more or until cheese melts. Divide tomato mixture and eggs evenly among 4 shallow bowls. Serve with garlic toasts topped with parsley.

Seattle Avocado Crab Quiche

Quiche was invented in Germany in an area that later became the Lorraine region of France so quiche is generally considered to be a French dish. Quiches are wonderful to make and have on board. They can be served for breakfast, brunch, as an appetizer, or as the main course at dinner time. They can be prepared ahead of time, refrigerated, frozen, served hot, warm, or at room temperature and can be filled with about anything you have on hand. They can be cooked in a pie dish and cut into servings or baked and cooked in large or mini muffin pans. You can make your own pie dough recipe or use prepared pastry shells, and if you want a "fancier" quiche they can be cooked in puff pastry or phyllo dough. Most can be prepared in a pie dish to be served as a main course, but we also served quiche with fruit bowls, salads, soups, and often as finger food. Enjoy the world of quiche. Create, experiment, and enjoy these easily made, tasty, and beautiful tarts. I've included quiches in the appetizer chapter as well, as we so often serve them as party food, so be sure to look at those.

YIELD: 4–6 servings

Ingredients:

1 (10 inch) uncooked, prepared pie crust (optional, homemade pie pastry or package mix)
2 tablespoons shallots, minced
3 tablespoons butter
4 eggs
1 cup heavy cream
1 tablespoon hot sauce, such as Tabasco sauce
¼ teaspoon salt
pepper, to taste
½ cup Monterey Jack cheese, shredded
1 cup fresh or canned crab
1 large avocado, deseeded, peeled, and sliced

Directions:

Preheat oven to 400°F. Pre-cook pastry shell for 10 minutes, remove from oven, and cool. In the meantime, in a small skillet, sauté shallots in the butter and set aside. In a medium-sized mixing bowl, beat eggs and then add heavy cream, hot sauce, salt, and pepper. Reduce oven heat to 350°F. Layer the cheese, crab, and avocado placed in a pinwheel design on top of pie crust. Slowly add the egg mixture, then place the quiche in the oven and bake for 25 to 35 minutes or until knife inserted in center comes out clean. Serve warm, cool, or at room temperature.

Note: If you buy a pre-packaged pie crust mix, don't roll it out if you don't want to. Sometimes package mixes come as a stick of dough, and some come needing to be combined and formed into a ball. Just put the mixed ingredients in the middle of the pie plate, start working with your fingers, and pull the crust and push it around until it fills the pie plate. Don't forget to vent with fork tines on bottom and sides. This is a fast and easy way to make a quiche crust.

Salmon Quiche

YIELD: 4–6 servings

Ingredients:

2 tablespoons butter
4 green onions, sliced
¼ cup white onion, chopped
1 can cream of mushroom soup, undiluted
½ cup sour cream
2 eggs, slightly beaten
2–3 teaspoons dried or fresh dill, plus extra for topping
salt and pepper, to taste
Montreal Steak Mixture Seasoning (optional)
garlic salt or powder, to taste (optional)
small pinches of red pepper (optional)
1 can red salmon, skin and bones removed, then drained and flaked
1 tablespoon flour
1 (10 inch) uncooked, prepared pie crust (optional, homemade pie pastry or a package mix)
1 cup sharp cheddar cheese, grated, divided

Directions:

Preheat oven to 350°F. In a medium skillet, sauté the green and white onions in butter until just nice and soft. Remove from heat and let cool. Scoop cooled onion mixture into a medium-sized bowl, add cream of mushroom soup, breaking up lumps, then add sour cream, eggs, dill, salt, pepper, and optional spices, and salmon and mix until ingredients are well blended. Sprinkle flour evenly over the top and gently mix in. Prick bottom and sides of uncooked pastry with a fork to let steam out as it cooks, then sprinkle ½ cup of cheese on the bottom of the pie shell. Scoop combined ingredients into pie shell, sprinkle ½ cup of cheese on top, and decorate with dill. Place in oven and bake 60 minutes until set. Remove quiche and let stand 15 minutes so it will hold its shape when cut. Serve hot or cold.

BLT Quiche

YIELD: *4–6 servings*

Ingredients:

4 eggs
1 cup light cream
⅛ teaspoon salt
¼ teaspoon black pepper
1 (10 inch) uncooked, prepared pie crust
4 slices bacon, cooked, drained, and chopped
½ cup frozen spinach, thawed, drained, and chopped
⅓ cup sun-dried tomatoes, chopped

Directions:

Preheat oven to 350°F. In an electric mixer, whisk together the eggs, light cream, salt, and pepper and set aside. Prick bottom and sides of uncooked pastry with a fork to let steam out as it cooks, then sprinkle bottom of pie with chopped bacon. Evenly add spinach and sun-dried tomatoes and pour the egg mixture on top. Place the pie dish on a baking sheet in the oven and bake for 40 to 45 minutes until top is golden brown. Remove from oven and let rest for 15 minutes before slicing.

Note: If you buy a pre-packaged pie crust mix, don't roll it out if you don't want to. Sometimes package mixes come as a stick of dough, and some come needing to be combined and formed into a ball. Just put the mixed ingredients in the middle of the pie plate, start working with your fingers, and pull the crust and push it around until it fills the pie plate. Don't forget to vent with fork tines on bottom and sides. This is a fast and easy way to make a quiche crust.

Crab Quiche

YIELD: 4–6 servings

Ingredients:

1 (10 inch) uncooked, prepared pie crust
1 cup (8 ounces) crab meat, picked over, chopped
2 cups (8 ounces) Swiss cheese
1 tablespoon flour
4 eggs
1½ cups half-and-half or milk
1 tablespoon lemon juice
½ teaspoon salt
¼ teaspoon Worcestershire Sauce

Directions:

Preheat oven to 375°F. Precook pastry shell for 6 minutes, remove from oven, and cool. In the meantime, combine crab, Swiss cheese, and flour and place evenly into the pie shell. Gently beat eggs with half-and-half or milk, lemon juice, salt, and Worcestershire Sauce and pour over cheese and crab mixture. Place in oven and bake 40 to 45 minutes or until knife inserted in center comes out clean. Let cool for at least 5 minutes and serve warm, cool, or at room temperature.

Note: If you buy a pre-packaged pie crust mix, don't roll it out if you don't want to. Sometimes package mixes come as a stick of dough, and some come needing to be combined and formed into a ball. Just put the mixed ingredients in the middle of the pie plate, start working with your fingers, and pull the crust and push it around until it fills the pie plate. Don't forget to vent with fork tines on bottom and sides. This is a fast and easy way to make a quiche crust.

Canadian Bacon Quiche

YIELD: 4–6 servings

Ingredients:

1 (10 inch) uncooked, prepared pie crust
6 tablespoons (3 ounces) cream cheese, softened
¼ cup milk
2 eggs
1 tablespoon fresh sage, chopped, or dried sage, crushed
salt and pepper, to taste
½ cup (2 ounces) Canadian bacon, diced
½ cup (2 ounces) sharp cheddar cheese, shredded
¼ cup green onions, sliced

Directions:

Preheat oven to 400°F. Precook pastry shell for 6 to 8 minutes, remove from oven, and cool. Reduce oven heat to 325°F. In the meantime, place cream cheese in a medium bowl and beat with an electric mixer on medium speed until cheese is light and fluffy. Gradually beat in milk, then add eggs and beat on low speed until combined. Stir in sage, salt, and pepper. Sprinkle bacon, cheddar cheese, and green onions over the bottom of the pie shell. Pour egg and milk mixture over bacon and cheddar and place in oven. Bake for 15 to 20 minutes or longer until knife inserted in center comes out clean. Let cool for at least 5 minutes and serve warm, cool, or at room temperature.

Note: If you buy a pre-packaged pie crust mix, don't roll it out if you don't want to. Sometimes package mixes come as a stick of dough, and some come needing to be combined and formed into a ball. Just put the mixed ingredients in the middle of the pie plate, start working with your fingers, and pull the crust and push it around until it fills the pie plate. Don't forget to vent with fork tines on bottom and sides. This is a fast and easy way to make a quiche crust.

Italian Sausage, Tomato & Cheddar Quiche

YIELD: 4–6 servings

Ingredients:

1 (10 inch) uncooked, prepared pie crust
2 teaspoons olive oil
1 large onion, finely chopped
6 ounces Italian sausage
½ teaspoon Kosher salt, divided
½ teaspoon pepper, divided
¾ cup parsley, chopped
1 cup grape tomatoes, halved
4 large eggs
¾ cup sour cream
½ cup milk
¼ teaspoon fresh nutmeg, grated (optional)
1 cup (4 ounces) extra sharp cheddar cheese, grated

Directions:

Preheat oven to 425°F. Precook pastry shell for 10 to 12 minutes until lightly golden, then remove from oven and cool. Reduce oven heat to 375°F. In the meantime, heat the oil in a large skillet over medium heat, add the onion, sausage, ¼ teaspoon salt, ¼ teaspoon pepper and cook, stirring occasionally until onions are soft and sausage is no longer pink, about 5 to 7 minutes. Stir in parsley and tomatoes and remove from heat. In a large bowl, whisk together the eggs, sour cream, milk, remaining salt and paper, and nutmeg if using. Gently stir in cooked onion mixture and the cheese. Pour everything into the pie crust and bake 35 to 40 minutes or until knife inserted in center comes out clean. Let cool for at least 5 minutes and serve warm, cool, or at room temperature.

Note: If you buy a pre-packaged pie crust mix, don't roll it out if you don't want to. Sometimes package mixes come as a stick of dough, and some come needing to be combined and formed into a ball. Just put the mixed ingredients in the middle of the pie plate, start working with your fingers, and pull the crust and push it around until it fills the pie plate. Don't forget to vent with fork tines on bottom and sides. This is a fast and easy way to make a quiche crust.

Roasted Asparagus & Goat Cheese Quiche

YIELD: 4–6 servings

Ingredients:

1 (10 inch) uncooked, prepared pie crust
½ pound asparagus, trimmed and cut into 1-inch pieces
1 tablespoon olive oil
½ teaspoon Kosher salt, divided
½ teaspoon pepper, divided
4 large eggs
4 green onions, sliced
2 tablespoons mint leaves, chopped
¾ cup sour cream
½ cup milk
¼ teaspoon fresh nutmeg, grated (optional)
1 cup (4 ounces) goat cheese, crumbled

Directions:

Preheat oven to 425°F. Precook pastry shell for 10 to 12 minutes until lightly golden, then remove from oven and cool. In the meantime, on a rimmed baking sheet toss asparagus with olive oil, ¼ teaspoon salt, and ¼ teaspoon pepper and place in oven and roast 6 to 8 minutes. Remove from oven and reduce oven heat to 375°F. In a large bowl, whisk together the asparagus, eggs, green onions, mint leaves, sour cream, milk, remaining salt and pepper, and nutmeg if using. Gently stir in the goat cheese and blend. Pour everything into the pie crust and bake 35 to 40 minutes or until knife inserted in center comes out clean. Let cool for at least 5 minutes and serve warm, cool, or at room temperature.

Note: If you buy a pre-packaged pie crust mix, don't roll it out if you don't want to. Sometimes package mixes come as a stick of dough, and some come needing to be combined and formed into a ball. Just put the mixed ingredients in the middle of the pie plate, start working with your fingers, and pull the crust and push it around until it fills the pie plate. Don't forget to vent with fork tines on bottom and sides. This is a fast and easy way to make a quiche crust.

Shrimp Breakfast Scramble

YIELD: *4 servings*

Ingredients:

1 can (4½ ounces) shrimp or ½ cup fresh shrimp cut in bite-size pieces
4 slices bacon, cooked until crisp, drained and crumbled, 1 tablespoon bacon grease reserved
¾ cup green pepper, chopped
½ cup onion, chopped
½ teaspoon salt
¼ teaspoon Tabasco (optional, any hot pepper sauce)
6 eggs, slightly beaten
¼ cup half-and-half or milk
½ teaspoon Worcestershire Sauce

Directions:

Drain shrimp and reserve. Sauté green pepper and onion in reserved bacon fat until tender, add salt and Tabasco and place in medium bowl. Add beaten eggs, half-and-half, Worcestershire Sauce, and bacon, blending well. Place all ingredients in a large skillet over medium heat and cook until eggs are firm, stirring occasionally.

Spinach, Feta & Egg Breakfast Quesadillas

You can make these ahead of time, freeze, and serve for an "on-watch" crew or quick breakfast underway.

YIELD: 6–8 servings

Ingredients:

2 teaspoons olive oil
1 red bell pepper, deseeded and chopped
½ red onion, peeled and chopped
8 eggs
¼ cup milk
¼ teaspoon salt
¼ teaspoon pepper

4 handfuls of spinach leaves, sliced as in a chiffonade
½ cup feta cheese, crumbled
1½ cups mozzarella cheese, shredded
5 tortillas
nonstick spray

Directions:

Add olive oil to a large nonstick pan over medium heat and cook the bell pepper and red onion until just soft, about 4 to 5 minutes. In the meantime, whisk eggs together with the milk, salt, and pepper and then add the egg mixture to the peppers and onions in the frying pan, stirring until eggs are nearly cooked through. Add the spinach and feta cheese and fold into the eggs, stirring until the spinach has wilted and the eggs are cooked through. Remove eggs from the heat. Heat a second large nonstick pan sprayed with oil, or put cooked eggs in a separate bowl, wipe out the fry pan, and respray with oil, then add one tortilla. Spread about ½ cup of the egg mixture over one half of the tortilla and top with ⅓ cup of shredded mozzarella cheese. Fold the second half of the tortilla over the cheese and egg and cook for 2 minutes or until nice and golden brown. Gently flip the tortilla and cook for another minute until golden brown. Cut in half and serve immediately. Continue cooking the remainder of the tortillas in the same manner, adding egg and cheese mixture equally on each tortilla. To make ahead and store in the fridge or freezer, cool cooked tortillas on a cooling rack, then wrap in plastic wrap and store in a tightly sealed container for 3 to 4 days in the fridge and up to 1 week in the freezer. To reheat refrigerated quesadillas, place in a frying pan and heat for 2 to 3 minutes. To reheat frozen quesadillas, place on a paper towel in the microwave for 30 to 60 seconds or bring to room temperature until completely thawed and then heat for 2 to 3 minutes in a frying pan to crisp up.

Chiffonade: To chiffonade basil, lettuce, spinach etc., stack the leaves so that they are flat; they do not have to be pointing the same direction. Then, roll them like you would a cigar. While still holding tightly, start cutting thin slices. That's it!

St. Croix French Toast Soufflé

YIELD: 12 servings

Ingredients:

cooking spray for baking pan

10 cups (12 ounces) sturdy white bread, cut into 1-inch cubes

1 (8 ounce) package cream cheese, softened to room temperature

8 large eggs

1½ cup whole milk

⅔ cups half and half

½ cup maple syrup

1 tablespoon cinnamon

½ teaspoon vanilla extract

2 tablespoons confectioners' sugar, for garnish

maple syrup, for serving

Directions:

Coat a 13 x 9-inch baking dish with cooking spray and place bread cubes evenly over the bottom. With an electric mixer, beat cream cheese at medium speed until completely smooth. Beat in eggs one at a time at low speed until completely blended. Beat in milk, half-and-half, maple syrup, cinnamon, and vanilla until smooth. Pour mixture over the top of the bread and gently press down, making sure that the bread is completely coated, then cover and refrigerate 1 hour or overnight. When ready to cook, preheat oven to 350°F, remove bread mixture from fridge, and gently press down again to completely re-soak the bread. Let stand at room temperature for 30 minutes while oven is preheating. Place in oven and bake 45 minutes or until set. Remove from oven and let sit for 10 minutes, then sprinkle top with confectioners' sugar and serve with additional maple syrup.

Tasty Breakfast Sandwich

YIELD: 4 servings

Ingredients:

4 (½-inch thick) red bell pepper rings

4 eggs

4 slices toasted Rye bread, toasted

1 cup fresh spinach or arugula

salt and pepper, to taste

Parmesan cheese, fresh shaved

Directions:

Arrange pepper rings in a single layer in a large nonstick skillet. Crack 1 egg into the center of each ring and cook approximately 3 to 5 minutes over medium heat until set, then flip over and continue until desired doneness of eggs is reached. Put one slice of toasted bread on each plate, top with the spinach and/or spinach arugula mixture, and top with the cooked egg in the red bell pepper ring. Sprinkle with salt and pepper and Parmesan. Shaved Parmesan makes a much more attractive presentation. Serve with juice, coffee, or tea and a side of fresh fruit.

Tomorrow's Breakfast Pie

YIELD: 4–6 servings

Ingredients:

8 slices bacon
½ cup bread crumbs
5 eggs
2½ cups frozen shredded hash brown potatoes, brought to room temperature
1 cup (4 ounces) Swiss cheese, shredded
½ cup cottage cheese
⅓ cup milk
2–3 green onions, chopped
½ teaspoon salt
¼ teaspoon black pepper
4 drops or more hot pepper sauce, to taste
green onions, sliced, for garnish

Directions:

In a large skillet cook bacon over medium heat until crisp. Drain bacon on paper towels, reserving 1 tablespoon drippings in skillet. When bacon is cool, crumble bacon and set aside. Stir bread crumbs into the reserved drippings in skillet and set in a small bowl; cover and chill until needed. Lightly grease a 9-inch pie plate and set aside. In a medium bowl, beat eggs until foamy and then stir in crumbled bacon, hash brown potatoes, Swiss cheese, cottage cheese, milk, green onions, salt, black pepper, and hot pepper sauce. Pour everything into greased pie plate. Cover and chill for 2 hours to 24 hours. When ready to cook, preheat oven to 325°F. Sprinkle pie with bread crumb mixture and bake uncovered about 50 to 60 minutes or until a knife inserted in the center comes out clean. If desired, sprinkle pie with additional sliced green onions for garnish.

Note: Because of the fairly bland ingredients, other than the bacon in this recipe, it is easy to add all kinds of different options, such as cooked sausage, ham, shrimp, smoked salmon, jalapeños, or just about anything you have on hand. Just be careful with the amount of liquids, as it can get a little sloppy before cooking, but it can be made and stored in a tightly covered container in the fridge with excellent results.

CHAPTER 9
Chicken & Poultry

Peter's Story

Years ago, Stanley and I had a yacht sales office in Annapolis, a wonderful two-bedroom rental home at Mears Marina. It was a perfect office with lots of space for our desks and seating for guests and a kitchen where I could whip up quick lunches or dinners for our clients. One bedroom was used for storing boat gear and the other was a bedroom for clients who were not prepared to pay the exorbitant Annapolis hotel prices. We were living on *Native Sun*, our *Valiant 40* in the marina, so it was a short walk up the dock to our office.

We received a call from a fellow named Peter in Colorado inquiring about a boat we were brokering. We immediately had a very friendly rapport, enjoying each other's sailing stories as we extolled the virtues of an ocean-ready sailing yacht. Peter agreed to come to Annapolis the following week to meet us and to preview this boat. Peter was on a tight schedule as his business season was just beginning, but he arrived in the early evening, saw the boat, decided it wasn't the boat for him, and returned to Colorado quite early the next day.

The following weekend, one of our clients called and said he had to sell his *Valiant 40* immediately due to family issues, and he had just lowered the price to reflect this necessity. We immediately called Peter, as we knew this was exactly what he had been looking for and it was now in his price range. He signed a contract, made a deposit into our corporate account, and left the next day to take delivery of a boat he had never seen from an owner he had never met in Southwest Florida.

When Peter had initially arrived in Annapolis, we all immediately felt like kindred spirits, and as we always closed the Annapolis office for the winter and cruised down to Florida, we were all excited about launching his new boat and cruising together in the company of Captain Charlie aboard *Leo* and Wade and Maryanne aboard *Welkin*, all of whom had bought their boats from us, and had become dear friends. Our plan was as usual, to make part of the trip down the intracoastal and part offshore, depending on late fall weather. After a brief stop in Florida to settle into our southern office which was mostly taken care of by phone calls and mail, we then would head over to the Bahamas for several months in the company of three other *Valiant 40s*.

The day after Peter returned home from Florida, we received a panicked call from him. He said "I don't even know you people and it was late at night and I've never seen an office quite like yours before and I just transferred a huge chunk of money to your account for a boat in Florida that I had only briefly seen after it was already loaded on a truck." We gave him our attorney's name and contact information, sent him a copy of our business license, had the marina management send him a notarized letter, and encouraged him to return the following weekend for a few days inspection of both us and the boat, which by then, had arrived in Annapolis by truck from Florida. Many of our clients who lived in the surrounding areas of Annapolis and some who were live-aboard sailors in Mears Marina with us gathered to welcome Peter back to Annapolis and to help assure and encourage him. Over the years, we have all laughed about this transaction and how really unusual it was, all of us being the most trusting people.

We ended up cruising with Peter and *Avatar* and first mate Boshie (whom he stole from Captain Charlie on *Leo*) for several years. It was quite a site whenever we anchored together or arrived at a marina to refuel and resupply, four *Valiant 40s*, sailed by owners and crew who were the best of friends. Peter had taken French cooking classes, and Captain Charlie was a fine cook, as were Wade and Maryanne, and so it was we shared many holiday feasts together from the east coast of the US throughout the Bahamas to the Virgin Islands and into the French islands of the Caribbean. Following is Peter's scrumptious rendition of a French stuffed chicken: Avatar Chicken Farci.

Avatar Chicken Farci

This is a very simple dish to prepare and will impress any guests on board.

YIELD: 6 servings

Ingredients:

1 pound zucchini, julienned
salt, to taste
1 whole chicken
1 onion, chopped
3 ounces ricotta or cream cheese
⅓ cup butter, softened
1½ teaspoons dried tarragon
1 egg
1 cup Parmesan cheese, grated
pepper, to taste

Directions:

Preheat oven to 450° F. Slice zucchini into julienned pieces and place on jelly roll pan or cookie sheet covered with paper towels. Sprinkle cut surfaces with a liberal amount of salt and let sit for 15 minutes. Drain the water and discard and pat the zucchini dry or wrap in dry paper towel until ready to use. Rinse and dry whole chicken and place on a counter or sheet pan large enough to hold the chicken. Cut out the back bone with scissors, then place breast side up and with the heel of your hand flatten the chicken—you'll hear a crunch! (The backbone and any other chicken parts can be tossed in boiling water with a few spices, onion, or any other leftover veggies and boiled down for chicken stock to use at a later time.) Starting at the bottom of the chicken, work your hand under the skin, pulling it gently (you don't want to rip the skin) away from the flesh, including the thighs and legs. Sauté onions and julienned zucchini 6 to 7 minutes until dried a bit. Mash ricotta or cream cheese, tarragon, egg, and add sautéed veggies. Add Parmesan ¼ cup at a time, mixing in to bring the stuffing to a firm, stiff consistency. Take handfuls of stuffing and shove between the skin and flesh of the chicken, smoothing out to even the stuffing, including the thighs and legs. It will all fit—keep stuffing. Place stuffed chicken in a roasting pan, sprinkle with salt and pepper, and roast for 10 minutes. Reduce heat to 375°F and continue roasting for 50 minutes. Baste frequently. Remove from oven, let rest at least 10 minutes, serve, and be prepared for a delicious French style chicken.

Baked Reuben Chicken

YIELD: 4 servings

Ingredients:

4 boneless, skinless chicken breasts
¼ teaspoon salt
pepper, to taste
1 (16 ounce) can sauerkraut, drained
4 slices Swiss cheese
1¼ cups bottled thousand island salad
    dressing
1 tablespoon parsley, chopped, for garnish

Directions:

Preheat oven to 325°F. Place chicken breasts in a greased baking pan, sprinkle with salt and pepper, and spread sauerkraut evenly over the breasts. Top with Swiss cheese and pour salad dressing over the cheese. Place in the oven and bake 1½ hours until done or juices run clear when a fork is inserted in the thick part of the chicken. Serve, making sure to scoop up all the juices and sauerkraut, sprinkle with parsley, and enjoy.

Bourbon Turkey Breast

YIELD: 4–6 servings

Ingredients:

1 cup bourbon
½ cup dark molasses
¼ cup brown sugar
1 tablespoon Kosher salt
1 teaspoon Tabasco
1 bone-in turkey breast

Directions:

In a medium saucepan, mix bourbon, molasses, and brown sugar and mix until sugar dissolves, then place saucepan over medium heat. Bring marinade to a simmer and then remove from heat. Add salt and Tabasco, mix well to blend, then with a rubber spatula, scoop all the marinade into a large bowl or large covered container that will hold the turkey and marinade. Place turkey breast skin-side down in the bowl and let stand for 1 hour, turning occasionally. When ready to cook, remove turkey breast from marinade, reserve marinade for basting, and place turkey breast in the oven on a rack over a large pan or in a roasting pan. Preheat oven to 350°F when ready to cook and cook turkey breast for about 45 minutes or according to directions on the turkey breast bag. Marinate occasionally and cook until inside temperature is 165°F. Remove from oven and let rest 10 to 20 minutes before slicing. If you have any turkey left over, it's delicious in a salad, in tacos, primavera, soup, sandwiches, fettucine, and almost any way you can think of.

Chicken Enchiladas with Salsa Verde Cruda

YIELD: 4 servings

Ingredients for the enchilada sauce:

3 garlic cloves, minced
1 tablespoon butter
1 tablespoon flour
1 cup chicken stock
2 teaspoons cumin
¼ teaspoon salt
¼ teaspoon fresh ground pepper
½ cup fat-free sour cream
1 cup mild or medium salsa verde
½ cup cilantro, chopped

Ingredients for the enchiladas:

8 flour tortillas
3–4 cups cooked chicken breasts, chopped or shredded
2 cups shredded Mexican blend cheese
3 avocados, peeled and chopped

Directions for the enchilada sauce:

Preheat oven to 375°F. In medium sauce pan, sauté garlic in butter for 1 minute on medium-high heat. Stir in flour and let it cook for about 2 more minutes, stirring constantly. Stir in the chicken stock, cumin, salt, and pepper and bring to a simmer. Remove from heat and stir in the sour cream, salsa verde, and cilantro until smooth (or at least as smooth as you can get it).

Directions for the enchiladas:

Lightly spray a 9 × 13-inch baking dish with nonstick spray. Add about ½ cup of the enchilada sauce to the bottom of the pan and spread out until bottom of the baking dish is evenly coated with enchilada sauce. Lay out a tortilla and add chicken, shredded cheese, and avocado to the end of the tortilla and roll. Place the rolled tortilla seam-side down and repeat until the pan is full. Pour the remaining enchilada sauce over the chicken enchiladas. Cover with 1 cup of cheese and bake for about 20 minutes or until cheese is bubbling.

Caraway Swiss Chicken

This delicious dinner is made to be cooked and frozen and reheated and served at a later date.

YIELD: *4 servings*

Ingredients:

1 (10 ounce) package frozen spinach
nonstick cooking spray
4 boneless, skinless chicken breasts, halved lengthwise to make 8 pieces
¾ cup milk
2 teaspoons cornstarch
1½ teaspoons chicken bouillon granules or 1½ chicken bouillon cubes
¼ teaspoon caraway seed
⅛ teaspoon pepper
2 ounces (overflowing ½ cup) Swiss cheese, torn into pieces

Directions:

Cook frozen spinach according to package directions. Drain well and place in a casserole dish with a tight-fitting lid. In the meantime, spray a large skillet with nonstick cooking spray. Add the 8 chicken pieces and cook over medium heat for 8 to 10 minutes until tender and no longer pink while turning occasionally to cook on both sides. Place cooked chicken on top of spinach. In a medium sauce-pan, combine milk, cornstarch, bouillon, caraway, and pepper and cook over medium heat, stirring constantly until thickened and bubbly. Add cheese and stir until melted. With a rubber spatula, scoop sauce evenly over top of chicken. Let cook a few minutes and then cover with foil, tightly seal the casserole dish, and freeze. To serve, remove casserole from freezer, remove lid, but keep the foil covering the dish. Preheat oven to 375°F and bake in the oven 45 to 50 minutes or until completely hot. Because of the saltiness of the bouillon, don't add additional salt to this dish.

Cheese-Stuffed & Bacon-Wrapped Chicken Breasts

YIELD: *4 servings*

Ingredients:

2 chicken breasts, boneless and skinless
4 tablespoons cream cheese, softened
2 tablespoons green onion, chopped
¼ cup pepper jack cheese, shredded
4–8 pieces of bacon

Directions:

Preheat oven to 375°F. Cut through the thick part of the chicken to make 4 equal-sized pieces. Pound breasts to about ¼-inch thickness. In a small bowl, mix softened cream cheese, green onions, and pepper jack cheese. Put ¼ of this mixture into the middle of each piece of chicken. Starting at the long side, roll chicken breast up, keeping the cheese mixture to the middle. Wrap 1 to 2 slices of bacon around each chicken breast and secure with toothpicks. Place on baking sheet and bake for 30 minutes, then broil the topside for about 5 minutes to fully brown and crisp bacon. Turn each breast over and broil for another 3 minutes or so to crisp up the bottom side.

Chicken Cakes with Horseradish Aioli

YIELD: 6 servings

Ingredients for horseradish aioli:

2 tablespoons mayonnaise
2 teaspoons prepared horseradish
2 cloves garlic, peeled, sliced, and minced
salt, to taste

Ingredients for chicken cakes:

2-3 cups cup cooked chicken, pulsed in food processor into small bits
¼ cup fresh cilantro, chopped
3 tablespoons mayonnaise
1 teaspoon Old Bay Seasoning
salt and pepper, to taste
2 large egg whites
1 cup fresh bread crumbs
2 teaspoons oil

Directions for horseradish aioli:

Mix all aioli ingredients together in a small bowl and blend well. Cover and refrigerate until serving.

Directions for chicken cakes:

In a medium bowl, thoroughly combine cilantro, mayonnaise, Old Bay Seasoning, salt and pepper, egg whites and bread crumbs, then scoop the minced chicken into the bowl. With a fork or your hands, mix all ingredients until well blended, then divide into 6 equal portions and shape into ½-inch thick patties. Refrigerate for 30 to 60 minutes. When ready to cook, heat oil in a large non-stick skillet over medium heat. Add patties and cook 5 minutes on each side until nicely browned. Serve with horseradish aioli or serve as a sandwich on a Kaiser-type roll with your choice of sliced onions, lettuce, and tomatoes.

Chicken in Rosemary Wine Sauce

YIELD: 4 servings

Ingredients:

4 boneless, skinless chicken breasts
2 teaspoons fresh rosemary sprigs, chopped
1 cup white wine
1 cup soy sauce
fresh rosemary sprigs, for garnish

Directions:

Preheat oven to 325°F. Place chicken breasts on a baking pan, sprinkle with 2 teaspoons fresh chopped rosemary, and place in oven. In a small bowl, combine white wine and soy sauce and mix well. Baste chicken every 10 to 15 minutes and bake for 1 hour or until juices run clear when pricked. To serve, place on dishes, spoon a little remaining sauce over chicken, and garnish with fresh rosemary sprigs.

Chicken Thighs in Ginger-Garlic Hoisin Sauce

YIELD: 4 servings

Ingredients:

½ cup peeled fresh ginger, coarsely chopped
2–3 large garlic cloves, peeled and chopped
½ cup hoisin sauce
2 tablespoons soy sauce
2 tablespoons sugar
¼ cup water
8 large boneless, skin-on chicken thighs

Directions:

Place all ingredients except chicken in food processor and process to a smooth purée. On the underside of each chicken thigh, cut 3 or 4 (½-inch thick) slices and rub purée over chicken thighs and into the cut slices. Place thighs in a large sealed container or re-sealable bag with any remaining purée, cover, and refrigerate 6 hours or overnight. To cook, preheat oven broiler, place thighs in a roasting pan skin-side up, and place under preheated broiler for 7 to 8 minutes or until skins are crunchy and brown. Turn thighs over and broil for 3 to 4 minutes more or until thighs are just cooked through. Place on a large serving platter or individual plates and enjoy.

Chicken with Hoisin Sauce

YIELD: 6–8 servings

Ingredients:

2 large chicken breasts, boneless and skinless
6 green onions
1 teaspoon sesame oil
3 tablespoons soy sauce
1 tablespoon Chinese rice wine or cooking sherry
salt, to taste
1 (1-inch) piece fresh ginger, peeled, finely chopped
5 cloves garlic, peeled, sliced, and minced
5 tablespoons peanut oil or other oil of choice
2 tablespoons hoisin sauce
1 tablespoon water, room temperature

Directions:

Cut chicken breasts into 1-inch cubes and place in a large bowl. Cut the green onions on an angle into ½-inch lengths and add to the chicken. Add the sesame oil, soy sauce, wine, and salt and mix chicken mixture until well blended. Cover and marinate for 15 to 20 minutes. In the meantime, peel the ginger and the garlic and mince. Heat a large skillet over high heat for 15 seconds, then carefully add the peanut or other oil and heat until tiny bubbles appear. Be careful, it will be very hot! Place ginger and garlic in hot skillet, stir for 10 seconds, then add hoisin sauce and stir-fry for 30 seconds while constantly stirring. Pour the water into the chicken mixture, stir well, then add to the skillet. Cook, stirring occasionally for about 5 minutes or until chicken is completely cooked through. Serve immediately over hot rice and with a steamed veggie of your choice on the side.

Chili Sauce & Grape Jelly Glazed Grilled Chicken

This recipe works well on baked or grilled skin-on or skinless chicken pieces such as breasts, thighs, etc.

YIELD: 8 servings

Ingredients:

1 (10 ounce) bottle grape jelly
1 (12 ounce) bottle chili sauce
8–10 chicken breasts

Directions for baking:

Preheat oven to 350°F. In a small saucepan, stir together grape jelly and chili sauce. Heat over medium-high heat until mixture comes to a boil and jelly is melted, stirring well to blend. Remove from heat. Arrange chicken pieces in a 13 x 9-inch baking dish, pour sauce evenly over chicken, and turn pieces to coat both sides. Place in hot oven and bake, uncovered, for 45–60 minutes, or until chicken is very tender. Check chicken halfway through and spoon sauce over all pieces. Because of the sugar in the grape jelly, you may want to cover with aluminum foil halfway through baking to keep the sauce from burning.

Directions for grilling:

Oil grill grates, then turn grill on to medium-high heat. In a small saucepan, stir together grape jelly and chili sauce. Heat over medium-high heat until mixture comes to a boil and jelly is melted, stir well to blend. Remove from heat. Place chicken on grill and sear 10 minutes and then turn and use a basting brush to "paint" the sauce on the second side. Continue to turn and baste, moving chicken around on the heat as necessary. Cook chicken about 30 minutes or until done, as the grilling time depends on the size of chicken pieces and whether they are bone in or out. Because of the sugar in the grape jelly, do not put marinade on the raw chicken as it will burn, so be sure to begin basting after the chicken has been seared and turned the first time.

Complete Chicken Sheet Pan Dinner

A sheet pan is generally around 10 x 15-inches with 1-inch thick sides, made so that your food won't slide off. These pans are just wonderful for roasting veggies, as marinade and juices won't spill into your oven.

YIELD: *4 servings*

Ingredients:

1 lemon, sliced in rings, to add while cooking
zest of 1 lemon
juice of 1 lemon
2 tablespoons olive oil
8 rosemary sprigs, leaves removed and finely minced
1 teaspoon garlic powder
1 teaspoon onion powder
1 teaspoon salt
1 teaspoon pepper
1 pound red potatoes, cut in fourths or large chunks
4 large chicken breasts, boneless and skinless
1 pound asparagus, thick stemmed are best
4–5 whole rosemary springs, to add while cooking

Directions:

Preheat oven to 415°F. Spray a sheet pan with nonstick spray or grease with olive oil. Slice one lemon into thin rings and set aside. Zest and juice another lemon into a medium bowl and whisk in olive oil, minced rosemary, garlic powder, onion powder, salt, and pepper, continuing to whisk until well blended. Add the prepared potatoes and toss them until totally covered with the marinade, then place potatoes onto sheet pan along the outside edges. Add and toss the chicken in the remaining marinade in the bowl until well coated. Place coated chicken into the middle of the sheet pan, preferably with a little space between each chicken breast. Place pan with potatoes and chicken in the oven and bake 10 minutes. In the meantime, trim the asparagus and coat the asparagus and the whole rosemary sprigs with any remaining marinade or a small amount of olive oil. Toss and turn the potatoes around so all sides will be roasted, and move the potatoes to the two ends of the pan with the chicken in the middle. Lay asparagus down the sides next to the chicken, and decorate with lemon slices over the chicken and sprigs of rosemary artfully placed around the other ingredients. Place back in the oven and bake for 10 more minutes or until chicken is done. Remove from oven and serve immediately.

Coral Cay Summer Lime Chicken Breast with Stir-Fry Broccoli

YIELD: 4 servings

Ingredients for marinade:

⅓ cup olive oil
juice of 3–4 limes
4 cloves garlic, peeled, sliced, and minced
3 tablespoons fresh cilantro, chopped
½ teaspoon salt
½ teaspoon black pepper
4 boneless, skinless chicken breasts

Ingredients for stir-fry broccoli:

6 sweet peppers, optional
1½ tablespoons sesame oil
½ teaspoon chili oil
garlic powder, to taste
¼ cup walnuts, chopped
4 cups fresh broccoli, cut into florets or small pieces
1 tablespoon soy sauce

Directions for marinade:

In a medium bowl, mix olive oil, lime juice, garlic, cilantro, salt, and pepper and blend well. Gently pound chicken breasts between two pieces of wax paper until tenderized and breasts are uniform in thickness, about ½-inch. Place chicken in a re-sealable plastic bag or lidded container, pour marinade over, and mix so that all the chicken is covered with marinade. Place in refrigerator for 2 hours or overnight to marinate. To cook, wipe BBQ grill grates with oil, turn heat to medium, place breasts on grill, and cook for 3 to 4 minutes. Turn chicken and cook an additional 3 minutes, being careful not to overcook.

Directions for stir-fry broccoli:

If grilling the optional sweet peppers, marinate long enough to coat all sides and grill on BBQ, just until they are barely cooked. In the meantime, place sesame oil, chili oil, and a shake of garlic powder into a large skillet over high heat. When oil is hot, reduce heat to medium, then add chopped walnuts and broccoli. Stir-fry and cook for 4 more minutes, then add soy sauce and cover and cook for only 1 more minute. To serve, plate breasts and broccoli and serve with optional grilled sweet peppers, if using.

Cornish Game Hens with Mushroom Sauce

YIELD: *2 servings*

Ingredients:

2 Cornish game hens
lemon pepper seasoning, to taste
olive oil for rubbing game hens and sautéing onions, celery, and mushrooms
½ cup onion, finely diced
4 stalks celery, diced
1 cup chopped mushrooms
1 cup heavy cream
6 tablespoons butter
4 tablespoons parsley, chopped
salt and pepper, to taste

Directions:

Preheat oven to 350°F. Pat game hens dry inside and out with a paper towel, then sprinkle with lemon pepper seasoning and rub in with a little olive oil. Place hens on a roasting pan or pan with a rack and bake for 45 to 60 minutes, until roasted and meat thermometer reads 170°F. To make the mushroom sauce, in a large saucepan sauté onion in olive oil over medium heat until translucent, then add celery and mushrooms and sauté a few minutes until mushrooms have released their delicious liquids and celery is translucent. Stir well to combine the veggies. Add heavy cream and cook, letting the sauce reduce. Remove pan from stove and add butter and parsley to mushroom sauce. Add salt and pepper to taste, and give it all a final whisk. To serve, remove game hens from the oven, place one on each plate, and cover game hens with mushroom sauce.

Maryanne & Wade's Story

Maryanne and Wade came from Kentucky and were sailing on the Chesapeake Bay in a *Valiant 40*, a sister ship to our *Native Sun*, when we first met them. We naturally gravitated toward each other, especially since they were both so fresh and excited about their first cruising experience, and because they each had a great sense of humor and we were sailing boats that would reach an anchorage at almost the same time, even after a day of competitive sailing.

Stanley is a much more relaxed sailor than I, for when I see a sail on the horizon, it is my inclination to take over the helm and begin what is generally a useless "race." It's difficult to pass a sailboat that is over a mile ahead, but I always try. That is how we met Maryanne and Wade, sailing alongside a sister ship and trying to be in the lead. We radioed one another and agreed to anchor for the evening in the same cove.

Maryanne was a wonderful cook and shared many recipes with us as we made our way down the Intracoastal Waterway to Florida, then across to West End in the Bahamas, and cruising for months together throughout the islands of the Bahamas.

Maryanne's Crab-Stuffed Key Lime Chicken Breasts

This is a hearty and delicious dish that Maryanne made for us on our cruise from Annapolis to Florida.

YIELD: 4 servings

Ingredients for chicken breasts:

1 tablespoon butter
1 tablespoon flour
½ cup cream
salt and pepper, to taste
1 cup crab meat, fresh or canned
1 cup mushrooms, chopped
seasoned bread crumbs
3 eggs, slightly beaten
4 boneless, skinless chicken breasts, beaten
    thin with a mallet
oil, for cooking

Ingredients for sauce:

2 tablespoons butter
2 tablespoons flour
1½ cups cream
salt and pepper, to taste
2 tablespoons dill
¼ cup white wine
juice of 2-4 limes, to taste
1 cup mushrooms, sliced

Directions for chicken breasts:

Preheat oven 350°F. In a large saucepan, melt butter and add flour and whisk to make a roux. Cook slowly over medium heat for 5 minutes. Add cream, continuously whisking to make a smooth sauce. Season with salt and pepper, taste and adjust seasonings. Add crab meat, mushrooms, and enough bread crumbs to bind everything together for a stuffing. Remove from stove and set aside. In the meantime, place beaten eggs in one shallow dish and more bread crumbs in a second shallow dish for breading. Fill each chicken breast with stuffing, roll to enclose, using a toothpick to hold together if necessary, then dip in egg mixture and then into breadcrumbs. In a large skillet, heat enough oil to generously cover the bottom, and sauté the chicken breasts, turning to cook both sides until breasts are a beautiful golden color. Place sautéed breasts in an ovenproof dish or skillet and cook 5 additional minutes.

Directions for sauce:

In a large saucepan over medium heat, melt butter, whisk in flour, and make a roux. Blend in cream, seasonings, wine, lime juice, and mushrooms. To serve, place a stuffed chicken breast on each plate or all of them on a serving platter and top with the hot cream sauce.

Chicken Scaloppini with Creamed Mushroom & Sherry Sauce

YIELD: 4 servings

Ingredients:

4 boneless, skinless chicken breasts, halved
½ cup all-purpose flour
6 teaspoons olive oil, divided
6 ounces (1½ cups) mushrooms, rinsed and quartered
2 tablespoons shallots, minced
½ teaspoon dried thyme
½ cup dry sherry
¼ cup chicken broth
2 tablespoons whipping cream
1 tablespoon chopped parsley
salt and pepper, to taste

Directions:

Preheat oven to 200°F to keep chicken warm between frying batches. Place chicken on a flat surface, cover with plastic wrap or parchment paper, and with a mallet pound chicken to ¼-inch thickness. Place ½ cup all-purpose flour in a pie plate or shallow container, roll chicken in flour, and lightly coat breasts. Heat a large nonstick skillet over medium-high heat, then add 2 teaspoons olive oil. Lay 2 pieces of chicken in pan and cook, turning once until golden and no longer pink in the center, about 4 to 6 minutes. Transfer to a platter and set in warmed oven. Coat the other 2 chicken breasts with flour, add 2 more teaspoons oil to the pan, and over medium-high heat add the chicken. Cook as before, and place them in the warmed oven. Don't wash the skillet. In the same skillet, heat 2 teaspoons olive oil, add mushrooms, shallots, and thyme to the hot skillet, stirring often over high heat until mushrooms are browned, 4 to 5 minutes. Add the sherry, chicken broth, and whipping cream to skillet and stir until mixture is boiling. Continue cooking, stirring occasionally until the mushroom sauce is slightly reduced, about 1 to 1½ minutes. To serve, remove chicken platter from oven, spoon sauce over chicken, and sprinkle with parsley, salt, and pepper.

Crepes Filled with Leftover Chicken

YIELD: 15–16 crepes

Ingredients:

1½ cups milk
4 eggs
1 cup all-purpose flour
1½ teaspoons sugar
⅛ teaspoon salt
8 teaspoons butter

Ingredients for crepe filling:

¼ cup butter
½ pound (2½–2¾ cups) mushrooms, sliced
¼ cup onion, chopped
¼ cup flour
2 cups milk
2 teaspoons chicken bouillon granules or
   2 cubes
½ teaspoon Italian seasoning
¼ teaspoon black pepper
½ cup sour cream
3 tablespoons sherry
2 cups cooked chicken, chopped
parsley, minced

Directions:

In a large bowl, whisk milk and eggs until well combined and set aside. In a small bowl, combine the flour, sugar, and salt and whisk into the milk and egg mixture. Mix well then place in refrigerator to chill for 1 hour. In an 8-inch skillet over medium heat, melt 1 teaspoon butter, then pour 2 to 3 tablespoons of crepe batter into the center of the skillet. Lift and tilt skillet to coat bottom evenly with batter and cook until top looks dry. With a non-metal spatula, carefully loosen the crepe and turn it over or use your fingers to turn it over. Cook 15 to 20 seconds longer. Remove from skillet and place on a wire cooling rack. Repeat with remaining batter, adding butter to the skillet as needed. Stack cooled crepes with wax paper or paper towels in between. Cooled crepes can be frozen by layering with wax paper between crepes, placing in a freezer container, sealing; freeze for up to 2 months. To use, let frozen crepes return to room temperature and use in any crepe recipe.

Directions for crepe filling:

In a medium saucepan, melt butter, add mushrooms and onion and cook until just tender. Whisk in flour and continue to whisk while adding milk. Add bouillon and seasonings and bring sauce to a boil. Stir in sour cream and sherry and blend thoroughly. Set 1 cup of sauce aside for garnish. Add chicken and minced parsley to remaining sauce in the pan. Spoon filling into prepared crepes, roll bottom up about ⅓ of the way, then bring the 2 sides together. Filling should be showing from the top of the crepe. Spoon the reserved sauce over the middle of the crepes and garnish with more parsley if desired.

Curried Chicken & Rice Phyllo Bundles

YIELD: 6 servings

Ingredients:

1 cup homemade or canned chicken broth
½ cup uncooked long grain rice
1½ cups cooked chicken breast, cut into cubes
1 cup frozen peas and carrots, thawed and drained
6 tablespoons mayonnaise
2 green onions, chopped
1 teaspoon salt
½ teaspoon pepper
½ teaspoon curry powder
¼ teaspoon garlic powder
¼ teaspoon ground turmeric
¼ teaspoon ground coriander
6 whole cloves
12 (14 x 9 inches) sheets phyllo dough
butter-flavored cooking spray
chives, for garnish

Directions:

Preheat oven to 375°F when ready to cook. In a small saucepan, bring broth and rice to a boil, then reduce heat, cover, and simmer for 15 to 18 minutes or until liquid is absorbed and rice is tender. Scoop rice into a large bowl and add chicken, peas and carrots, mayonnaise, green onion and seasonings. Place one sheet of phyllo dough on a work surface and lightly spray with butter-flavored cooking spray. Top with another sheet of phyllo and lightly spray this second sheet. (Remaining phyllo sheets must be covered with plastic wrap and a damp towel to prevent them from drying out.) Place ½ cup filling in the center of the sprayed phyllo sheets. Bring all 4 corners together to make a bundle and twist the top, then tie with a long chive to make a pretty presentation. Repeat with remaining phyllo sheets and chicken mixture ingredients. Place bundles on a baking sheet coated with cooking spray. Bake for 12 to 15 minutes or until lightly golden brown.

Curried Honey-Glazed Drumsticks

YIELD: *6 servings*

Ingredients:

12 skinless chicken drumsticks
2 tablespoons Dijon mustard
¼ cup fresh lemon juice
¼ cup honey
¼ teaspoon curry
½ teaspoon salt

Directions:

Rinse chicken and pat dry. In a large bowl, combine mustard, lemon juice, honey, curry, and salt and mix well to blend. Place chicken in the marinade and turn in to coat evenly. At this point, you can transfer the chicken and marinade into a tightly sealed container and chill in the refrigerator overnight. When ready to cook, preheat oven to 375°F, remove chicken from the marinade, place on a large, lightly greased oven baking sheet and bake for 1 hour. Turn drumsticks and baste occasionally until drumsticks are cooked and the sauce has turned into a thick golden glaze. Serve immediately with any remaining sauce spooned over the chicken.

Dan-Dan Chicken Noodles

YIELD: 4 servings

Ingredients:

½ pound Chinese-style noodles or 3 packages chicken Ramen noodles, reserve flavor packages
1 tablespoon fresh ginger, minced
2 garlic cloves, peeled, sliced, and finely minced
2 tablespoons corn starch
3 tablespoons soy sauce
1–2 teaspoons oyster sauce
1 pound ground chicken
⅔ cup chicken broth
2 tablespoons peanut butter, creamy old-fashioned style
1 tablespoon rice vinegar
2 teaspoons Asian chili garlic sauce or sriracha chili sauce
2 teaspoons hot chili oil or more to taste
2 teaspoons sesame oil
2 tablespoons canola oil
3–4 green onions, sliced
1½ red bell peppers, stemmed, deseeded, and cut into slivers
½ pound fresh snow peas, trimmed
½ cup salted, roasted peanuts, chopped, divided
green onions, sliced, for garnish

Directions:

When making Dan-Dan Chicken Noodles, it's best to have all the ingredients prepared and measured before starting. Though there are a lot of ingredients, this is an easy meal to prepare and so delicious that it's well worth the prep time. In a large pot of boiling water, cook noodles according to package instruction. If using Ramen, do not use flavor packages. Drain and rinse noodles with cold water. In the meantime, in a large bowl, add ginger, garlic, cornstarch, soy sauce, and oyster sauce and mix well to combine. Add chicken and mix to cover all chicken pieces with sauce. In a medium bowl, whisk together chicken broth, peanut butter, rice vinegar, chili sauce, chili oil, and sesame oil until well combined. Heat a large skillet (not nonstick) on high heat, add 2 tablespoons canola oil, and while tilting skillet swirl oil so that it evenly covers the bottom. Add the chicken mixture, stirring to separate chicken pieces, and cook, continuing to stir until chicken is lightly browned. Add bell peppers and stir for 1 minute. Add chicken broth mixture, stirring until slightly thickened, then add snow peas and cooked noodles to skillet. With 2 large forks or tongs, toss everything until snow peas are bright green and noodles are well coated and heated through, about 1 to 2 minutes. Taste and adjust seasonings. Add ¼ cup peanuts and toss. To serve, plate Dan-Dan Noodles in large bowls or rimmed dishes and top with remaining peanuts and sliced green onions.

Dijon Chicken Diane

YIELD: *4 servings*

Ingredients:

2 tablespoons butter, divided
2 tablespoons olive oil, divided
4 boneless chicken breasts, pounded with a mallet to ½-inch thick
½ teaspoon salt or more to taste
¼–½ teaspoon pepper or more to taste
⅛ teaspoon garlic, peeled, sliced, and finely minced
3 tablespoons green onions, chopped
juice of ½ large lime or lemon
3 tablespoons parsley, chopped
2–3 teaspoons Dijon mustard, to taste
2 tablespoons brandy or cognac
¼ cup chicken broth
1 teaspoon Worcestershire sauce (optional)

Directions:

Preheat a large sauté pan over medium heat and add 1 tablespoon butter and 1 tablespoon olive oil. Add the chicken, sprinkle with salt and pepper, increase heat to medium-high, and sauté 2 to 3 minutes on each side. Do not cook longer or chicken will be overcooked and dry. Place chicken on a warm serving platter. While whisking constantly, add the garlic, green onions, lime or lemon juice, parsley, mustard, and brandy or cognac to the sauté pan and cook for 15 seconds. Whisk in chicken broth and Worcestershire sauce, if using, and stir until sauce is smooth. Whisk in remaining butter and oil until well blended. To serve, pour sauce over chicken and serve immediately. Serve with pasta with a cream or cheese sauce, steamed broccoli, and a nice cool, crisp salad.

Grilled Basil Chicken Breasts

YIELD: 4 servings

Ingredients:

¾ teaspoon black pepper
4 large, boneless, skinless chicken breasts, halved lengthwise to make 8 pieces
⅓ cup butter, melted
¼ cup fresh basil, chopped + 2 tablespoons fresh basil
½ cup butter, softened to room temperature
1 tablespoon Parmesan cheese, grated
¼ teaspoon garlic powder
salt and pepper, to taste
fresh basil sprigs, for garnish

Directions:

Evenly press ¾ teaspoon pepper into meaty sides of 8 chicken breast pieces. In a small bowl combine ⅓ cup melted butter with ¼ cup chopped basil and stir well. Brush all sides of chicken pieces with the melted butter mixture. Reserve the remaining melted butter marinade for basting. In another small bowl, combine and beat with an electric mixer ½ cup softened butter, 2 tablespoons chopped basil, Parmesan cheese, garlic powder, salt, and pepper until completely smooth and blended. Transfer to a small serving bowl and set aside. Place chicken breasts on a preheated grill and cook over medium heat for 8 to 10 minutes on each side, basting frequently with reserved melted butter mixture. Place grilled chicken on a large warmed serving platter and spread the herbed Parmesan butter over the hot chicken. Serve immediately and top with fresh basil.

Grilled Chicken in Jalapeño Lime Marinade

YIELD: 4 servings

Ingredients:

4 skinless, boneless chicken breasts, washed and patted dry
6 limes (½ cup), juiced
½ cup olive oil
2 tablespoons fresh cilantro, chopped
2 teaspoons salt
1 teaspoon black pepper
3 jalapeño peppers, stemmed, deseeded, and finely chopped

Directions:

With a mallet, pound chicken breasts so that they're approximately the same thickness throughout, about ¾" thick. Set aside. In a small bowl, juice the limes until you think you have gotten all the juice out, then run a fork around the inside to get those last drops of juice. Whisk in the oil, cilantro, salt, and pepper and stir well to combine. Add jalapeños, and if you love it hot you can add a few jalapeño seeds as well. Scoop marinade into a re-sealable bag or sealed container, then add the chicken to the marinade, coating with the marinade and adding more juice and oil if necessary. You can refrigerate marinating chicken for up to 3 days, but be sure to turn chicken over in the marinade at least once a day to evenly marinate. Oil grill grate and turn grill on medium-high heat, place chicken on grill, and cook over medium heat for about 4 minutes. Turn and cook an additional 3 minutes until done and a thermometer reads 160°F.

Grilled Chicken with Apple Salsa

YIELD: 4 servings

Ingredients for salsa:

½ cup fresh lime juice
1 (¾ cup) Anaheim chili pepper, deseeded and chopped
½ cup onion, chopped
salt and pepper, to taste
1 (2 cups) apple, halved, cored, and chopped
lime wedges for garnish

Ingredients for marinade:

¼ cup dry white wine
¼ cup apple juice
½ teaspoon lime peel, grated
½ teaspoon salt
pepper, to taste
4 boneless, skinless chicken breasts

Directions for salsa:

In a large bowl, mix the first 4 salsa ingredients, then prepare apples and immediately place in salsa bowl to keep the apples from turning brown. Gently mix everything together, tightly cover, and chill in the refrigerator for 30 minutes.

Directions for marinade:

Combine all ingredients except the chicken breasts and mix well to blend. Place chicken breasts in a re-sealable bag or lidded container, pour marinade over chicken, massaging the re-sealable bag or spooning marinade over chicken breasts to complete coat, then place in the fridge and marinate for 30 minutes. When ready to cook, spray grill or wipe with oil and heat to medium-hot. Bring salsa to room temperature to serve. Remove chicken from the fridge and remove from marinade. (You can use some of the leftover marinade to baste on the chicken while it's cooking.) Grill chicken, turning once until chicken tests done. To serve, place grilled chicken on a serving platter and serve with apple salsa spooned on top and optional lime wedges, if using.

Grilled Chicken with Goat Cheese & Sun-Dried Tomatoes

YIELD: *6 servings*

Ingredients:

2 tablespoons butter plus ⅔ cup cold butter, sliced
1 tablespoon garlic, minced
1 tablespoon yellow onion, minced
½ cup dry white wine
¼ cup fresh lemon juice
1½ cups sun-dried tomatoes, chopped
¼ cup fresh basil, chopped
½ teaspoon Kosher salt
½ teaspoon pepper
6 boneless, skinless chicken breasts, halved, brushed with olive oil for grilling
½ teaspoon salt
½ teaspoon black pepper
8 ounces goat cheese, room temperature

Directions:

In a large skillet, melt 2 tablespoons butter over medium heat, add garlic and onion, and sauté until tender. Whisk wine and lemon juice into skillet, increase heat to medium-high, continue whisking, and simmer to reduce by half. Reduce heat to low and stir in remaining butter one slice at a time until incorporated. Stir in sun-dried tomatoes, basil, salt, and pepper and blend well, then remove from heat and set aside. To grill chicken breasts, wipe BBQ grates with oil, then turn on high. Brush chicken breasts with enough olive oil to cover all surfaces, sprinkle with salt and pepper, place on BBQ, and grill for 15 to 20 minutes or until cooked through. Just before chicken is done, place equal amounts of goat cheese on each chicken breast. To serve, place chicken breasts on a large platter or individual plates and spoon prepared sauce over chicken.

Jamaican Pineapple Chicken

YIELD: 6 servings

Ingredients:

6 fresh pineapple slices
6 boneless, skinless chicken breasts
1 chicken bouillon cube
½ cup boiling water
1 (10¾ ounces) can condensed cream of
   chicken soup
¼ teaspoon salt
1 cup (¼ pound) cheddar cheese, shredded

Directions:

Preheat oven to 375°F. Place pineapple slices in a lightly oiled baking dish and top each slice with a chicken breast. In a medium bowl, dissolve bouillon cube in ½ cup boiling water. Add soup and salt and mix to blend. Pour soup mixture over chicken, place in oven, and cook for 40 minutes until chicken is done. Remove from oven, sprinkle cheese evenly over top of chicken breasts, and return to oven until cheese melts.

Mardi Gras Cajun BBQ Chicken

YIELD: 6 servings

Ingredients:

½ cup Worcestershire Sauce
1 teaspoon Cajun seasoning
1 teaspoon garlic powder
2½ tablespoons brown sugar
1½ tablespoons ketchup
3 boneless, skinless chicken breasts, halved, to
   make 6 servings

Directions:

In a large bowl, combine all ingredients except the chicken and mix well. Place the halved chicken breasts in the bowl and coat thoroughly with the Cajun marinade, or scoop everything into a re-sealable bag, seal tightly, lay still in a container so it doesn't leak, and refrigerate overnight. To grill, remove chicken from the marinade and discard remaining marinade. Grill 6 to 8 minutes on each side, being careful not to cook too long, until chicken is no longer pink and juices run clear.

The Sea Cliff Hotel's Story

After a few years of sailing thousands of offshore miles, we came to the realization that our cruising kitty needed to be replenished immediately. We were in the harbor at St. Thomas in the United States Virgin Islands, where we had been recruited by a local sailing company to take cruise ship passengers on sailing and snorkeling tours. We were scheduled for two to three day-charters per week, and though we were making a small living, it wasn't enough to cover our needs and build a kitty, so we decided after our first week of cruise ship day chartering to sail over to Honeymoon Bay on the West side of Water Island, a private island at that time, the main feature being the Sea Cliff Hotel. The hotel had a beach club for their guests, and our thought was that maybe we could supplement our day chartering business by working at the hotel, a perfect solution as we could anchor right in front of the beach club and still be close on chartering days to quickly motor over to the cruise ship docks to pick up the charter guests.

The stars were aligned that day. After we beached the dingy at the beach club, we went up to the bar to talk with the manager and scout things out. By the time we left to return to *Native Sun* we both had jobs and inquiries about providing exclusive charters for their hotel guests. Stanley would be teaching sailing to the hotel guests on their fleet of Hobie Cats and little Sunfish sailboats on days we weren't working with the cruise ships, and on Wednesday evenings he would be the sous chef for the hotel's fabulous Wednesday evening beach events. My job was to be behind the bar, mixing drinks and cooking typical lunchtime beach fare during the day and serving dinner on Wednesday evenings.

This time was magical for us, and we had some of the best years of our lives in this very special place of the US Virgin Islands. The stories could fill a separate book, but this is a book about cooking and the people who shared their favorite recipes with us. Our dearest friends over these next few years were Jan and Byron, who were the managers of the beach club, Terri and Alan, the managers of the Sea Cliff hotel, and Bill, who was also called "The Governor of Water Island," as he was the person responsible for helping with the needs of the few island residents as well as managing the island's security services, utilities, ferry service, main cistern upkeep, and overseeing the management of this exclusive hotel. I am including Bill's Chicken and Artichoke Fettuccine, which has been a favorite of ours for a very long time, and a couple of recipes from Jan and Byron and Terri and Alan.

Mayor Bill's Chicken & Artichoke Fettuccine

YIELD: 4 servings

Ingredients:

8 ounces (½ package) fettuccine
2 (14 ounce) cans artichoke hearts packed in water, drained
2–3 cups cooked chicken, cut in chunks or shredded
2 tablespoons butter
½ onion, diced
2 large garlic cloves, peeled, sliced, and diced
2 cups fresh mushrooms, sliced
1 package dry Knorr Leek Recipe Mix
1 teaspoon dried basil
1–2 teaspoons dried dill, to taste
2 cups milk
½ cup sharp cheddar cheese, shredded
½ cup Parmesan Cheese
1 tablespoon flour
parsley, chopped

Directions:

Place fettuccine in 2½ quarts boiling, unsalted water and cook until tender, for 10 to 12 minutes. In the meantime, drain artichoke hearts and coarsely cut chicken into chunks. Set aside. Melt butter in a large saucepan over medium heat, add onion and garlic, and cook until just translucent. Add artichokes and mushrooms and cook until mushrooms are tender, about 2 minutes. Add dry leek soup mix, basil, and dill and stir well. Add milk, sharp cheddar, and Parmesan and stir until cheese is melted. Add prepared chicken, sprinkle in flour, and stir until sauce is the consistency of warm pudding. Reduce heat to lowest setting and simmer, stirring occasionally, while fettuccini finishes cooking. Drain fettuccini and place some on each serving plate, top with parsley for garnish, and serve.

Oven Baked Orange Chicken

YIELD: 4–6 servings

Ingredients

2 eggs, beaten
2 cups bread crumbs
½ cup all-purpose flour
5 boneless, skinless chicken breasts, cut into bite-sized pieces
1½ cups orange juice, fresh squeezed
¼ cup soy sauce
3 tablespoons brown sugar, packed
3 tablespoons mirin or dry sherry
1½ tablespoons sriracha
3 garlic cloves, peeled, sliced, and minced
1½ teaspoons fresh ginger, finely grated
1 tablespoon cornstarch
toasted sesame seeds, for garnish
green onions, finely sliced, for garnish

Directions:

Preheat oven to 425°F. Spray a large rimmed baking sheet with cooking spray and set aside. Put beaten eggs in a pie plate or shallow dish. Put the bread crumbs and flour in a separate pie plate or shallow dish. Dredge each chicken piece in the egg, then in the bread crumb mixture and add to the prepared baking tray. Repeat until all chicken pieces are breaded and on the baking sheet. Place in oven and bake for 10 minutes, turn the pieces, then continue to cook for another 10 minutes or until chicken is thoroughly cooked. In the meantime, in a medium saucepan, add the orange juice, soy sauce, brown sugar, mirin or dry sherry, sriracha, garlic, and ginger. Bring to a low boil, stir occasionally, and turn heat down to low. When the chicken is just about done, add the cornstarch to the orange juice mixture and bring to a boil. Heat until thickened enough to coat a spoon, and remove from heat. To serve, place the cooked chicken in a large serving bowl and top with the orange sauce; toss lightly to coat. Sprinkle with sesame seeds and green onions to garnish and serve with steamed white rice. Share the Love!

Port-au-Prince Haitian Jerk Chicken

YIELD: 6 servings

Ingredients:

1–2 teaspoons grated lime rind
¼ cup fresh lime juice
1 tablespoon ground allspice
1 tablespoon brown sugar
1–2 tablespoons jalapeño pepper, stemmed, deseeded, and finely chopped
2 tablespoons olive oil
1 teaspoon dried thyme
1 teaspoon ground cinnamon
½ teaspoon ground nutmeg
3–4 garlic cloves, peeled, sliced, and finely chopped
1 teaspoon salt
1 teaspoon black pepper
6 boneless, skinless chicken thighs
3 large boneless, skinless chicken breasts, halved to make 6 pieces
½ cup onion, chopped
cooking spray
parsley springs, for garnish (optional)
lime slices, for garnish (optional)

Directions:

With an electric mixer or food processor, combine the first 12 ingredients and mix until well blended. Pour marinade into a large re-sealable plastic bag, add chicken and onion, seal bag, and squeeze marinade so that chicken and onion are well coated. Refrigerate 2 hours or overnight. To cook, spray grill with cooking spray and heat grill. Remove chicken from the marinade and discard remaining marinade. Place chicken pieces on the grill, cover and cook 5 minutes, then turn and cook on the other side 5 minutes or until juices run clear and chicken is done. Serve with optional parsley and lime slices if using, and dish up cooked rice and some veggies for a wonderful, flavorful meal.

Sesame Honey Chicken

YIELD: 4 servings

Ingredients for chicken:

4 boneless and skinless chicken breasts, cubed
1 cup cornstarch for dipping chicken
2 tablespoons coconut oil

Ingredients for sauce:

5 tablespoons ketchup
8 tablespoons honey
4 tablespoons sugar
2 tablespoons brown sugar
3 tablespoons white vinegar
4 tablespoons soy sauce
salt, to taste
1½ teaspoons garlic powder
½ teaspoon onion powder
3 tablespoons corn starch mixed with 2 tablespoons water
green onion, sliced, for garnish
toasted sesame seeds, for garnish

Directions for chicken:

Preheat oven to 350°F. In a large bowl, mix cubed chicken with the cornstarch and using your hands, turn chicken over and over to coat thoroughly. Heat a skillet with a small amount of coconut oil, just enough to fry the chicken, and pan-fry coated chicken until slightly golden brown but not fully cooked, about 3 to 5 minutes.

Directions for sauce:

In a large bowl, combine sauce ingredients and whisk to mix thoroughly. Once chicken is done being pan fried, remove it from the skillet and place in a baking dish, whisk the sauce again to combine, and pour the sauce over chicken as evenly as possible so that all the chicken has sauce on it. Place in the oven and bake for 25 minutes. To serve, scoop up on a nice pile of hot rice, garnish with sliced green onions, and sprinkle with toasted sesame seeds. If there's sauce remaining, spoon it over each serving.

So Good, So Fast Chicken Thighs

YIELD: 4 servings

Ingredients:

½ cup Dijon mustard
¼ cup maple syrup
1 tablespoon rice wine vinegar
salt and pepper, to taste
8 (1½ pounds) boneless, skinless chicken thighs
fresh rosemary, chopped, for garnish

Directions:

Preheat oven to 450°F. In a large bowl, mix the mustard, syrup, and rice wine vinegar until well blended. Salt and pepper the chicken thighs, place chicken in marinade bowl, and turn to completely cover all the thighs so they are completely coated. At this point, you can transfer the marinade and chicken into a tightly sealed container and refrigerate for 1 hour and up to overnight. After marinating chicken thighs, they can be cooked on the BBQ grill, marinating frequently with the remaining sauce until done, or else place chicken on a lightly greased ovenproof baking dish and with a rubber spatula, scoop all of the marinade on top of the chicken. Place chicken in the oven and bake for about 40 minutes or until a meat thermometer reads 165°F. Halfway through baking, baste the tops of the chicken with the sauce in the pan. To serve, remove from oven and let rest for 5 minutes. Place the chicken on a large serving dish or individual dinner plates, whisk any remaining sauce that is in the baking dish and spoon over top of chicken thighs. Sprinkle fresh rosemary on top and serve.

Tomato, Sherry & Cream Skillet Chicken

YIELD: 4 servings

Ingredients:

salt and pepper, to taste
ground nutmeg, to taste
2 large boneless, skinless chicken breasts, halved to make 4 servings
1½ tablespoons butter
¼ cup onion, finely chopped
2 cups (⅓ pound) mushrooms, sliced
¼ cup parsley, chopped
¼ tsp dried basil leaves
⅓, cup dry sherry
1 teaspoon Dijon mustard
1 medium tomato, peeled, deseeded and diced
½ cup whipping cream, not whipped

Directions:

Lightly sprinkle salt, pepper, and nutmeg on all sides of chicken breasts. In a large skillet over medium heat, melt butter; add chicken and lightly brown one side of chicken. When ready to turn and cook chicken on the other side, add the onion and mushrooms, placing them around the edges of the skillet. Sprinkle the chicken breasts evenly with parsley and basil, then pour the sherry in the skillet and bring to a boil. Cover and reduce heat and simmer just until the thickest part of the chicken is white when pricked with a knife point, about 20 minutes. When finished cooking, place on a warmed serving platter and keep warm. In the same skillet, stir mustard into the liquid in the pan and blend well. Add diced tomatoes and cream and bring to a boil. Cook, stirring occasionally until sauce is shiny, slightly reduced in quantity, and just barely thickened. Taste the sauce, adjust the seasonings, and pour over the chicken. Serve 2 pieces of chicken with lots of sauce on each plate. Delicious served with steamed broccoli, a salad, and crusty bread.

Trinidad's Honey Ginger Marinated Drumsticks

YIELD: 6 servings

Ingredients:

2 tablespoons soy sauce
¼ cup honey
¼ cup hoisin sauce
3–4 garlic cloves, peeled, sliced, and finely diced
1 tablespoon fresh ginger, peeled, sliced, and finely diced
12 chicken drumsticks
2–3 teaspoons sesame seeds, toasted
cilantro, for garnish

Directions:

In a large bowl, mix the soy sauce, honey, hoisin sauce, garlic, and ginger, mix well, and set aside. Make 3 to 4 slits on each side of the chicken drumsticks with a sharp knife, about ¼-inch deep, just lightly scored to reduce cooking time and to allow marinade to better soak into the chicken. Place chicken in marinade and turn chicken to completely cover with marinade. Place chicken drumsticks in a large container and using a rubber spatula, scoop all the marinade onto the chicken. Tightly seal and refrigerate overnight. When ready to cook, preheat broiler with rack positioned 8 to 10 inches from the heating source and line a large baking sheet or jelly-roll baking pan with heavy duty foil. Place the chicken so that pieces are not touching; scoop all the marinade evenly on top of drumsticks, place the pan in the oven, and broil for 15 to 20 minutes until chicken is browned and crisp and has no traces of pink juices when pierced. Turn drumsticks often and watch the cooking carefully until the marinade is nicely glazing the drumsticks and the chicken is thoroughly cooked. Transfer the cooked drumsticks to a large serving platter, sprinkle sesame seeds on top, and garnish with cilantro springs or leaves.

Water Island Chicken in Sour Cream Sauce

YIELD: 4 servings

Ingredients:

6 tablespoons butter, divided
4 large boneless, skinless chicken breasts
¾ cup sauterne wine, divided
1 small onion, sliced
1 shallot, chopped
1 cup sour cream
salt and pepper, to taste

Directions:

In a large skillet over medium heat, melt 4 tablespoons butter, add chicken breasts, and cook until lightly brown. Turn breasts, cook a few more minutes to brown a little, pour ½ cup wine over chicken, cover, and simmer 20 to 25 minutes or just until tender. Don't overcook or the breasts will be dry. In a small saucepan, melt remaining butter and cook onions and shallots until soft and translucent. Add remaining wine and slowly stir in the sour cream. Taste and adjust seasonings. Heat only long enough to warm sauce. To serve, pour evenly over plated chicken.

CHAPTER 10
Desserts

Desserts

Our dear friend Captain Charlie had a younger sister who made a yearly trip from her home in California to sail with him on board *Leo* for a few months of winter cruising. She was "Aunt B" to everyone. When we first met, though there was a twenty-five-year age difference, Aunt B and I became instant friends, enjoying a cherished friendship until her passing many years later. Aunt B was funny, always joyful, adventurous, and full of life-enriching anecdotes, many about her own antics as a young woman. She was not an ardent sailor like her brother, Captain Charlie, but she stood a safe watch for night crossings, was a great companion to everyone, and she turned a "wicked spoon" when it came to cooking and what she called, "the art of the stove." She shared her most precious and secret recipes with me, and I am certain she'd be honored to pass her secret Brownie, delicious Tomato Aspic, and Eggplant Creole recipes to fellow yachties.

Aunt B's Secret Brownies

YIELD: 50 small brownies

Ingredients:

1 stick butter
vegetable oil
4 squares unsweetened chocolate
4 large eggs
2 cups sugar
½ teaspoon salt
1 teaspoon vanilla
1 cup flour
2 cups walnuts, chopped

Directions:

Preheat oven to 350° F. In a 1-cup measuring cup, stand 1 stick of butter up on end. Fill the rest of the measuring cup to the ¾-cup mark with vegetable oil, then scoop oil and butter out into the top of a double boiler with a rubber spatula. Place double boiler over low-medium heat and add squares of chocolate, stirring while it's melting and blending. In a medium bowl, beat the eggs, add sugar, salt, and vanilla and beat until well combined. Beat flour into egg mixture a little bit at a time to make sure mixture is creamy and smooth. Add flour mixture to melted chocolate mixture, add in walnuts, and blend. Pour ingredients into a 15 x 10-inch lightly greased baking pan and bake approximately 30 minutes. Brownies should be semi-soft to the touch. Cool on a cooling rack, cut into 50 pieces, and enjoy Aunt B's secret recipe.

Amaretto Mocha Truffles

YIELD: 40 truffles

Ingredients:

9 ounces bittersweet chocolate, chopped
1 cup heavy cream
¼ cup amaretto
¾ cup coffee beans, finely ground

Directions:

Place chopped chocolate in a medium bowl. In a small saucepan over medium heat, bring cream and amaretto to a simmer. Pour over chocolate and let sit until chocolate is softened, about 3 minutes. Whisk until smooth and thick. Cover and chill until mixture is firm enough to roll into balls, at least 3 hours or up to 3 days. Place ground coffee in a small bowl. Scoop out a small tablespoonful of chilled truffle mixture and roll a ball (wear disposable gloves, if you like), then roll in ground coffee. Place on a parchment-lined baking sheet. Repeat with remaining truffle mixture. Chill truffles until firm, at least 1 hour. Store in airtight container in the refrigerator and serve while very cold, as they stick and melt when warm.

Apple Latkes

YIELD: 4 servings

Ingredients:

4 tart or sweet apples, to taste
2–3 tablespoons sugar plus extra for serving
3 tablespoons brandy or dark rum
2 eggs, yolks and whites separated
2 tablespoons vegetable oil
pinch of salt
1 cup all-purpose flour
14 tablespoons water, milk, or beer
oil for frying, preferably sunflower oil
ground cinnamon, for serving
sour cream (optional)

Directions:

Peel the apples, cut each apple into 4 thick slices, and remove cores. Mix sugar and brandy or dark rum in a shallow dish and mix to blend, then place apple slices in the dish, turning them over so they are well coated. Cover and refrigerate for 30 minutes, turning slices over occasionally so they are well coated with the brandy mixture. In the meantime, in a medium bowl beat the egg yolks with vegetable oil and salt. Add the flour and mix well, then gradually beat in the water, milk, or beer until well mixed and there are no lumps. Cover and chill for 1 hour. When ready to cook, beat the egg whites until they are stiff and have peaks, then gently fold into the chilled flour mixture. Remove apples from fridge and heat a large skillet with a minimum of ¾-inch oil over medium-high heat. Dip apple slices into the batter, 4 to 5 at a time, making sure they're very well covered with lots of batter. Carefully lift one slice of apple at a time and lower in the hot sizzling oil. The oil must be sizzling hot, but not so hot that the batter is browned before the apples are soft inside. Fry apples in batches, turning slices over to brown on both sides. With a slotted spatula, remove latkes from the skillet and drain on paper towels before serving. Serve with sugar and cinnamon to sprinkle on top and a bowl of chilled sour cream to dollop on top.

Bread Pudding with Buttercream Whiskey Sauce

YIELD: 10 servings

Ingredients for bread pudding:

12–14 cups day-old white bread, cut into 1-inch cubes
7 tablespoons butter, room temperature
2 cups heavy cream
4 cups whole milk
6 large eggs
1¾ cups brown sugar plus 2 tablespoons
4½ teaspoons vanilla extract
1½ teaspoons cinnamon
½ teaspoon nutmeg, freshly ground
¼ teaspoon salt
½ cup raisins
powdered sugar, for garnish
Buttercream Whiskey Sauce, for serving

Ingredients for buttercream whiskey sauce:

2 cups heavy cream
½ cup milk
½ cup white sugar
2 tablespoons cornstarch
¾ cup whiskey
⅛ teaspoon salt
2 tablespoons butter, room temperature

Directions for bread pudding:

Preheat oven to 350°F. Place bread in a large bowl and set aside. Melt 6 tablespoons butter in a small saucepan and pour over the bread cubes. With a large rubber spatula, toss the bread in the butter, making sure bread is evenly covered. Grease a 9 x 13-inch casserole dish with remaining butter and set aside. In a large bowl, combine heavy cream, milk, eggs, brown sugar, vanilla, cinnamon, nutmeg, salt, and raisins. Whisk and blend cream mixture completely, then scoop mixture over the bread and stir well to combine. Cover and set aside at room temperature for 30 to 45 minutes. Scoop bread mixture into the prepared casserole dish, place in the center of the oven, and bake for 50 to 60 minutes or until set. Serve warm with powdered sugar sprinkled on top and warm Butter Cream Whiskey Sauce.

Directions for butter cream whiskey sauce:

In a large saucepan, combine cream, milk, and sugar over medium heat. In a small bowl, whisk cornstarch and ¼ cup whiskey until well blended. Pour whiskey sauce into cream mixture and bring to a boil. Immediately reduce heat to a low simmer, continue to stir, and cook for 5 minutes. Remove from heat, add salt, and stir in the butter and remaining whiskey.

Captain's Cookies

YIELD: 48 cookies

Ingredients:

1 cup butter, room temperature
2 eggs
6 tablespoons corn syrup
½ teaspoon salt
2 cups rolled oats
2 cups flour
1 cup coconut
1 cup white sugar
2 teaspoons baking soda
½ teaspoon allspice

Directions:

Preheat oven to 350°F. In a large bowl using an electric mixer add all ingredients one at a time until well blended. Roll dough into 48 small balls, place on a baking sheet, and press top with fork to make marks. Place in oven and bake for 12 to 15 minutes or until done.

Creamy Fudge

YIELD: 1-8-inch square pan of fudge

Ingredients:

4 (1 ounce) squares unsweetened chocolate
2 (3 ounce) packages cream cheese, softened
　　to room temperature
4 cups powdered sugar
dash of salt
½ teaspoon vanilla
½ cup walnuts, chopped plus extra for garnish

Directions:

Lightly butter an 8-inch square pan and set aside. Put 2 inches of water in the bottom of a double-boiler and place over low-medium heat. Melt chocolate in top of double-boiler. In a large bowl, break up cream cheese using a wooden spoon and beat cream cheese until smooth and soft. Slowly stir in powdered sugar and salt, blending gently so powdered sugar stays in the bowl. Add the melted chocolate, using a rubber spatula to get all of the chocolate out of the pan. Mix well so it's completely blended, add vanilla and chopped nuts and mix again. Press chocolate mixture into prepared pan, cover, and refrigerate until firm. To serve, cut into squares and top with extra walnuts.

Crème Brûlée à la Grand Marnier

Custards need to chill overnight, so make them the day before you're planning on serving.

YIELD: 6 servings

Ingredients:

6 large egg yolks
½ cup white sugar plus 6 teaspoons
1⅓ cups whipping cream, not whipped
⅔ cup milk
2½ teaspoons orange peel, grated
1½ tablespoons Grand Marnier

Directions:

Preheat oven to 325°F. Lightly butter 6 (¾ cup) custard cups or soufflé dishes. In a medium bowl, beat egg yolks and ½ cup sugar to blend. In a medium saucepan over medium-high heat, bring cream, milk, and orange peel to a simmer. Gradually whisk hot cream mixture into yolks, just a little at a time to keep from cooking the yolks. Stir in Grand Marnier and divide custard into prepared dishes. Set dishes in a large baking pan and add enough hot water to the pan to come halfway up the sides of soufflé dishes. Bake custards about 40 minutes or until just set in centers. Gently remove from water, taking care not to drip any water into custards, cool on a cooling rack, then cover and refrigerate overnight. To serve, preheat broiler, put custard dishes on a baking sheet, sprinkle 1 teaspoon sugar over each custard and broil until sugar browns. Watch closely to avoid burning and rotate baking sheet for even browning, only about 2 minutes. Remove from broiler and refrigerate for 1 hour. You can make the brûlée up to 6 hours ahead of time, keeping refrigerated until serving.

Cuban Orange Flan

YIELD: 4 servings

Ingredients:

5 whole eggs, plus 1 egg yolk
⅓ cup sugar
1½ cups fresh orange juice
1 orange rind, grated
Cointreau, small amount blended into whipped cream (optional)
whipped cream, for topping (optional)

Directions:

Preheat oven to 325°F. In a medium bowl using an electric mixer beat 5 whole eggs, 1 egg yolk, and sugar until creamy. While still beating, add orange juice and grated rind. Pour evenly into 4 custard cups or ramekins and place cups in a baking pan. Pour hot water into the baking pan halfway up the custard cup sides and bake for 30 to 40 minutes or until a knife inserted in the middle of custard comes out clean. Remove from baking pan, being careful not to drip any pan water onto custard tops. Cool on a cooling rack. To serve, mix a little of the optional Cointreau into the whipped cream and top each custard with a dollop of whipped cream.

Deep Dish Apple Pie with Parmesan-Topped Pastry

YIELD: 6–8 servings

Ingredients for pie filling:

6 cups apples, peeled, cored, and sliced
½ cup sugar
2 tablespoons flour
¾ teaspoon cinnamon
¼ teaspoon nutmeg
¼–½ teaspoon cardamom (optional)
salt, to taste
1 tablespoon lemon juice
1 tablespoon butter

Ingredients for Parmesan pastry:

1¼ cups flour, sifted
½ teaspoon salt
½ cup shortening
½ cup Parmesan cheese, shredded
4 tablespoons cold water

Directions for pie filling:

Preheat oven to 350°F. In a large bowl, mix prepared apple slices with sugar, flour, and spices, turning well so all apple slices are covered. Turn into an 8 x 8-inch square baking pan (or shallow 6-cup baking dish) and sprinkle with lemon juice and butter. Cover with foil and bake about 15 minutes. Remove from oven and remove foil. In the meantime, prepare the Parmesan pastry.

Directions for Parmesan pastry:

In a large bowl combine flour and salt, then use a pastry blender to cut in shortening to make a crumble texture. Add Parmesan cheese and mix lightly with a fork. Sprinkle cold water, mixing with a fork to make a stiff dough. Scoop dough onto a lightly floured surface and shape into a rectangle, then roll into a 9 x 11-inch rectangle. Cut off 2 inches from the long side, making a 9-inch square to fit the top of the pan. Cut decorations such as 6 small leaves from the remainder of the pastry to decorate the top of pastry. When pie filling has cooked, remove the foil and top the pan or dish with the 9-inch square of Parmesan pastry and cut a few slits in the top. Decorate top of pastry with pastry decorations and crimp edges of pastry against sides of pan or dish. Return to oven and bake about 45 to 50 minutes until pastry is browned.

Pineapple Rum Cake

YIELD: 12 servings

Ingredients for the pineapple glaze:

½ cup packed light brown sugar
1 cup dark rum, divided
¼ cup butter, softened to room temperature
½ pineapple, cored and cut into circular
    ¼-inch thick slices

Ingredients for the cake:

2 sticks (1 cup) butter
2 cups sugar
4 large eggs
1 teaspoon vanilla extract
1 teaspoon dark rum
2½ cups all-purpose flour
½ teaspoon Kosher salt
½ cup pecans, crushed
ice cream for serving, optional

Directions for the pineapple glaze:

Combine brown sugar and 1 cup rum together in a small saucepan over medium heat. Bring mixture to a simmer and continue to simmer until reduced by ⅓, stirring occasionally to keep sugar from burning. Whisk in the butter till completely combined, then remove saucepan from heat. Add the pineapple slices, gently stirring to completely coat them with the glaze, then let mixture sit for about 3 minutes to cool a bit. With a slotted spoon, transfer the pineapple slices to the bottom of a 9-inch square cake pan, arrange slices to cover the bottom of the cake pan, and set cake pan aside. Reserve the remaining rum glaze.

Directions for the cake:

Preheat oven to 350°F. In a large mixing bowl combine 2 sticks butter and the sugar and beat on high speed until light and fluffy, about 3 minutes. Scrape down bowl and then add eggs one at a time, beating between eggs until well blended and eggs are fully incorporated. Add vanilla and rum and beat for 1 minute. Add the flour and salt and mix well as this batter will be relatively thick. When combined, scoop the batter over the glazed pineapple slices, then sprinkle crushed nuts evenly over the batter. Place in oven and bake about 1 hour and 10 minutes, testing with a clean knife until the knife comes out clean. Remove from oven and cool on a rack for 15 minutes, then place a serving plate over the cake pan. Quickly and gently flip the plate and cake pan over together so the pineapples are on top on the plate. To serve, place the remaining rum glaze and remaining rum in a small saucepan and warm slowly until heated through. Cut the cake into squares and serve with ice cream, then top with the warm rum glaze.

Ensenada Chocolate Cookie Bars

YIELD: 24–36 bars

Ingredients:

½ cup butter
1½ cups graham cracker crumbs
1 (14 ounce) can sweetened condensed milk
1 (6 ounce) package semi-sweet chocolate chips
1½ cups flaked coconut
1 cup chopped walnuts

Directions:

Preheat oven to 350°F. In a metal 13 x 9-inch baking pan, melt butter in the oven, then remove pan from oven. Evenly sprinkle graham cracker crumbs over butter and pour condensed milk evenly over crumbs. Evenly add chocolate chips, coconut, and walnuts on top and press down. Return pan to oven and bake 25 to 30 minutes or until lightly browned. Cool on cooling racks and serve.

Pumpkin Mousse

This is a very simple recipe to put together on short notice and is guaranteed a lovely presentation.

YIELD: 8 servings

Ingredients:

1 (14 ounce) can sweetened condensed milk
1 (15 ounce) can pumpkin purée
¼ teaspoon Kosher salt
1 teaspoon ground cinnamon
1 teaspoon ground allspice
1 teaspoon ground nutmeg
⅛–¼ teaspoon ground cloves, to taste
3 cups heavy cream

Directions:

In a medium saucepan, heat condensed milk over medium heat. While stirring constantly with a rubber spatula, cook 10 to 12 minutes until milk is a slightly darker color. Remove saucepan from stove and cool 10 minutes. When cool, stir in pumpkin purée and spices, return pan to medium heat and continue to cook, stirring often until mixtures bubbles, about 4 minutes. Remove from stove and strain mixture into a large bowl through a fine mesh sieve, pressing solids down with a rubber spatula to work it through the sieve. Set aside to cool. In a separate large bowl, whip cream with an electric mixer on medium speed until it forms peaks. Transfer ⅓ whipped cream into a small bowl, cover tightly, and chill until ready to garnish mousse. Mix a few spoonfuls of remaining whipped cream into the pumpkin mixture to blend, then gently fold in remaining whipped cream and transfer mousse into 8 individual glasses, small bowls, or a 2-quart dish. Cover and chill 3 to 4 hours. To serve, gently whip reserved cream to bring the peaks back, then top each serving with a dollop of whip cream. Pumpkin mousse can be made 2 days ahead, then tightly covered and refrigerated.

Frango Truffle Mints

YIELD: 30 truffles

Ingredients:

1 (12 ounce) package semi-sweet chocolate
    chips
½ cup (1 stick) butter
1½ cups powdered sugar, sifted
2 eggs, unbeaten
2 teaspoons vanilla
¼–½ teaspoon peppermint extract

Directions:

Melt chocolate in a pan over hot water, then let cool. With an electric mixer, cream the butter and powdered sugar together. Add eggs and beat well. Add flavored extracts and cooled chocolate and blend until smooth and thick. Drop teaspoons of frango mix onto waxed paper and refrigerate overnight. Frango mints tend to stick to waxed paper as they warm, so serve immediately from the refrigerator or place into a little paper candy cup and serve. They are also delicious stirred into a cup of hot coffee!

Fresh Peach Cobbler

YIELD: 6–8 servings

Ingredients:

¾ cup flour
pinch of salt
2 teaspoons baking powder
2 cups sugar, divided
¾ cup milk
½ cup butter, melted
2 cups fresh peaches, sliced
cardamom, to taste
cinnamon, to taste
ginger, to taste
nutmeg, to taste

Directions:

Preheat oven to 350°F. Sift flour, salt, and baking powder together in a large bowl. Mix in 1 cup sugar, slowly stir in milk, and mix to make a batter. In a small pan, melt butter and pour into a baking pan. Pour batter evenly over melted butter but do not stir. In a large bowl, mix sliced peaches with remaining sugar and spices. I find that heavy on the spices is better than light, but taste and adjust to your liking. Make sure all the peaches are totally covered with the sugar and spice mixture. Carefully spoon peaches over the batter, scraping the bowl with a rubber spatula to make sure you get all the peach sauce, and place in oven and bake 1 hour. Serve hot or cold with cream.

Fried Bananas with Honey & Cinnamon

YIELD: 2 servings

Ingredients:

olive oil or coconut oil, for frying
2 barely ripe bananas, sliced
2 tablespoons honey
2 tablespoons water
cinnamon, for garnish

Directions:

In a large skillet over medium heat, warm oil, place banana slices in pan, and pan-fry for 1 to 2 minutes. Then, turn and fry for 1 to 2 minutes on other side. In the meantime, whisk honey and water together in a small bowl. Remove bananas from skillet, place on plates, and pour honey mixture over bananas. To serve, cool a bit and sprinkle with cinnamon.

Ginger Snaps

YIELD: 48 cookies

Ingredients:

2 cups sifted flour
1 tablespoon ground ginger
2 teaspoons baking soda
1 teaspoon cinnamon
½ teaspoon salt
¾ cup shortening
1 cup sugar plus extra for rolling cookies
1 egg
¼ cup molasses

Directions:

Preheat oven to 350°F. In a medium bowl, mix and sift together flour, ginger, baking soda, cinnamon, and salt. Sift again two more times, then return to sifter and set aside. In a separate large bowl, beat shortening with an electric mixer until creamy. While continuing to beat, gradually add 1 cup sugar, then the egg and molasses and blend until well combined. Sift ¼ of the flour mixture over the molasses mixture, blend well, and repeat until all the flour mixture is incorporated. Place extra sugar in a shallow bowl. Form teaspoons of dough into small balls by gently rolling between the palms of your hands, then roll in the extra sugar and place balls about 2 inches apart on ungreased baking sheets. Bake 12 minutes or until tops are slightly rounded and cracked in appearance. Cool on cooling racks.

Granny Apple Galette

A fruit galette is one of the easiest dessert pies to make and they're simply delicious served hot or cold, as a standalone desert, or with a topping of cinnamon sauce or ice cream.

YIELD: 6–8 servings

Ingredients:

5 tablespoons sugar, divided
1 cup flour plus extra for rolling dough
1 teaspoon salt, divided
8 tablespoons (1 stick) cold butter, divided
2 eggs
2 large Granny Smith apples
1 teaspoon cinnamon

Directions:

In a large mixing bowl, combine 1 tablespoon of sugar, 1 cup of flour, and ½ teaspoon salt. Add 6 tablespoons of cold butter in small chunks and work into flour mixture with your fingers or pastry cutter until combined and mixture looks like coarse flour, with pea-sized chunks of butter. In a small bowl, beat one egg until creamy, then pour it into the flour mixture and combine with a fork. Mixture should just barely come together into a dough. Turn the dough out onto a floured surface and knead it, without overworking it, until it becomes smooth. Form dough into a disc, wrap in plastic wrap, and refrigerate for a minimum of 2 hours. Preheat oven to 375°F when ready to bake. To prepare the apple filling, cut apples in half, remove core and stem, and slice into thin, ⅛-inch uniform slices. Melt 2 tablespoons of butter and set aside. In a small bowl, mix remaining sugar, remaining salt, and cinnamon and set aside for sprinkling on top of the apple mixture. Roll out the dough to ⅛-inch thickness into an oval, round or rectangle shape. This is a rustic pie, so looking perfect is not important. Place dough on a rimmed baking sheet or jelly roll pan lined with foil or parchment paper. Arrange apple slices on dough, leaving 1 inch of space around the edges. Brush apples with melted butter and sprinkle top with ⅔ of the sugar and cinnamon mixture. Fold the edges of the dough over the apples and crimp roughly where necessary. Beat remaining egg and brush the dough with egg, then sprinkle with the remaining sugar and cinnamon mixture. Bake for about 40 minutes or until the crust is golden brown and apples are juicy.

Irish Cream Truffles

YIELD: 40 pieces

Ingredients:

1 (12 ounce) package semi-sweet chocolate
    morsels
¼ cup heavy cream
¼ cup Baileys Original Irish Cream Liqueur
2 egg yolks
1 tablespoon butter, unsalted
chocolate chunks, finely chopped, for garnish
nuts, finely chopped
Dutch cocoa mix blended with a small amount
    of powdered sugar, for garnish

Directions:

In a large saucepan over lowest heat, melt chocolate, cream, and Baileys together until blended. Whisk in egg yolks one at a time. Whisk in butter until melted and well blended. Scoop chocolate mixture into a bowl and cover and refrigerate overnight. To assemble, remove from fridge and with a spoon mold mixture into ¾-inch truffle balls, setting truffles on waxed paper while making. Set up a few small dishes of nuts or other garnishes of your choice and roll truffles to cover. Refrigerate until serving.

Lemon Bars

YIELD: 16 bars

Ingredients for lemon bars:

¾ cup flour
¾ cup sugar
¼ teaspoon salt
1 stick butter, room temperature soft
2 eggs
2 tablespoons fresh lemon juice
2 tablespoons lemon zest

Ingredients for lemon glaze:

¾ cup powdered sugar
2 tablespoons fresh lemon juice
1 tablespoons lemon zest

Directions for lemon bars:

Preheat oven to 350°F. In a large bowl, combine flour, sugar, and salt. With an electric mixer, add the softened butter and mix well. In a medium bowl, whisk the eggs with the lemon juice and zest, then mix into the flour mixture, stirring until well blended. Pour ingredients into a lightly greased 8 x 8-inch baking pan, place in oven, and bake for 25 minutes. Remove from oven and cool on a cooling rack.

Directions for lemon glaze:

Combine all glaze ingredients until well blended, then pour evenly over the cooled lemon bars.

Lemon Raisin Rice Pudding

YIELD: 6–8 servings

Ingredients:

3 eggs, beaten
1⅓ cups milk
⅓ cup white sugar or ½ cup brown sugar
1 tablespoon butter, room temperature
1 teaspoon vanilla
⅛ teaspoon salt
2 cups cooked white rice
½ teaspoon grated lemon rind
lemon juice, to taste
⅓ cup raisins (optional, chopped date)
cinnamon or nutmeg, to taste

Directions:

Preheat oven to 325°F. In a large bowl, combine beaten eggs, milk, sugar, butter, vanilla, and salt and mix well. Add cooked rice, lemon rind, lemon juice, and raisins and mix until well blended. Pour mixture into a greased baking dish, sprinkle with cinnamon or nutmeg, place in oven, and cook for 45 to 50 minutes or until pudding is set. Serve hot or chilled. Pudding can be thinned with a little milk or half-and-half.

Lemon-Lime Macaroon Bars

YIELD: 16–32 bars

Ingredients for the bars:

2 cups sweetened flaked coconut, toasted
1½ cups all-purpose flour
¾ cup powdered sugar
2 tablespoons cornstarch
¼ teaspoon Kosher salt
1 cup cold butter, cut into chunks

Ingredients for the filling:

¼ cup flour
2 cups white sugar
4 large eggs
¼ cup fresh lemon juice
2 teaspoons lemon zest
¼ cup fresh lime juice
2 teaspoons lime zest
powdered sugar, for dusting

Directions for the bars:

Preheat oven to 350°F. In a large bowl, combine toasted coconut, flour, sugar, cornstarch, and salt. With an electric mixer, add the butter and mix well until dough is crumbly and has small pieces. Press dough into the bottom and up the sides of a lightly greased 8 x 8-inch baking pan, then place in oven and bake for 25 minutes until light gold. Remove from oven and let cool at least 20 minutes.

Directions for the filling:

Combine all ingredients until well blended, then pour evenly over the cooled lemon bars. Cut bars in small or large pieces and top with powdered sugar.

Lime Meltaways

YIELD: 36 bars

Ingredients:

¾ cup (1½ sticks) butter, room temperature
1 cup powdered sugar, divided
zest of 2 limes, finely grated
2 tablespoons fresh lime juice
1 tablespoon vanilla extract
1¾ cups plus 2 tablespoons all-purpose flour
2 tablespoons cornstarch
¼ teaspoon Kosher salt or sea salt

Directions:

Preheat oven to 350°F when ready to cook. In a large bowl using an electric mixer on medium speed, whisk butter and ⅓ cup powdered sugar until pale and fluffy. Add lime zest, lime juice, and vanilla and continue to mix until fluffy. In a medium bowl, whisk together flour, cornstarch, and salt to blend, then add flour mixture to the large bowl of butter mixture and mix on low speed until just combined. Put parchment paper on 2 (8 x 12-inch) baking pans, divide dough in half, and place each half on a baking pan. Roll dough up in parchment paper to form a 1¼-inch thick log, pressing a ruler along edge of parchment at each turn to help narrow the log. Refrigerate logs until cold and firm, at least 1 hour. Remove from fridge and gently peel the parchment from logs. Cut logs into ¼-inch thick round discs. Place rounds 1 inch apart on baking sheets lined with parchment paper. Bake cookies about 13 minutes until barely golden, being sure to rotate sheets halfway through. Transfer cookies to cooling racks to cool slightly, 8 to 10 minutes. While still warm, place remaining ⅔ cup sugar in a re-sealable plastic bag, add meltaways, and toss to cover with sugar. Lime meltaways can be stored in airtight containers at room temperature up to 2 days or refrigerated in tightly sealed container up to 1 week.

Mango Lime Rice Pudding

YIELD: 8–10 servings

Ingredients:

3 cups milk
1 (3-inch) cinnamon stick
2 cups water
¼ teaspoon salt
1 cup rice, jasmine or basmati
peel of 1 lime, removed with a vegetable peeler into strips
½ cup sugar
1½ tablespoons fresh lime juice
¼ teaspoon vanilla extract
¼ teaspoon coconut extract
1 large firm mango, divided
grated lime zest, for garnish

Directions:

In a small saucepan, bring milk and cinnamon stick to a simmer, then cover and remove from heat. In a large 2-quart saucepan, bring water and salt to a boil, stir in rice, and lay ½ of the strips of lime peel on top of rice. Cover saucepan and reduce heat to low, simmering 20 minutes or until rice is tender and water has been absorbed. Discard lime peel. Leave rice in the saucepan and fluff with a fork. Pour warm milk mixture over rice, stir in sugar, and mix to blend. Bring pot back to a simmer over medium heat until little bubbles appear around the edge of the pan, reduce to medium-low heat, stir frequently, and simmer 15 to 20 minutes until pudding is thick and creamy. Remove pan from heat, stir in lime juice and vanilla and coconut extracts. Let cool for 5 minutes and remove the cinnamon stick. In the meantime, slice along each side of the mango's long, flat seed and cut the side strips off the seed. Remove the peel from the side strips and dice half of the mango flesh, reserving the other half, sliced into thin strips for garnish. Stir diced mango flesh into pudding and let cool 20 to 30 minutes before serving. Dish rice pudding into bowls; garnish each serving with sliced mango, remaining lime slices, and a sprinkling of lime zest.

Mini Cheesecakes

YIELD: 18 servings

Ingredients:

1 cup graham cracker crumbs
2 tablespoons sugar plus ¾ cup
3 tablespoons butter, melted
3 (8 ounce) packages cream cheese, softened at
   room temperature
1 teaspoon vanilla
3 eggs
1 cup unsweetened shredded coconut, toasted
   plus 2 tablespoons

Directions:

Preheat oven to 325°F. In a medium bowl mix graham cracker crumbs, 2 tablespoons sugar, and melted butter, then press mixture into the bottom of 18 paper-lined muffin cups. In a large bowl using an electric mixer, beat cream cheese, vanilla, and remaining sugar until smooth. Add eggs one at a time, mixing on low speed until well blended. Spoon cream cheese mixture over the 18 muffin crumb crusts. Place muffin tins in the oven and bake 25 to 30 minutes or until centers are almost set. Completely cool on cooling racks, then refrigerate for 2 hours to set. Top each cheesecake with 1 tablespoon toasted coconut to serve.

Mint Choco' Chip Ice Cream

Yup, you can make ice cream on board without a churn!

YIELD: 8–10 servings

Ingredients:

1 (14 ounce) can sweetened condensed milk
2 teaspoons peppermint extract
1 tablespoon crème de menthe liqueur
2 cups heavy whipping cream, chilled
pinch of coarse salt
1 cup bittersweet chocolate, chopped

Directions:

In a large bowl, stir condensed milk, peppermint extract, and crème de menthe and mix well. In a second bowl using an electric mixer beat whipping cream with pinch of coarse salt just until peaks form. Gently fold whipped cream into the milk mixture a little at a time until there are no streaks left. Gently fold in chopped chocolate pieces, and scoop ice cream into a loaf pan. Cover and freeze a minimum of 6 hours up to 3 to 4 weeks.

Old-Fashioned Pie Crust

YIELD: 2 (9-inch) pie crust bottoms and tops

Ingredients:

4 cups white flour
1 tablespoon sugar
1½ teaspoons salt
1¾ teaspoons shortening
1 egg
1 tablespoon apple cider vinegar
½ cup very cold water

Directions:

In a very large bowl, mix flour, sugar, and salt. Add shortening and cut in with a pastry blender, two knives, or an electric mixer set at low speed until the shortening is cut into small pea-sized crumbs. In a small bowl, beat egg, vinegar, and water together and mix liquid mixture 1 tablespoon at a time into the flour, only using as much liquid as necessary to form a ball. Flour your hands and remove dough from bowl, divide into 4 mounds of dough, and roll out each one on a floured surface with a rolling pin. Handle dough as little as possible, as handling the dough will toughen it.

Banana Nut Bread

YIELD: 2 loaves

Ingredients:

½ cup butter, room temperature
1–1½ cups sugar, to taste
2 eggs
10 very ripe mashed bananas
2 teaspoons baking soda
2 teaspoons baking powder
juice of 1 large key lime
3 cups flour
1 teaspoon salt
1 teaspoon cinnamon
1 teaspoon nutmeg
½ cup walnuts, chopped
½ cup raisins (optional)

Directions:

Preheat oven to 350°F. Beat butter, sugar, and eggs with an electric mixer in a medium bowl until well blended. Put mashed bananas in a large bowl, add baking soda, baking powder, and lime juice and mix well. Add egg mixture to banana mixture and beat. Continue to beat and add flour a little at a time followed by salt, cinnamon, nutmeg, walnuts, and raisins if using, just until all ingredients are blended. Lightly grease and flour 2 loaf pans. Evenly pour ingredients into pans and bake 35 to 45 minutes or until a knife inserted in the middle comes out clean. Remove from oven, cool on cooling racks, then run a knife around edges of pan and invert to release banana bread. Serve warm or at room temperature or one of our favorite ways: toast a few slices in the morning and slather with butter.

Pear & Ginger Galette

YIELD: 6–8 servings

Ingredients:

dough for single pie crust (see Old-Fashioned Pie Crust on pg. 198)
2 Bosc pears, peeled and sliced into thin wedges
¼ cup brown sugar, packed
4½ teaspoons cornstarch
1 tablespoon fresh ginger, grated
¼ teaspoon salt
1 egg
1 teaspoon water

Directions:

Preheat oven to 400°F. Place oven rack in bottom third of the oven. Prepare dough for a single pie crust or use a pre-made pie crust, then place it onto a parchment-lined rimmed baking sheet or jelly roll pan. Pie crust can be rolled into a circle, oval, or rectangle. In a large bowl, toss sliced pears with the brown sugar, cornstarch, ginger, and salt until well coated. Arrange overlapping pear slices onto the pastry. Fold edges of the pastry over the pears, leaving the center uncovered. Beat the egg with water and brush the egg wash over the pastry. Place pan on rack in bottom third of oven and bake until pastry is deep golden and pears are tender, approximately 40 minutes. Remove to a cooling rack, dip pastry brush into the bubbly juices, and brush over the pears to glaze them. Let stand 10 minutes before cutting. Serve warm wedges with vanilla ice cream.

Raspberry Bars

YIELD: 12–16 bars

Ingredients for raspberry layer:

1 cup all-purpose flour
1 teaspoon baking powder
¼ cup sugar plus 2 tablespoons
½ cup butter, room temperature
1 egg, well beaten
1 tablespoon milk
1½ cups raspberries, crushed or 1 cup raspberry jam

Ingredients for topping:

¾ cup sugar
1 egg, well beaten
1½ tablespoons butter, melted
2 cups coconut, flaked

Directions for raspberry layer:

Preheat oven to 375°F. In a medium bowl, sift together flour, baking powder, and sugar. Add butter and mix well. Add beaten egg and milk. Scoop mixture into an 8 x 8-inch pan and press into bottom and corners. Evenly spread crushed raspberries or jam on top. If berries are extra juicy, stir in 2 additional tablespoons of sugar into the berries.

Directions for topping:

Beat sugar and egg until blended and continue beating while adding melted butter and coconut. Spread mixture evenly over berry layer and bake for 25 minutes or until done. Remove from oven and cool on cooling rack. Cut into 1-inch squares and serve warm or cool.

Rosemary Lemon Cupcakes

YIELD: 15 cupcakes

Ingredients for cupcakes:

1¾ cups flour
2 teaspoons fresh rosemary, finely chopped
1½ teaspoons baking powder
½ teaspoon salt
½ cup butter at room temperature for 30 minutes
1 cup white sugar
1½ teaspoons lemon extract
½ teaspoon vanilla extract
2 eggs at room temperature for 30 minutes
⅔ cup milk
2 teaspoons lemon zest
3 tablespoons fresh lemon juice
lemon glaze

Ingredients for lemon glaze:

1 cup powdered sugar
5–5½ teaspoons fresh lemon juice
1 teaspoon lemon zest

Directions for cupcakes:

Preheat oven to 350°F. Line 15 muffin tins with paper baking cups and set aside. In a medium bowl, combine flour, rosemary, baking powder, and salt and set aside. Place butter in a large bowl and using an electric mixer on medium-high, cream butter for 30 seconds. Add sugar, lemon extract, and vanilla and beat for 2 minutes until light and fluffy. Scrape bowl a few times during beating. Add eggs one at a time, beating well after each egg. Alternately add flour mixture and milk to creamed butter mixture on low speed just until combined. Stir in lemon zest and lemon juice to combine. Spoon batter into lined muffin tins and bake 22 to 25 minutes or until a toothpick inserted in the center comes out clean. Cool on cooling rack for 5 minutes, remove cupcakes in their paper cups from muffin tins, and cool.

Directions for lemon glaze:

While cupcakes are cooling, combine powdered sugar and enough fresh lemon juice for spreading consistency, then stir in 1 teaspoon lemon zest. Spoon lemon glaze on cupcakes and let stand 10 minutes before serving.

*Note: If you don't have cake flour, you can make a good substitute as follows:

All-purpose flour (just under one cup)

2 tablespoons cornstarch

Directions for cake flour:

Place 2 tablespoons of cornstarch in a 1 cup measuring cup. Fill the rest of the cup with all-purpose flour. Use in place of the cake flour called for in any recipe. One cup of substitute is equal to one cup of cake flour, so scale the recipe up or down as needed, to fit your recipe.

Rugelach Cookies

Yield: 64 cookies

Ingredients for cookies:

2 cups all-purpose flour plus more for dusting
¼ teaspoon salt
8 ounces cream cheese, cold and cubed
1 cup butter, cold and cubed
1 egg yolk
1 teaspoon vanilla extract
powdered sugar, for dusting

Ingredients for filling:

2 cups walnuts
¼ cup melted butter
¼ cup honey
¼ cup granulated sugar
1 teaspoon vanilla extract

Directions for cookies:

Place 2 cups flour and ¼ teaspoon salt in a food processor and pulse a few times to combine. Add cream cheese cubes and then butter cubes, pulsing until you have coarse crumbs. In a small bowl, whisk the egg yolk, then whisk in the vanilla and when combined, add egg mixture to the processor and run it until the dough starts to clump together and form large pieces. Scoop dough onto a lightly flour-dusted work surface and form it into a ball. Divide the ball into 4 equal portions and flatten each one out into 1-inch thick disks. Wrap each separately in plastic wrap, place in fridge, and chill dough for 1 hour. Make filling (directions below) while chilling dough. When ready to bake, preheat oven to 375°F and line 2 large baking sheets (or one at a time) with parchment paper. Generously sprinkle work surface, the dough, and the rolling pin with powdered sugar to prevent everything from sticking. Roll each dough portion into a ⅛-inch thick circle. Evenly spread ¼ of the filling in a thin layer over the surface of the circle of dough from edge to edge. Press the filling gently into the dough with your hands. Slice the circle of dough using a pastry or pizza cutter into 16 wedges just like a pizza. Starting at the wide end of each wedge, roll up the dough and place on your baking sheet with the small tip of the cookie tucked under. Place baking sheet with the cookies on it in the fridge and chill for 20 to 30 minutes. In the meantime, work on the remaining 3 balls of dough, spreading with filling, cutting, and rolling into cookies. Bake the cookies one tray at a time until golden cookies are brown, about 18 to 22 minutes. Cool on the baking sheet 5 minutes and then transfer to a cooling rack. Repeat until all the cookies are baked.

Directions for filling:

While chilling dough, put walnuts in the food processor and pulse into tiny crumbs. Place the melted butter in a medium bowl; add the nut crumbs, honey, sugar, and vanilla extract. Mix well to combine.

CHAPTER 11
Drinks

Banana Daiquiri

YIELD: Serves 1

Ingredients:

1½ ounces light rum
1 tablespoon triple sec
1 ounce lime juice
1 ounce banana liqueur
½ banana
½ ounce heavy cream
½ cup crushed ice

Directions:

Blend all ingredients in a blender on high speed until mixture is smooth. Pour into cocktail glass.

Blue Cuban

YIELD: Serves 1

Ingredients:

1 large ice cube
1 ounce white rum
1 ounce sweet white vermouth
1 ounce blue Curacao
1 twist of orange peel, to garnish

Directions:

In a rocks glass or tumbler, place ice cube, add rum, vermouth, and blue Curacao. Vigorously stir, garnish with orange peel, and serve.

Canuck Old-Fashioned, Eh?

YIELD: 1 serving

Ingredients:

2 ounces rye whiskey or bourbon
1 teaspoon pure maple syrup
dash of angostura bitters
1 teaspoon cold water
orange peel, for garnish

Directions:

In an old-fashioned glass or tumbler, mix whiskey, maple syrup, bitters, and water in an old-fashioned glass, stirring until syrup is dissolved. Add a single large ice cube to the tumbler, pour in the old-fashioned, and garnish with a small slice of orange peel.

Champagne Jello Shots

YIELD: 4–6 servings

Ingredients:

2 cups hot water
4 (1 ounce) unflavored gelatin packets
1 bottle cream soda or diet root beer
¾ (25 ounce) bottle champagne,
    approximately 2¾ cups
sanding sugar or sprinkles, for decoration
    (optional)

Directions:

In a medium saucepan, boil two cups of water and remove from heat. Sprinkle gelatin on top and stir until gelatin is completely dissolved, about 3 to 4 minutes. Let cool for a few minutes, then add soda and champagne. Pour into a small baking dish, loaf pan, or 13 x 9-inch pan lined with wax paper. Refrigerate 3 to 5 hours or overnight. To serve, run a fine blade around edges, invert pan, remove wax paper, and cut into squares with a sharp knife. Garnish by dipping in sanding sugar or sprinkles if using, and serve with festive toothpicks.

Dark 'N Stormy (Bermuda's National Drink)

YIELD: 1 serving

Ingredients:

2 ounces dark rum
4–5 ounces ginger beer
ice
lime wedge

Directions:

Combine rum and ginger beer in a tumbler or old-fashioned glass, add ice, stir, and top with lime wedge.

Foxy's Pineapple Cocktail

YIELD: 1 serving

Ingredients:

1½ ounces light rum
¾ ounce pineapple juice
drop of lemon juice

Directions:

Combine all ingredients, use a shaker to mix, and add crushed ice.

Grand Island South Shore

YIELD: 1 serving

Ingredients:

2 ounces rum
½ ounce fresh lemon juice
½ ounce simple syrup
2 ounces ginger beer
ice
fresh mint springs

Directions:

Combine rum, lemon juice, simple syrup, and ginger beer in a tumbler or old-fashioned glass, add ice, stir, and top with mint sprigs.

Greycliff Hotel Bahama Mama

YIELD: 1 large serving

Ingredients:

¾ ounce rum
½ ounce Nassau Royale Liqueur
½ ounce Cointreau
½ ounce grenadine
¼ ounce lemon juice
2 ounces fresh orange juice
1 dash angostura bitters
cherry, for garnish (optional)
orange slice, for garnish (optional)

Directions:

Mix all ingredients together. If you have a container that you can shake, fill it with ice, pour ingredients over ice, and shake away. Pour into a 12-ounce glass and fill with ice. If you don't have a shaker, simply pour your Bahama mama into a 12-ounce glass and fill with ice. Garnish with a maraschino cherry and/or an orange slice.

Ice Cream & Baileys

Stanley and one of his best friends in high school, Roger, played in a rock and roll band around the Kirkland, Washington area. Eventually they parted ways when Stanley went to the University of Washington and Roger moved to England, but all these years later they still keep in contact and laugh about their rock and roll days. Roger shared his "almost famous" cocktail recipe.

YIELD: 2 servings

Ingredients:

3 scoops coffee ice cream
2 jiggers Baileys Irish Cream
1 jigger milk

Directions:

Drop ice cream scoops into a blender; add Bailey's and milk, and blend. To serve, put ice in 2 tumblers and pour blender ingredients over top.

Jan & Byron's Beach Club Margarita

YIELD: 2–4 servings

Ingredients:

1 small can frozen lime juice
¾ to full can tequila or more, to taste
½ can triple sec
ice
coarse salt, for glass rim
lime slices, for garnish

Directions:

Dump frozen lime juice, tequila, and triple sec into a blender. Add ice and blend until margarita is full and thick. Taste and adjust. Sprinkle coarse salt on a saucer, lightly dampen the rim of serving glass by running the cut side of a lime wedge around the rim of serving glass, then invert on salted saucer and twist so that salt adheres to rim. Pour margarita into glass and serve with a lime slice for garnish. In Jan and Byron's words, "Drink with gusto."

Mango Mama

YIELD: 2 servings

Ingredients:

1 ripe mango, deseeded, peeled, and diced
1 small can frozen orange/pineapple
    concentrate
¾ cup rum
ice

Directions:

Blend all ingredients in mixer with ice until mixed but frothy.

Unusual, but Really Delicious Martini

YIELD: 1 serving

Ingredients:

lemon pepper
lemon and lime, sliced in circles, for garnish
ice cubes
5 ounces Clamato juice
1 ounce citrus vodka
½ teaspoon hot sauce
¼ teaspoon hot sauce with chipotle
1 teaspoon Worcestershire sauce
1 teaspoon lemon juice
1 teaspoon lime juice

Directions:

Place lemon pepper on a saucer, rub rim of a tall glass with lime, and rub into the lemon pepper to coat edge of glass. Fill the glass with ice cubes and add the rest of the ingredients. Stir well and garnish with lemon and lime slices.

Infused Vodka Martini

YIELD: 1 large bottle infused vodka

Ingredients for infusing vodka:

1 large jar with a tight-fitting lid
2 carrots, peeled and sliced to fit into jar
2 celery stalks, sliced to fit into jar
1 sweet red bell pepper, deseeded and diced
1 leek, cleaned, halved lengthwise, and sliced
1 small sweet onion, peeled and sliced
1 jalapeño pepper, deseeded and sliced
2–4 basil leaves
1 bottle of vodka or more, to taste

Ingredients for infused vodka martini:

celery salt
lime wedge
ice cubes
1½ ounces infused vodka
1 teaspoon Worcestershire sauce
½ teaspoon hot sauce
juice of ⅛ fresh lime
1 teaspoon horseradish
4 ounces Clamato juice
salt and pepper, to taste
assorted garnishes, such as a skewer of
    prosciutto strips or grape tomatoes

Directions for infusing vodka:

Infusing vodka can take 2 weeks to completely assimilate flavors, but the taste is so unusual and so good, it's worth the time and refrigerator space. In a large jar with a tight-fitting lid for a good seal, combine all the ingredients. Seal tightly, shake, and leave in fridge or cool dark place for at least 2 weeks.

Directions for infused vodka martini:

Place celery salt on a saucer, rub rim of a tall glass with lime wedge and rub into the celery salt to coat edge of glass. Fill glass with ice, then add all ingredients, stir to mix, and serve.

Dirty Martini

YIELD: 2 servings

Ingredients:

¾ cup (6 ounces) vodka
1 splash dry vermouth
1 ounce brine from olive jar
4 stuffed green olives
ice (optional)

Directions:

In a large glass or shaker, combine vodka, vermouth, and olive brine. Shake or mix well, add green olives, pour into 2 martini glasses, and serve over ice or straight up.

Espresso Martini

YIELD: 1 serving

Ingredients:

1 ounce cold espresso
1 ounce White Crème de Cacao
1½ ounce Kahlua Coffee Liqueur
1½ ounce vodka
ice cube

Directions:

In a large glass or shaker, mix espresso, Crème de Cacao, Kahlua, vodka, and ice cube and mix well or vigorously shake to combine ingredients. Serve in martini glass over ice or straight up.

Christmas Cranberry Martini

YIELD: Serves 1

Ingredients:

1½ ounces vodka
½ ounce cranberry juice
1 teaspoon dry vermouth
ice cube
1 twist lime peel, for garnish

Directions:

In a large glass or shaker, mix vodka, cranberry juice, vermouth, and ice cube and mix well or vigorously shake to combine ingredients. Serve in martini glass over ice or straight up. Garnish with lime twist.

Mojitos

We sailed to Cuba a few years ago on a sanctioned sailboat race, and though the "rules" were that we were not to spend any money there, we somehow downed more than our fair share of mojitos. We found we just loved these refreshing drinks, especially in Cuba, the home of the mojito. Here is the collection of Mojito recipes we collected, just as they were given to us. The first rule of mojito making that every one of our servers mentioned was to remember to wash your limes and lemons before you slice them. If you slice through unwashed fruit, you can contaminate the fruit flesh with all sorts of germs from pickers, handlers, and who knows what else from the tree to your galley. Essentially there are six ingredients in a mojito: mint, lime, rum, sugar, club soda or water, and ice. Some bartenders insisted on crushing the mint leaves with a mortar and pestle, some tore the leaves by hand, and some poured a hot liquid over mint leaves to make an infused liquid base. If you lean toward the crushed or bruised mint leaves and you don't have a mortar and pestle, place mint leaves in a small bowl and crush with the back of a spoon. Don't be so aggressive with the mint leaves that you end up with a paste. You want to bruise the mint leaves just enough so they release their flavor. Try experimenting with different rums and flavored rums or have a mojito tasting party, just like a wine tasting party.

Simple Syrup

YIELD: 1 cup

Ingredients:

1 cup sugar (optional, ⅔ cup white sugar and
⅓ cup brown sugar for a much richer taste)
1 cup water

Directions:

In a small saucepan, bring sugar and water to a boil; simmer and stir until the sugar is dissolved, about 3 minutes. Remove from the heat and cool completely. For most 1 serving recipes, only 1 jigger of simple syrup is used so you will not use this entire amount in one recipe. Save remaining syrup for future use. Simple syrup stores in the fridge for up to 2 weeks.

Mint Simple Syrup

YIELD: 1 cup

Ingredients:

1 cup chopped mint leaves, packed
1 cup sugar
1 cup water

Directions:

Wash, pick over, remove stems, and chop mint leaves. In a medium saucepan, combine sugar, water, and packed mint leaves. Bring ingredients to a boil, lower heat, and simmer for 2 to 3 minutes. Remove from heat and let cool. When completely cooled, strain syrup and store in an airtight container in refrigerator.

Optional: Warm sugar and water in a heatproof bowl and pour ½ cup hot simple syrup over 1 packed cup of mint leaves. Cover and refrigerate overnight. Strain, cover, and refrigerate for up to 1 week.

Classic Mojito

YIELD: 8 servings

Ingredients:

2 large limes, cut into wedges
4 cups water, divided
⅔ cup sugar plus extra for garnish
¼–½ cup light rum
2 limes, quartered, for garnish

Directions:

Reserve 1 wedge of lime and put remaining wedges in a blender, add 2 cups water and the sugar and blend about 30 to 45 seconds or until limes are unevenly, not uniformly chopped. Strain lime mixture through a fine-mesh sieve into a large serving pitcher to remove the lime chunks. Stir in remaining cups of water. Cover and chill for 1 to 12 hours. To serve, stir rum into the chilled lime mixture. Run the cut side of a lime wedge around the rims of 8 serving glasses and dip rims in extra sugar. Garnish with quartered limes.

Havana Party Mojito

YIELD: 12–15 servings

Ingredients:

2 cups fresh lime juice
1–2 cups superfine sugar, to taste
1 cup mint leaves, torn
6 cups ice, crushed
1 bottle amber rum
club soda
lime wedge, for garnish
mint sprig, for garnish

Directions:

In a large glass punch bowl or similarly large container, combine lime juice, sugar, and mint leaves and muddle until sugar is dissolved. Add crushed ice and 1 bottle rum. Stir well and pour into 4-ounce (½ cup) tumblers and top with a splash of club soda. Garnish with lime wedge and mint sprig.

Mint Mojito

YIELD: 1 serving

Ingredients:

1-ounce jigger mint syrup
1 handful mint leaves
crushed ice
1½–2 ounces light rum, to taste
½ lime, to squeeze into mojito
club soda or water
mint sprig, for garnish
slice of lime, for garnish

Directions:

Pour 1-ounce jigger of mint syrup into a tall glass. Add a handful of mint leaves to the glass and muddle it all together to bruise leaves. Add crushed ice and muddle some more. Pour in rum and squeeze in the juice of half a lime. Add a splash of club soda, stir, and garnish with a mint sprig and a slice of lime. If you want to make a larger batch, you can easily increase recipe by the number of servings.

Wine & Rum Mojito

YIELD: 1 serving

Ingredients:

1 ounce simple syrup
handful of fresh mint leaves (6–12 leaves)
crushed ice (optional, several ice cubes)
2 ounces rum
1 ounce lime juice
dash of angostura bitters
sparkling wine (optional, ginger beer or
    ginger ale)
mint sprig, for garnish

Directions:

Pour 1 ounce of simple syrup into a tall glass, add fresh mint leaves, and gently muddle to bruise the mint leaves. Add crushed ice or several ice cubes and muddle again. Add rum, lime juice, and bitters, and stir vigorously. Add a splash of sparkling wine or ginger beer or ginger ale and garnish with 1 to 2 mint sprigs and enjoy.

Planters Punch

YIELD: 1 serving

Ingredients:

1¼ ounces dark rum
2 ounces orange juice
2 ounces pineapple juice
dash of angostura bitters
⅙ ounce grenadine
1 maraschino cherry, for garnish
slice of orange, for garnish

Directions:

Blend all ingredients well, and serve with orange garnish and ice cubes in a tall glass.

Puerto Rican Rum Runner

YIELD: 1 serving

Ingredients:

1 ounce light rum
2 ounces Tia Maria Coffee Liqueur

Directions:

Mix both ingredients and serve over ice.

Rum Daiquiri

YIELD: 1 serving

Ingredients:

2 ounces Bacardi Light Rum
1 teaspoon sugar
squeeze of lime juice

Directions:

Mix all ingredients well and serve over ice.

Rum Kahlua

YIELD: 1 bottle

Ingredients:

1 cup boiling water
3 cups sugar
4 tablespoons (2 ounces) instant coffee
1 bottle rum (optional, vodka)
1 vanilla bean, halved (optional, 2 tablespoons vanilla extract)

Directions:

Mix water, sugar, and instant coffee in a large saucepan and simmer 10 to 15 minutes until sugar is completely dissolved. Cool to room temperature. Pour into a large container, add rum, and stir to combine, then add vanilla bean halves or vanilla extract. Tightly cap the container and let stand for 2 to 3 weeks.

St. Croix Pina Colada

YIELD: 1 serving

Ingredients:

1¼ ounces gold rum
½ ounce Coconut Liqueur
3 ounces pineapple juice
1½ ounces cream
½ ounce simple syrup
1 maraschino cherry, for garnish

Directions:

Blend all ingredients well and serve with cherry garnish and ice cubes in a tall glass.

Yellow Bird

YIELD: 1 serving

Ingredients:

1¼ ounce light rum
½ ounce Banana Liqueur
½ ounce Galliano Liqueur
2 ounces orange juice
2 ounces pineapple juice
1 maraschino cherry, for garnish
slice of orange, for garnish

Directions:

Blend all ingredients well and serve with orange garnish and ice cubes in a tall glass.

CHAPTER 12
Meat

Baked Chinese Egg Roll Wraps

YIELD: 20 egg rolls

Ingredients:

1 pound ground pork, any flavor
1½ teaspoons ginger, minced
1 large garlic clove, peeled, sliced, and minced
2 cups Chinese (Napa) cabbage, shredded and finely chopped
¼ pound bean sprouts
½–¾ cup carrot, peeled and shredded
4 green onions, finely chopped
3 tablespoons oyster sauce
1 package large egg roll wraps (generally 20 wraps per package)
sweet chili sauce, for dipping (optional)
soy sauce, for dipping (optional)
Chinese hot mustard, for dipping (optional)
duck sauce, for dipping (optional)

Directions:

Preheat oven to 400°F. Prepare a baking sheet with nonstick cooking spray and set aside. In a large skillet over high heat, stir-fry ground pork, ginger, and garlic together for 2 to 3 minutes until pork is lightly browned. Add cabbage, bean sprouts, carrots, and green onions and cook another 2 minutes. Stir in oyster sauce, remove from heat, and let mixture cool. Separate egg roll wraps, placing them in a diamond pattern (corner ends facing up, down, left, and right) and one at a time, place 2 tablespoons of filling in center of egg roll wrap, shaping it from left to right but leaving a border so the filling doesn't reach the edges. Fold the bottom corner over the filling and then fold in the side corners like an envelope. Use your fingertip or brush with water on the top corner and tightly roll up wrap from the bottom up, sealing the roll with the top corner. Place on prepared baking sheet, seam-side down. Lightly brush the tops with olive oil or spray with nonstick cooking spray and put on middle rack of oven and bake until golden brown, about 10 to 12 minutes. Serve immediately with optional dipping sauces.

Balsamic Pork Tenderloin with Plum Reduction

YIELD: 4 servings

Ingredients:

1 pork tenderloin
salt, to taste
pepper, to taste
1 tablespoon olive oil
1½ plums, pitted and chopped in small pieces
2 tablespoons balsamic vinegar
1 tablespoon brown sugar
1 tablespoon honey
1 cup blueberries, smashed

Directions:

Preheat oven to 400°F. Season pork tenderloin with salt and pepper on all sides. In a heavy ovenproof skillet, heat olive oil over high heat until oil shimmers, then carefully lay tenderloin into the hot oil. Cook about 1 minute, then gently loosen meat from the bottom of the skillet as the bottom of the tenderloin can burn at this point. Cook until the tenderloin is seared a golden-brown color, about 3 minutes per side. In the meantime, line a baking sheet with foil. When tenderloin is browned, transfer it to the foil-lined baking sheet. Place tenderloin in oven and roast until an instant read thermometer inserted into the center of the tenderloin reads 145°F, about 15 minutes. Remove the pork from the oven and allow to rest for 10 to 12 minutes before slicing into medallions. While the tenderloin is roasting, in a medium-sized saucepan cook the plums, balsamic vinegar, brown sugar, honey, and blueberries over medium-low heat, stirring often until fruit is soft, about 10 minutes. Transfer sauce to a blender and blend until smooth, then return sauce to the saucepan and simmer until it is reduced and thickened to the consistency of apple butter, about 5 minutes. To serve, plate tenderloin slices and top each with a good-sized portion of plum sauce.

Beef Bourguignon

YIELD: 4–6 servings

Ingredients:

12–18 pearl onions
2 pounds sirloin, cubed
salt, to taste
pepper, to taste
4 tablespoons butter, divided
2 tablespoons brandy or more, to taste
2 tablespoons flour
1 teaspoon tomato paste
¾ cup beef broth
¾ cup red wine
4–6 sprigs parsley, chopped
1–2 bay leaves
4 stalks fresh thyme
1 pound of mushrooms, cleaned and thickly sliced

Directions:

Preheat oven to 325°F. Remove pearl onion skins, pour hot water over onions, and let them sit for 20 minutes. Cut off the roots and the skins will slip off. Set onions aside. Cube sirloin into bite-sized pieces, then season beef with salt and pepper and set aside. Over medium-high heat, melt 2 table-spoons butter in a Dutch oven or other lidded large saucepan. Add prepared meat and cook until lightly browned. Pour brandy over meat, carefully ignite, and let burn until brandy has burned off. Sprinkle flour over meat, stir, add tomato paste, and stir again. Add beef broth, red wine, parsley, bay leaves, and thyme, bring to a boil, then reduce heat, cover, and simmer for 1 hour. In a skillet over medium heat, brown the prepared white onions in remaining butter, add in the mushrooms, and cook for 1 minute. Mix onions and mushrooms in with the meat mixture, cover, and cook an additional 30 minutes. Taste and adjust seasonings and remove any herb sprigs and bay leaves before serving. Serve over mashed potatoes, large buttered noodles, or simply in good-sized individual bowls with plenty of garlic bread to sop up the sauce.

Caesar Burgers

YIELD: *4 servings*

Ingredients:

1 pound ground round
¼ cup Parmesan cheese, grated
1 tablespoon anchovy fillets, minced
1 egg
2 teaspoons lemon juice
1 teaspoon Worcestershire sauce
¼ cup olive oil
2 garlic cloves, peeled, sliced, and smashed
4 hamburger buns, halved
mayonnaise, to garnish
mustard, to garnish
tomato, sliced, to garnish
lettuce, to garnish

Directions:

In a medium-sized bowl, mix ground round, cheese, anchovies, egg, lemon juice, and Worcestershire sauce until well combined. Gently form 4 equal-sized hamburger patties. Heat oil and garlic in a large skillet until garlic is a light golden color. Remove and discard garlic and scoop out ½ of the oil and reserve. Pan-fry the cut sides of 2 buns until golden brown. Remove to a platter, then add reserved oil and pan-fry remaining buns and remove them to a platter. In the same skillet, pan-fry the patties over medium-high heat, about 3 minutes on each side. Place cooked patties on toasted bottom buns, add garnishes, and top with toasted bun tops.

Chinese Dumplings

YIELD: *36 small or 8 large dumplings*

Ingredients:

water to fill 1 inch in saucepan
2 cups Napa cabbage, sliced and packed
1 pound ground pork
1 large green onion, chopped
1½ teaspoons fresh ginger, peeled and minced
2 tablespoons soy sauce
1 tablespoon dry sherry
2 teaspoons cornstarch
36 (3½ x 3½-inch) wonton wrappers or 8 large egg roll wrappers
1 large egg white, beaten
water, (½–1-inch) in large skillet for cooking
soy dipping sauce

Directions:

Heat 1 inch of water to boiling in a 2-quart saucepan over high heat. Add cabbage, pushing it down into saucepan, and heat to boiling. Cook 1 minute and immediately remove cabbage from the water and rinse with cold running water to stop cooking. Drain well, then using your hands, squeeze out as much water as possible. Finely chop cabbage and squeeze out any remaining moisture. Place cabbage in a medium-sized bowl, add pork, breaking it up with a fork as you add it, then add green onions, ginger, soy sauce, sherry, and cornstarch and mix well until it's all blended. Arrange half of the wonton wrappers on a sheet of waxed paper and brush each wonton lightly with beaten egg white. Spoon 1 well-rounded teaspoon full of filling into the center of each wonton wrapper. Bring 2 opposite corners of each wonton wrapper up over filling and pinch and pleat edges together to seal in the filling. Repeat with the remaining wrappers, beaten egg white, and filling. In a deep, nonstick 12-inch skillet, heat ½-inch water to boiling over high heat. Place all the dumplings, pleated side up, in 1 layer in water in a large skillet. Gently move dumplings around with a soft spatula to keep them from sticking to the bottom of the skillet. Bring to a boil, reduce heat, and cover and simmer about 5 minutes until dumplings are done. In the meantime, prepare the soy dipping sauce. Using a slotted spoon, transfer cooked dumplings to a large serving platter. When all dumplings are plated, tip plate a little bit to drain any water that has accumulated. Serve immediately with soy dipping sauce.

Soy Dipping Sauce

YIELD: ½ cup

Ingredients:

¼ cup soy sauce
¼ cup seasoned rice vinegar (optional, white wine vinegar)
2 tablespoons fresh ginger, peeled and cut into very thin slivers

Directions:

Mix all ingredients in a small serving bowl, set aside until ready to serve dumplings.

Chinese Pork Chops

YIELD: 4 servings

Ingredients:

2 cloves garlic, peeled and crushed to a paste
5 tablespoons soy sauce
2 tablespoons hoisin sauce
1 tablespoon honey
1 tablespoon sugar
4 well-trimmed, center-cut pork chops, 1-inch thick

Directions:

Place garlic, soy sauce, hoisin sauce, honey, and sugar in a large re-sealable bag or container with a tight-fitting lid. Add pork chops and turn to make sure all meat is marinated. Place in refrigerator overnight or up to 24 hours to marinate. Remove pork chops from marinade and arrange on a baking sheet. Reserve marinade. Place pork chops under broiler and cook 4 minutes, rotating pan once. Remove pork chops from the broiler, turn chops over, and spoon some of the reserved marinade over the tops. Return to broiler, and cook until just done and still tender, about 4 to 7 minutes or more.

Cocktail Meatballs in Sherry Mushroom Sauce

YIELD: 40 meatballs

Ingredients for meatballs:

2 pounds ground beef
1 cup bread crumbs
½ cup ketchup
¼ cup green pepper, finely chopped
2 packages Hidden Valley Green Onion
    Dip Mix
2 eggs
½ teaspoon oregano
½ teaspoon garlic powder
salt, to taste
pepper, to taste

Ingredients for sauce:

2 cans cream of mushroom soup
2½ cups sour cream
¼ cup sherry
¼ cup onion, peeled, sliced, and finely minced
1 tablespoon fresh parsley, minced
⅛ teaspoon oregano
½ teaspoon garlic powder

Directions for meatballs:

Preheat oven to 350°F. In a large bowl, mix all ingredients and shape into small cocktail-sized meatballs. Place on a very lightly greased baking sheet and bake for 20 to 30 minutes until done and brown. With a slotted spoon remove meatballs and drain off fat.

Directions for sauce:

Mix all sauce ingredients in a large saucepan over low heat, being careful not to boil, as sour cream may curdle. Add cooked meatballs and simmer about 45 minutes, then place in a warming dish for hors d'oeuvres or for a dinner, serve over rice, noodles, or mashed potatoes with plenty of sauce on top.

Creamy Horseradish Burgers

YIELD: 6 servings

Ingredients:

2 pounds ground beef
2 tablespoons steak sauce
¾ teaspoon seasoned salt
6 tablespoons (3 ounces) cream cheese, room temperature and softened
1–2 tablespoons prepared horseradish, to taste
1 teaspoon Dijon mustard
6 hamburger buns, very lightly toasted
mayonnaise, to garnish
lettuce, to garnish
tomato slices, to garnish
cheese slices, to garnish

Directions:

Preheat grill for 10 minutes. In the meantime, in a medium bowl, combine beef, steak sauce, and seasoned salt. Mix well and shape into 12 thin, equal-sized patties. Set aside. In a small bowl, blend cream cheese, horseradish, and mustard. Spread about 1 tablespoon of cream cheese mixture in the center of each of the 6 patties. Top with remaining 6 patties and press edges firmly to seal. Grill patties on medium heat until burgers feel slightly firm, 10 to 14 minutes, carefully turning over once while cooking. Serve on lightly toasted buns with mayonnaise, lettuce, tomato slices and cheese slices if using.

Dijon-Thyme Pork Tenderloin Medallions

YIELD: 4 servings

Ingredients:

1 tablespoon fresh thyme, finely chopped
2 tablespoons Dijon mustard
3–4 large garlic cloves, peeled, sliced, and smashed
1 pound pork tenderloin
1 tablespoon butter
¼ cup milk
¼ cup dry white wine
2 teaspoons flour
salt, to taste
pepper, to taste

Directions:

Remove stems from thyme, chop, and place in a medium-sized bowl. Add mustard and garlic and mix well. Reserve herb mixture. Cut tenderloin into 8 equal-sized medallions, as there will be 2 medallions per serving. Add medallions to herb mixture and coat each medallion with herb mixture, pressing and turning to coat completely. Preheat a large skillet on medium heat. Place butter in hot pan; add pork with herbs and cook 5 to 6 minutes on each side until browned and an instant read thermometer reads 160°F. In the meantime, in a small bowl, combine milk, wine, and flour, whisking to thoroughly combine. Add to skillet with pork, cooking and stirring 2 to 3 minutes or until sauce thickens. To serve, place 2 medallions on each of 4 plates and spoon sauce evenly over each plate. Season with salt and pepper to taste.

Down Island Goat Chili

YIELD: 4–6 servings

Ingredients:

2 pounds goat meat, finely diced
1 tablespoon bacon drippings
2 onions, peeled and chopped
2–4 garlic cloves, peeled and chopped
1 teaspoon salt. to taste
½ teaspoon black pepper, to taste
2 tablespoons chili powder
1 teaspoon sage
1 teaspoon cumin
2 (15 ounce) cans Spanish-style tomato sauce
2 cups water
1 (23 ounce) can ranch-style beans
lettuce, shredded, for serving
cheddar cheese, shredded, for serving
diced onion, for serving
chili powder, to sprinkle on top for serving
tortilla chips, for serving

Directions:

In a large skillet over medium heat, sauté goat in bacon drippings, using enough drippings to keep meat from sticking to pan. Goat is a very dry meat with not much fat content, so slow and long cooking is generally required. Add onions, garlic, and seasonings. Stir in tomato sauce, water, and beans. Simmer for 1 hour or more, depending on tenderness of the meat and to your preference. To serve "Down Island Style," place shredded lettuce on a plate or bowl, dish up goat stew and top with cheese, onion, chili powder, and tortilla chips if desired.

Beef & Broccoli Stir-Fry

YIELD: 4 servings

Ingredients:

⅔ cup reduced sodium soy sauce
½ cup chicken stock
¼ cup honey
2 tablespoons rice wine vinegar
2 tablespoons brown sugar, packed
3 cloves garlic, minced
1 tablespoon sesame oil
1 tablespoon cornstarch
1 teaspoon sriracha or more, to taste
1 teaspoon ground ginger
¼ teaspoon red pepper flakes
¼ cup water, room temperature
1 tablespoon olive oil
1 pound flank steak, thinly sliced across the grain
1 head broccoli, cut into florets

Directions:

In a medium bowl, whisk together soy sauce, chicken stock, honey, vinegar, brown sugar, garlic, sesame oil, cornstarch, sriracha, ginger, red pepper flakes, and water and set aside. In a large skillet over medium-high heat, heat olive oil. Add sliced flank steak and cook, flipping once or twice until browned, about 3 to 4 minutes. Stir in broccoli florets and reserved soy sauce mixture and cook until broccoli is just slightly tender and sauce is slightly thickened, about 3 to 4 minutes. To serve, top hot white rice with stir fry and enjoy.

Glazed Pork Chops

YIELD: 4 servings

Ingredients:

½ teaspoon paprika
½ teaspoon cayenne pepper
½ teaspoon garlic powder
½ teaspoon salt
½ teaspoon black pepper
olive oil, for sautéing
4 thick-cut pork chops
4 tablespoons brown sugar, divided

Directions:

Preheat oven to 350°F. Combine paprika, cayenne, garlic powder, salt, and pepper in a small bowl. Rub the pork chops generously with the spice mix and set aside. Heat olive oil in a large ovenproof skillet over medium-high heat. When oil is very hot, add pork chops and cook for 3 to 5 minutes on each side until they are caramelized brown. Once they are a lovely brown, top each pork chop with 1 tablespoon of brown sugar. Turn each chop over so that there is melted brown sugar on both sides of chops. Put skillet in oven on middle rack and cook for 15 minutes, making sure chops are cooked through. To serve, place a chop on each plate and pour a bit of the glaze in the pan over the top of each chop.

Enchilada Pie

YIELD: 6 servings

Ingredients:

1 tablespoon olive oil
1 cup green or red bell pepper
1 pound ground chicken or ground turkey
2 teaspoons ground cumin
1 (15 ounce) can cut tomatoes with garlic and onion
½ cup canned or jarred enchilada sauce
1 (4 ounce) can green chilies
1 cup fresh, canned, or frozen corn kernels, drained
¼ cup black olives, pitted and sliced plus extra to garnish
3 (8-inch) corn or flour tortillas
2 cups Mexican blend cheese, shredded
shredded lettuce, to garnish
sour cream, to garnish

Directions:

Preheat oven to 325°F. Heat oil in a large, deep skillet over medium heat. Add bell pepper and sauté for 3 to 4 minutes until pepper is just slightly soft. Add chicken or turkey and cook while breaking up meat with a wooden spoon for 5 minutes or until meat is no longer pink. Sprinkle with cumin; add tomatoes, enchilada sauce, and green chilies. Stir and bring to a simmer and continue simmering 10 minutes to combine flavors. Remove pan from stove and stir in corn and olives. Line the bottom of a 3-quart casserole dish with 2 tortillas. Spoon half of enchilada mixture on top and ⅓ cup of the shredded cheese. Top with 1 more tortilla, the remaining filling, half the remaining cheese, then the last tortilla. Cover with foil and bake on center rack for 30 minutes. Uncover, sprinkle with remaining cheese, and bake 10 more minutes until cheese melts and bubbles. To serve, let stand 5 to 10 minutes before cutting in wedges. Serve on shredded lettuce and top with sour cream and additional olives.

Fiery Korean Gochujang Flank Steak

YIELD: 4 servings

Ingredients:

6 tablespoons Korean Gochujang red pepper
   paste
3 tablespoons mirin or rice wine vinegar
1 tablespoon soy sauce
3 teaspoons toasted sesame oil
4 large garlic cloves, sliced and mashed
1 tablespoons fresh ginger, peeled and
   chopped
1 (2 pound) flank steak

Directions:

Mix Gochujang, mirin or rice vinegar, soy sauce, sesame oil, garlic, and ginger until it's a smooth paste. Place flank steak in a large re-sealable storage bag and scoop marinade on top of meat. Seal bag tightly and massage marinade into meat, making sure all sides of meat are thoroughly coated. Refrigerate 6 hours or overnight, massaging and turning bag occasionally. When ready to cook, remove steak from marinade, place on a hot grill, and cook to your liking. The hot marinade will crisp up or burn off the steak, leaving a beautifully cooked and tasty flank steak.

Fluffy Meatloaf

YIELD: 4–6 servings

Ingredients:

1½ pounds ground beef
½ pound ground pork
2 cups torn bread
1 egg, beaten
1½ cups milk
1 onion, peeled, sliced, and minced
2 teaspoons salt
¼ teaspoon pepper
½ teaspoon dry mustard
¼ teaspoon sage
BBQ sauce or ketchup
parsley, chopped

Directions:

Preheat oven to 350°F. Mix all ingredients except the BBQ sauce and parsley in a large bowl until completely combined. Pack into a lightly greased 9 x5 x 3-inch loaf pan. With the outside edge of your palm, press into top of meatloaf, making diagonal grooves. Alternating BBQ sauce and chopped parsley, fill grooves. Place on middle shelf in oven and bake 90 minutes. During cooking, check for accumulated liquid and carefully spoon out hot liquid occasionally so it doesn't spill over. Don't take all the liquid out, as you do not want a dry meatloaf. If meatloaf is getting too brown, slide a piece of lightly oiled aluminum foil over the top. Remove from oven, drain off more of the accumulated liquid, let stand 1 minute, slice, and serve.

Foxy's Pork 'N Rice

YIELD: 4 servings

Ingredients:

2 cups white rice, uncooked
1 tablespoon oil
1 pound pork tenderloin, cut in chunks
1 medium onion, peeled and chopped
2 medium carrots, peeled and chopped
1 (14 ounce) can pineapple chunks, drained
1 (14 ounce) can water
¼ cup BBQ sauce, your favorite
1 teaspoon ground ginger
1 green pepper, stemmed, deseeded, and chopped

Directions:

In a large pot, cook rice according to directions. In the meantime, heat oil in a large skillet, add tenderloin chunks, and cook while stirring, until pork is mostly cooked. Add onion and carrots and cook until pork is no longer pink inside. While stirring, add pineapple, water, BBQ sauce, ground ginger, green pepper and cooked rice. Bring to a boil, cover, remove from heat, and let stand 5 minutes. To serve, stir well and scoop generous portions into 4 bowls or onto 4 plates.

Ginger Beef

YIELD: 4–6 servings

Ingredients:

1½ pounds beef sirloin, sliced to bite size
¼ cup beef stock
1½ tablespoons soy sauce
2 teaspoons dry sherry
1 teaspoon sugar
red chili flakes, to taste
2 tablespoons oil
1–2 garlic cloves, sliced and mashed
2 tablespoons fresh ginger, chopped
3 green onions, diagonally sliced into ½-inch pieces plus extra to garnish
1 tablespoon cornstarch
1 tablespoon water
sesame seeds, toasted, to garnish

Directions:

Chill the steak in the freezer for 30 minutes before you slice it; this will make it easier to cut in thin slices. Slice the steak first crosswise in ½-inch thick slices, then cut each slice lengthwise into strips. In a medium-sized bowl, combine beef stock, soy sauce, sherry, sugar, and red chili flakes if using. Mix well and set aside. Heat the oil in a wok or a large sauté pan over high heat until it is nearly smoking. As the oil is heating up, pat the beef dry and separate it into small batches no larger than the palm of your hand. Working in batches, sauté beef until just brown outside but rare inside, no more than 1 minute. Transfer beef to a bowl as it cooks. When all of the beef is cooked, put the garlic into the pan and stir-fry for 30 to 45 seconds. Add the ginger and cook for 30 to 45 seconds more. Add the green onions and meat back to pan. Pour in beef stock mixture, cover, and simmer about 3 minutes. Mix cornstarch and water and gradually stir into the pan. Cook for 1 minute until thickened, stirring constantly. Taste and adjust seasonings. Serve immediately over steamed rice with sesame seeds and sliced green onions to garnish.

Goat Meatloaf

YIELD: 6 servings

Ingredients:

1 can cream of mushroom soup
2 pounds goat meat, ground
1 envelope dry onion soup/dip mix
½ cup dry bread crumbs
1 egg, beaten
¼ cup water or milk

Directions:

Preheat oven to 350°F and reduce to 325°F when ready to cook. In a large bowl, mix ½ can mushroom soup, goat meat, onion soup mix, bread crumbs, and egg. Lightly grease an 8 x 4-inch loaf pan and add mixture, pressing in and firmly shaping into the loaf pan. Place on middle rack and bake at 325°F for 1 hour and 15 minutes or until done. Mix remaining mushroom soup, ¼ cup water or milk, and 2 tablespoons drippings from loaf in bowl. Heat in microwave 2 minutes or until heated through. To serve, slice meatloaf and place on plates, and spoon microwaved sauce over slices.

Jamaican Curried Goat

YIELD: 6–8 servings

Ingredients:

3 pounds goat meat, cut into 1-inch cubes
2 large limes, halved
1 large onion, peeled and sliced
5 garlic cloves, sliced and finely chopped
1 teaspoon thyme
2 teaspoons salt
1 teaspoon pepper
2 tablespoons canola oil
1 teaspoon sugar
5 green onions, chopped
2 teaspoons curry powder
2 medium potatoes, peeled and cut into ½-inch cubes
¼ cup water

Directions:

Put cubed goat meat into a large re-sealable container or bag. Squeeze limes over meat and ream out the halves with a fork to get out as much juice and pulp as possible. Seal container and let stand for at least 30 minutes. Open container and rinse goat meat with cold water. Place meat back in sealable container; add onion, garlic, thyme, salt, and pepper. Rub spices all over meat, making sure all surfaces have spices on them. Cover tightly and let marinate a minimum of 2 hours. In a large pot over medium heat, heat the oil and sugar. Stir until sugar is brown. Add goat meat with marinade, green onions, and curry powder and stir. Cover the pot and reduce the heat to low. Simmer slowly, stirring occasionally until meat is nearly tender, about 40 minutes. Add potatoes and water and stir. Cover and simmer for another 15 minutes until potatoes are cooked but not soft. Crush potatoes to thicken sauce if desired. To make more sauce, you can add a little water and cook for 10 minutes more.

Kalamata-Buttered New York Oven Steaks

YIELD: 6 servings

Ingredients for kalamata butter:

1 large head of garlic, roasted
1 clove fresh garlic, sliced and chopped
1 shallot, sliced and chopped
2 anchovy fillets
½ cup pitted Kalamata olives
1 teaspoon fresh marjoram, chopped or ¼–⅓ teaspoon dried marjoram, to taste
⅓ cup butter, diced
salt, to taste
pepper, to taste

Ingredients for steaks:

6 (8 ounce) New York steaks
salt, to taste
pepper, to taste
1 tablespoon olive oil

Directions for kalamata butter:

Combine roasted garlic, fresh garlic, shallot, anchovies, olives, and marjoram in a food processor. While machine is running, add the diced butter a few pieces at a time and process until Kalamata butter is smooth. Scrape the bowl, mix in salt and pepper, taste, and adjust seasonings. Scoop a 6-inch strip of kalamata butter onto a 12-inch piece of plastic wrap, leaving at least a 1-inch border from the end. Fold one side of plastic wrap over butter and roll up tightly to form a log, then place in refrigerator until ready to serve.

Directions for steaks:

Preheat oven to 350°F. Season both sides of the steaks with salt and pepper. Heat the olive oil in a large ovenproof sauté pan over high heat until oil is smoking. Add the steaks and sear 2 to 3 minutes per side to sear. Set the pan in the oven and cook 6 to 8 minutes for medium doneness or less for rare. To serve, place steaks on a large platter or 8 serving plates and top each with a ½-inch slice of kalamata butter to taste.

Goat Skewers Dipped in Herb Vinaigrette

YIELD: 4 skewers

Ingredients:

¼ cup fresh chives, minced
¼ cup fresh cilantro leaves, stemmed, packed
¼ cup fresh parsley leaves, stemmed, packed
3 tablespoons red wine vinegar
½ teaspoon freshly ground black pepper
¼ teaspoon salt
⅔ cup olive oil
1½ pounds goat meat, cut into 1-inch cubes from the leg
1 teaspoon mild paprika
½ teaspoon ground cardamom
4 metal kebab skewers

Directions:

Place chives, cilantro, parsley, vinegar, pepper, and salt in a food processor and chop. While the food processor is whirring, pour the olive oil through the open feed tube in a slow stream to make a light sauce. Place half of this vinaigrette in a large bowl, reserving the remainder in a separate bowl in the fridge to use as a garnish. Add the cubed goat meat, paprika, and cardamom to the herb vinaigrette, stir well, cover, and refrigerate for at least 4 hours or up to 12 hours to marinate. Thread marinated goat meat cubes onto skewers and set them aside at room temperature while you prepare the grill, heating to high, about 550°F. As the grill is heating up, bring the reserved vinaigrette out of the fridge and bring to room temperature. Grill until meat is done to your preference. Put reserved room temperature sauce on serving plates, then push kebabs off the skewers and serve with rice. If there's enough leftover vinaigrette, place in a small bowl for dipping goat meat.

Ground Beef Curry

YIELD: *4 servings*

Ingredients:

2 cups white rice, uncooked
1 pound ground beef
4 tablespoons vegetable oil
1 medium onion, peeled and chopped
¼ teaspoon turmeric
¼ teaspoon cinnamon
¼ teaspoon ground cloves
½ teaspoon salt
¼ teaspoon pepper
¼ teaspoon ground ginger
1 teaspoon curry powder or more to taste
2 garlic cloves, sliced and chopped
1 (8 ounce) can tomato sauce
1¾ cups water
½ cup green peas, frozen

Directions:

Cook rice according to directions, set aside, and cover to keep warm. In a large skillet, cook ground beef until no pink remains. Remove meat from pan, drain off fat, and reserve. Add oil and onion to the skillet and sauté till lightly brown. Add turmeric, cinnamon, cloves, salt, pepper, ginger, curry powder, and garlic. Cook 1 minute, then add cooked beef, tomato sauce, water, and frozen peas. Stir just to mix and then simmer uncovered for 20 minutes while stirring occasionally. To serve, plate rice and top with beef curry mixture.

Ham & Corn Custard

YIELD: 6 servings

Ingredients:

2 cups (¾–1 pound) cooked ham, cubed
1 (17 ounce) can whole kernel corn, drained
3 eggs, beaten
¼ cup all-purpose flour
1 tablespoon sugar
¾ teaspoon salt
¼ teaspoon pepper
2 cups milk
¼ cup butter, softened and divided
27 Saltine crackers (1 cup), finely rolled into crumbs
1 teaspoon fresh basil, finely chopped
parsley sprigs, to garnish

Directions:

Preheat oven to 325°F. Spread cubed ham in the bottom of a lightly greased 11¾ x 7½ x 1¾-inch heat-resistant glass baking dish. In a large bowl, combine corn, eggs, flour, sugar, salt, pepper, milk, and 2 tablespoons butter. Mix thoroughly, then pour over ham. Place baking dish on the middle rack of the oven and bake for 30 minutes. Combine Saltine crumbs with basil and remaining butter. Remove custard from the oven and sprinkle crumb mixture over the top, return to oven, and bake an additional 10 minutes or until custard is set. To serve, garnish with parsley.

Herb-Infused Honey Pork Loin

YIELD: 4 servings

Ingredients:

1–1¼ pound pork tenderloin
Kosher salt plus extra to taste
freshly cracked black pepper, to taste
2 tablespoons olive oil
¼ chicken stock
3 tablespoons fresh thyme plus extra for garnish
¼ cup thyme or lavender honey
1 tablespoon unsalted butter, room temperature

Directions:

Preheat oven to 375°F. Take the pork out of the refrigerator at least 15 minutes before you want to use it. With a paper towel, gently pat the tenderloin dry, then season liberally on all sides with salt and pepper. Heat the olive oil in a skillet over medium to high heat. When the oil begins to shimmer, sear the pork until golden brown on all sides, about 3 minutes per side or 12 minutes total. Take the pork out of the pan, add the chicken stock, and over medium heat scrape up all the brown bits from the bottom of the pan, then remove from heat and reserve the sauce. While the pork is searing, whisk together in a small bowl the thyme and flavored honey and butter until completely incorporated. Season the mixture with salt and pepper to taste. Carefully rub the seared pork all over the outside with the flavored honey mixture. Line a rimmed baking sheet with aluminum foil and light oil, then place the seasoned pork on the baking sheet. Use a rubber spatula to spoon any of the honey mixture that runs off the meat back on top of the pork loin. Pour the chicken stock from the searing pan into the baking sheet. Roast the pork in the oven until the pork reaches an internal temperature of 165°F. Take the pork out of the oven, tent with foil, and allow to rest for 10 minutes before slicing. Slice into medallions and serve with the pan sauce and garnish with a few extra sprigs of fresh thyme.

Honey Baked Spiral Ham

YIELD: 8–10 servings

Ingredients:

3½–5-pound ham, smoked, spiral cut, and fully cooked
½ cup apple juice
½ cup fresh orange juice
½ cup brown sugar, firmly packed
½ cup honey

Directions:

Preheat oven to 350°F. In a baking pan large enough to hold ham, place ham wide, cut-end down. In a small-sized bowl, mix apple juice and orange juice, then pour the juice mixture over the ham and bake for 20 minutes, basting frequently with juices. In the meantime, in another bowl, mix brown sugar and honey together until well combined and reserve. Remove ham from oven and brush mixture over ham. Bake uncovered for 1 additional hour or until internal temperature reads 140°F on an instant read thermometer. Remove ham from oven onto a safe surface and carefully using a butane torch in small sweeping strokes caramelize the glaze to the crust. Serve hot, warm, or at room temperature.

Lasagna Roll-Ups

YIELD: 4–8 servings

Ingredients:

16 uncooked lasagna noodles
1 pound ground beef
½ pound pork sausage
½ cup chopped onion
6 cups tomato pasta sauce, divided
2 (15 ounce) containers ricotta cheese
1 (9 ounce) box frozen spinach, thawed, drained, and squeezed dry
2 teaspoons Italian seasoning (optional, dried basil leaves)
1 egg
2 cups (8 ounces) mozzarella cheese shredded, divided

Directions:

Preheat oven to 350°F. Line a 15 x 10 x 1-inch baking pan with foil and set aside. Cook lasagna noodles as directed on package, then drain, rinse with hot water, and drain again. In a large skillet over medium-high heat, cook ground beef, sausage and onion, stirring frequently until meat is no longer pink. Drain fat from skillet. Stir 1½ cups pasta sauce into skillet with meat, reduce heat to low, and simmer uncovered 10 minutes, stirring occasionally. Remove from heat. Mix ricotta, spinach, Italian seasoning, and egg in a small bowl. When thoroughly blended, spread 3 tablespoons of the cheese mixture over each cooked lasagna noodle, leaving a 1-inch border at one of the short ends of the noodle. Spoon about ¼ cup meat mixture over ricotta mixture on each lasagna noodle and then firmly roll noodle toward unfilled end. Place rolled noodles seam-side down on prepared baking pan, then loosely cover with foil. Place pan in freezer for about 30 minutes or until lasagna noodles are firm. To freeze for up to 3 months, place prepared frozen lasagna noodles in an airtight freezer container for a quick meal at a later time. To cook totally frozen lasagna, spray 2 (13 x 9-inch) baking dishes with nonstick cooking spray and place 8 lasagna noodles in each baking dish. Cover baking dishes with foil and place in refrigerator to thaw for at least 8 hours but no longer than 24 hours. Heat oven. Pour 1½ cups pasta sauce over and around roll-ups in each baking dish. Cover tightly with foil; bake 30 to 40 minutes or until hot and bubbly. Sprinkle each baking dish with about 1 cup mozzarella cheese and bake uncovered 3 to 5 minutes longer or until cheese is melted. Let stand 5 minutes before serving. To cook lasagna noodles that were firmed for 30 minutes in the fridge, place 8 noodles in each of 2 prepared baking dishes, pour 3 cups pasta sauce over and around and bake as above.

Welsh Rarebit (Rabbit)

YIELD: 4 servings

Ingredients:

2 eggs, slightly beaten
½ cup half-and-half or light cream
4 tablespoons butter
4 cups (16 ounces) cheddar cheese, shredded
1 tablespoon Worcestershire sauce
½ teaspoon dry mustard
dash cayenne pepper
2 English muffins, split, toasted, and buttered
Canadian bacon, 4 (½-inch thick) slices, warmed
4 (½-inch thick) slices tomato

Directions:

Since this is a quick cooking recipe, it's best to have all ingredients prepared before starting to cook. In a small bowl, combine eggs and cream, mix well, and set aside. In a 2-quart heavy saucepan over medium heat, melt butter. Add cheese, stirring constantly until cheese is melted. Stir in Worcestershire sauce, mustard, and cayenne. Remove from heat, stir in egg and cream mixture until well blended, then return to medium heat and cook until thickened, stirring constantly. To serve, place 1 warmed English muffin on each plate, top with a warmed slice of Canadian bacon, and a slice of tomato. Spoon ¾ cup sauce over each plate and serve with a small salad and bowl of sliced fresh fruit.

Maryanne's Moussaka

YIELD: 4–6 servings

Ingredients:

1 pound eggplant
4 small zucchinis
3 tablespoons salad oil
1 large onion, peeled and sliced
2 tablespoons fresh parsley, chopped
1 large (7 ounce) jar sliced mushrooms, drained
1 small (4 ounce) jar pimentos, drained
2 pounds ground round
1 teaspoon salt
1 teaspoon oregano
2 tablespoons red wine vinegar
1 small can tomato paste
tabasco sauce, to taste
1 can cheddar cheese soup
¼ cup Parmesan cheese, grated
Parmesan cheese, to garnish

Directions:

Preheat oven to 350°F. Wash and dry eggplant and zucchinis, remove stems, peel strips off and cut into quarters lengthwise, then into ¼-inch slices. In a large skillet, heat oil, add eggplant, zucchinis, onion, and parsley and cover and cook over medium heat 15 minutes or until tender. Stir in mushrooms and pimentos, remove from heat, drain off liquids, and reserve skillet ingredients into a large bowl. In the same skillet, sauté ground round until brown, then pour off fat and stir in salt, oregano, red wine vinegar, tomato paste, and tabasco. Cook while stirring about 3 minutes. In a small saucepan, heat cheese soup without diluting, stirring constantly until it comes to a boil. In a 2-quart, lightly greased casserole or large ovenproof baking pan, place a layer of veggies and then a layer of cooked meat mixture and repeat until all ingredients are layered in the casserole. Pour cheese soup evenly on top. Sprinkle Parmesan on top and bake uncovered for 30 minutes or until moussaka is nice and bubbly.

Mini Meatloaves

YIELD: 12 muffin-sized meatloaves

Ingredients:

vegetable oil, for greasing
2 pounds ground beef
1 medium onion, peeled and chopped into small pieces
2 celery ribs, cut into small pieces
1 green bell pepper, stemmed, deseeded, and finely chopped
1 large egg, beaten with a small amount of milk or water
1 cup bread crumbs
2 tablespoons grill seasoning mix
1 cup smoke-flavored barbecue sauce
½ cup tomato salsa
1 tablespoon Worcestershire sauce

Directions:

Preheat oven to 450°F. Brush a 12-muffin (½ cup each) tin with vegetable oil. In a large bowl, mix ground beef, onion, celery, and green pepper and mix well with your hands to combine ingredients. Add beaten egg, bread crumbs, and grill seasoning and mix well. In a small bowl, whisk together the BBQ sauce, salsa, and Worcestershire sauce and pour half this sauce mixture into the bowl with the meatloaf mixture; reserve the other half of the sauce. Mix all together again to combine all ingredients. Using an ice cream scoop or good-sized spoon, fill each muffin tin with meat mixture and top each little meatloaf with a spoonful of reserved sauce. Place muffin tin in oven and bake about 20 minutes, then cup 1 little meatloaf open to test for doneness. Pour off any grease, and then run a thin blade around meatloaves to easily remove from pan. Serve with mashed potatoes and green veggies.

Gravy-Smothered Hamburger Steak

YIELD: 8 servings

Ingredients:

1 pound ground beef
1 egg
¼ cup bread crumbs
1 teaspoon Worcestershire sauce
½ teaspoon onion powder
½ teaspoon garlic powder
⅛ teaspoon black pepper
½ teaspoon seasoned salt
1 tablespoon vegetable oil
1 cup thinly sliced onion
2 tablespoons flour
1 tablespoon cooking sherry
1 cup beef broth
½ teaspoon seasoned salt

Directions:

Mix together the ground beef, egg, bread crumbs, Worcestershire sauce, onion powder, garlic powder, pepper, and seasoned salt and form into 8 balls, then flatten into patties. Heat the oil over medium heat in a large skillet, add patties and onions and cook until the patties are brown, approximately 4 minutes per side. Remove patties, leaving onions in the pan, and place patties on a plate and keep warm while making the gravy. Sprinkle the flour over the onions and pan drippings, then stir the flour and drippings, loosening all of the bits of beef while stirring. Over medium heat, gradually mix in the sherry, beef broth, and seasoned salt and continue stirring while simmering, approximately 5 minutes, until the gravy thickens. Turn heat to low, return patties to the gravy, cover, and simmer for another 15 minutes. Serve alone or over rice or noodles.

Pina Colada Pork Chops

YIELD: 4 servings

Ingredients:

3 large limes, divided and juiced
4 thick boneless pork chops
½ cup canned coconut milk
salt, to taste
cayenne pepper, to taste
4 green onions, minced, to garnish
½ cup cilantro, minced, to garnish

Directions:

Juice limes one at a time into individual little bowls. Place pork chops in a large re-sealable bag, add lime juice, tightly seal, and marinate for 1 to 2 hours. When ready to cook, place marinated chops on a medium-hot grill and cook for 4 to 5 minutes per side. In the meantime, place coconut milk in a small saucepan over low heat so it does not boil, season with salt and cayenne, add juice of second lime, and cook for 5 minutes over low heat. When chops are thoroughly cooked, place on a large platter, spoon sauce over chops, and garnish with green onions and cilantro and any remaining sauce.

Next Watch Stew

YIELD: 4 servings

Ingredients:

1 can golden mushroom soup
1 can onion soup
2 pounds stew meat
1 can potatoes, whole or cut, drained
1 can carrots, drained
canned veggies, drained

Directions:

Preheat oven to 350°F. In a large, lightly greased casserole, mix all ingredients. Do not add salt or water. Bake on middle rack for 3 hours. Serve over rice in large bowls to the crew on the next watch.

Rosemary & Garlic Roasted Pork Loin

YIELD: 4–6 servings

Ingredients:

2 teaspoons fresh rosemary leaves or more to taste
2 teaspoons Kosher salt
5 cloves garlic
2 tablespoons olive oil
1 (4 pound) pork loin roast

Directions:

Preheat oven to 350°F. Mash or pulse rosemary, salt, garlic, and olive oil until a paste is formed.

Place roast on a wire rack on a baking sheet pan to catch all the juices with the fat cap side up. Spread rosemary and garlic paste over the roast and press into the meat to adhere. Place in oven and bake about 1 hour and 20 minutes, checking with a meat thermometer to show temperature at 145°F to 165°F. When ideal temperature is reached, remove from oven. Length of time depends on the weight and thickness of the roast, so watch that meat thermometer. Remove from oven and let rest 10 to 20 minutes before carving. Drizzle servings with pan juices.

Soufflé de Anything

YIELD: 4–6 servings

Ingredients:

1 large onion, peeled, sliced, and minced
4 tablespoons butter
¼ teaspoon garlic powder
½ teaspoon ginger
1 teaspoon nutmeg
pinch of salt
½ teaspoon pepper
few dashes Tabasco sauce, to taste
1 cup leftovers, meat, seafood, vegetables or any combination
1½ cups evaporated milk
3 tablespoons butter, melted
8 eggs, slightly beaten
1 cup flour
1 cup cheddar cheese, grated
Parmesan cheese, grated for topping

Directions:

Preheat oven to 325°F. In a large skillet over medium heat, sauté onions in butter until soft and transparent. Add garlic powder, ginger, nutmeg, salt, pepper, and Tabasco and mix well. Add the 1 cup of leftover ingredients, evaporated milk, melted butter, and eggs, then gently incorporate the flour a little bit at a time, then the cheddar cheese. Stir and cook over low heat for a couple of minutes until the mixture thickens. Pour soufflé mixture into a large 6-cup soufflé dish or similar baking dish that has been greased and floured. Lightly sprinkle optional Parmesan on top, if using. Place soufflé dish in a shallow pan with 1 inch of water and bake 50 to 60 minutes, or until it is done when tested with a knife inserted in the center that comes out clean.

Spinach-Stuffed Flank Steak

YIELD: 6 servings

Ingredients:

1 (1½–2 pounds) flank steak
1 (10 ounce) package frozen chopped spinach, thawed, and squeezed dry
4 ounces sun-dried tomatoes, finely chopped
4 ounces feta cheese, crumbled
2 tablespoons seasoned bread crumbs
2 tablespoons olive oil, divided
1 egg, lightly beaten
¾ teaspoon salt, divided
½ teaspoon pepper, divided

Directions:

Preheat oven to 425°F. Coat a rack with nonstick cooking spray and place it in a shallow pan. Open up flank steak on a good-sized work surface. Starting at a long side, slice steak halfway through as in filleting, but not cutting all the way through, so that you can open it like a book and flatten it out to an even thickness. Your flank steak should now be thinner and twice as big as when you placed it on the work surface. In a medium bowl, combine dry chopped spinach, sun-dried tomatoes, feta cheese, bread crumbs, 1 tablespoon oil, and beaten egg until well mixed. Season steak with ½ teaspoon salt and ¼ teaspoon pepper. Spoon spinach mixture into the center of the long side of steak from one end to the other and press it into the meat, leaving a 1-inch border on all sides. Starting at a short end, tightly roll steak up, shoving stuffing back in if it starts to slip out. Tie stuffed flank steak every 2 inches with cotton cooking twine and rub all over with remaining oil, salt, and pepper. Heat a large nonstick skillet over medium-high heat, gently place stuffed flank steak into hot pan, and brown on all sides for about 5 minutes. Carefully transfer stuffed flank steak to prepared rack, place on middle shelf of oven, and cook for 35 to 40 minutes or until an instant read thermometer registers 135°F. Remove meat from oven, tent with aluminum foil, and let rest 10 minutes before slicing. Any pan juices left in the roasting pan are really good lightly dribbled over sliced meat.

Stuffed Cabbage Rolls

YIELD: 12 rolls

Ingredients for cabbage rolls:

1 pound ground beef
¼ cup chopped onion
½–1 cup cooked white rice
2 tablespoons parsley, chopped
½ teaspoon salt
¼ teaspoon pepper
1 egg
1 large head of green cabbage

Ingredients for sauce:

1 cup canned tomatoes
½ cup lemon juice
1 cup tomato sauce
¾ cup brown sugar

Directions for cabbage rolls:

In a large skillet, cook ground beef until just beginning to brown, then add onion and cook until onion is slightly soft. Drain meat mixture and put in a large bowl. Add cooked rice, parsley, salt, pepper, and egg and mix well, then set aside. Cut core out of cabbage and gently pull leaves off, starting at the core end. You may have to use a small knife to separate each leaf from remaining core. Fill a large pot over medium-high heat with water and bring to a boil. Place cabbage leaves in water in batches and steam cabbage leaves only until soft enough to roll. Gently remove leaves as they soften, drain, and set aside. Place 1 tablespoon of meat mixture at the heart end of each cabbage leaf. Roll leaf up, tucking ends in to form a "package" and secure with a toothpick if necessary. Set rolls in a large pot with the sauce and simmer about 2 hours. Skim any fat off before serving.

Directions for sauce:

Place all ingredients in a large pot and combine well. Add prepared cabbage rolls to pot, bring to a simmer, and simmer about 2 hours.

Stuffed Meatloaf

YIELD: 6 servings

Ingredients:

2 pounds hamburger
1 teaspoon dry mustard
2 eggs, beaten
⅓ cup chili sauce
2 teaspoons salt, divided
1 (4 ounce) can sliced mushrooms
½ cup cheese, grated
⅛ teaspoon pepper
¼ teaspoon thyme

Directions:

Preheat oven to 325°F. In a large bowl, combine hamburger, dry mustard, beaten eggs, chili sauce, and 1½ teaspoons salt and mix well. Lightly grease a loaf pan and press ½ of the hamburger mixture into the pan. In a small bowl, combine sliced mushrooms, grated cheese, ½ teaspoon salt, pepper, and thyme and mix until well combined. Pack cheese mixture on top of meatloaf in the pan and then press remaining ½ meatloaf on top of cheese mixture. Place on middle rack of oven and cook 1½ to 2 hours.

Oyster-Stuffed Flank Steak

YIELD: 4–6 servings

Ingredients:

4 cups bread, torn into small pieces
⅓ cup butter, melted
¼ –½ cup onion, peeled, sliced, and minced
2 teaspoons salt
¼ teaspoon pepper
1 teaspoon sage
1 teaspoon dry mustard
1 teaspoon thyme
1 (8 ounce) can of oysters, drained
1 cup water, more or less, to moisten
1 large flank steak

Directions:

Preheat oven to 425°F. In a large bowl, gently mix all ingredients except water and flank steak. Add a little oyster juice to moisten stuffing. Mix well and let stand for 5 minutes. Stuffing should have a moist texture, so if it needs additional moistness, add a little water, mix, let stand, then check for proper consistency. In the meantime, prepare the flank steak for stuffing. There are two ways to prepare the flank steak depending on the thickness of the meat. For a thicker cut of steak, lay flank steak out on a work surface with the long side (the grain of the meat), lying left to right (parallel to the front edge of work surface) and the short side facing up and down on the work surface. With a very sharp boning knife, cut the steak open like a book, starting at the side closest to the edge of the work surface, but being very careful not to cut through the top edge. Use just the tip of your knife when you're close to the upper seam, cutting into the seam little by little, getting closer and closer to the edge until it's being held together only by the last ½ to ¼ inch or so. Pull open the meat, laying it out flat, and then gently pound the seam with the palm of your hand so that it forms a rectangular shape. It's now ready to stuff. The easier and good option for a thinner piece of flank steak is to lay it out the same as above and beat with a mallet to soften and shape flank steak more evenly. It's now ready to stuff if you're using the pounded method. Spoon the stuffing onto the steak, leaving a 1-inch border. Start rolling flank steak away from you, keeping it as tight as possible while trying to prevent stuffing from squeezing out the ends. Lay it seam-side down and grab a good length, 18 inches or so, of kitchen twine. Place twine on underside in the middle of the rolled steak and start rolling string around meat, tying about every 1½ inches from middle to left and then middle to right. If there is just too much stuffing to fit, it can be cooked for a short time alongside the flank steak in a small greased ramekin. Place steak on a baking pan, put on middle rack of oven, and cook for 1 hour or until done with a nice crust on top. If you have pan juices during cooking, baste the meat occasionally with them. To serve, let stand at room temperature for 10 to 15 minutes to assimilate juices back into meat, slice, and remove string before serving.

Stuffed Sweet Peppers From Bolongo Bay

YIELD: 4 servings

Ingredients for sweet pepper stuffing:

2 tablespoons olive oil
2 large garlic cloves, sliced and chopped fine
1 medium onion, sliced and chopped
1 pound ground round
4 sweet peppers, any color, tops cut off and
    reserved, deseeded, and cored
reserved sweet pepper tops, finely chopped
sprinkle of red pepper flakes (optional)
⅓ cup parsley, chopped
1–1½ cups dried Italian bread crumbs
1½ cups cooked rice
3–4 tablespoons grated Parmigiano-Reggiano
    cheese
¼ cup capers, rinsed and drained
1¼ teaspoons Kosher salt
black pepper, to taste

Ingredients for marinara sauce:

1 large clove of garlic, sliced and chopped fine
2 tablespoons olive oil
1 (28 ounce) can peeled Italian tomatoes
⅓ cup fresh basil, chopped
¼ cup fresh oregano, chopped
⅓ cup parsley, chopped
small dash red pepper flakes (optional)
Kosher salt, to taste
black pepper, to taste
Parmesan cheese, to garnish

Directions for sweet pepper stuffing:

Put olive oil in a large skillet over medium-high heat. Add garlic, onion, ground round, chopped pepper tops, and red pepper flakes, if using, and sauté for 4 minutes. Add parsley, remove pan from heat, spoon grease off and discard. Place bread crumbs and rice in a large bowl, scoop ground round ingredients from the skillet into the bowl, and mix well. Add cheese, capers, salt, and pepper and mix all ingredients well. Using a small spoon, stuff peppers with mixture, drizzle a very small amount of olive oil over the peppers, and reserve peppers while making sauce.

Directions for marinara sauce:

Preheat oven to 350°F. In a large skillet over medium-high heat, sauté garlic in olive oil just until soft. Be sure you don't burn the garlic. Add the tomatoes, basil, oregano, parsley, pepper flakes if using, salt, and pepper. Reduce heat and simmer 30 minutes. Scoop a little marinara sauce in the bottom of a very lightly oiled baking dish and place the stuffed peppers in the sauce, propping them up with toothpicks inserted in the sides if needed. Spoon each pepper with more marinara sauce and sprinkle Parmesan cheese over the tops. Pour any remaining sauce on the bottom of the pan all around the peppers and place in oven on middle rack. Bake uncovered for 1 hour or until a fork easily pierces the pepper skin. Check stuffed peppers after 30 minutes and if sauce is dry, add a little water. Let cool 5 minutes, then serve. Since there might be stuffing remaining, as peppers vary so much in size, freeze remaining stuffing and use to stuff mini peppers for hors d'oeuvres, or my favorite, add to chicken or beef broth for a delicious beef and rice soup.

Swedish Meatballs in Cream Sauce

YIELD: 6 servings

Ingredients for the meatballs:

1 pound ground beef
¼ cup onion, finely minced
¼ cup bread crumbs
¼ teaspoon allspice
¼ teaspoon nutmeg
½ teaspoon garlic powder
1 tablespoon parsley, chopped
1 egg
⅛ teaspoon pepper, to taste
½ teaspoon salt, to taste
1 tablespoon olive oil
1 tablespoon butter

Ingredients for the sauce:

4 tablespoons butter
3 tablespoons flour
2 cups beef broth
1 cup heavy cream
1 tablespoon Worcestershire sauce
1 tablespoon Dijon mustard
salt and pepper, to taste

Directions for the meatballs:

In a medium-sized bowl, combine ground beef, onion, bread crumbs, allspice, nutmeg, garlic powder, parsley, egg, pepper, and salt. Mix until combined. When thoroughly combined, roll mixture into 12 large, same size meatballs or divide into 20 smaller meatballs for cocktail size. Place 1 tablespoon olive oil and 1 tablespoon butter in a large skillet over medium-high heat. Add the meatballs and cook, turning continuously until meatballs are brown on both sides and thoroughly cooked. Transfer meatballs to a plate and cover with foil to keep warm.

Directions for the sauce:

Add butter and flour to the skillet and cook while continuously whisking until mixture turns brown. Slowly stir in beef broth and heavy cream. Add Worcestershire sauce and Dijon mustard and bring to a simmer until sauce starts to thicken. Continue to whisk, add salt and pepper, taste, and adjust seasonings. Add the meatballs back to the skillet and simmer for another 1 to 2 minutes. Serve over noodles or rice as an entrée.

Teriyaki Spareribs

YIELD: 4 servings

Ingredients for spareribs:

4 pounds (2 racks) spareribs
1 cup chicken stock
½ cup soy sauce
½ cup honey
½ cup white vinegar
2 large garlic cloves, sliced and minced
1 tablespoon fresh ginger, grated
Chinese dipping sauces, to serve

Ingredients for parboiling:

1 medium onion, peeled and quartered
2–3 cloves
1 bay leaf
1 celery top
1 teaspoon dried thyme
dash salt
¼ teaspoon black pepper

Directions for spareribs:

Preheat grill when ready to cook. Remove backbone from rib racks and have butcher saw racks horizontally into 2 portions to give you about 3-inch wide racks. It's a bit messy, but you can saw these ribs in half with a hack saw. It's best to do it ahead of time and freeze the ribs until you decide a nice rib dinner is just what you want. Lay the slabs of baby back ribs on a cutting board and with a knife with a sharp blade such as a boning knife, cut the ribs into smaller slabs of three to four ribs. Place the ribs into a large pot of cold water, enough that the ribs are covered. Add parboiling ingredients to the pot, bring the water to a boil, then reduce to a simmer. Cook ribs until they are tender, about 40 to 45 minutes until the pink and red color of the outer layers of the raw ribs have turned a light brown. Using tongs, remove the ribs from the pot, place them on a baking sheet, and let cool. Make a marinade by combining remaining ingredients for spareribs, except for Chinese dipping sauce. Place cooled ribs in a large re-sealable bag, spoon marinade over ribs, seal tightly, and massage marinade into ribs. Refrigerate 4 hours or overnight, massaging marinade into ribs occasionally. Preheat grill (or lace 3 ribs on spit) and grill about 45 minutes, basting frequently until they are done and have a nice brown crust. To serve, place on a large platter surrounded by Chinese dipping sauces of your choice, BBQ sauce, or a small bowl of each.

Chinese Dipping Sauces

Ingredients for Chinese mustard sauce:

¼ cup boiling water
¼ cup dry mustard
2 teaspoons vegetable oil
½ teaspoon salt

Ingredients for Chinese red sauce:

3 tablespoons ketchup
3 tablespoons chili sauce
1–2 tablespoons horseradish, not the cream style
1 teaspoon fresh lemon juice
dash of hot pepper sauce, to taste

Ingredients for Chinese plum sauce:

1 cup plum preserves
⅓ cup dry sherry
½ teaspoon ground cloves
½ teaspoon ground anise
½ teaspoon ground fennel
½ cup (1 small can) dry mustard

Directions for Chinese mustard sauce:

In a small bowl, place dry mustard and add boiling water and mix well. Whisk in oil and salt.

Directions for Chinese red sauce:

Combine all ingredients in a small bowl and whisk to mix well.

Directions for Chinese plum sauce:

In a blender or with an electric mixer, combine all ingredients except mustard and mix well. Add a little mustard, a small amount at a time, blending well until sauce is hot and spicy to your liking.

CHAPTER 13
Pasta & Rice

Almond Rice Pilaf

YIELD: 4 servings

Ingredients:

2½ tablespoons butter, divided
1 cup white rice
2¼ cups chicken stock
⅛ teaspoon salt
⅓ cup almonds, sliced or slivered
¼ cup celery, diced
¼ cup onion, diced

Directions:

In a medium saucepan with a lid, melt 2 tablespoons butter over medium heat, then add rice and sauté for 3 to 5 minutes, until some of it begins to turn light brown. While the rice is cooking, heat chicken stock to a boil, then quickly add the hot chicken stock and salt to the saucepan. Cover the saucepan with the lid, reduce heat to low, and simmer for 20 minutes. As the rice mixture is cooking in a medium skillet over medium heat, sauté almonds until they are a golden brown. When rice mixture has finished cooking, remove from the heat, add almonds, celery, and onion, put lid back on, and let it sit 5 minutes or until all the liquid has been absorbed and you have a nice fluffy pilaf.

Deborah's Story

When Stanley and I were day chartering out of the Sea Cliff hotel on Water Island, USVI along with our other charter guests, we welcomed a single lady named Deborah. Stanley had met Deborah the previous day as they were on the same small hotel ferry from Sub Base to Water Island. Deborah had rented one of the beautiful Sea Cliff Villas during the Christmas holiday season and was returning from purchasing her groceries for the week. Though the hotel had a first-class restaurant, Deborah said she loved to cook, so we were invited to dinner a few days later and confirmed that she was a first class cook for sure. Years later we still laugh about Stanley saying to Deborah within the first five minutes of meeting her, "Oh you have to meet my wife, Sylvia, you're exactly the same." Within the first half hour of our leaving the hotel dock with our charter guests that morning, Deborah was at the helm of *Native Sun* delighting us with her stories, her sailing abilities, and her immediate friendship toward us and my father, who was spending the holidays with us. Deborah and I knew we were definitely "sisters" for life.

During our chartering years, Stanley and I spent our summers at an old family cabin deep in the Canadian Bush five hundred miles north of Seattle. The summer following our week with Deborah in the Caribbean, we invited her and her boyfriend Bob to come up to this very special but extremely rustic cabin. Coming from Philadelphia, neither Bob nor Deborah had any idea of how far removed we were from civilization, but they came prepared, except for the ingredients they would need to make the wonderful food they planned to cook over the next week. We have neither electricity nor running water in the cabin, and the grocery store is an all-day trek away. Going to a grocery store involves an eight-mile boat ride down lake, then a twenty-mile ride in a jeep over meadows and on logging roads, and an additional twenty miles down the highway to a small village called 100 Mile House, B.C., Canada. Within a day or so of their arrival at the cabin, the decision was made and agreed upon that they would have Stanley take them to town and acquire groceries for Bob and Deborah's much anticipated Italian cooking, something we had not thought about until they started talking about all the different food they loved to cook.

As it turned out, over the years we have always said they were the best guests in every way that we ever had at our cabin. The fabulous food they prepared during their visit is still a topic of conversation at the cabin, and in the years since, we are still honored to be guests at their Florida home where we are served the most delicious dinners. When we leave, our car is packed with containers of sauces, pasta, and even desserts to bring home. One of our most favorite sauces is the Bolognese sauce that they make, and following is the recipe they shared with us, which we know will be a favorite of yours. Deborah was raised on the Eastern shore of the Chesapeake Bay and makes the most fantastic crab cakes. Don't miss them on page 320.

Casa Pietrangelo Bolognese Sauce

YIELD: 20–24 cups

Ingredients:

olive oil
3 pounds lean ground round or pork sausage
1 large head fresh garlic, cloves peeled, sliced, and finely chopped
Italian seasoning, to taste
3 (28 ounce) cans Italian crushed tomatoes
1 large can, drained or 1–2 cups fresh mushrooms, sliced
3 cups red wine
hot red pepper sauce, to taste
2 small cans Italian tomato paste
salt, to taste
pepper, to taste

Directions:

In a deep saucepan, pour in ¼-inch of olive oil and add the ground round or pork sausage, breaking it up as it cooks. Constantly stir and make sure the meat is well broken up. Add some of the prepared garlic and Italian seasoning. When meat is brown, add crushed tomatoes, stirring occasionally, and bring to a simmer. Add the mushrooms, red wine, red pepper sauce, and remaining garlic and continue to simmer with a lid lightly open to reduce fluid. Add tomato paste, salt, and pepper and continue to simmer with occasional stirring for 1 hour, making sure it doesn't stick to the bottom of the pot. Taste, adjust seasonings, and refrigerate when cool for at least 24 hours to blend flavors. Use what you need for dinner and freeze the rest for a future delicious dinner.

Avocado Cilantro Lime Rice

YIELD: 4–6 servings

Ingredients:

4–5 cups rice, cooked
1 clove garlic, minced (optional)
½ white onion, minced (optional)
1 jalapeño, stemmed, deseeded, and chopped (optional)
oil for sautéing (optional)
2 avocados, peeled and pitted
2 tablespoons fresh lime juice
¼ cup fresh cilantro, chopped
¼ teaspoon plus ⅛ teaspoon ground cumin
salt and pepper, to taste

Directions:

Cook rice according to directions and set aside in a large bowl. If you're using the optional garlic, onion, and jalapeño, place them in a medium sauté pan with a small amount of oil and cook until just tender. Add to rice. In a large mixing bowl, mash avocados and stir in lime juice, cilantro, cumin, salt, and pepper until fairly smooth and well blended. Add avocado mixture to the warm cooked rice, stirring well. Press warm rice into a cup or medium ramekin, then turn upside down and plate it or dish up from the large rice bowl.

Linguini Carbonara

YIELD: 4–6 servings

Ingredients:

1 pound linguini
2 tablespoons reserved pasta cooking water
2 eggs
1 tablespoon milk
3 tablespoons olive oil
3–4 large garlic cloves, minced
1 cup peas, frozen, fresh, or canned
½ teaspoon red pepper flakes
1 cup cooked bacon or pancetta, crumbled
½ cup Parmesan cheese, crumbled
2 tablespoons parsley, chopped
salt and pepper, to taste

Directions:

Bring a large pot of water to a rolling boil; add linguini and cook according to package instructions. Drain the linguini, reserving a little of the pasta water to add to the egg mixture, set linguini aside. Beat eggs with 1 tablespoon milk and reserved 2 tablespoons pasta water and set aside. In a large pot, heat olive oil, add the garlic and peas, and cook on low heat until garlic is translucent. Toss in the red pepper flakes, then the cooked linguine. Gently add bacon or pancetta and the egg mixture the egg mixture, and white wine while tossing gently. Turn heat off and add cheese, parsley, and salt and pepper to taste. Gently toss and serve on warm plates or in pasta bowls.

Chicken & Broccoli Alfredo

YIELD: 4 servings

Ingredients:

½ (16 ounce) package linguine
1 cup broccoli florets, fresh or frozen
2 tablespoons butter
1 pound skinless, boneless chicken breasts, cut into 1½-inch pieces
1 (10¾ ounce) can cream of mushroom soup
½ cup milk
½ cup Parmesan cheese, grated plus extra for garnish
¼ teaspoon ground black pepper

Directions:

Prepare linguine according to package directions in a large saucepan. Add broccoli the last 4 minutes of cooking time, being sure not to overcook broccoli. Drain linguine and broccoli well in colander. In a large skillet over medium-high heat, melt butter and add chicken pieces, stirring often, and cook until well browned. Stir soup, milk, Parmesan, black pepper, and cooked linguine with broccoli in the skillet mixture with the chicken. Cook until mixture is hot and bubbling. Serve with additional Parmesan for garnish.

Coconut Rice

YIELD: 6 servings

Ingredients:

1 cup white rice
1 jalapeño pepper, stemmed, halved
    lengthwise, seeds and membrane scraped
    out
1 (12 ounce) can frozen coconut milk,
    defrosted
½ cup water
¾ teaspoon salt
1 teaspoon lime zest
2 tablespoons fresh lime juice
2 small green onions, minced
1 fresh lime, cut into 6 wedges

Directions:

In a large 2-quart saucepan, combine rice, jalapeño, coconut milk, water, salt and lime zest. Bring to a boil and continue cooking at a low boil for 3 minutes while stirring well. Cover the pan, reduce heat to low, and cook for 15 minutes. Remove from heat and let stand, covered, for 5 minutes. Stir in lime juice and green onions and plate with lime wedges on the side. Squeeze fresh lime juice over rice.

Creamy Risotto

YIELD: 6–8 servings

Ingredients:

2 tablespoons butter
2 tablespoons shallots, minced
1 cup Arborio rice
3 cups chicken stock, divided
1 cup heavy cream
3 tablespoons Parmesan cheese
salt and pepper, to taste

Directions:

In a medium-sized braising pan or high-sided skillet, melt butter over medium heat, add shallots and cook until shallots are golden brown, about 10 minutes. Add rice and cook for 2 minutes, stirring frequently. Slowly add ¼ cup chicken stock and stir until it is completely absorbed, then add 2¾ cups of chicken stock ¼ cup at a time, stirring continuously with a smooth, gentle motion (preferably with a wooden spoon) until the liquid is completely absorbed before adding more. When all the stock has been completely absorbed, add the heavy cream and Parmesan cheese and stir in gently. This delicious risotto will take about 40 to 50 minutes to cook and must be stirred frequently. Season with salt and pepper to taste.

Garlic Rice

YIELD: 4 servings

Ingredients:

4 tablespoons oil
3–4 cloves garlic, minced
1 cup rice, uncooked
2 cups water
1½ teaspoons salt

Directions:

In a medium saucepan, warm oil. Add garlic and cook until garlic becomes translucent. Add the rice and mix well to coat rice in oil and garlic. Add water and salt and stir well to mix. Bring to a boil. Once water is boiling, turn heat to low and cover. Cook until water is gone, about 12 to 15 minutes. Fluff with a fork before serving. To serve, press warm rice into a cup or medium ramekin, then turn upside down and plate it, or dish up from a large rice bowl.

Lemon & Garlic Fettucini

YIELD: 4 servings

Ingredients:

8 ounces fettucine or enough to serve 4
1 large lemon, grated for zest and juiced for minimum of 2 tablespoons lemon juice
3–5 large garlic cloves, peeled, sliced, and finely minced
4 tablespoons olive oil, divided

Directions:

In a large saucepan, bring 3 quarts of water to a boil, then reduce heat to simmer until you're ready to add the fettucine. Place fettucine in the boiling water in the large saucepan, then reduce to medium heat and cook fettucine 9 minutes to al dente, still slightly firm. Grate lemon with a fine grater and place in small saucepan. Cut the lemon in half, remove seeds, and squeeze juice out, then run a spoon inside of lemon to catch pulp and add in with lemon juice to the saucepan. Add finely minced garlic and 1 tablespoon olive oil. When the pasta is cooked, reserve ½ cup cooking water, then drain the pasta. Place drained pasta back into the pot, add the ½ cup reserved pasta cooking water, then add the warm lemon and garlic mixture in the small saucepan and lightly toss to coat pasta.

Marsh Harbor Peas 'N Rice

YIELD: *8 servings*

Ingredients:

2–3 slices bacon, cut into ½-inch pieces
1 large onion, chopped
½ cup green pepper, chopped
2 cups rice, preferably long grain
1 can stewed tomatoes
2 bay leaves
1 teaspoon thyme
1 teaspoon oregano
salt and pepper, to taste
1½ cups boiled or canned pigeon peas or black-eyed peas
1 pound conch marinated in lemon juice, chopped or cut into strips
1 pound shrimp, shelled and deveined
sausage, sautéed and broken into pieces, to taste (optional)

Directions:

Fry bacon pieces to a tender consistency, reserving 3 tablespoons of bacon drippings. Add onion and sauté until translucent, then add peppers and cook until soft. Add rice and stir until rice is covered with bacon drippings and slightly cooked. Add tomatoes plus juice, herbs, and seasonings. Add enough water to cover rice and bring to boil, then lower to simmer and cover. Cook for 15 minutes. Add peas, conch, shrimp, and sausage if using. Stir well, cover, and continue simmering for another 10 minutes. Check rice. Continue cooking until water is absorbed. Adjust seasonings. Serve as main course or as a side to cracked conch.

Mexican Rice

YIELD: 6 servings

Ingredients:

1 tablespoon olive oil
2 cloves garlic, minced
1 onion, diced
1½ cups basmati rice, uncooked
1 (8 ounce) can tomato sauce
1½ cups vegetable broth
1 cup corn kernels
½ cup diced carrots
½ cup frozen peas
¼ teaspoon chili powder
¼ teaspoon cumin
1 can black beans, rinsed (optional)
Kosher salt and freshly ground black pepper, to taste
2 Roma tomatoes, diced
2 tablespoons fresh cilantro leaves, chopped

Directions:

Heat olive oil in a large skillet over medium heat. Add garlic and onion and cook, stirring frequently until onions have become translucent, about 2 to 3 minutes. Stir in rice until toasted, about 2 minutes. Stir in tomato sauce and vegetable broth and bring to a simmer, about 2 minutes. Stir in corn, carrots, peas, chili powder, cumin, and black beans if using; season with salt and pepper, to taste. Bring to a boil; cover, reduce heat, and simmer until rice is cooked through, about 13 to 16 minutes. Stir in tomatoes. To serve, press warm rice into a cup or medium ramekin, then turn upside down and plate it, or dish up from a large rice bowl. Garnish with fresh cilantro, if desired.

Caribbean Red Beans & Rice

YIELD: 4 servings

Ingredients:

⅔ cup white rice
1⅓ cup water
1 tablespoon butter or margarine
1 (15 ounce) can kidney beans, drained and
   rinsed well
1 medium green pepper, stemmed and
   chopped
1 large clove garlic, peeled, sliced, and minced
salt, to taste

Directions:

Combine rice, water, and butter or margarine in a 1½-quart casserole dish. Cover and microwave on high for 5 minutes. Remove from microwave, add kidney beans, green pepper, and garlic. Cover and microwave on medium for 12 minutes or until liquid is absorbed. Let stand 5 minutes, salt to taste, and serve.

Stanley's Favorite Vodka Cream Pasta

YIELD: 2 servings

Ingredients:

½ tablespoon olive oil
½ tablespoon butter
2 cloves garlic, peeled, sliced, and minced
1 large shallot, peeled, sliced, and minced
½ cup vodka
½ cup chicken stock
1 (14½ ounce) can diced tomatoes
salt and pepper, to taste
¼ cup heavy cream
10 fresh basil leaves, shredded or torn

Directions:

Place olive oil, butter, garlic, and shallot in a large skillet over medium heat and gently sauté for 3 to 5 minutes. Add vodka to the pan and cook about 2 to 3 minutes to reduce by half. Add stock and tomatoes and bring sauce to a full bubble, then reduce heat to simmer. Season with salt and pepper and simmer about 10 minutes. Stir cream into the sauce and when it returns to a bubble, remove from heat. Dish up your favorite pasta and toss the hot pasta with the vodka sauce topped with fresh basil.

Olive Parmesan Fettuccine

YIELD: 4 servings

Ingredients:

1 (6 ounce) can pitted black olives, drained
¼ cup olive oil
4–5 teaspoons lemon juice
3 cloves garlic, peeled, sliced, and minced
½ cup Parmesan cheese, shredded plus extra
   to garnish
½ cup fresh basil leaves, finely chopped
1 (9 ounce) package fettuccine, cooked
   according to directions, drained

Directions:

In a food processor or blender, place olives, olive oil, lemon juice, and garlic and coarsely purée. Scoop into a medium-sized bowl, add cheese and basil, and mix well. Toss with hot fettuccine and more Parmesan if desired.

Pasta With Cherry Tomatoes, Basil, Lemon & Clams

YIELD: 4 servings

Ingredients:

12 ounces spaghetti, linguini, or fettucine
¼ cup olive oil
3 large garlic cloves, peeled, sliced, and minced
1 pound cherry tomatoes, halved
3 (6 ounce) cans chopped clams, drained, and
   juices reserved
½ cup fresh basil, thinly sliced
1 cup Parmesan cheese, grated plus extra to
   garnish
¼ cup fresh lemon juice
salt and pepper, to taste

Directions:

Cook pasta a minute or two less than package directions, until just tender but still firm to bite.

Drain pasta and return to same cooking pot. While pasta is cooking, make clam sauce by first heating olive oil in a large skillet over medium-high heat. Add garlic and sauté about 2 minutes until garlic releases its fragrance, then add tomatoes and sauté until they begin to soften, about 5 minutes. Add drained clams and basil and stir while cooking 1 minute. In the pasta pan with the drained pasta, add clam sauce, 1 cup Parmesan, and lemon juice and toss over medium-high heat until heated through, adding reserved clam juice in ¼ cup measurements if pasta is too dry. Season with salt and pepper, taste, and adjust seasonings. Garnish with additional Parmesan and serve.

Ravioli with Sage Butter

YIELD: *6 servings*

Ingredients:

2 (9 ounce) packages refrigerated or frozen ravioli
1 tablespoon olive oil
12–15 fresh sage leaves plus 2 tablespoons sage, coarsely chopped
6 tablespoons butter
½ teaspoon fresh thyme, chopped
½ teaspoon salt
¼ teaspoon pepper
2 tablespoons parsley, chopped

Directions:

Cook ravioli following package directions and drain when cooked. In the meantime, heat olive oil in medium-sized skillet over high heat; add sage leaves and fry about 1 minute on each side or until lightly crisped. Transfer fried sage to paper towels to drain. In the same skillet, melt butter over medium-high heat until butter has browned slightly. Stir in 2 tablespoons chopped sage, thyme, salt, and pepper. Place drained ravioli on a large serving platter, pour sage butter over top, and sprinkle with chopped parsley. Garnish with reserved fried sage leaves and serve immediately.

Sausage-Stuffed Manicotti

YIELD: 6–8 servings

Ingredients:

14 manicotti shells, uncooked
1 pound pork sausage
1 pound ground beef
1 teaspoon Italian seasoning
1 teaspoon nutmeg
1 teaspoon fennel (optional)
4 large garlic cloves, peeled, sliced, and minced
1 medium onion, peeled, sliced, and minced
2 cups (8 ounces) mozzarella cheese, shredded
1 (3 ounce) package cream cheese, chopped into small cubes
¼ teaspoon salt
pepper, to taste
6 cups meatless spaghetti sauce, divided
¼ cup Parmesan cheese, grated

Directions:

Preheat oven to 350°F. Cook manicotti shells according to package directions. In the meantime, cook sausage and ground beef in a large skillet over medium heat until meat is no longer pink. Add Italian seasoning, nutmeg, and fennel if using. Add garlic and onion, cook 1 minute longer, drain fat, and remove skillet from heat. Let cool for 10 minutes. Drain shells and rinse in cold water. When meat mixture has cooled, stir in mozzarella cheese, cream cheese, salt, and pepper. Pour 2 cups of meatless spaghetti sauce in a greased 13 x 9-inch baking dish. With narrow spoon, stuff each shell with about ¼ cup meat mixture and arrange evenly over spaghetti sauce. Pour remaining 4 cups of spaghetti sauce, sprinkle top with Parmesan cheese, cover with foil, and bake for 40 minutes, then remove foil cover and bake 5 to 10 minutes longer until bubbly and heated through. To freeze manicotti, cover and freeze uncooked casserole. To bake, thaw partially in refrigerator overnight and then remove from refrigerator 30 minutes before baking. Bake according to directions but insert an instant read thermometer in the center of casserole and cook until it reads 165°F.

T's Extreme St. Croix Mac 'N Cheese

YIELD: 6 servings

Ingredients:

1 pound elbow macaroni, cooked
1 cup butter, cut into small pieces
½ pound Colby cheese, shredded
½ pound Monterey Jack cheese, shredded
½ pound sharp cheddar cheese, shredded
1 pound Velveeta cheese, cut in chunks
1 cup whole milk
2 (12 ounce) cans evaporated milk
3 eggs
salt, to taste
1 tablespoon white or black pepper
1 tablespoon sugar
1 cup American cheese, shredded

Directions:

Preheat oven to 350°F. Lightly oil a 9 x 13-inch dish and add cooked macaroni. Add the butter, Colby, Monterey Jack, sharp cheddar, and Velveeta cheeses evenly to the pasta. In a separate bowl combine whole milk and evaporated milk. Blend eggs into milk mixture until well blended and pour over the macaroni. Season with salt, pepper, and sugar and toss to combine. Sprinkle remaining shredded American cheese evenly over the top and bake for 30 to 45 minutes or until top is lightly browned.

Tuna, Capers & Olive Linguine

YIELD: 6 servings

Ingredients:

1 pound linguine
¼ cup olive oil
2 cloves garlic, peeled, sliced, and chopped
1½ tablespoons capers, chopped
½ cup pitted black olives, finely chopped
4 tablespoons parsley, chopped
salt and pepper, to taste
1 small can tuna fish, drained and flaked

Directions:

Cook linguine according to package instructions. While it's cooking, place olive oil in a large skillet and sauté garlic, capers, and olives. Add in some reserved pasta water, then add the parsley and salt and pepper to taste and cook a few minutes longer. Remove from heat and stir in the flaked tuna. Drain the pasta and dish it up with hot tuna sauce on top.

CHAPTER 14
Salads & Dressings

Aunt B's Tomato Aspic

YIELD: 8 servings

Ingredients:

3 cups tomato juice, divided
2 tablespoons gelatin
2 tablespoons apple cider vinegar
½ teaspoon celery seed
½ teaspoon Worcestershire sauce
2 tablespoons onion, grated
black pepper, generous amount

Directions:

In a medium saucepan add 1 cup of tomato juice, sprinkle gelatin on top, and let stand until soft. Heat tomato-gelatin mixture on medium heat, stirring often until melted. Add remaining tomato juice and all other ingredients, stir well, and scoop everything into a medium-sized bowl or square pan and refrigerate to firm up. To serve, scoop out or cut into squares and place on a plate with a little lettuce. Especially good if topped with garlic mayo!

Balsamic Vinaigrette Dressing

YIELD: ½ cup

Ingredients:

2 tablespoons balsamic vinegar
1 tablespoon red wine vinegar
1 tablespoon Dijon mustard
1 teaspoon light brown sugar
1 large garlic clove, peeled, sliced, and minced
½ teaspoon salt
¼ teaspoon black pepper
¼ cup olive oil

Directions:

In a small bowl, combine all ingredients except oil. Whisk and mix well, then slowly add the oil while mixing well. Cover and chill.

Best Creamy Caesar Salad Dressing

YIELD: 6–8 servings

Ingredients:

3 cloves garlic, peeled, sliced, and minced
¾ cup mayonnaise
2 teaspoons anchovy paste or more to taste
2 rounded tablespoons Parmesan cheese, grated
1 teaspoon Worcestershire sauce
1 teaspoon Dijon mustard
1 tablespoon fresh lemon juice
Kosher salt and freshly ground black pepper, to taste

Directions:

In a bowl, combine the garlic, mayo, anchovy paste, Parmesan, Worcestershire sauce, mustard, and lemon juice. Whisk to combine well. Add salt and fresh ground pepper, taste, and adjust seasonings. Put in refrigerator and chill.

Blue Cheese Dressing

YIELD: 1½ cups

Ingredients:

1 cup vegetable oil
1 teaspoon sugar
1 teaspoon salt
2 teaspoons paprika
3 tablespoons lemon juice
4 ounces blue cheese
½ onion, minced

Directions:

Combine all ingredients in a bowl and beat well, preferably with an electric mixer. Place in a container with tightly fitting lid and refrigerate.

Brazilian Black Bean Salad

YIELD: 6 servings

Ingredients:

1–2 tablespoons jalapeño, stemmed, sliced, and minced
⅓ cup vegetable oil
¼ cup fresh lime juice
3 tablespoons fresh cilantro, chopped
1 large garlic clove, peeled, sliced, and minced
½ teaspoon ground cumin (optional)
½ teaspoon salt
1 (16 ounce) can black beans, drained and rinsed
½ cup red onion, chopped
½ cup sweet red pepper, chopped
½ cup sweet yellow pepper, chopped
fresh lemon, sliced, for garnish

Directions:

In a large lidded bowl or container, combine jalapeño, oil, lime juice, cilantro, garlic, cumin, and salt. Mix well and add beans, red onion, and peppers and toss to coat well. Taste and adjust lime and salt if necessary. Cover and refrigerate overnight to meld all the flavors. Serve with slices of fresh lemon if using.

Caesar Salad Dressing à la "Tabasco"

One afternoon in Annapolis, we pulled up to the fuel dock just behind a large red boat named Tabasco. *We heard a "Yoo-hoo, do you need help tying up?" As soon as we tied up, I stepped off the dock to thank the nice blonde lady who had offered help. Her name was Beverly and she was the cook on the private yacht owned by a member of the McIlhenny family, creators of the famous Tabasco Sauce. As happens with most boaters when they meet, friendships bloom rapidly, so within the next 20 minutes we were invited as guests for dinner aboard* Tabasco *that evening. Beverly made a Caesar salad dressing that had all of us asking for the recipe, and it is still one of my favorite Caesar dressings, though it seems to change each time depending on the size of the lemons, etc. Each time I make this dressing, I continue to taste and adjust ingredients, sometimes using 2 cans of anchovies and 2 juiced lemons, but always with a lot of garlic.*

YIELD: 1 quart-sized jar

Ingredients:

1 egg, room temperature and coddled
3–4 garlic cloves, peeled, sliced, minced, and
    smashed
¼ teaspoon ground oregano or more to taste
½ teaspoon dry mustard or enough to
    emulsify the dressing when the bottle is
    shaken
2 tablespoons Worcestershire sauce
fresh ground pepper, to taste
1–2 cans anchovies with oil, smashed, and
    chopped
¼–½ cup Parmesan cheese, grated
1–2 lemons, juiced
olive oil, to fill quart jar ¾ full

Directions:

In microwave in a large coffee cup, heat enough water to boiling to cover 1 egg in the shell. When water is boiling, remove from microwave and carefully and slowly lower egg into hot water. Let sit while making remainder of dressing so it will be coddled by the time you're ready to make the salad. In a small bowl, add smashed garlic, oregano, dry mustard, Worcestershire, and pepper and mix well. Carefully open anchovies, add the oil to the bowl, remove the anchovies, and on a cutting board chop them as finely as you can, then smash with the wide side of a knife blade and add them to the bowl. Add Parmesan and lemon juice and whisk all ingredients well. Using a rubber spatula, scoop the bowl ingredients into a quart jar, screw the lid on tightly, shake, then taste and adjust flavors to your liking. Wash romaine, tear into pieces, and wrap in a clean dish towel or paper towels to dry. Just before dressing your salad, crack coddled egg with a spoon and make sure the whole egg is scooped into the dressing jar, whisk to combine, replace lid, and shake hard.

Captain Charlie's Vinaigrette

When making vinaigrettes, I find the proportions should be 2 parts vinegar to 4 parts oil, or 1 part vinegar to 2 parts oil if you're making a smaller amount. This is a nice ratio, and doesn't make your dressing too oily or too tart. The dry mustard in vinaigrettes creates a nice emulsion which keeps your ingredients from separating. I adjust the amount of garlic*, dry mustard, and pepper almost every time I make vinaigrette as different brands of oil or the size and type of garlic tend to vary the outcome slightly. After you've minced your garlic, sprinkle it with the salt listed in the dressing ingredients. Let it sit a couple of moments, then smash the garlic. I have great results doing this with a mortar and pestle, but you can do it with a knife blade as well. If you're using a knife blade, after you've smashed it, start chopping, scooping into a little pile, and chop again. The salt breaks down the fiber in the garlic and you'll end up with a nice mushy garlic, which infuses its flavor into the oil while also making a nice blended vinaigrette without the shock of a slice of garlic in your salad.

YIELD: ⅓ cup

Ingredients:

2–3 cloves garlic, peeled, sliced, and minced
½ teaspoon salt
2–3 green onions, sliced
¾ teaspoon paprika
¾ teaspoon dry mustard
13 twists of fresh ground pepper
2 tablespoons vinegar
1 tablespoon olive oil
3 tablespoons cooking oil

Directions:

Mince the garlic cloves, sprinkle with the salt, smash to a nice paste, and put in a bowl. Slice green onions and add to the bowl, then add paprika, dry mustard, and pepper. Add vinegar and slowly blend in the olive and cooking oil. Charlie used a variety of vinegars, sometimes white, sometimes apple cider, sometimes malt, and my favorite of his dressings was made with red wine vinegar. Experiment with these vinegars and I promise, one will stand out. Stir to blend. Now, you can either simply add your washed and torn lettuce to this bowl and toss with the dressing and you're ready to serve, or, as I most often do, double the recipe and keep in an airtight bottle, then shake and spoon out what you need and refrigerate the rest.

---

* Most of my garlic is the fine garlic that comes from Joe's Garden in Bellingham, Washington. In the Veggies (pg. 354) chapter, there is a story about Joe's Garden and the award-winning garlic they grow there, along with details on how you can have this fabulous garlic shipped to you.

Captain Charlie's Malt Vineger Potato Salad

YIELD: ⅓ cup

Ingredients:

5 medium-sized potatoes
1 teaspoon salt plus more to taste
1 large onion, peeled and sliced
1 garlic clove, peeled, sliced, and minced
¼ teaspoon pepper
¾ teaspoon dry mustard
¾ teaspoon paprika
⅛ cup malt vinegar
1 bunch of parsley, lightly chopped
¼ cup cooking or corn oil

Directions:

Scrub potatoes, place in a large pot, and cover with 1 inch of cold water. Bring to boil over high heat. Add 1 teaspoon salt and boil 12 to 20 minutes until potatoes are fork-tender and firm but not mushy or falling apart. Drain the potatoes and allow to slightly cool just enough that they're easy to handle. Peel and cut potatoes into ¼-inch slices and place in a large bowl. Add the sliced onion. While the potatoes are boiling, make the dressing by first mincing the garlic cloves; sprinkle with salt to taste, smash to a nice paste, and place in a separate bowl. Add pepper, dry mustard, paprika, and vinegar, reserving the chopped parsley and oil for later. Blend well. Pour dressing over potatoes and onions while gently stirring so you don't break up the potatoes until they're well coated. Cover bowl with plastic wrap and let marinate for about 30 minutes at room temperature, then add chopped parsley and oil and mix gently. Serve with a slotted spoon if there is too much liquid at the bottom. Serve immediately or cover and refrigerate overnight and let it come to room temperature before serving.

Captain Charlie's German Potato Salad

YIELD: ⅓ cup

Ingredients:

2 pounds small Yukon Gold (or yellow) potatoes
1½ teaspoons salt, divided, plus more to taste
¾ cup beef broth or stock, heated until very warm
1 cup yellow onion, peeled, sliced, and minced
¼ cup white wine vinegar
freshly ground black pepper
3 tablespoons vegetable oil
fresh parsley, finely chopped

Directions:

Scrub the potatoes and place in a large pot covered with 1 inch of cold water. Set over high heat and bring to a boil. Add 1 teaspoon salt and boil until potatoes are tender but not overcooked, about 12 to 20 minutes depending on the size of the potatoes. Drain the potatoes and allow to slightly cool. When just cool enough to handle, peel them with a small paring knife and cut into ¼-inch slices. Place the potato slices in a large bowl and pour the warm beef broth over the top. Top with the minced onion and white wine vinegar. Season with the remaining salt and freshly ground black pepper, to taste. Use a large spoon to gently stir until all of the potatoes until coated. Cover the bowl with plastic wrap and allow to marinate at room temperature for 30 minutes. Stir in the vegetable oil and parsley and serve immediately, using a slotted spoon if too much liquid remains at the bottom of the bowl. Alternatively, you may cover and refrigerate the potato salad overnight, then allow it to come to room temperature for 30 minutes before gently stirring and serving.

Honey Dressing for Fruit Salad

YIELD: 2 cups

Ingredients:

½ cup sugar
1 teaspoon dry mustard, to emulsify
1 teaspoon onion, grated
dash paprika
1½ teaspoon celery seed
1 teaspoon salt
¼ white vinegar
1 cup honey
1 cup vegetable oil

Directions:

In a bowl, combine sugar, dry mustard, grated onion, paprika, celery seed, and salt and mix well to combine. Add white vinegar, honey, and vegetable oil and mix well. Store in glass jar and chill. This dressing lasts a long time and goes a long way. Mix well before each use. Pour over any combination of fruit for a fresh and tasty fruit salad.

Honey Mustard Dressing

YIELD: 2½ cups

Ingredients:

2 cups mayonnaise
1 cup honey
8 tablespoons Dijon mustard

Directions:

In a small bowl, combine mayonnaise, honey, and Dijon mustard. Mix well, cover, and chill.

Maryanne's Seafood-Stuffed Avocado Salad

YIELD: 8 servings

Ingredients:

½ pound cooked shrimp
½ pound crab meat
2 celery stalks, finely chopped
2 green onion stalks, finely chopped
1 teaspoon hot sauce
1 teaspoon fresh lemon juice
zest of 1 lemon, grated
1 teaspoon Old Bay seafood seasoning
1 tablespoon fresh parsley, chopped
3 tablespoons mayonnaise
1 teaspoon grainy mustard
1 teaspoon red pepper flakes (optional)
2 tablespoons whipped cream cheese or heavy cream
4 avocados, halved, shells removed, and placed on plates

Directions:

Mix all ingredients except avocados in a good-sized bowl and chill for at least 1 hour to meld flavors. When ready to serve, slice 4 avocados in half, remove the seeds, and scoop out halves (optional, spritz a bit of lemon juice on flesh to keep them looking fresh) and immediately fill with seafood mixture. Place onto lettuce leaves such as a Boston lettuce cup, a small pile of arugula, or even a small banana leaf in 8 small serving dishes or one large decorated serving platter with 8 piles of lettuce leaves so guests can serve themselves. Seafood salad is also delicious on toast or pita points, served as a seafood sandwich, or simply topping a fresh green salad.

Maryanne's Salmon & Avocado Salad

YIELD: 4 servings

Ingredients:

1 can red salmon, drained, picked over, skin
  and bones removed
2 tablespoons celery, finely chopped
2 hard-boiled eggs, chopped
4 tablespoons mayonnaise
½ tablespoon curry powder or more to taste
2 avocados, halved, deseeded, scooped out of
  shell, brushed with lemon juice
juice of 1 lemon
lettuce, for serving
paprika, for garnish

Directions:

In a medium bowl, flake picked-over salmon,
mix in celery and eggs, and gently toss. In a
small separate bowl, mix mayonnaise with curry
powder until well combined, pour over salmon,
and gently mix, then cover tightly and refrigerate. When you're ready to serve, prepare the
avocados and set on 4 individual small plates on
top of lettuce leaves, mixed assorted greens, or
arugula. Fill avocado halves with chilled salmon
mixture and garnish with a dusting of paprika.

Mexican Avocado Chicken Salad

YIELD: 2 servings

Ingredients:

1 avocado, halved and deseeded
¼ cup plain Greek yogurt
1 Roma tomato, halved, seeds removed, and
  finely minced
juice of 1 lime
2 tablespoons corn, frozen, fresh, or canned
½ jalapeño, stemmed, halved, seeds and
  membrane removed
1 tablespoon shallot, minced
2 tablespoons fresh cilantro, finely minced
1 cooked, skinless, boneless chicken breast,
  diced
salt and pepper, to taste

Directions:

In a medium bowl, scoop out the avocado and
mash it coarsely, reserving avocado shell for
serving. Mix in the yogurt, tomato, lime juice,
corn, jalapeño, shallot, cilantro, and diced
chicken. Stir until well combined and then
season with salt and pepper. Taste and adjust
seasonings. Mix well and scoop the chicken
salad into the avocado halves or into pita pockets
if desired.

Oriental Salad Dressing

YIELD: ¾ cup

Ingredients:

3 tablespoons honey
1½ tablespoons rice wine vinegar
¼ cup mayonnaise
1 teaspoon Dijon mustard
⅛ teaspoon sesame oil

Directions:

In a small bowl, mix all ingredients together and whisk to combine. Refrigerate before using.

Pear, Spinach & Shaved Parmesan Salad

YIELD: 8 servings

Ingredients:

8 cups fresh baby spinach, washed
2 Bosc pears, quartered lengthwise, cored, and thinly sliced
2 ounces Parmesan cheese, shaved
2 tablespoons balsamic vinegar
1 tablespoon whole-grain mustard
1 teaspoon sugar
1 teaspoon salt
¼ teaspoon freshly ground pepper
½ cup extra virgin olive oil

Directions:

In a large bowl, combine spinach, pears, and cheese. In a small bowl, whisk together vinegar, mustard, sugar, salt, and pepper and whisk in oil to make dressing. Plate spinach and drizzle dressing on salad.

Simple Ramen Dressing

YIELD: 1½ cups

Ingredients:

4 tablespoons sugar
1 teaspoon salt
¼ teaspoon black pepper
6 tablespoons vinegar

1 cup oil
2 packets noodle flavoring

Directions:

Whisk all ingredients together until combined.

Asian Honey Ramen Dressing

YIELD: 1½ cups

Ingredients:

⅔ cup vegetable oil
⅓ cup honey
⅓ cup rice wine vinegar
2 teaspoons soy sauce
¼ teaspoon sesame oil
salt and black pepper, to taste

Directions:

Whisk all ingredients together until combined.

Ramen Salad

YIELD: 6–8 servings

Ingredients:

1 head cabbage, chopped
¾ cup green onion, sliced
2 packages ramen noodles, smashed into bite-
    sized pieces (flavoring packet reserved)
1 cup slivered almonds
4 tablespoons sesame seeds

Directions:

Preheat oven to 425°F. Mix all Simple Ramen Dressing (pg. 284) or Asian Honey Ramen Dressing (pg. 285) ingredients and refrigerate until ready to assemble the salad. In a large bowl, combine the prepared cabbage and green onions, mix well, and set aside. Spread the crumbled ramen noodles, slivered almonds, and sesame seeds onto a baking sheet and stir a bit to combine. Bake for about 5 minutes or until the almonds, sesame seeds, and noodles are golden and lightly toasted. Remove baking sheet from the oven and toss the ramen mixture well to combine, then return baking sheet to the oven and toast for an additional 3 minutes. Keep a sharp eye on the ramen mixture, as it can burn rapidly. Remove from oven and set aside to cool. When cool, add all ingredients to the bowl of cabbage and onions including the dressing and toss well. Serve immediately. If you cover tightly and refrigerate, it will keep up to 3 days, but the ramen loses its crunchiness the longer it sits.

Raspberry Vinaigrette

YIELD: 1 cup

Ingredients:

½ cup raspberry wine vinegar
½ cup vegetable oil
½ cup white sugar
2 teaspoons Dijon mustard
¼ teaspoon dried oregano
¼ teaspoon black pepper
¼-½ teaspoon powdered mustard, to emulsify

Directions:

In a jar with a tight lid, combine all ingredients and shake well to combine. Chill.

Chunky Salad on a Stick

YIELD: 8 servings

Ingredients:

2 cucumbers cut into ½-inch rounds
16 cherry tomatoes
½ head iceberg lettuce, cut into small chunks
8 wooden skewers
ranch dressing, to serve

Directions:

Wash and dry cucumbers and tomatoes. To serve, skewer 1 slice cucumber, 1 chunk lettuce, 1 cherry tomato, and another cucumber slice, chunk of lettuce, cherry tomato, and last slice of cucumber on each skewer. Lay skewers on a serving dish or platter, drizzle with ranch dressing, and let your guests enjoy a fresh salad on a stick. Use your imagination with ingredients, such as small shrimp and small chunk of sweet pepper with tomato and cucumber and drizzling with Catalina dressing, or even a threaded anchovy filet with Caesar dressing.

Roy & Jill's Story

When I was three years old, my father took me on vacation to a rustic wilderness hunting and fishing lodge deep in the interior of British Columbia, Canada, five hundred miles north of the Seattle, Washington border. The owners were his best friends, and over the years they became my second family. My first memory of their eldest son, Roy, just a year older than I, was on a hot summer day when he and his younger brother were playing in the creek that ran into the lake. He's the closest thing I'll ever have to a brother, and when he married his high school sweetheart, Jill, she became my sister along with his other siblings.

Two years after Stanley and I first started sailing, we had just taken delivery of our second boat, an *Ericson 27*, when we decided to go to visit the lodge for a long weekend. Roy and Jill happened to be there visiting that weekend, which was the first time Stanley met them. Immediately, the four of us were like family. That evening, I asked Stanley if we could invite them to go sailing with us for a weekend. His comment was, "Roy's a cowboy, a rancher, and he's only been on a lake skiff to help with the fishermen, and Jill has never done anything like this." I reminded him that we hadn't either when we first discovered sailing, and so the invitation was extended and immediately accepted.

From the moment they stepped aboard, Roy didn't sit down most of the weekend; he just hung onto the shrouds and stared, while Jill fell into the sailing style like she was a sailor by birth. We saw the same stars in their eyes that we had only a few years before. Over the next few years, they sailed back from Hawaii, made passages to Alaska, cruises to the Bahamas, a trip up the Intracoastal Waterway to Annapolis, and numerous weekend cruises with us.

The next step was their purchase of the *Valiant 32* plug from the Valiant Factory in Bellingham, Washington. Roy became a welder after leaving the lodge, and with his natural familial artistic talent, he created a work of art from the cockpit chairs to the gorgeous interior of their beautiful Valiant named *Shashay*. Roy has sailed on many Swiftsure International Races from Victoria Canada to Hawaii, and together he and Jill have spent many summers cruising from Vancouver down to the mouth of the Columbia River on the Oregon border and throughout the American San Juan Islands and the Canadian Gulf Islands. Jill often made us corn chowder on our voyages together, and offered her recipe for her delicious Salmon & Fennel Salad with Roasted Lemon Vinaigrette.

Roy & Jill's Salmon & Fennel Salad with Roasted Lemon Vinaigrette

YIELD: *4 servings*

Ingredients:

2 bulbs of fennel, sliced
2 lemons, halved crosswise
4–6 large cloves of garlic in their skins
salt and pepper, to taste
3 tablespoons olive oil, divided
4 serving size pieces of salmon
1 tablespoon honey
2 tablespoons rosemary, chopped
8 cups salad greens

Directions:

Preheat oven to 400° F. In a large roasting pan, toss fennel, lemons, and garlic cloves (in their skins) with 1 tablespoon olive oil. Add salt and pepper to taste. Roast until fennel softens, about 6 to 8 minutes, then nestle salmon pieces in the fennel, salt and pepper lightly, and roast an additional 12 to 15 minutes and remove from oven. Remove the garlic cloves and squeeze garlic out of their skins into a small bowl and mash. Squeeze the pulp and juice out of the roasted lemons and stir in 1 tablespoon honey, the chopped rosemary, and the remaining olive oil. Divide the greens onto 4 plates, dish up the fennel on each, and top with 1 piece of salmon. Drizzle the dressing on top to serve.

Stan & Sandy's Story

When Stanley and I were based out of St. Thomas in the US Virgin Islands and doing day chartering for upscale hotels, cruise ship directors, and booking agencies, it was imperative that every mechanical part of *Native Sun* and our dinghy was in perfect working order every single day. As one of the premier charter boats, we could not afford to ever say "we have a mechanical problem and we're down for the day." We met and became friends with Stan and Sandy at the old Yacht Haven Marina by the cruise ship docks, where they had a nearby engine and dingy sales and service company within the marina complex. We completely relied on Stan's expertise to keep our dingy and dingy motors operating at peak performance.

This area was part of the old Navy harbor-side workshops from World War II and some buildings were Quonset huts made of corrugated steel. For us, every visit and many other cruisers' visits there as well was an afternoon of great adventure and fun. Within one of these buildings, there was a consignment business that specialized in marine supplies and consignments from ship wrecks and yacht refits with many parts and pieces being sold by cruisers who were filling up their cruising kitty. This was also the home of the abandoned parrots of St. Thomas. For whatever reason, some cruisers thought that part of the cruising lifestyle included having a bird on board. We love birds, but we have seen how confined, destructive, and disruptive they can be on board and by the time many sailors arrived in St. Thomas, they were trying to relieve themselves of the responsibility and nuisance of having a bird aboard. Fortunately, the "coconut telegraph" was active and most of these sailors had heard that there was a big-hearted man at the marine supply place at Yacht Haven that would accept a bird, regardless of size or type, and keep them safe and cared for, for life.

It takes a special human being to accept the responsibility and expense of caring for hundreds of abandoned birds and it was an amazing site to see these gorgeous birds simply perching on steering wheels or sitting on ceiling fans as they went around in circles, and some even walked on the floors accompanying people as they strolled through the building. There were parrots, parakeets, budgies, cockatiels, and macaws in a mesmerizing rainbow of colors and sizes, every one of them gorgeous and loving the company of sailors who came just to visit this menagerie. Many people were delighted to find this special place when they had just come in for a dingy or outboard repair issue or were looking for a boat part. The walls, floors, ceiling, and shelves were strewn with all things "marine" that one could imagine. Stan and Sandy often invited us for dinner and Sandy's spinach salad with her special dressing was always our favorite. Even now, I double this recipe and always keep a large jar of it in the refrigerator.

Sandy's St. Thomas Spinach Salad Dressing

YIELD: 2½ Cups

Ingredients

½ cup oil
¼ cup ketchup
2 tablespoons Worcestershire sauce
⅓ cup red wine vinegar
¼ cup sugar
salt, pepper, and garlic powder, to taste
½–1 teaspoon dry mustard (optional)

Directions:

Mix all ingredients several hours before using. I add the dry mustard to help emulsify the oil and vinegar and to help make this wonderful dressing a bit creamier. Serve over salad greens.

CHAPTER 15
Sauces, Gravy & Pesto

Pesto

Ah, pesto! Pesto is one of my favorite condiments and can be used in so many delicious ways. The word pesto comes from the Italian word *pestare,* meaning to pound or crush something with a pestle, which is fitting, as traditionally it is made with a mortar and pestle, though most cooks now prepare it in a blender or food processor. There are so many variations and no limits on what ingredients can be used to make this versatile and diverse sauce, which can be served either hot or cold in combination with just about any other food you can think of. There are no pesto rules, just use what tastes good to you and your guests. If you have enough ingredients, a fun way to serve your pesto to guests is to serve bruschetta with several kinds of pesto on a serving tray and let your guests dig in. You'll be surprised and delighted with all the various comments.

I use pesto as a tasty dip, meat and seafood marinade, sandwich spread, on crackers and bruschetta, on pizza, in soups, (especially tomato soup or bisque), on popcorn, scrambled eggs, burgers, chowders, on grilled cheese sandwiches, in Focaccia bread made with pesto and mozzarella, and even on corn on the cob. Let your imagination help you create your own pesto, inspired by what you have on board at the time. It's fun and easy to make, can be easily frozen, and will last for months in the fridge or freezer. As with any recipe, your personal taste will dictate what adjustments you may want to make. Since the ingredients for all these different types of pestos are so different, I highly recommend that you taste as you're blending and adjust lightly. I personally almost always add more pepper and/or garlic. It all depends on the main ingredient I'm using for my pesto.

To store in the fridge, keep it in a small glass jar or a sealable container, and after each use, just add a bit of olive oil to the top to keep the air off the pesto. I like to make a double recipe if I'm going to freeze pesto. When it's all done, put it into a large plastic re-sealable bag, cut a small corner off of one end, squeeze the pesto into ice cube trays, cover with plastic wrap, and put in the freezer. When they're frozen solid, take them out of the trays and store in a clean re-sealable bag. These little "squares" can simply be thawed or added directly to food that you're preparing on the stove. Be cautious when using pestos in your recipes as the mix is of quite strong flavors, some spicier than others, and it's easy to overdo it and ruin your dish.

Classic Basil Pesto

YIELD: 2½ cups

Ingredients:

4 cups fresh basil leaves, packed
4 garlic cloves, peeled, slivered, and minced
⅔ cup pine nuts or walnuts
1 cup Parmesan cheese, grated
1 cup olive oil
1 teaspoon Kosher salt
1 teaspoon black pepper

Directions:

In a food processor, combine the basil, garlic, pine nuts, and Parmesan. With the machine running, pour in the olive oil through the food tube in a slow, steady stream and process until smooth, stopping to scrape down the sides of the bowl as needed, using only the amount of olive oil needed to make a creamy pesto. Season with salt and pepper to taste and adjust the seasonings. Pour into cold sterilized jars. Pour a little of the remaining oil over the top and seal tightly. Store in the refrigerator for up to 1 month or freeze.

Arugula Pesto

YIELD: 1 cup

Ingredients:

½ cup walnuts or almonds, chopped
1 garlic clove, peeled, sliced, and minced
2 cups packed arugula leaves
½ cup freshly grated Parmesan cheese
Kosher salt, divided
freshly ground pepper
1 cup olive oil, divided

Directions:

In a food processor, combine the walnuts or almonds, garlic, arugula, Parmesan, and 1 teaspoon salt and pulse to blend. With the machine running, pour in the olive oil through the food tube in a slow, steady stream and process until smooth, stopping to scrape down the sides of the bowl as needed, using only the amount of olive oil needed to make a creamy pesto. Season with salt and pepper to taste and adjust the seasonings. Pour into cold sterilized jars. Pour a little of the remaining oil over the top and seal tightly. Store in the refrigerator for up to 1 month or freeze.

Creamy Avocado Pesto

YIELD: 1 cup

Ingredients:

1 ripe avocado, peeled, pitted, and diced
1 cup fresh basil leaves, packed
⅓ cup pine nuts or walnuts
3 cloves garlic, peeled, sliced, and minced
¼ cup Parmesan cheese, grated
juice of 1 lemon
2 tablespoons olive oil
salt and pepper, to taste

Directions:

In a food processor, combine the avocado, basil, nuts, garlic, and Parmesan. With the machine running, pour in the lemon juice and olive oil through the food tube in a slow, steady stream and process until smooth, stopping to scrape down the sides of the bowl as needed, using only the amount of olive oil needed to make a creamy pesto. Season with salt and pepper to taste and adjust the seasonings. Pour into cold sterilized jars. Pour a little of the remaining oil over the top and seal tightly. Store in the refrigerator for up to 1 month or freeze.

Beurre Blanc (White Wine & Butter) Sauce

YIELD: 1 cup

Ingredients:

4 tablespoons dry white wine
4 tablespoons white wine vinegar
2 tablespoons shallots, finely minced
salt and pepper, to taste
2 sticks unsalted butter, chilled, cut into 16
    pieces

Directions:

In a medium saucepan, combine wine, vinegar, shallots, salt, and pepper. Bring to a gentle simmer until reduced to about 1½ tablespoons of sauce. Remove from heat and immediately whisk in 2 pieces of chilled butter. Continue whisking, adding another piece or 2 as the butter is mixed into the liquid, until all 16 pieces have been incorporated into the sauce. Remove from heat and adjust seasonings according to taste. Sauce should be thick and creamy. Serve immediately. Reheat the sauce by gradually whisking in 2 to 3 tablespoons of hot liquid such as water, cream, or stock.

Beet Tops Pesto

YIELD: 1 –2 cups

Ingredients:

5–6 cups beet top greens, from about 2 bunches of beets
¼ cup walnuts, chopped
¼ cup Parmesan cheese, grated
2 garlic cloves, peeled, sliced, and minced
zest from ½ lemon
juice from ½ lemon
½ cup olive oil
salt and pepper, to taste

Directions:

In a food processor, combine the beet top greens, walnuts, Parmesan, garlic, lemon zest, and juice. With the machine running, pour in the olive oil through the food tube in a slow, steady stream and process until smooth, stopping to scrape down the sides of the bowl as needed, using only the amount of olive oil needed to make a creamy pesto. Season with salt and pepper to taste and adjust the seasonings. Pour into cold sterilized jars. Pour a little of the remaining oil over the top and seal tightly. Store in the refrigerator for up to 1 month or freeze.

Brussels Sprout Pesto

YIELD: 1 cup

Ingredients:

2 cups Brussels sprouts, halved
4 garlic cloves, peeled, slivered. and minced
¼ cup almonds, peeled and slivered
juice of 1 lemon
3 tablespoons Parmesan cheese, grated
¼ cup olive oil
Kosher salt, to taste
pepper, to taste

Directions:

Bring a large pot of salted water to a boil, plunge the sprouts in, and cook for 2 to 3 minutes, only until just tender. Remove sprouts and place in a strainer and rinse immediately with cold water to stop the cooking. When cool, place the sprouts in a food processor; add garlic, almonds, lemon juice, and Parmesan. With the machine running, pour in the olive oil through the food tube in a slow, steady stream and process until smooth, stopping to scrape down the sides of the bowl as needed, using only the amount of olive oil needed to make a creamy pesto. Season with salt and pepper to taste and adjust the seasonings. Pour into cold sterilized jars. Pour a little of the remaining oil over the top and seal tightly. Store in the refrigerator for up to 1 month or freeze.

Chive Pesto

YIELD: 1 cup

Ingredients:

½ cup fresh chives, chopped and packed
½ cup fresh flat-leaf parsley, chopped and
    packed
2 tablespoons slivered almonds, walnuts, or
    pine nuts
1 large garlic clove, peeled, sliced, and minced
2 teaspoons fresh lemon juice
½ cup olive oil

Directions:

In a food processor, combine the chives, parsley, nuts, garlic, and lemon juice and pulse to blend. With the machine running, pour in the olive oil through the food tube in a slow, steady stream and process until smooth, stopping to scrape down the sides of the bowl as needed, using only the amount of olive oil needed to make a creamy pesto. Season with salt and pepper to taste and adjust the seasonings. Pour into cold sterilized jars. Pour a little of the remaining oil over the top and seal tightly. Store in the refrigerator for up to 1 month or freeze.

Cilantro Pesto

YIELD: 1–2 cups

Ingredients:

4 cups fresh cilantro, packed
4 tablespoons pumpkin seeds
½ cup Monterey Jack cheese, shredded
2 large garlic cloves, peeled, sliced, and minced
2 tablespoons water
2 tablespoons fresh lime juice
2 tablespoons olive oil
salt and pepper, to taste

Directions:

In a food processor, combine the cilantro, pumpkin seeds, shredded cheese, garlic, water, and lime juice and pulse to blend. With the machine running, pour in the olive oil through the food tube in a slow, steady stream and process until smooth, stopping to scrape down the sides of the bowl as needed, using only the amount of olive oil needed to make a creamy pesto. Season with salt and pepper to taste and adjust the seasonings. Pour into cold sterilized jars. Pour a little of the remaining oil over the top and seal tightly. Store in the refrigerator for up to 1 month or freeze.

Coconut-Cilantro Pesto

YIELD: 1 cup

Ingredients:

1 cup fresh cilantro leaves, packed
1 large garlic clove, peeled, sliced, and minced
1 cup almonds or walnuts
2 tablespoons fresh lemon juice
6 tablespoons coconut oil, melted
salt and pepper, to taste

Directions:

In a food processor, combine the cilantro, garlic, nuts, and lemon juice and pulse to blend. With the machine running, pour in the coconut oil through the food tube in a slow, steady stream and process until smooth, stopping to scrape down the sides of the bowl as needed, using only the amount of olive oil needed to make a creamy pesto. Season with salt and pepper to taste and adjust the seasonings. Pour into cold sterilized jars. Pour a little of the remaining oil over the top and seal tightly. Store in the refrigerator for up to 1 month or freeze.

Dandelion Pesto

YIELD: 1–2 cups

Ingredients:

2 cups dandelion leaves, tightly packed
¾ cup chopped walnuts
½ cup Parmesan cheese, grated
4 large cloves garlic, peeled, sliced, and minced
2 tablespoons lemon juice
2 teaspoons lemon zest
red pepper flakes, to taste
¾ cup olive oil
½ teaspoon Kosher salt
pepper, to taste

Directions:

In a food processor, combine the dandelion leaves, walnuts, cheese, garlic, lemon juice, zest, and red pepper flakes if using. With the machine running, pour in the olive oil through the food tube in a slow, steady stream and process until smooth, stopping to scrape down the sides of the bowl as needed, using only the amount of olive oil needed to make a creamy pesto. Season with salt and pepper to taste and adjust the seasonings. Pour into cold sterilized jars. Pour a little of the remaining oil over the top and seal tightly. Store in the refrigerator for up to 1 month or freeze.

Dill Pesto

YIELD: 1–2 cups

Ingredients:

4 cups fresh dill, packed
2 tablespoons pine nuts
2 cloves garlic, peeled, sliced, and minced
½ cup Parmesan cheese, freshly grated
2 tablespoons water
2 teaspoons fresh lemon juice
2 tablespoons olive oil
salt and pepper, to taste

Directions:

In a food processor, combine the dill, pine nuts, garlic, cheese, water. and lemon juice. With the machine running, pour in the olive oil through the food tube in a slow, steady stream and process until smooth, stopping to scrape down the sides of the bowl as needed, using only the amount of olive oil needed to make a creamy pesto. Season with salt and pepper to taste and adjust the seasonings. Pour into cold sterilized jars. Pour a little of the remaining oil over the top and seal tightly. Store in the refrigerator for up to 1 month or freeze.

Garlic Anchovy Pesto

YIELD: 1 cup

Ingredients:

2 ounces (2 tablespoons) anchovy fillets
12 garlic cloves, peeled, sliced, and minced
1 egg
¼ medium onion, minced
½ cup Parmesan cheese, freshly grated
2 tablespoons red wine vinegar
½ cup olive oil
salt and pepper, to taste

Directions:

In a food processor, combine the anchovies, garlic, egg, onion, cheese, and red wine vinegar. With the machine running, pour in the olive oil through the food tube in a slow, steady stream and process until smooth, stopping to scrape down the sides of the bowl as needed, using only the amount of olive oil needed to make a creamy pesto. Season with salt and pepper to taste and adjust the seasonings. Pour into cold sterilized jars. Pour a little of the remaining oil over the top and seal tightly. Store in the refrigerator for up to 1 month or freeze.

Green Olive Pesto

YIELD: 1 cup

Ingredients:

1 cup pitted green olives
1 cup fresh parsley
⅓ cup pistachios, toasted
1 large garlic clove, peeled, sliced, and minced
1 tablespoon fresh rosemary
zest of 1 lemon
juice of 1 lemon
½ cup Parmesan cheese, freshly grated
¼ cup olive oil

Directions:

In a food processor, combine the olives, parsley, pistachios, garlic, rosemary, lemon zest, juice, and cheese. With the machine running, pour in the olive oil through the food tube in a slow, steady stream and process until smooth, stopping to scrape down the sides of the bowl as needed, using only the amount of olive oil needed to make a creamy pesto. Season with salt and pepper to taste and adjust the seasonings. Pour into cold sterilized jars. Pour a little of the remaining oil over the top and seal tightly. Store in the refrigerator for up to 1 month or freeze.

Kale Pesto

YIELD: 1 cup

Ingredients:

8 ounces kale, rinsed, trimmed, and chopped
½ cup walnuts, chopped and roasted
1 cup Parmesan cheese, freshly grated
4 garlic cloves, peeled, sliced, and minced
2 teaspoons lemon juice
½ cup olive oil
1 teaspoon salt
½ teaspoon pepper

Directions:

Bring a large pot of salted water to a boil. Have a large bowl of cold water ready. First, drop the chopped kale into the boiling water. When the water returns to a boil, swirl the kale around a few times until it becomes limp. Drain the kale and plunge immediately into the cold water. Drain again, then place the kale on a clean dishtowel and roll up loosely in towel to dry moisture. In a food processor, combine the kale, walnuts, cheese, garlic, and lemon juice. With the machine running, pour in the olive oil through the food tube in a slow, steady stream and process until smooth, stopping to scrape down the sides of the bowl as needed, using only the amount of olive oil needed to make a creamy pesto. Season with salt and pepper to taste and adjust the seasonings. Pour into cold sterilized jars. Pour a little of the remaining oil over the top and seal tightly. Store in the refrigerator for up to 1 month or freeze.

Meyer Lemon Pesto with Mint

YIELD: 1 cup

Ingredients:

1 Meyer lemon, deseeded and cut into pieces
¼ cup fresh basil, chopped
¼ cup fresh mint, chopped
1 large garlic clove, peeled, sliced, and minced
¼ cup Parmesan cheese, grated
¼ cup olive oil
salt and pepper, to taste

Directions:

In a food processor, combine the lemon, basil, mint, garlic, and cheese. With the machine running, pour in the olive oil through the food tube in a slow, steady stream and process until smooth, stopping to scrape down the sides of the bowl as needed, using only the amount of olive oil needed to make a creamy pesto. Season with salt and pepper to taste and adjust the seasonings. Pour into cold sterilized jars. Pour a little of the remaining oil over the top and seal tightly. Store in the refrigerator for up to 1 month or freeze.

Red Pepper Pesto

YIELD: 1 cup

Ingredients:

2 red bell peppers, roasted
2 tablespoons pine nuts
2 garlic cloves, peeled, sliced, and minced
½ cup fresh basil leaves
½ cup Parmigiano-Reggiano cheese, grated
2 tablespoons water
1 tablespoon fresh lemon juice
1 tablespoon white wine vinegar
2 tablespoons olive oil
salt and pepper, to taste

Directions:

Preheat oven to broil. Place the peppers in the oven and roast, turning frequently until blackened on all sides. Remove and place peppers in a brown paper bag. Allow them to cool. After the peppers are cooled, peel and deseed them. In a food processor, combine the roasted peppers, pine nuts, garlic, basil, cheese, water, lemon juice, and white wine vinegar. With the machine running, pour in the olive oil through the food tube in a slow, steady stream and process until smooth, stopping to scrape down the sides of the bowl as needed, using only the amount of olive oil needed to make a creamy pesto. Season with salt and pepper to taste and adjust the seasonings. Pour into cold sterilized jars. Pour a little of the remaining oil over the top and seal tightly. Store in the refrigerator for up to 1 month or freeze.

Sage Pesto

This is a very bold pesto, so use sparingly.

YIELD: 1 cup

Ingredients:

1 cup sage leaves
¼ cup roasted walnuts
1 large garlic clove, peeled, sliced, and minced
4 green onions, coarsely chopped
¼ cup Parmesan cheese, grated
½ cup olive oil

Directions:

In a food processor, combine the sage, walnuts, garlic, green onions, and cheese. With the machine running, pour in the olive oil through the food tube in a slow, steady stream and process until smooth, stopping to scrape down the sides of the bowl as needed, using only the amount of olive oil needed to make a creamy pesto. Season with salt and pepper to taste and adjust the seasonings. Pour into cold sterilized jars. Pour a little of the remaining oil over the top and seal tightly. Store in the refrigerator for up to 1 month or freeze. For added decoration, top pesto with sage flowers; they are edible and have a slightly milder flavor than the leaves.

Spinach Pesto

YIELD: 1 cup

Ingredients:

2 cups fresh baby spinach
2 cups basil leaves, loosely packed
1 cup Parmesan cheese, grated
2 tablespoons fresh oregano
1–2 large garlic cloves, peeled, sliced, and minced
½ cup chopped walnuts, toasted
½ teaspoon salt
1 tablespoon lemon juice
2 teaspoons lemon zest
1 cup olive oil

Directions:

In a food processor, combine the spinach, basil leaves, cheese, oregano, and garlic and pulse until chopped. Add walnuts, salt, lemon juice, and zest and pulse. With the machine running, pour in the olive oil through the food tube in a slow, steady stream and process until smooth, stopping to scrape down the sides of the bowl as needed, using only the amount of olive oil needed to make a creamy pesto. Taste and adjust the seasonings. Pour into cold sterilized jars. Pour a little of the remaining oil over the top and seal tightly. Store in the refrigerator for up to 1 month or freeze.

Sun-Dried Tomato Pesto

YIELD: 1 cup

Ingredients:

1 cup sun-dried tomatoes in olive oil
½ cup walnuts, chopped
2 large garlic cloves, peeled, sliced, and minced
¾ cup Parmesan cheese, grated
¾ tsp salt
¼ tsp pepper
½ cup olive oil

Directions:

In a food processor, add sun-dried tomatoes and pulse for 3 to 4 pulses until chopped, then add walnuts, garlic, cheese, salt, and pepper and pulse. With the machine running, pour in the olive oil through the food tube in a slow, steady stream and process until smooth, stopping to scrape down the sides of the bowl as needed, using only the amount of olive oil needed to make a creamy pesto. Taste and adjust the seasonings. Pour into cold sterilized jars. Pour a little of the remaining oil over the top and seal tightly. Store in the refrigerator for up to 1 month or freeze.

Alfredo Sauce

YIELD: 3–4 servings

Ingredients:

2 tablespoons butter
1 cup whipping cream
salt, to taste
freshly ground black pepper, to taste
½ cup Parmigiano-Reggiano cheese, freshly grated

Directions:

Melt butter in a large saucepan over medium heat, making sure the butter does not brown. Carefully add the cream into the saucepan with the melted butter. Add salt and pepper to taste. While stirring with a wooden spoon to keep sauce from browning, bring the cream mixture to a boil, then reduce heat to a simmer and gently cook the sauce until it begins to thicken, stirring frequently with a wooden spoon for 3 to 5 minutes. Remove from heat, let pan cool a few minutes, then add the cheese a little at a time, stirring to combine until cheese is thoroughly incorporated into the sauce. Serve with pasta and garnish with additional Parmigiano-Reggiano cheese.

Chicken Fettuccine Alfredo

Ingredients:

1½ cups cooked chicken, chopped
¼ cup drained oil-packed sun-dried tomatoes
alfredo sauce, to taste
½ cup Parmigiano-Reggiano cheese, freshly
    grated

Directions:

Stir chicken and sun-dried tomatoes into
alfredo sauce. Heat until all ingredients are
thoroughly warm, remove from heat, let pan
cool a few minutes, then add the cheese a little
at a time, stirring to combine until cheese us
thoroughly incorporated into the sauce. Serve
with fettuccine and garnish with additional
Parmigiano-Reggiano.

Seafood Fettuccine Alfredo

Ingredients:

12–16 ounces cooked lobster, tuna, crab, or
    shrimp, lightly chunked
1 tablespoon fresh basil or dill, chopped
alfredo sauce
½ cup Parmigiano-Reggiano cheese, freshly
    grated
capers, to taste (optional)

Directions:

Stir seafood and herbs into the alfredo sauce.
Heat until all ingredients are thoroughly warm,
remove from heat, let pan cool a few minutes,
then add the cheese a little at a time, stirring to
combine until cheese is thoroughly incorporated
into the sauce. Add drained capers if using.
Serve with pasta and garnish with additional
Parmigiano-Reggiano.

Meatball Alfredo Appetizers

Ingredients:

appetizer-sized meatballs, cooked
alfredo sauce
½ cup Parmigiano-Reggiano cheese, freshly
    grated

Directions:

Stir cooked meatballs into the alfredo sauce.
Heat until all ingredients are thoroughly warm,
remove from heat, let pan cool a few minutes,
then add the cheese a little at a time, stirring to
combine until cheese is thoroughly incorporated
into the sauce. Serve with pasta and garnish with
additional Parmigiano-Reggiano.

Apple Cider Gravy

*YIELD: **About 3 cups***

Ingredients:

¼ cup butter
¼ cup flour
3 cups turkey or chicken stock
1 cup apple cider
2 teaspoons sage, finely chopped
Kosher salt and freshly ground black pepper,
   to taste

Directions:

In a medium saucepan, melt butter. Whisk in flour and cook, stirring frequently until golden blonde in color, about 2 minutes. Gradually add in turkey or chicken stock in a steady stream, whisking constantly, then add apple cider. Bring to a boil, reduce to a simmer, and cook until reduced to 3 cups, about 10 to 15 minutes. Stir in sage and season with salt and pepper to taste. Taste, adjust seasonings, and serve immediately or store in an airtight container in refrigerator for up to 1 week, reheating over medium-low heat before serving.

Soy Dipping Sauce

*YIELD: **¾ cup***

Ingredients:

½ cup soy sauce
1½ teaspoons sesame oil
2 tablespoons rice wine or white vinegar
2 teaspoons hot chili sauce
2 scallions, finely minced

Directions:

In a small bowl, mix all ingredients thoroughly to combine. Keep tightly covered and refrigerated. Serve with California rolls or tempura shrimp or veggies.

Wasabi Cream Sauce

YIELD: ½ cup

Ingredients:

1 tablespoon wasabi powder
1 tablespoon water
¼ cup sour cream
¼ cup mayonnaise

Directions:

In a small bowl, mix all ingredients thoroughly to combine. Keep tightly covered and refrigerated. Serve with California rolls or tempura shrimp or veggies.

Hard Sauce

YIELD: 6 servings

Ingredients:

⅓ cup butter, room temperature
1 cup powdered sugar
1 teaspoon vanilla

Directions:

In a medium bowl using an electric mixer, cream butter. While beating, gradually sift in powdered sugar until creamy and fluffy. Add vanilla and mix thoroughly. Chill. To serve, bring to room temperature for 2 hours and spoon on warm desserts.

Hot Chocolate Sauce

YIELD: 1 cup

Ingredients:

⅔ cup (1 small can) evaporated milk
1 cup (6 ounces) semisweet chocolate pieces

Directions:

Combine ingredients in the top of a double boiler and cook over hot water until chocolate is melted. Serve hot.

Blender Béarnaise Sauce

YIELD: 12 servings

Ingredients:

1 small shallot, peeled, sliced, and minced
¼ cup champagne or white wine vinegar
¼ cup dry white wine
3 tablespoons fresh tarragon, chopped, divided
½ teaspoon salt
¼ teaspoon black pepper
1½ sticks butter
3 egg yolks

Directions:

In a small pot, combine shallot, champagne or vinegar, white wine, 1 tablespoon tarragon, salt, and pepper. Bring to a simmer and cook until reduced by half, about 5 minutes. Let cool for 2 minutes. Then, melt butter in a separate small pot until steaming. Let cool for 2 minutes. Place champagne/tarragon mixture in a blender and while running on low, drop in egg yolks one at a time. Slowly pour in warm butter. Increase speed, blending until well combined. Pour into a bowl and stir in remaining tarragon. Serve warm.

Butter Rum Sauce

Delicious on grilled pork chops!

YIELD: 1¾ cups

Ingredients:

1 cup dark brown sugar, packed
½ cup (1 stick) butter
½ cup dark rum
½ cup Dijon mustard
2 tablespoons apple cider vinegar
½ teaspoon black pepper

Directions:

In a medium saucepan, combine all ingredients and bring to a boil. Reduce heat to medium-low and simmer for 20 minutes, whisking occasionally until thickened. To serve, brush on thick pork chops and grill, brushing sauce on chops several times during grilling. Grill for 5 to 7 minutes per side or until internal temperature registers 160°F.

Chinese Mustard Sauce

Ingredients:

¼ cup dry mustard
¼ cup boiling water
2 teaspoons vegetable oil
½ teaspoon salt

Directions:

In a small bowl, place dry mustard, add boiling water, and mix well. Whisk in oil and salt.

Chinese Red Sauce

Ingredients:

3 tablespoons ketchup
3 tablespoons chili sauce
1–2 tablespoons horseradish
1 teaspoon fresh lemon juice
dash of hot pepper sauce, to taste

Directions:

Combine all ingredients in a small bowl and whisk to mix well.

Chinese Plum Sauce

Ingredients:

1 cup plum preserves
⅓ cup dry sherry
½ teaspoon ground cloves
½ teaspoon ground anise
½ teaspoon ground fennel
½ cup (1 small can) dry mustard

Directions:

In a blender or with electric mixer, combine all ingredients except mustard and mix well. Add mustard a small amount at a time, blending well until sauce is hot and spicy to your taste.

Cocktail Sauce

YIELD: 2 cups

Ingredients:

2 cups ketchup
2 teaspoons Worcestershire sauce
1 tablespoon lemon juice
2 teaspoons prepared horseradish
dash of hot sauce (optional)
black pepper (optional)

Directions:

Mix all ingredients together until well combined, cover, and refrigerate up to 1 hour to meld flavors.

Cream Cheese Alfredo Sauce

YIELD: 2–4 servings

Ingredients:

1 (8 ounce) package cream cheese, cut into small bits
¾ cup Parmesan cheese, grated
½ cup butter
½ cup half-and-half
1 teaspoon garlic powder

Directions:

In a large saucepan over medium heat while constantly stirring, combine little chunks of cream cheese, Parmesan, butter, half-and-half, and garlic powder and mix well until thoroughly heated and smooth. Pour immediately over prepared pasta, toss, and serve.

Vodka Sauce

YIELD: 2-4 servings

Ingredients:

1 onion, peeled, sliced, and diced
½ cup butter
1 cup vodka
2 (28 ounce) cans crushed tomatoes
¼ teaspoon dried oregano
2 tablespoons fresh parsley, chopped
1 tablespoon dried basil
pinch red pepper flakes
1 pint heavy cream

Directions:

In a skillet over medium heat, sauté onion in butter, until slightly brown and soft. Pour in vodka and let cook for 10 minutes. Mix in crushed tomatoes, oregano, parsley, basil, and pepper flakes and cook for 30 minutes. Pour in heavy cream and cook for another 30 minutes.

Honey Rum Sauce

YIELD: 10 servings

Ingredients:

2½ cups light brown sugar
1¼ cups honey, strained
pinch of salt
½ cup hot water
½ pound butter, room temperature
½ cup rum

Directions:

In a large saucepan, combine brown sugar, honey, salt, and hot water. Mix well to combine, then add butter. Place over heat and slowly bring mixture to a rolling boil, then immediately remove from heat and let cool. Add rum and mix well to combine. Best served over apple pie.

Horseradish Orange Sauce

YIELD: 4 servings

Ingredients:

2 tablespoons prepared horseradish
1 tablespoon Dijon mustard
8 ounces orange marmalade
sea salt, to taste
pepper, to taste

Directions:

In a small bowl, combine horseradish, Dijon mustard, and orange marmalade. Taste and adjust flavors. Season with salt and pepper and refrigerate to chill. Best served with crab claws and coconut shrimp.

Key Lime Dipping Sauce

YIELD: *4 servings*

Ingredients:

1 cup mayonnaise
5 tablespoons Dijon mustard
4 key limes, juiced
sea salt, to taste
pepper, to taste

Directions:

In a small bowl, combine mayonnaise, Dijon mustard, and lime juice. Taste and adjust flavors. Season with salt and pepper and refrigerate to chill.

Lemon Sauce

YIELD: *3 cups*

Ingredients:

2 tablespoons cornstarch
1 cup sugar
2 teaspoons lemon zest
2 cups water
¼ cup fresh lemon juice
¼ cup butter, room temperature
¼ teaspoon salt

Directions:

In a medium saucepan over medium heat, combine cornstarch, sugar, and lemon zest and slowly add water while mixing. Continue stirring and heat until thickened. Remove from heat and add lemon juice, butter, and salt. Mix all ingredients well and serve warm over cakes, fruit cobblers, or other desserts.

Orange Butter Sauce

YIELD: 4 servings

Ingredients:

6 tablespoons butter
grated rind of 2 oranges
grated rind of 2 lemons
juice of 4 oranges
juice of 2 lemons
2 tablespoons sugar
salt, to taste
1 teaspoon cornstarch
1 tablespoon cool water
½ cup orange-flavored liqueur

Directions:

In a medium saucepan, melt butter, then add the grated orange and lemon rinds and the juice of oranges and lemons. Mix well and cook over medium heat, stirring frequently until the sauce is reduced by about half. Add the sugar, stirring well until sugar is dissolved. In a small bowl, mix the cornstarch and water with a fork until well blended, then add to the saucepan and cook for 1 minute until sauce is thickened. Stir in the orange-flavored liquor and remove from heat. Best served with Cornish game hens; baste hens repeatedly with sauce during the last 15 minutes of roasting and serve any remaining sauce alongside the hens.

Peanut Dipping Sauce

YIELD: 1½ cups

Ingredients:

½ cup smooth peanut butter
½ cup hoisin sauce
2 green onions (¼ cup), coarsely chopped
1½ tablespoons fresh lime juice
¼ cup water
1 tablespoon soy sauce
2 teaspoons fresh ginger, finely grated
hot pepper sauce, to taste

Directions:

In a small bowl, combine the peanut butter, hoisin sauce, green onions, lime juice, water, soy sauce, ginger, and hot pepper sauce into a food processor or blender and purée until smooth. Add additional water if necessary to thin sauce to a pourable consistency. Cover and refrigerate until ready to serve. Best served with shrimp, chicken, pork, veggies, skewered grilled chicken, or tossed with defrosted peas in linguine.

Steakhouse Tiger Dill Sauce

Ingredients:

⅔ cup sour cream
3 teaspoons prepared horseradish
¼ cup mayonnaise
¾ teaspoon sugar
¼ teaspoon dill, dried

Directions:

In a small bowl, combine all ingredients and mix until completely blended. Cover and refrigerate for 12 to 24 hours before serving alongside any beef entrée.

Tangy Honey BBQ Sauce

The chef on the yacht Tabasco *gave us this recipe while docked in Annapolis during a summer cruise to the Chesapeake. This is a nice quick BBQ sauce with only a few ingredients and little cooking time, which makes it particularly suited to making on board. We've enjoyed it on chicken, ribs, chops, meat of all sorts, and even as a dip for grilled shrimp.*

YIELD: 3 cups

Ingredients:

½ cup honey
¼ cup ketchup
½ cup yellow mustard
½ cup white vinegar
1 cup light brown sugar
1½ teaspoons paprika
1½ teaspoons Kosher salt
fresh pepper, to taste

Directions:

Place all ingredients in a medium-sized saucepan over medium-high heat and whisk to combine. Bring to boil, reduce to a simmer, and simmer for 5 minutes. Take pan off the heat and let sauce come to room temperature before serving. Store sauce in a tightly sealed container in the fridge.

Thai Sweet Chili Sauce

YIELD: 1½ cups

Ingredients:

½ cup rice or white vinegar
½ cup white sugar plus 2 tablespoons
¼ cup water plus 3–4 tablespoons
3 tablespoons fish sauce
2 tablespoons sherry
3 cloves garlic, peeled, sliced, and minced
½–1 tablespoon dried chili flakes, crushed
½–1 tablespoons cornstarch

Directions:

In a medium saucepan over medium-hot heat, place vinegar, sugar, ¼ cup water, fish sauce, sherry, garlic, and chili flakes and bring to a rolling boil. Reduce heat to medium, stir well, and boil for 10 more minutes or until reduced by half. In a small bowl, combine cornstarch and 3–4 tablespoons cold water and mix well with a fork to combine, then stir into saucepan, continuing to cook for 2 minutes until the sauce thickens. Remove from heat, taste, and adjust seasonings. Pour into a small lidded jar and serve with seafood, fish, chicken, or as a dip for wings, spring rolls, and shrimp.

Tzatziki Sauce

YIELD: 2 cups

Ingredients:

½ large cucumber
2 cups plain yogurt
2 tablespoons fresh parsley, chopped
2 tablespoons fresh mint, chopped
1 tablespoon fresh lemon juice
Kosher salt and black pepper, to taste

Directions:

Peel, deseed, and small dice cucumber. In a medium bowl, combine prepared cucumber, yogurt, parsley, mint, lemon juice and salt and pepper to taste. Blend well, cover, and refrigerate.

CHAPTER 16
Seafood

Bahamian Cracked Conch

YIELD: *4 servings*

Ingredients:

4 conches, cleaned, and pounded very thin with a metal mallet
1 cup lime, sour orange, or lemon juice
dash of Tabasco, to taste
2 eggs, beaten
½ cup evaporated milk
½ teaspoon salt
¼ teaspoon pepper
½ cup flour
oil, for frying

Directions:

Marinate conch in lime juice and Tabasco for 30 minutes, then drain. In a medium bowl mix together eggs, evaporated milk, salt, and pepper. Pour the flour into a pie plate and dip pounded conch in the egg and milk mixture, making sure they're totally covered, then roll each conch in flour, making sure each conch is fully covered. Heat cooking oil ¼-inch deep to a pot, enough to cover each conch when it's time to fry. Once oil is hot, start adding conch and cook them until they're a beautiful light golden brown. Using a slotted spoon, remove cooked conch from the oil and place on a dish lined with several layers of paper towels to soak up the grease. Serve with a side of lime, hot sauce, coleslaw, fries, peas, or rice.

Baked Fish Sticks with Tartar Sauce

YIELD: 8 fish sticks

Ingredients for fish sticks:

1½ cups bread crumbs, lightly toasted
1 teaspoon Kosher salt
¼ teaspoon cayenne pepper
¼ cup flour
2 large eggs, beaten
1½ pounds boneless fish such as cod or halibut fillets, cut into strips
2 tablespoons vegetable oil
lemon wedges, for serving
tartar sauce, for serving

Ingredients for tartar sauce:

½ cup mayonnaise
2 tablespoons lemon juice
1 tablespoon sweet pickle relish
½ tablespoon onion, minced
salt and pepper, to taste

Directions for fish sticks:

Position oven rack to upper third of oven. To toast bread crumbs, spread them on a large oiled baking sheet and place under your oven's broiler for 1 to 2 minutes. Watch carefully to avoid burning. In a shallow dish, combine toasted bread crumbs, salt and cayenne. In a separate dish, add flour. In another separate dish, beat eggs. Set up a breading station, dip fish in flour, dip in beaten eggs, then coat with bread crumbs. Preheat oven to 450°F and arrange fish on a parchment-lined and oiled baking sheet. Bake for 10 to 12 minutes, turning halfway through until cooked through. The fish should be opaque, tender, and flaky. Serve with the following tartar sauce.

Directions for tartar sauce:

Mix together all ingredients in a small bowl. Season to taste with salt and pepper and adjust seasonings. Refrigerate for at least 1 hour before serving. Serve with fish sticks and lemon wedges.

Calamari in Puttanesca Sauce

YIELD: 4 cups

Ingredients:

1 (9 ounce) pouch calamari or squid rings and tentacles
¼ cup olive oil
1 cup onion, peeled, sliced, and finely chopped
6 cloves garlic, peeled and finely diced
1 teaspoon shallots, peeled, sliced, and finely diced
2 (28 ounce) cans Roma plum tomatoes, torn into pieces plus juice
½ teaspoon dried chili flakes
2 tablespoons anchovy fillets, finely chopped
½ cup capers, rinsed and drained
¼ cup white wine
2 (13¾ ounce) cans artichoke hearts, drained and quartered
1 cup pitted and halved Kalamata olives, tightly packed
green and black pitted and halved olives
2 tablespoons tomato paste
1 teaspoon dried basil
1 teaspoon dried oregano
2 tablespoons fresh parsley, chopped, for garnish
Parmesan cheese, grated, for garnish
crusty bread, for serving

Directions:

Cut calamari into rings; slice the rings into halves, and score each ring on the inside edge to help calamari soak up the sauce. In a large pot, heat the olive oil over medium-high heat. Add onion and sauté until lightly caramelized and soft, about 5 minutes, then add garlic and shallots and cook another 2 minutes. Add calamari and gently sauté for just a few minutes until it naturally releases its juices, being careful not to overcook. Remove calamari with a slotted spoon and set aside. Add tomatoes and remaining ingredients to the pot and simmer until sauce has thickened, stirring occasionally, about 40 minutes. Taste, adjust seasonings, and add a little more tomato sauce if necessary. Gently toss reserved calamari into the sauce, sprinkle with Parmesan and fresh parsley for garnish, and serve with a nice crusty bread.

Chorizo & Mussels

YIELD: *2 servings*

Ingredients:

1 tablespoon olive oil
8 ounces Mexican chorizo, casings removed
1 medium white onion, peeled, and thinly sliced
2 garlic cloves, peeled, sliced, and minced
1¼ teaspoons ground cumin
1 teaspoon Kosher salt
1 (12 ounce) bottle strong beer
2 tablespoons butter
2 pounds mussels, scrubbed and de-bearded
½ cup cilantro, coarsely chopped
hot sauce, for serving
crusty toasted bread, for serving
1 garlic clove, peeled, sliced, halved lengthwise

Directions:

Place a Dutch oven or large cooking pot over medium heat, add oil, and warm. Add chorizo, onion, garlic, cumin, and salt, stirring frequently to break up chorizo. When onions are soft and chorizo is cooked through, about 10 minutes, add beer and butter, increase heat to medium-high, and bring to a boil. Cook 1 minute to reduce slightly. Add washed mussels, cover, and cook until mussels open, about 5 to 8 minutes, then scoop out and discard any mussels that have not opened. Spoon mussels into bowls, ladle chorizo mixture and broth over mussels, and top with cilantro. Shake hot sauce on sparingly to taste. Rub toasted bread with cut side of sliced garlic clove to serve alongside or with the broth.

Deborah's Maryland Crab Cakes

YIELD: 8 crab cakes

Ingredients:

2 pounds canned or bottled crab, not drained
1 cup mayonnaise, preferably Hellman's
2 teaspoons Worcestershire Sauce
2 tablespoons Dijon mustard
salt and pepper, to taste
2 tablespoons Old Bay Seasoning
2 eggs

Directions:

Preheat oven to 350°F. Line a baking sheet with parchment paper, then spray parchment with cooking spray and make sure it covers parchment evenly. Mix all ingredients gently and with a large ice cream scoop or spoon, scoop crab mixture into 8 evenly sized mounds, using your hands to shape. Place on middle rack of oven and cook for 30 minutes or until edges are nice and brown and the crab cakes have firmed up. Serve with tartar sauce or hot sauce of your choice.

Double Seafood Sauce

This is a wonderful sauce we learned to make from Chef Roy at The Seacliff Hotel in St. Thomas. Serve it over grilled or baked fish.

YIELD: 6 servings

Ingredients:

6 tablespoons butter, divided
½ cup sweet or yellow onion, chopped
1½ tablespoons flour
½ cup clam juice
2 cups whipping cream
splash of white wine
½ teaspoon salt
¼ teaspoon white pepper
dash cayenne pepper
1 cup small shrimp, uncooked
6 ounces (¾ cup) crabmeat

Directions:

Melt 3 tablespoons of butter in a large saucepan. Add the onion and cook until soft but not brown. Stir in the flour a little at a time and cook about 2 minutes, stirring constantly. Slowly pour in the clam juice and whipping cream. Taste and add a splash of white wine to taste and season with salt, pepper, and cayenne. Continue to cook, stirring, about 3 minutes. In a separate saucepan, melt the remaining 3 tablespoons butter. Add the shrimp and cook about 2 minutes. Add the crabmeat and cook 1 minute. Stir into cream mixture and serve over grilled or baked fish.

Grouper Ceviche

YIELD: *4 servings*

Ingredients:

1½ cups lime juice
½ cup grapefruit juice
1 pound raw, skinned grouper, diced
1¾ cups fresh tomatoes, diced
1¼ cups white onion, peeled, sliced, and diced
½ cup fresh cilantro, rough chopped
salt and pepper, to taste
2 mangos, peeled, deseeded, and cubed
2 avocados, peeled, deseeded, and cubed
tortilla chips, for serving
lemon wedges, to garnish

Directions:

In a large bowl, mix the lime, grapefruit juice, and prepared grouper. Cover and chill and let fish marinate for 30 minutes. In the meantime, chop the tomatoes, onion, and cilantro. When ready, drain the grouper and mix with the tomato mixture. Add salt and pepper and taste to adjust flavors. Mix in prepared mangos and avocados, cover, and refrigerate to let flavors meld, for 1 hour. Serve in one large bowl with tortilla chips for dipping or in separate martini glasses or small bowls with lemon wedges for garnish.

Oven-Baked Jumbo Shrimp Scampi

YIELD: *8 servings*

Ingredients:

2¼ (21–25 shrimp per pound) pounds jumbo raw shrimp
½ cup (1 stick) butter
1 teaspoon salt
6 large garlic cloves, peeled, sliced, and minced
⅓ cup parsley, chopped, divided
3 teaspoons lemon peel, grated
3 tablespoons lemon juice
2–3 lemons, cut into wedges, for serving

Directions:

Preheat oven to 400°F. Shell, devein, wash, and drain shrimp on a paper towel. Place melted butter on a 13 x 9 x 2-inch baking dish, evenly spreading it around. Add the salt, garlic, and half of the parsley. Arrange the shrimp in a single layer in the baking dish and place uncovered in the oven for 5 minutes. Remove from oven and turn shrimp with tongs , sprinkle evenly with grated lemon, lemon juice, and remaining parsley. Return to oven and bake 8 to 10 minutes just until tender and being careful not to overcook. Immediately remove from oven and place on a heated platter. Pour butter and garlic mixture from the pan evenly on the shrimp, garnish with lemon wedges, and serve.

Lemon & Garlic Fettucini with Pan-Seared Scallops over Basil Pesto

YIELD: 4 servings

Ingredients:

8 ounces fettuccine

zest of 1 large lemon

2 tablespoons lemon juice

3–5 large garlic cloves, peeled, sliced, and finely minced

4 tablespoons olive oil, divided

16 large scallops

½ teaspoon salt

¼ teaspoon pepper

1 cup prepared basil pesto, divided into 4 servings or more if desired

2 tablespoons Parmesan cheese, shredded

Directions:

Grate lemon with a fine grater and place in small saucepan. Cut the lemon in half, remove seeds, squeeze juice out, then spoon out as much pulp as you can get and add with lemon juice to the saucepan. Add finely minced garlic and 1 tablespoon olive oil. Stir well to blend and place on low heat. In a large saucepan, bring 3 quarts of water to a boil, then reduce heat to a simmer until you're ready to add the fettuccine. Sprinkle scallops with salt, pepper and 1 to 2 tablespoons olive oil to coat well. Heat a large nonstick skillet on high temperature until very hot, place scallops in the hot skillet, and cook about 2 minutes on each side or until they are well browned and milky white in the center. Turn the scallops over in the pan, then immediately place the fettuccine in the boiling water, reduce heat to medium, and cook 9 minutes to al dente or slightly firm. When the pasta is cooked, set aside ½ cup of the cooking water and drain pasta. Place drained pasta back into the pot, add the ½ cup of reserved pasta water, then add the warm lemon and garlic mixture in the small saucepan and lightly toss to coat pasta. To serve, place equal portions of pasta on 4 warmed plates. Spread ¼ cup of pesto on each plate and place 4 scallops on top alongside the flavored pasta. Garnish with ½ tablespoon Parmesan cheese on each plate.

Lemon Shrimp à la Roger

YIELD: 4 servings

Ingredients:

1 cup flour or more if needed

1 tablespoon lemon pepper

salt, to taste

¾ –1 pound medium-large shrimp, cleaned, shelled, and deveined

¼ cup olive oil, divided

¼ cup ginger, grated, divided

2 tablespoons lemon zest, divided

¼ cup lemon juice

2 tablespoons butter

1 head romaine lettuce, cut into bite-size pieces

1 tomato, diced

½ cup Parmesan cheese, shredded

Directions:

Put flour in a large bowl, add lemon pepper and salt, and mix well. Toss shrimp with flour and lemon pepper and salt mixture. In a large sauce pan, heat half the olive oil, half the ginger, and half the lemon zest over medium-high heat. Add shrimp and cook until they are golden, then remove from pan, place on folded paper towels, and set aside. Reduce heat to medium, then add lemon juice, butter, and the remainder of olive oil, ginger, and lemon zest to sauce-pan. Add romaine lettuce to the pan, return cooked shrimp to the pan, and stir until lettuce is just wilted. Add diced tomato and shredded parmesan to garnish.

Maine Coast Lobster Pie

Yield: 4–6 servings

Ingredients for the topping:

2½ tablespoons salted butter, melted
½ cup crushed Ritz-style butter crackers
½ teaspoon paprika
2 tablespoons Parmesan cheese, grated

Ingredients for the filling:

3 tablespoons plus 5 tablespoons butter, divided
¼ cup dry sherry
2 cups (12 ounces) cooked lobster meat, chopped
3 tablespoons all-purpose flour
1½ cups half-and-half
4 large egg yolks
chives, minced, to garnish

Directions for the topping:

Preheat oven to 350°F. Set rack to the middle position. In a small bowl, stir together all topping ingredients and set aside.

Directions for the filling:

Melt 3 tablespoons of butter in a large skillet over medium-high heat. Add sherry, bring to a boil, and boil for 1 minute. Add the lobster, stirring to coat lobster, then remove skillet from the heat and remove lobster from the skillet. Reserve juices from the skillet, strain the juices into a measuring cup, and set aside. Melt remaining butter over medium-low heat in a 3-to 4-quart sauce pan. Slowly add the flour while stirring and cook, continuing to stir, until the mixture is nice and smooth and glossy. Add half-and-half into the reserved lobster mixture, mixing gently, then whisk that into the butter/flour mixture. Increase the heat to medium-high and simmer, stirring continuously until the sauce thickens, about 3 minutes. Spoon ½ cup of this sauce into a small bowl and add the egg yolks one at a time, beating well after each addition until everything is blended. Add this mixture back to the sauce and stir over low heat until the sauce is smooth and thick, about 3 minutes. Remove saucepan from the heat, add the lobster mix gently, then pour the mixture into a medium-size casserole dish and sprinkle the topping evenly over the lobster filling. Place casserole in the oven and bake until lightly golden brown, about 10 to 15 minutes. Serve hot and garnish with chives.

Veggie-Seafood Skewered Grill

YIELD: *4 servings*

Ingredients:

12 ounces fish
¼ large red onion, cut into 1½-inch chunks
½ red bell pepper, cut into 1½-inch chunks
½ green bell pepper, cut into 1½-inch chunks
½ orange bell pepper, cut into 1½-inch chunks
½ yellow bell pepper, cut into 1½-inch chunks
olive oil, to taste
salt and black pepper, to taste
1–2 lemons, halved and charred on the grill

Directions:

Preheat grill to hot. Soak wooden skewers for 30 minutes or up to 24 hours. Water is generally used to soak, but soaking skewers in beer, different types of juice, or wine is a wonderful way to impart some different flavor to the skewers. Cut fish into 1½-inch chunks so that you have 12 pieces of similar size. Separate the layers of the chunked onion, then thread alternate layers of onion, several pieces of different colored peppers, then a chunk of fish, and continue until there are approximately 3 good-sized chunks of fish with 4 layers of veggies on each skewer. Brush the skewers all around with lots of olive oil to keep them from sticking to the grill, sprinkle with salt and pepper to taste, and place on hot grill. Watch carefully as these can burn easily. Turn once during grilling. You'll want a nice easy char for a beautiful presentation and to soften the veggies a bit. Serve with rice and squeeze charred lemon on skewers and rice or over a bed of mixed greens.

Jack & Arla's Story

On one of our cruises between Seattle and Alaska, we anchored one evening just north of Seymour Narrows, one of the most dangerous straits in North America with recorded tides that can rise twenty feet and currents that rush through the Narrows at ten to fifteen knots. Many boats have been lost there due to treacherous currents, swirling eddies, and turbulent tide-rips, and though we had waited for slack tide to pass through Seymour Narrows, our nerves were pretty shot by the time we found a suitable anchorage for the night. Being from Seattle, Stanley and I are used to calm tidal shifts of eight feet or so. Several hours after we had gone to bed, we heard the most frightening sound, something like a train going full speed across our bow, and we quickly went on deck to see what was going on. Even north of the Narrows, the water was screaming past us as the tide went out. We quickly threw out a second anchor and began a rotating cockpit watch until the morning.

Sometime in the early morning, a large private motor yacht entered the bay and dropped anchor. They hailed us on the VHF as the motor yacht *Tahoe* and inquired about an overnight anchorage there. We said we would dingy over and tell them all about our evening. The owners were Jack and Arla from Oregon and they said they cruised up to Alaska every summer, but had never anchored in this particular bay. We all laughed at how terrified we were the night before and it was agreed that both boats would never anchor overnight again in that bay.

Jack and Arla had several large freezers on board and said they made the Inside Passage trip every year to fish for salmon and to catch crab. Judging by what we saw on a tour of their boat, they had already been quite successful. They served us a pickled salmon dish with little toast points and then graciously shared their delicious recipe, which I make several times a year.

Jack & Arla's Pickled Salmon

YIELD: 2–2½ quart jars

Ingredients:

2½ pounds salmon filets, boned and skinned
1 tablespoon salt plus 1 teaspoon
2 cups white vinegar
2 cups water
¼ cup Wesson-type oil
1½ tablespoons whole pickling spice
5 small onions, thinly sliced

Directions:

Cut salmon into ¾-inch chunks and spread them in a single layer on waxed paper or in a shallow glass baking dish. Sprinkle with 1 tablespoon salt and let stand uncovered 30 minutes. Rinse salmon well to remove all salt and pat dry. In the meantime, in a medium saucepan combine the vinegar, water, oil, pickling spice, and 1 teaspoon salt. Bring to boiling, then reduce heat, partially cover, and simmer 30 minutes. Layer salmon chunks and onion slices equally into two (2½ quart) wide-mouth jars. Pour boiling hot pickling liquid over salmon, cover loosely, and cool. When cool, tightly cover well and refrigerate for 24 hours. Keeps well refrigerated for up to a month. Serve with crackers, toast points, or in very small bowls as a side dish accompaniment.

Salmon with Pesto Mayo

YIELD: 4–6 servings

Ingredients:

2–3 pounds skinless, boneless fresh or frozen salmon fillets
2 tablespoons firm-textured bread, crumbled
1 tablespoon Parmesan cheese, grated
¼ cup mayonnaise
3 tablespoons prepared basil pesto

Directions:

Thaw fish in fridge overnight if frozen. Preheat broiler. Cut fillets into number and size of desired servings. Place the bread crumbs in a shallow baking pan, place in heated broiler, and broil for 1 to 2 minutes or until lightly toasted, stirring once. When completely cool, mix Parmesan cheese into bread crumbs and set bread crumbs aside. Place fish on a greased unheated rack on a broiler pan, tucking under any thin edges so they won't overcook. Broil for 4 to 6 minutes per ½-inch thickness or until fish just begins to flake easily with a fork. Turn fillets over and broil another minute or two, checking constantly for doneness and not overcooking. In the meantime, mix mayonnaise and pesto together and combine well and set aside. Spoon mayonnaise mixture over fillets. Sprinkle with crumb mixture. Broil 1 to 2 minutes more or until crumbs are lightly browned.

Scallops with Herbed Brown Butter

YIELD: 4 servings

Ingredients:

1 tablespoon olive oil
1 pound sea scallops, side muscle removed if attached
Kosher salt, to taste
freshly ground pepper, to taste
2 tablespoons (¼ stick) cold butter, cut into small pieces
4 sprigs herbs of your choice or availability
2 teaspoons wine or fresh lemon juice

Directions:

In a large skillet, heat oil over medium-high heat. Season scallops with salt and pepper, place in hot oil, and cook until deep golden brown, about 3 minutes. Turn scallops over and add butter and herbs to pan. Continue cooking, spooning butter over scallops often, until scallops are cooked through and opaque and butter is brown and smells nutty, about 3 minutes longer. Add wine or optional lemon juice. Serve scallops with brown butter pan sauce.

Sea Bass with Lemons, Capers & Kalamata Olives

YIELD: 8 servings

Ingredients:

3 tablespoons olive oil, divided
8 sea bass fillets (about 5 ounces each), skin on
1 teaspoon salt, divided
½ teaspoon freshly ground black pepper, divided
2 lemons, peeled and thinly sliced, segments halved
juice of 2 lemons
2 tablespoons fresh oregano, chopped
2 tablespoons capers, rinsed
¾ cup pitted Kalamata olives, roughly chopped

Directions:

Preheat broiler. Place 1 tablespoon oil on a large plate and coat fillets on both sides with oil. Carefully remove pan from broiler and place on stovetop. Arrange fillets on hot pan skin-side down and sprinkle with ¼ teaspoon salt and ¼ teaspoon pepper. Broil fish 6 minutes. In the meantime, in a medium-sized bowl, mix together lemon slices, lemon juice, oregano, capers, olives, remaining oil, and remaining salt and pepper. Place fish on platter and top with sauce.

Sole Meunière

YIELD: 2 servings

Ingredients for sole:

½ cup flour
4 (3–4 ounce) sole fillets
Kosher salt
freshly ground black pepper
2 tablespoons vegetable oil
2 tablespoons (¼ stick) butter

Ingredients for sauce:

¼ cup (½ stick) butter, cut into 4 pieces
2 tablespoons fresh Italian parsley, chopped
1 tablespoon fresh lemon juice
lemon wedges, for garnish

Directions for sole:

Place flour in a pie dish. Rinse fish and pat with paper towels. Sprinkle both sides of fish with Kosher salt and freshly ground pepper, then dredge both sides of fish fillets with flour, shake off excess flour, and place fillets on a platter. In a large skillet over medium-high heat, heat oil until it is hot and shimmers. Add butter to oil and quickly swirl skillet to coat; this will make a foam, but when foam subsides, add the floured and seasoned fish. Cook until golden on bottom, about 2 or 3 minutes, then carefully turn fish over and cook until golden all over and fish is opaque in the center, about 1 to 2 minutes. Divide fish between 2 warmed plates and tent with foil to keep warm while making the sauce. Pour off drippings from skillet and wipe with paper towels.

Directions for sauce:

Place wiped skillet over medium-high heat. Add ½ stick of butter which has been cut into 4 pieces and cook until butter is golden, about 1 to 2 minutes. Remove skillet from heat, stir in parsley and lemon juice, and stir to mix, then spoon evenly over fish. Serve with lemon wedges to squeeze over fish.

Squid, Fennel & Lemon Fettuccine

YIELD: 4 servings

Ingredients:

5 tablespoons olive oil, divided
1 pound squid (bodies and tentacles), bodies sliced ¼-inch thick
Kosher salt, to taste
pepper, to taste
1 large fennel bulb, thinly sliced lengthwise, plus 2 tablespoons fronds
2 garlic cloves, thinly sliced
¾ teaspoon red pepper flakes, crushed
½ lemon, seeds removed, very thinly sliced, divided
1 (12 ounce) package fettuccine
½ cup parsley, to garnish

Directions:

You will be cooking squid in two batches. In a large skillet, heat 2 tablespoons of the olive oil over high heat. Season prepared squid with salt and pepper and cook while continuing to stir, about 3 minutes or until squid is just barely cooked. Make sure not to overcook squid or it will have a rubbery texture. With a slotted spoon, remove squid from the skillet to a small bowl and set aside. Reduce heat to medium-high and heat 2 tablespoons oil in skillet (no need to wipe out). Add fennel bulb slices, season with salt and pepper, and cook while stirring occasionally, until golden brown and soft, 10 to 12 minutes (some browned bits should stick to skillet). Add garlic, red pepper flakes, and half of the lemon slices; cook, tossing occasionally until garlic and lemon are soft, about 2 minutes. Meanwhile, cook fettucine in a large pot of boiling salted water, stirring occasionally until al dente. Drain pasta, reserving 1½ cups cooking liquid. Add fettuccine to skillet along with 1 cup cooking liquid. Toss, scraping up any browned bits, and season with salt and pepper. Cook, tossing and adding the remaining cooking liquid as needed until sauce coats pasta, about 3 minutes. Add squid and give it all another toss to combine. Toss parsley, fennel fronds, remaining lemon slices, and remaining 1 tablespoon oil in a small bowl and season with salt and pepper.

Steamed Mussels with Fennel, Tomatos, Ouzo & Cream

YIELD: 4 servings

Ingredients:

2 shallots, finely chopped
4 cloves garlic, finely chopped
1 bulb fennel, trimmed, cored, and thinly sliced
1 large tomato, cubed
½ cup white wine
¼ cup ouzo
½ cup heavy cream
4 pounds mussels, cleaned and debearded
⅓ cup fresh basil leaves, torn

Directions:

Heat olive oil in a medium saucepan over medium heat. Stir in shallots and garlic and cook until tender. Stir in fennel and tomato and continue cooking about 5 minutes. Mix white wine, ouzo, and heavy cream into the saucepan, and bring to a boil. Gradually stir in mussels, half of the basil, and salt. Cover saucepan and continue cooking about 5 minutes until the mussels have opened. Garnish with remaining basil to serve.

Stove Top Pan-Fried Fish Cakes

YIELD: 12 fish cakes

Ingredients:

¼ cup cooking oil
1 yellow onion, peeled, sliced, and diced
1 carrot, peeled, sliced, and finely diced
1 celery stalk, sliced and finely diced
1 teaspoon salt, divided
1 lime, zested, divided
1 pound cod fillet
freshly ground black pepper, to taste
⅓ cup heavy cream
¼ cup chopped cilantro leaves and stems
1 jalapeño, stemmed, deseeded, membrane
  removed, and finely diced
3½ cups fresh bread crumbs, divided
4 eggs, divided
1 cup all-purpose flour
lime juice, to serve

Directions:

Heat a large skillet to high, then add ¼ cup cooking oil. Add the onion, carrot, celery, and ½ teaspoon salt, then lower heat to medium and cook, stirring occasionally until the vegetables are soft and lightly browned, about 20 minutes. Remove from heat and scoop mixture onto a plate to completely cool. Grate ½ teaspoon lime zest and set it aside. Cut cod fillet into ¼-inch pieces, place in a medium bowl, and season with the remaining salt, then grind a bit of pepper over fillets. In a food processor or blender, combine ¼ of the fish mixture with the cream and pulse or blend until smooth, scraping down the sides as needed. Add the fish purée back to the bowl of ¼-inch fish pieces along with the cooled vegetable mixture, cilantro, jalapeño, remaining lime zest, 1½ cups bread crumbs, and 2 eggs. Scoop everything into a large bowl and stir with your hands to mix everything well. Beat the remaining eggs in a wide, shallow bowl, put the flour in a second bowl, and the remaining bread crumbs in a third bowl, setting up a "breading station." Pat the fish mixture down in the bowl, smooth the top, and divide it in half. Now, separate each half into 3 parts to make mixture into sixths. Line a baking sheet with parchment paper. Scoop one half of each sixth of mixture with your hands, form into a ball, then flatten into a patty. Place each patty in the flour bowl, turn over, coat completely, then shake off excess, place in beaten egg mixture, turn to coat, let excess egg drip off, then place into crumb mixture, coating completely. Set fish cake on the baking sheet and repeat with the remaining mixture until you have 12 fish cakes. Cover baking sheet with plastic wrap and place with all 12 fish cakes in the fridge for 30 minutes to 6 hours. When ready to cook, heat a large skillet to medium-high and heat the oven to warm for holding one batch of fish cakes as you fry the rest. Add ¼-inch of oil to the skillet and add as many fish cakes as will fit in a single layer. Fry, adjusting the heat as needed until one side of each cake is golden brown, about 4 minutes. Turn fish cakes over and brown the other side. Check a fish cake to be sure it's cooked through, then keep the batch warm in the oven while you fry the rest. Squeeze lime juice over fish cakes just before serving.

Sylvia's Chardonnay Mussels with Lemon-Garlic Fettuccine

YIELD: 6 servings

Ingredients for chardonnay mussels:

2 pounds fresh or frozen mussels
1⅓ pounds fettuccine
2 tablespoons olive oil
2 tablespoons butter
3–4 cloves garlic, peeled, sliced, and minced
½ cup onion, minced
2 medium jalapeños, stemmed, deseeded, sliced, and diced
1 teaspoon fresh rosemary leaves, chopped
1 cup Chardonnay
1 cup Monterey Jack cheese, shredded
1 cup Swiss cheese, shredded
1 tablespoon flour
½ cup heavy cream
parsley, chopped, for garnish

Ingredients for lemon-garlic fettuccine:

1 large lemon, zested
4 tablespoons lemon juice
2–4 large garlic cloves, peeled, sliced, and mashed
1 tablespoon olive oil
½ cup reserved pasta water

Directions for mussels:

If using fresh mussels, rinse in cool water and clean any beards and sand from outside of shells. Discard any open mussels. Cook fettuccine according to package instructions, drain, toss with oil, put in a large serving dish, keep warm, and follow directions for lemon-garlic pasta below. In a large pot heat butter, then add garlic, onion, jalapeños, and chopped rosemary for 1 minute. Add wine and mussels. Turn heat to high and steam mussels in wine sauce for 3 to 5 minutes until shells just open. Remove mussels with a slotted spoon and arrange over pasta. Keep warm. If using frozen mussels, cook according to directions, place mussels over pasta to keep warm, and add all mussel juices in package to wine sauce. Put the shredded cheeses in a re-sealable bag, add flour, and toss to coat cheese. Add the cheese and heavy cream to the wine sauce and simmer just until sauce begins to thicken, stirring occasionally, and remove from heat. To serve, scoop out the cheese and wine sauce and pour over mussels and pasta. Garnish with parsley and serve with a good crusty French bread and salad.

Directions for lemon-garlic fettuccine:

Put all of the above ingredients into a good-sized pot and stir to blend. Place on stove top over low heat. In a separate large pot, cook the fettuccine according to package directions. Reserve ½ cup of pasta water and drain remaining fettuccine. Return drained pasta into the pot with the lemon-garlic fettuccini ingredients, swirl, and mix well to cover pasta. When ready to serve, plate pasta with the lemon-garlic sauce, top with mussels, and garnish with parsley. This is my go-to way to serve pasta in 99 percent of my pasta dishes.

CHAPTER 17
Soup

Beach Party Chili

YIELD: 16 servings

Ingredients:

1 pound bacon, semi-frozen and cut into small pieces
1 large onion, peeled, sliced, and diced
1 red bell pepper, stemmed, deseeded, and chopped
1 green bell pepper, stemmed, deseeded, and chopped
6 cloves garlic, peeled, sliced, and minced
1 large jalapeño, stemmed, halved, seeds and membranes removed, chopped
4½ tablespoons chili powder
1½ tablespoons cumin
1½ tablespoons paprika
1½ tablespoons chipotle powder
2 teaspoons dried oregano
2 teaspoons salt
½ teaspoon cayenne powder
3 pounds ground beef
1 can strong beer
1 (14 ounce) can black beans, rinsed and drained
1 (14 ounce) can red kidney beans, rinsed and drained
1(24 ounce) can crushed tomatoes
1 (24 ounce) can diced tomatoes
salt, to taste
shredded cheese (optional, for garnish)
sour cream (optional, for garnish)
corn chips (optional, for garnish)
green onions, sliced (optional, for garnish)

Directions:

If you put your bacon in the freezer for a few hours or even overnight, and cut with kitchen shears, it's much easier to cut into pieces. In a large pot or Dutch oven over medium heat, cook bacon pieces until almost done, then add onion and bell peppers and cook until soft. Add garlic, jalapeño, chili powder, cumin, paprika, chipotle powder, oregano, salt, and cayenne powder. Stir well and continue to cook 2 minutes or so, just until aromatic. Add ground beef and cook until it is no longer pink, breaking it up into small pieces as it cooks. Stir in can of beer, beans, crushed tomatoes with juice, and diced tomatoes with juice. Reduce heat, cover, and simmer for 1½ hours, checking occasionally and adding a little more water or beer if necessary. Stir every 10 minutes or more if your stove is too hot. Add salt, taste, and adjust seasonings. Garnish chili with optional toppings.

Carrot Soup

YIELD: 4–6 servings

Ingredients:

2 tablespoons butter
¼ cup onion, peeled, sliced, and chopped
1 rib celery, sliced and peeled
2 cups carrots, peeled and sliced
2 cups chicken broth
¼ cup dry white wine
1 cup half-and-half
¼ teaspoon nutmeg
1 teaspoon salt
pepper, to taste

Directions:

In a large saucepan over medium heat, melt butter. Add onion and celery and cook until tender. Add carrots and cook 5 minutes more. Add broth and wine and bring soup to a boil. Cover, reduce heat, and simmer 20 minutes until carrots are tender. Remove from stove and let soup cool at least 30 minutes. With a blender or in a food processor and working in batches, purée soup mixture and return to saucepan. Add half-and-half, nutmeg, salt, and pepper and bring to a simmer for 10 minutes.

Chilled Corn Soup

YIELD: 6 servings

Ingredients:

6 ears fresh corn, husked and halved crosswise
6 cups chicken broth, divided
3 shallots, peeled, sliced, and chopped
1 onion, peeled, sliced, and chopped
salt and pepper, to taste
6 tablespoons sour cream
¼ English cucumber, minced
2 tablespoons green onions, chopped

Directions:

Place corn in a large heavy pot, add 5 cups broth, shallots, and onion and bring to a boil. Reduce heat, cover pot, and simmer until corn is very tender, about 25 minutes. Using tongs, transfer corn to a large bowl to cool, reserving broth. Cut corn kernels off cobs. Return 4 cups corn kernels to broth (reserving any remaining corn for another use). Working in batches, purée cooled soup in blender or food processor until very smooth. Strain soup through fine sieve set over large bowl, pressing on solids with back of spoon. Mix in remaining broth to reach a consistency of heavy cream. Season with salt and pepper, taste, and adjust seasonings. Cover and refrigerate 4 hours until cold or overnight. To serve, ladle soup into 6 bowls, top each with a dollop of sour cream, and sprinkle with minced cucumber and green onions.

Cold Curry Soup

*YIELD: **4 servings***

Ingredients:

2 tablespoons butter
2 tablespoons curry powder
1 cup milk
1 quart chicken broth
6 egg yolks
1 cup (½ pint) heavy cream
fresh parsley, chopped, for garnish

Directions:

Put butter in a large saucepan over medium-low heat. Add curry powder and milk, stir well, and bring to a boil. Lower heat, add chicken broth, and warm over low heat. In the meantime, place egg yolks in a bowl and mix with a fork, then add cream to yolks and keep gently mixing with the fork. Slowly add egg and cream mixture to broth, stirring constantly over low heat until thickened, but do not let boil. Remove from heat, chill, and serve ice cold. Garnish with chopped parsley.

Corn Chowder "Sashay"

YIELD: *6 servings*

Ingredients:

6 slices bacon, cut in ½-inch pieces
1 onion, chopped
2 cloves garlic, chopped
½ teaspoon paprika
¼ teaspoon red pepper flakes, crushed
1 can drained corn
3 cups chicken or vegetable broth
1 cup half-and-half
salt and pepper, to taste
4 green onions, sliced, for garnish

Directions:

Cook the bacon, drain, and remove to a paper towel. Reserve 2 tablespoons of the drippings and cook chopped onion in reserved bacon drippings until soft. Add garlic and cook until soft, then add paprika and red pepper flakes and cook for 2 minutes while stirring. Add corn, broth, and half-and-half and simmer for about 15 minutes. Transfer half of the soup to a blender, add salt and pepper, and blend till creamy. Return blended soup to the pot of remaining soup and heat through. Add the cooked bacon; give it a good stir, and dish up, garnishing with green onions. Serve with a nice loaf of bread.

Cream of Avocado Soup

YIELD: 8–10 servings

Ingredients:

3 large avocados, peeled, pitted, and mashed
6 cups clear chicken broth
2 teaspoons white wine vinegar
2 tablespoons lemon juice
2 teaspoons garlic salt
½ teaspoon Tabasco sauce
2 cups half-and-half
bacon, fried crisp, crumbled, to garnish (optional)
toasted almond chips or slices, to garnish (optional)
fresh tomatoes, finely diced, to garnish (optional)
green onions, diced, to garnish (optional)
sour cream, to garnish (optional)

Directions:

In a large bowl or pan, combine and mix all ingredients, then with a blender or in a food processor, place all ingredients in batches and purée until completely smooth. Place in fridge to chill. In the meantime, prepare any of the optional garnishes, place in small bowls, and when ready to serve, spoon soup into serving bowls and place bowls of garnish on the table for your guests to select which they'd like to add to their soup.

Cream of Cauliflower Soup

YIELD: 6–8 servings

Ingredients:

2 strips bacon, chopped
1 large onion, peeled, sliced, and chopped
2 shallots, peeled, sliced, and chopped
2 garlic cloves, peeled, sliced, and chopped
2 tablespoons butter
½ cup dry white wine
1 bay leaf
1 head cauliflower, stalks trimmed, chopped
3 cups chicken or vegetable stock
salt and pepper, to taste
1 teaspoon curry powder
1 teaspoon nutmeg
½ teaspoon thyme
1 tablespoon dry sherry
1 cup half-and-half, whole milk, or heavy cream
2 cups Swiss cheese, shredded
2–3 tablespoons fresh dill or chives, chopped, to garnish

Directions:

Place a large soup pot or Dutch oven over medium heat. Add the bacon and stir for 1 minute to cook slightly. Add the onion, shallots, garlic, and butter. Cook for 5 to 7 minutes, stirring occasionally until softened. Add the white wine and raise heat to medium-high to bring soup to a boil. Add the bay leaf, cauliflower, and chicken or vegetable stock and season with a few pinches of salt and pepper. Bring to a boil, stirring once or twice. Once soup is boiling, turn heat to low, cover, and let simmer for 20 to 25 minutes. Remove pan from heat, remove bay leaf, and add curry powder, nutmeg, and thyme. Cool for at least 15 minutes, then using a handheld blender or food processor and working in batches, purée to a thick and creamy texture. Once the soup has been blended, return to the pot and cook over medium heat until heated through. Add the sherry, half-and-half, then taste, adjust seasonings, and bring soup just to a boil. Turn off heat and add in the Swiss cheese, stirring until it melts. Serve in bowls and garnish with fresh dill.

Cream of Crab Soup

YIELD: 6 servings

Ingredients:

¼ cup onion, peeled, sliced, and minced
¼ cup butter
2 tablespoons flour
¼ teaspoon celery salt
dashes Worcestershire sauce
½ teaspoon salt
¼ teaspoon pepper
1 cup strong chicken broth
4 cups light cream
1 pound fresh crabmeat
2 tablespoons parsley, chopped
12 tablespoons sherry, divided

Directions:

In a large pot or Dutch oven, cook onion in butter until golden. Add flour, celery salt, Worcestershire sauce, salt, and pepper and stir constantly over medium heat until it begins to thicken. Slowly add broth and cook 5 more minutes. Slowly add cream, stirring constantly, and slowly cook until thickened. Then add crabmeat and parsley and cook until crabmeat is hot. Ladle immediately into 6 bowls and add 2 tablespoons sherry to each bowl.

Cream of Tomato Soup

YIELD: 4 servings

Ingredients:

1 cup peeled tomatoes
2 tablespoons butter
2 tablespoons flour
1 teaspoon salt
⅛ teaspoon pepper
¼ teaspoon baking soda
4 cups milk
1 small onion, peeled, sliced, and minced

Directions:

In a large saucepan melt butter. While whisking, add flour and mix, then add tomatoes. Cook 5 minutes, add salt, pepper, and baking soda. Remove from heat and add milk and onion and mix well. Put back on stove top and bring to a boil, adjust seasonings, and serve.

Captain Phillip's Story

In May of 1999, we were invited by our dear friend Phillip to sail on his lovely yacht *Peregrina*, which he had entered in a sanctioned sailboat race between St. Petersburg, Florida and Havana, Cuba. We had never heard of The Havana Cup, but it made no difference. We jumped at this opportunity to visit such a secretive place as Cuba was in those days, and also to sail with Phillip, a true gem of the sea. We sailed to the Dry Tortugas, a series of small islands in the Gulf of Mexico just 65 miles off the tip of Key West, a few days before the race was to begin. After anchoring for the night, we read up on the history and significance of the Dry Tortugas. The next morning, having read about sunken wrecks and gold coins which had been discovered over the years, Stanley and I decided to try our luck while snorkeling. Of course, we found nothing valuable, other than the undersea beauty of this place. We also found to our surprise and delight another sailboat anchored nearby, the yacht *Windwalker*, with owners and old friends Fred and Iris on board. We spent a delightful evening together on board *Peregrina*, introducing old friends to old friends and talking about the wonder that of all places on earth, we'd all be in the little harbor here in the Dry Tortugas on the same day. These coincidences are part of the great and many surprises we've come to expect while cruising.

We had a small crew on *Peregrina,* so Captain Phillip assigned the cooking of meals to each of us on a rotating schedule, which worked out perfectly, as we were all sailors and all shared a love of cooking on board. When we arrived in Hemingway Marina, we all went our separate ways to tour the old city of Havana, as we realized that the points of interest were different for each of us. We had life changing experiences over the next several days, meeting the friendliest and most wonderful local people, intimately learning from our tour guides and people we met in the square the history of Cuba, and what the present conditions were from the locals' perspective. We tasted local food in places that did not cater to tourists, much of which sounded familiar to us, but with a definite Cuban twist to each item we ate.

Our guides told us about eating our meals at "Paladares" rather than the tourist restaurants. Paladares are often restaurants that are actually the living room of a family's home with sometimes one or up to three or four small tables set up for dining. In one Paladares, we were served what seemed like a very complicated gazpacho. It was so delicious and we raved so much while we were eating it that the owner came out of his kitchen with the recipe written on the back of our check. I'm not sure that so many diverse ingredients were readily available on a regular basis to these people, but perhaps many of his spices, oils, and condiments were given to him by fellow visiting sailors, so when we got back to *Peregrina* we scoured our supplies for items we mostly likely would not use soon or which could easily be replenished once we were stateside. We made a special trip to gift these people with as much food, condiments, bars of soap, shampoo, candy, and miscellaneous items we thought they needed or could use. Our gifts were such a little thing to us, but were accepted with a flood of tears. Over the past several years, I have worked with the recipe I was given. It was written in English of sorts, so I've added and replaced ingredients to make what is an extremely close replica of the gazpacho we were served in Havana. I call it Conch Republic Grilled Seafood Gazpacho.

Captain Phillip's Gazpacho

YIELD: 6 servings

Ingredients:

2 cups English cucumber, peeled, deseeded, and coarsly chopped plus extra for garnish
4 cups fresh tomatoes, deseeded, and chopped (optional, canned tomatoes)
½ red sweet pepper, stemmed, deseeded, and diced
½ orange or yellow sweet pepper, stemmed, deseeded, and diced
½ small jalapeño pepper, stemmed, deseeded, and diced
¼ cup sherry
2 teaspoons garlic, chopped
½ cup onion, peeled and chopped plus extra for garnish
3 tablespoons olive oil
Tabasco sauce, to taste
salt, to taste
1 cup croutons, for garnish
2 tablespoons cilantro, chopped

Directions:

In a food processor or blender, purée cucumber, tomatoes, sweet pepper, red and orange or yellow peppers, jalapeño pepper, sherry, garlic, onion, and olive oil until almost smooth. Season with Tabasco and salt to taste. Place in a large tightly covered container and place in refrigerator for 4 to 6 hours. To serve, divide evenly between 6 bowls. Place croutons, chopped onion, chopped cucumber, and cilantro in small bowls so that your guests can garnish their own bowl of gazpacho.

Conch Republic Grilled Seafood Gazpacho

YIELD: 8 servings

Ingredients:

½ cup semi-sweet wine
½ cup whole basil leaves
3½ cups tomato juice
3½ cups red onions, diced
1 serrano chili, stemmed, deseeded, and chopped
3 cups fresh tomatoes, deseeded and diced
2 cloves garlic, peeled and chopped
1 poblano pepper, stemmed, deseeded, and chopped
1 cucumber, peeled, deseeded, and diced
2 green onions, chopped
½ cup red wine vinegar
1 teaspoon ground cumin seed, toasted
1 teaspoon ground coriander seed, toasted
¼ cup olive oil
salt and pepper, to taste
8 sea scallops
8 large prawns, shelled, deveined
juice of ½ lemon
¼ cup fresh assorted herbs, chopped
basil and saffron oil (optional)
fresh basil sprigs, for garnish

Directions:

In a medium stainless saucepan, bring the wine to a boil, then remove from heat and add the basil leaves. Let basil leaves steep for 15 minutes in the hot wine, then strain the wine, removing the leaves. Add tomato juice to wine mixture, blend, and set aside. In a blender, purée red onions, the serrano chili, tomatoes, garlic, poblano pepper, cucumber, and green onions until smooth. Scoop blended ingredients into a large bowl and begin whisking while adding the wine and tomato mixture, vinegar, cumin, coriander, and olive oil until well blended. Taste and adjust seasonings with salt and pepper and additional serrano and vinegar if necessary. Cover gazpacho tightly and refrigerate until ready to serve. In the meantime, with the grill on medium-high heat, sprinkle scallops and prawns with a small amount of salt and pepper, place them on the grill, and cook carefully until done. Be careful not to overcook the seafood as it can rapidly turn rubbery if overcooked. To serve, remove gazpacho from refrigerator and divide between eight serving bowls. Place a scallop then a prawn on top of each bowl, add a small amount of optional basil oil and saffron oil on top, and garnish with a small sprig of basil.

Green Onion & Leek Vichyssoise

YIELD: 8–10 servings

Ingredients:

¼ cup (½ stick) butter
4 medium leeks, washed and sliced (white part only)
1 onion, peeled and thinly sliced
2 pounds potatoes, peeled and thinly sliced
1 quart chicken broth
1 tablespoon salt
2½ cups milk
2 cups half-and-half or light cream
green onions, chopped, to garnish

Directions:

Put butter in a large, deep saucepan, add leeks and onion, and lightly brown over medium heat. Add potatoes, broth, and salt, then increase heat and bring to a boil and boil for 30 minutes or just until potatoes are very tender. Remove from heat and cool a bit, then put into a blender and purée until mixture is nice and smooth. Return mixture to the saucepan, add milk, and bring to a boil. Remove from heat and cool completely. Strain cooled mixture through a fine sieve, add half-and-half, stir well, and refrigerate until well chilled. To serve, spoon vichyssoise into soup bowls and garnish with green onions.

Cool Puerta Vallarta Gazpacho

YIELD: 2 servings

Ingredients:

2 medium cucumbers, peeled and rough chopped
2 cloves garlic, peeled and crushed
1 pint sour cream
½–¾ cup plain yogurt
salt and pepper, to taste
¼–½ cup chicken stock (optional)
3 dashes Tabasco
green onions, chopped, for garnish
parsley, chopped, for garnish
slivered almonds, lightly toasted, for garnish

Directions:

Place cucumbers in food processor. Add garlic, sour cream, yogurt, salt, and pepper and blend well. Adjust consistency by adding chicken stock if too thick, or more yogurt if too thin. Add Tabasco and adjust seasoning to taste. Place in covered container and chill overnight. Serve in 2 bowls and garnish with chopped green onions, parsley, and a sprinkling of lightly toasted slivered almonds.

Onion Soup

YIELD: 8–10 servings

Ingredients:

1 tablespoon olive oil
2½ pounds mild onions, peeled, halved lengthwise, and thinly sliced
2 cloves garlic, peeled, sliced, and minced
8 cups beef stock
1 cup water
2 teaspoons salt
¼ teaspoon black pepper
5 English muffins
Worcestershire sauce, to taste
soy sauce, to taste
10 thin slices Provolone cheese
10 teaspoons Parmesan cheese, grated or shaved plus extra for sering

Directions:

Preheat oven to 325°F. In a large heavy pot, heat oil over medium-low heat, add onions, and cook, stirring only occasionally so that onions brown evenly and don't burn. Add the garlic and stir for 1 minute until fragrant, then increase the heat to medium-high, add the beef stock, water, salt, and pepper and bring soup to a boil, then lower heat and simmer for 45 minutes. In the meantime, cut English muffins in half so you have 10 rounds, place on a cookie sheet, and bake 10 to 15 minutes. When soup is cooked, add Worcestershire and soy sauce to taste and adjust seasonings. Remove from heat, increase your oven heat to broil, then ladle soup into individual, ovenproof soup bowls, top each with an English Muffin crouton, a slice of Provolone cheese, and a sprinkle of Parmesan. Place bowls on a rimmed cookie sheet or baking sheet so they won't spill when setting on the wire racks. Broil about 5 minutes, keeping a sharp eye on them, just until cheese is melted and beginning to become golden brown. Sprinkle each with a bit more Parmesan and serve immediately.

Owen's Clam Chowder with Bacon & Potatoes

YIELD: 4–6 servings

Ingredients for clam stock:

1 tablespoon butter
½ cup onions, peeled, sliced, and roughly chopped
2 pounds Manila clams in shells
2 cups dry white wine

Ingredients for soup:

¼ cup bacon, small diced
1 tablespoon butter
¼ cup onion, peeled, sliced, and large diced
¼ cup celery, sliced and large diced
2 cups reserved clam stock
1 cup Yukon Gold potatoes, peeled and diced into ½-inch cubes
1 cup heavy cream
2 cups milk
reserved clams
salt and pepper, to taste
oyster crackers, to serve

Directions for clam stock:

In a large pot over medium heat, melt butter, then add onions and cook only a few minutes until onions begin to soften. Add clams and wine, bring to a gentle simmer, and cook for 10 minutes or until all clams have opened. Remove from heat and get rid of any clams that have not opened. Strain remainder through a fine strainer, reserve the liquid for later, shuck clams, and reserve them in a separate bowl.

Directions for soup:

If you put your bacon in the freezer for a few hours or even overnight and use kitchen shears, it's much easier to cut into pieces. In a large pot or Dutch oven over medium heat, cook bacon pieces in butter until almost done, then add onion and celery and cook just until they begin to soften. Add reserved clam stock, potatoes, and cream and simmer until vegetables are tender. Add milk, reserved clams, and cook for only 30 seconds, just to barely heat ingredients. Season with salt and pepper, taste, and adjust seasonings. Spoon into serving bowls and serve with oyster crackers.

Pork Noodles

YIELD: 6 servings

Ingredients:

2 pounds pork or chicken tenderloin, sliced in
   thin strips
2 tablespoons sesame oil, divided
2 tablespoons Asian seasoning mix
4 (3 ounce) packages instant ramen noodles
2 medium carrots, peeled and julienned
1 medium red pepper, stemmed, deseeded,
   and sliced thin
4 cups water
6 green onions, sliced, green parts separated
   from white parts
soy sauce, for serving

Directions:

Combine meat with 1 tablespoon sesame oil, Asian seasoning mix, and 2 of the instant noodle seasoning packets. Mix well. Add remaining sesame oil to a large 12-inch skillet over medium-high heat and add half the meat, stirring while cooking for 2 to 3 minutes or until meat is browned. Remove meat from skillet, set aside, and keep warm. Repeat with remaining meat, remove from skillet, and set aside when cooked. Add carrots and red pepper to skillet and cook 2 minutes until crisp. Add water and remaining 2 seasoning packets, stir, and scrape bottom of skillet to loosen browned bits from the bottom, then add noodles and white parts of green onions. Cover and simmer for 4 to 5 minutes until noodles are softened. Add meat mixture and stir well, remove skillet from heat, and let stand covered 3 to 5 minutes until meat is heated through. To serve, dish up in bowls and garnish with green onion tops. Add soy sauce for flavor if desired.

Quick Cream of Tomato Soup

YIELD: 4 servings

Ingredients:

4 cups tomato juice
⅓ cup onions, peeled, sliced, and chopped
¼ cup (½ stick) butter
¼–⅓ cup flour
2 tablespoons sugar
1 teaspoon salt
¼ teaspoon pepper
4 cups (1 quart) cold milk

Directions:

In a large saucepan, heat tomato juice and onion and boil for 10 minutes. Remove from heat and with a slotted spoon, remove onions. In a small saucepan, melt butter and slowly add and mix flour to make a roux, then slowly add to the saucepan with the tomato juice and mix well. Return mixture to medium heat and cook until it thickens. Add sugar, salt, and pepper and remove from heat. Beat in cold milk, 1 cup at a time, then return to stove and heat but do not boil.

West African Peanut Soup

YIELD: 6 servings

Ingredients:

1 tablespoon oil
2 cups onion, peeled, sliced, and chopped
½–1 teaspoon cayenne, to taste
1 teaspoon fresh ginger, peeled and grated
1 cup carrots, peeled, sliced, and coarsely chopped
2 cups sweet potato, peeled, sliced, and coarsely chopped
4 cups vegetable broth or water
2 cups V8 juice or tomato juice
1 cup smooth peanut butter
1 tablespoon sugar, optional
1 cup green onions, sliced, to garnish
Tabasco sauce, optional to serve

Directions:

Heat oil in a large pot over medium heat. Add onion and sauté until soft and transparent, about 5 minutes. Reduce heat to low, add cayenne and ginger, and stir to combine, then add carrots and sauté a few minutes longer just until carrots start to soften. Add sweet potato and broth, increase heat and bring to a full boil, then reduce heat to medium-low and cook 15 to 20 minutes, until all vegetables are tender. Remove from heat and let cool, 30 minutes. Working in batches and using a blender or food processor, purée vegetables and cooking liquid, adding V8 juice as you're blending. Return purée to the pot and place over low heat. Stir in peanut butter, stirring constantly until smooth and heated through. Taste, add sugar if needed (the sweetness of the soup depends on flavor of potatoes and sweet potatoes), and mix. To serve, immediately place in soup bowls, garnish with green onion slices, and pass around the Tabasco for those who want a spicier soup.

CHAPTER 18
Veggies

Karl and Carol's (& Joe's Garden) Story

It was a sunny Bellingham day in 1958 when Karol, a bright and curious seven-year-old, pressed her face against the window of the family's old Nash Rambler and saw a sign that read "Joe's Garden." Joe's Garden was a small local truck garden that provided fresh produce, including the finest garlic, to the local Bellingham stores. The garlic that Joe had brought from his home in Italy is still considered by many to be one of the best strains of garlic available. Joe's Garden's awards, state fair ribbons, media coverage, newspaper articles, and magazine photo stories could well fill a small trunk. Bellingham was a small town, a good place to farm and raise a family, and this beautiful garden and setting never left Karol's memory—eventually, it would change her life forever.

In 1959, a third generation Southsider from Bellingham, Carl Weston, was celebrating his fifteenth birthday with a trial job at Joe's Garden—a job that would last for ten years. Since Joe's Garden closed for the winter seasons, Carl knew that he needed a full-time job, so he applied for and began working a new job at Uniflite, a power boat builder.

In the spring of 1970, Karol was eighteen and newly engaged when she and her sister drove into Joe's Garden to pick up a few fresh veggies and garlic for the family dinner. It had been eleven years since Karol was first struck by this beautiful garden, this very special small piece of land. A handsome, blonde, well-built young man with a crate of lettuce on his strapping shoulders came up to them to help with their selection, and it was one of those moments that was meant to be. Karol and Carl took one look at each other, and Karol slipped her engagement ring from another man off of her finger. Six months later, when Karol was nineteen and Carl just twenty-five, they were married. Both went to work at Uniflite shortly after, where my husband Stanley and I first met Karol and Carl and formed a fast friendship that has continued for nearly forty years.

In 1974, my husband Stanley Dabney, vice president and co-founder of Valiant Yachts, and I were in Bellingham at the Uniflite factory going over final production ideas with Nathan Rothman, Valiant Yachts president, and Carl Weston, who was now a lead man in the company's contracts division. Carl was presented the new Valiant sailboat project by Uniflite because of his motivation and intense pride in doing everything better than it had ever been done before. Carl still stopped by Joe's Garden to buy veggies and fresh garlic for his family, but mostly he wanted to let Joe know that he would be interested in buying the garden if Joe and his wife Ann ever decided to sell. The day that Carl and Karol got the call from Joe and Ann that the farm was available for sale was a day that would change their whole world. On March 3, 1983, Carl and Karol left boat manufacturing behind them and became full-time farmers and owners of their much-loved Joe's Garden. With Joe as their teacher, guardian, and patriarch of the garden, Carl and Karol learned even more than they thought was possible. The presence of Joe and Ann has been an influence of friendship and family and warmth that has entwined these two families for many years.

Carl and Karol have been married for forty-plus years. It has been one of those very special relationships that is truly a happy joining of two people. They are best friends and working partners. In those years, not much has changed at Joe's Garden except for the addition of rows and rows of fresh flowers, a beautiful sight to behold, and as it turned out, a profitable market item. Karol spends her days putting together big, beautiful, and fragrant bouquets for customers, but Joe's Garden still provides produce for the community. Customers have become good friends, former workers return to show their children where they happily worked on warm summer days, and people visit from all over the world, filling Carl and Karol with precious memories and friendships.

Carl and Karol travel the world in the garden's off season. Reminiscent of French family vineyards, today Carl and Karol live in a fabulous Chateau style house just above the farm, which they designed and built. It is filled with family warmth, joy, and love. Every room looks out over the beauty of the garden, a garden filled with garlic, basil, vegetables of all sorts, and colorful and fragrant fresh flowers; it is a special place within a special place.

The garlic from Joe's Garden continues to win accolades from gourmet chefs from the Virgin Islands to Alaska and from the regular clients who come by car and truck to buy fresh and braided garlic from Joe's hand. When these folks pull out of the garden, their cars and trucks are loaded up with fresh and fragrant flowers, herbs, vegetables, and one of the world's greatest and best kept secrets—garlic from Joe's Garden. It is still said with pride, "From Joe's!"

The knowledge and success of contained space gardening that Carl and Karol have achieved is unlike that of any other garden; knowledge that he and Karol are passing to their sons. Carl tests experimental seed varieties for various companies and guards the garden's soil and seeds with the future in mind. All of the weeding and harvesting is done by hand, and there have been no sprays used for over twenty-five years. By practicing sustainable agriculture, Joe's Garden will continue on for future generations of Joe's Garden aficionados.

A Note from Karol

"We were so proud of the first boat we built and sailed for many years. We have now built a second boat, but we will always have the best memories of building our first boat with our family. During the summer months, after a hard day's work in the garden, we walk home, looking back at the sight of peas in long rows and all the colors that vegetables and flowers can grow, and we bask in the knowledge that tomorrow we will start another growing day—and we will never have to fight traffic commuting to work!"

Karol's Swiss Chard with Linguine & Walnuts

My good friend Karol likes to dress the top with more cheese, and has found that the mixed-color chard works just as well as the standard green chard.

YIELD: 6 servings

Ingredients:

1½ cups shelled walnuts, chopped
2 pounds Swiss chard, washed
4 tablespoons olive oil
5 shallots, minced
salt and pepper, to taste
1 pound linguine, cooked according to package directions
½ pound Monterey Jack cheese, grated

Directions:

Place walnuts in a large skillet and toast over medium heat for about 10 minutes. Set aside. Trim the Swiss chard, discarding tough stems and coarsely chopping the leaves. Both the lush dark green leaves and the thick white ribs of the chard plant can be eaten, each cooked in different ways. The leaves can be steamed, sautéed, or stuffed. (The stems are delicious stewed or in a chard gratin.) It is best to separate the leaves from the ribs before cooking by loosely folding the leaf in half along the stem, grasping the folded leaf in one hand, and separating the stem by pulling the stem away with your other hand. Heat the oil in a large skillet over medium heat. Add the shallots and cook about ten minutes until soft. Add the chard and season with salt and pepper. Cook until leaves have wilted. Meanwhile, cook the pasta, drain, and reserve ¼ cup of the cooking water. Add the pasta and liquid to the chard mixture. Stir in cheese and walnuts and serve.

Karol's Orange-Infused Beet & Pasta Salad

This pasta salad is pink in color and wonderful to eat! The textures and sweet and citrus flavors just sparkle in your mouth.

YIELD: *4 servings*

Ingredients:

½ pound penne pasta, cooked according to package directions
4 medium cooked beets
1 teaspoon orange zest
¼ cup orange juice
1 shallot, minced
2 cloves garlic, minced
1½ teaspoons rice vinegar
½ teaspoon sugar
1 tablespoon stone ground mustard
¼ cup olive oil
¼ cup hazelnuts, chopped, for garnish
chives or green onions, chopped, for garnish

Directions:

Cook the pasta and drain water. Chop beets into bite-sized pieces and toss with the pasta and orange zest. In a small saucepan, bring the orange juice, shallots, garlic, rice vinegar, and sugar to a boil. Lower the heat and simmer for about 2 minutes until the liquid is syrupy. Stir in mustard and drizzle in oil while whisking. Pour the warm vinaigrette over the pasta and stir. Garnish with hazelnuts and chives.

NOTE FROM THE AUTHOR:

As a garlic aficionado, I continue after all these years to only cook with Joe's Garden Garlic. They ship their fabulous garlic anywhere that I am and will do the same for anyone, so please do yourself a favor and contact them for your delivery order at www.joesgarden.com.

Asparagus with Toasted Bread Crumbs

YIELD: 4 servings

Ingredients:

zest from ½ lemon plus more to garnish
1 pound asparagus, washed and trimmed to same length
1 tablespoon butter or more to taste
1 cup bread crumbs
salt, to taste
freshly ground black pepper, to taste

Directions:

Set zest of ½ lemon aside in a small bowl, then grate a little more of the lemon to garnish asparagus and set aside in a small bowl. In the meantime, melt butter over medium heat in a large skillet. Add bread crumbs and zest of ½ lemon and cook, stirring frequently, until the crumbs are golden and lightly toasted, 3 to 5 minutes. Add more butter as it's cooking if you prefer a more buttery topping. Transfer the crumbs to a plate and season with salt and pepper. To cook asparagus, put it in a micro-wave container, add about ½–¾ inches of water but not enough to cover asparagus, and microwave for 3 to 4 minutes. Check tenderness but do not overcook; microwave for another 60 seconds if necessary, checking doneness with a fork halfway through. Drain asparagus, pat dry, and transfer to a serving dish. To boil asparagus, bring a large pot of water to a boil. Cook asparagus just until tender, 1 to 2 minutes, depending on the thickness of the spears. Drain and pat dry and transfer to a serving dish. To serve, top asparagus with crumb mixture and serve immediately. This sautéed crumb mixture is also wonderful on salads, casseroles, fish, meat, and veggies such as cauliflower.

Aunt B's Eggplant Creole

YIELD: 4–6 servings

Ingredients:

1 medium eggplant, peeled and diced
3 tablespoons butter plus extra for topping eggplant
3 tablespoons flour
3 large tomatoes or 1 (28 ounce) can whole tomatoes with juices
1 green pepper, stemmed, deseeded, and chopped
1 small onion, peeled, sliced, and chopped
2–3 garlic cloves, peeled, sliced, and minced
1 teaspoon salt
3–4 tablespoons brown sugar, to taste
1 bay leaf
7–10 whole cloves, to taste
fresh thyme, to taste
bread crumbs, to top
cheese, grated, to top

Directions:

Preheat oven to 350°F. Grease a large casserole dish or baking pan. In a large saucepan over medium-high heat, boil the peeled and diced eggplant for 10 minutes, then drain and place eggplant in the prepared casserole dish. In a large saucepan, whisk butter and flour together until mixed, then add tomatoes, green pepper, onion, garlic, salt, brown sugar, bay leaf, cloves, and thyme and cook 5 to 8 minutes, until well blended and bubbly. Pour over eggplant in the casserole dish, then top with bread crumbs, dots of butter evenly placed all over the top, and grated cheese of your choice. Place in oven and cook 30 minutes or until browned and nice and bubbly. This is also delicious frozen and reheated.

Charred Brussels Sprouts

YIELD: 4 servings

Ingredients:

1 pound small to medium Brussels sprouts, trimmed and halved
4 tablespoons olive oil, divided
4 teaspoons honey, divided
½ teaspoon Kosher salt
4 garlic cloves, minced
4 anchovy fillets, minced
¼ teaspoon red pepper flakes
2 teaspoons lemon juice

Directions:

In a large bowl, toss the sprouts with 1 tablespoon oil, 2 teaspoons honey, and salt. Set aside. In a 12 to 14-inch heavy skillet, combine the remaining oil, garlic, anchovies and red pepper flakes. Place over high heat and cook, stirring occasionally until the garlic begins to turn a light yellow/gold color. Remove skillet from heat, scrape the pan ingredients into a bowl, and set aside. Return the skillet to high heat and add the sprouts (reserve the bowl) and make sure all sprouts are cut-side down in a single layer. Cook without moving sprouts until they are deep brown and a bit blackened in spots, 3 to 7 minutes depending on your stove and type of skillet. Use tongs and flip the sprouts cut-side up and cook until charred and just tender, another 3 to 5 minutes. As they finish cooking, return sprouts to the bowl and toss with the garlic mixture, remaining honey, and lemon juice. Season with salt and a small amount of red pepper flakes.

Brussels Sprouts Gratin

YIELD: 4–6 servings

Ingredients:

1 pound Brussels sprouts, trimmed and halved lengthwise
Kosher salt and freshly ground black pepper, to taste
½ teaspoon dried chili flakes
½ cup heavy cream
¼ cup extra sharp cheddar cheese, grated
¼ cup smoked Gouda, grated
½ cup bread crumbs
2 tablespoons butter, melted

Directions:

Preheat oven to 450°F. Bring a large pot of salted water to a boil. Add Brussels sprouts and cook over medium-high heat until just tender, about 4 to 5 minutes. Drain and season with salt and pepper. Add chili flakes to sprouts and toss gently to combine. Spray a baking dish with non-stick cooking spray and scoop Brussels sprout mixture evenly into the baking dish. Pour the heavy cream over the sprouts. In a small bowl, combine both cheeses, bread crumbs, and melted butter and mix to combine, then sprinkle evenly over the Brussels sprouts. Place on middle rack in oven and bake 20 to 25 minutes until the top is golden brown.

Buttery Asparagus with Hollandaise Sauce

YIELD: 4–5 servings

Ingredients:

1¼ tablespoons white wine vinegar
1¼ tablespoons fresh lemon juice
3 egg yolks
pinch of salt
½ cup (1 stick) unsalted butter, melted plus 2 tablespoons
20–30 asparagus spears, trimmed
salt and pepper, to taste
hot sauce, to taste

Directions:

In a medium-size heatproof bowl, combine the vinegar, lemon juice, egg yolks, and a pinch of salt and whisk until thoroughly combined. Set bowl over a pan of simmering water on low heat and whisk for about 3 minutes, until the mixture is thick enough to leave a trail when the whisk is lifted. In the meantime, melt ½ cup butter in a small pan over low heat. Add egg yolk mixture to butter just a little at a time, whisking constantly. Season to taste and keep warm while cooking the asparagus. In a large pan of boiling water add asparagus and cook 3 to 6 minutes, depending on their size, until just tender. Drain asparagus, return to the pan, and quickly toss in 2 tablespoons of butter. To serve, slide the buttery asparagus onto a warmed serving plate and spoon the Hollandaise sauce over. Add salt, pepper, and hot sauce to taste.

Calico Baked Beans

YIELD: 12 servings

Ingredients:

1 pound ground beef
1 large onion, peeled, sliced, and chopped
2 tablespoons butter
1 pound bacon, cooked, drained, and cut into
    1-inch pieces
½ cup white sugar
½ cup brown sugar
¼ cup ketchup
¼ cup barbeque sauce
2 tablespoons prepared mustard
2 tablespoons molasses
¾ teaspoon chili powder
1 teaspoon salt
½ teaspoon pepper
1 (16 ounce) can kidney beans, drained
1 (16 ounce) can lima beans, drained
1 (28 ounce) can pork and beans

Directions:

Preheat oven to 350°F. In large skillet, brown beef and onion in butter over medium heat. Drain well and place meat mixture in large casserole. Add cooked bacon and mix well. In a medium bowl, combine sugars, ketchup, barbeque sauce, mustard, molasses, chili powder, salt, and pepper and mix well; set aside. Add kidney beans, lima beans, and pork and beans to casserole, then pour sugar mixture on top. Blend well. Cover casserole, place on middle rack of oven, and bake 45 minutes. Uncover casserole and bake additional 15 minutes. This casserole can remain covered in low oven for 1 hour. It's also perfect divided and frozen.

Cheesy Baked Hash Brown Patties

YIELD: 9 servings

Ingredients:

4 red potatoes
½ cup butter, melted
1 cup cheddar cheese, shredded
2 eggs, whisked
¼ cup green onions, chopped
1 tablespoon garlic salt
1 teaspoon oregano
½ teaspoon pepper
1 jalapeño, stemmed, halved, deseeded,
    membranes removed, finely chopped

Directions:

Preheat oven to 400°F. Peel and grate the potatoes, put into a large bowl of ice water, mix around with your hands to remove starch, then strain or squeeze grated potato shreds to dry as much as possible and transfer to a large bowl. Add butter, cheese, eggs, green onions, garlic salt, oregano, pepper, and jalapeño and mix together. Using your hand, pack the patties into the shape you want and place them on a lightly sprayed baking sheet. Bake for 40 to 45 minutes or until brown and crispy. Allow to cool for 5 minutes.

Chili Carrots

YIELD: 4 servings

Ingredients:

4 medium carrots, peeled and sliced in ½-inch pieces
1 tablespoon olive oil
1 tablespoon honey
½–1 teaspoon chili powder
salt and pepper, to taste

Directions:

In a large skillet, cook carrots in olive oil, stirring constantly until just beginning to be tender. In a small bowl, combine honey and chili powder, add to carrots and oil and cook while stirring for 1 additional minute or until everything is well mixed and carrots are cooked to your desired doneness. Season with salt and pepper, stir, and serve.

Glazed Pearl Onions

YIELD: 4–6 servings

Ingredients:

1 pound pearl onions
1 tablespoon cooking oil
1 large clove garlic, peeled and thinly sliced
½ cup orange marmalade
½ teaspoon salt
⅛ teaspoon black pepper
1 tablespoon green onions, thinly sliced

Directions:

In a medium-sized saucepan, cook onion in enough boiling water to cover them for 1 minute. Drain well, reserving some of the boiling water, and cool onions a few minutes, then slip peels off and cut root ends off. Place prepared onions in the same saucepan with a small amount of boiling, lightly salted water for 10 minutes or until tender. Drain well and set aside. In a large oiled skillet over medium-high heat, add garlic and cook and stir 30 seconds until garlic is golden brown. Immediately stir in marmalade and continue to stir until marmalade has melted, then stir in onions, salt, and pepper and cook 3 to 5 minutes. Continue to stir until marmalade is slightly thickened and onions are coated. Stir in green onions, mix well, and serve.

Creamy Mashed Potatoes

YIELD: 8–10 servings

Ingredients:

4 pounds Yukon Gold potatoes, peeled, cut into 2-inch pieces
6 large garlic cloves, peeled, sliced, and minced
1 tablespoon salt plus 2 teaspoons
1¼ cups whole milk
4 thyme sprigs
¾ cup (1½ sticks) plus 2 tablespoons unsalted butter, divided
2 teaspoons salt
¾ teaspoon freshly ground black pepper
½ cup sour cream

Directions:

Scrub potatoes, rinse, peel, and cut into 2-inch pieces. Place potatoes, garlic, and 1 tablespoon salt in a large pot filled with cold water. Cover and bring to a low boil, then reduce heat and simmer (do not boil) until potatoes are very tender but not falling apart or mushy when pierced with the tip of a paring knife, about 20 to 25 minutes. In the meantime, heat milk, thyme, and ¾ cup butter in a small pot over medium heat, stirring until butter is melted, then remove from heat and set aside. Drain potatoes and garlic, return to pot, and toss and shake over low heat until moisture evaporates, about 1 to 2 minutes. With a potato ricer, food mill, or masher, immediately press potatoes and garlic into a large bowl without letting them cool. Discard thyme from milk mixture and gradually stir into potatoes. Season with remaining salt and pepper. Fold in sour cream and stir with a spoon until incorporated and very smooth, being careful not to overmix. Taste and adjust seasonings. Serve topped with remaining butter and more pepper to taste.

Pan-Browned Brussels Sprouts

YIELD: 2–3 servings

Ingredients:

3 tablespoons butter
1–2 tablespoon olive oil
2 large garlic cloves, peeled and thinly sliced
½ pound Brussels sprouts, trimmed and
    halved lengthwise
2–4 tablespoons pine nuts
coarse salt, to taste
freshly ground black pepper
¼ cup shaved Parmesan, for serving

Directions:

In a 10-inch heavy skillet, melt 1½ tablespoons butter with oil over moderate heat, add garlic, stirring constantly until pale golden. Transfer garlic with a slotted spoon to a small bowl and reserve. Reduce heat to low and arrange sprouts in skillet cut-sides down in one layer. Sprinkle sprouts with pine nuts and salt to taste. Cook sprouts without turning until crisp-tender and undersides are golden brown, about 10 minutes, then cover and cook about 5 more minutes to bring up color and increase moisture. With tongs, transfer sprouts to a plate, browned sides up. Add cooked garlic and remaining butter to skillet and cook over moderate heat, stirring, until pine nuts are more evenly pale golden in color, about 1 minute. Spoon mixture over sprouts and sprinkle with freshly ground black pepper and shaved Parmesan.

Pesto Potatoes

YIELD: 6–8 servings

Ingredients:

6 medium russet potatoes, peels left on
¾ cup prepared pesto
Parmesan cheese

Directions:

Preheat oven to 450°F. Scrub potatoes and cut into large bite-sized cubes and place in a large re-sealable plastic bag. Add pesto sauce, using more if necessary, to the bag and shake and massage bag until pesto is coating all the potato pieces. Pour the contents of the bag out onto a cookie sheet, squeezing bag to get out all the pesto. Arrange the potatoes so they are lying flat, sprinkle with Parmesan cheese to get a nice coating, and bake for 25 to 30 minutes or until they begin to look lightly toasted and feel done when pierced with a fork.

Pickled Fennel with Orange Zest

YIELD: 1 large jar

Ingredients:

¾ cup orange juice
¾ cup white vinegar
1 tablespoon sugar
1 teaspoon black peppercorns
2 fennel bulbs plus fennel sprigs
1 teaspoon Kosher salt
zested strips of 1 orange

Directions:

In a medium saucepan, bring orange juice, vinegar, sugar, and peppercorns to a boil, stirring constantly until sugar is fully dissolved. Remove from heat and set aside to cool. Cut fennel bulbs into slices and place in a large bowl. Sprinkle 1 teaspoon of Kosher salt on top, toss fennel well, and let it stand for 1 hour. Zest the orange into strips, making sure not to include any of the white membrane. Drain the fennel slices, discard the brine, rinse fennel under cold water, and drain again. Toss the orange zest strips into the bowl of drained fennel and mix well. Pack fennel slices and orange zest into jars and add a few of the fennel sprigs. Pour the orange juice brine over jar, tightly seal, and refrigerate for 24 to 48 hours or longer before serving. Pickled fennel is delicious to munch on or you can toss it in with a shrimp or chicken salad, serve it as a small side with meat dishes, or mounded on top of a cooked fish.

Cheesy Potato Soufflé

YIELD: 4 servings

Ingredients:

3 small baking potatoes, peeled and cut into
    1-inch cubes
1 egg
1 cup ricotta cheese
½ cup half-and-half
1 cup Gruyere cheese, grated, divided
1½ teaspoons Kosher salt
fresh pepper, to taste

Directions:

Preheat oven to 350°F. Place cubed potatoes in a medium saucepan, cover with cold water, and bring to a boil. Lower heat, cover, and simmer until tender, 12 to 15 minutes, but check after 10 minutes. Drain potatoes and run through a ricer, thoroughly mince potatoes, and mash. In a medium-sized bowl, whisk the egg with the ricotta until smooth and while still whisking, add half-and-half, then ¾ cup Gruyere. Stir in prepared potatoes and mix well to blend completely. Season with salt and pepper and mix to blend. Scoop ingredients into a small very lightly greased casserole dish and bake 30 minutes until soufflé is set and heated through. Sprinkle remaining Gruyere on top, return to oven, and bake until cheese is just melted. Gently divide among 4 plates and serve.

Potatoes au Gratin

YIELD: 4–6 servings

Ingredients:

6–7 small potatoes, skin scrubbed clean and diced

2 tablespoons butter, room temperature

½ cup milk

1½ cups heavy cream

2 tablespoons all-purpose flour

3–5 garlic cloves, peeled, sliced, and minced

1 teaspoon salt

pepper, to taste

1½ cups sharp cheddar, yellow or white, shredded

handful of fresh chives or green onions, thinly sliced

Directions:

Preheat the oven to 400°F. Dice the potatoes and place them in a buttered shallow baking or casserole dish and set aside. In a medium bowl, combine the milk and cream and add flour, garlic, salt, and pepper while whisking. Scrape milk mixture out and pour over potatoes. Cover dish with foil, place in oven, and bake for 30 minutes. Remove the foil and bake uncovered for another 20 to 30 minutes. Pull au gratin out of the oven, sprinkle with sharp cheese, and bake for another 3 to 5 minutes or until cheese is melted and bubbly. Sprinkle chives on top and serve immediately.

Grilled Balsamic Asparagus

YIELD: 4 servings

Ingredients:

2 pounds (24 pieces) large asparagus spears, trimmed to uniform sizes

balsamic vinegar, to taste

extra virgin olive oil, to taste

coarse sea salt, to taste

freshly ground black pepper, to taste

hard Parmesan cheese, for shaving as garnish

Directions:

Preheat oven to 400°F. Arrange asparagus spears in a single layer on a large rimmed baking sheet, then splash balsamic vinegar on top and refrigerate for 30 minutes. When ready to grill, coat asparagus with olive oil and salt and pepper. Place asparagus in a vegetable basket over a hot grill, turning frequently for 6 to 8 minutes or until some of the spears begin to crisp. To serve, place on a large platter and use a vegetable peeler to shave Parmesan over the spears.

Ricotta Spinach Pie

YIELD: 6–8 servings

Ingredients:

2 tablespoons butter
¼ cup green onions, chopped
1 (10 ounce) package frozen chopped spinach,
    thawed and drained
1 (15 ounce) container ricotta cheese
4 eggs, beaten plus 1 beaten egg to glaze pie
½ cup grated Parmesan cheese
⅓ cup prosciutto, finely chopped
¼ teaspoon nutmeg
¼ teaspoon salt
pepper, to taste
pastry shell for a 9-inch double crust pie

Directions:

Preheat oven to 425°F. In a large skillet over medium heat, melt butter, add green onions, and cook until soft. Let cool slightly and add the spinach, mixing onions and spinach well, and cook until all the butter is absorbed. Scoop all the spinach mixture into a large bowl and spoon ricotta into mixture a bit at a time, mixing well to combine. Add the 4 beaten eggs, Parmesan, prosciutto, nutmeg, salt, and pepper and mix everything together until well blended. Set aside. Roll out half the pastry and line a 9-inch pie plate, prick the crust with a fork, place in the oven, and bake 12 minutes or until lightly golden. Remove from the oven, brush outer edge with the remaining beaten egg, reserving some for the pastry top. Scoop all the spinach filling into the crust. Roll out the remaining pastry, place over the filling, seal the edges, and cut several slits in the top pastry. Place oven rack in lowest position, put pie in the center of the rack, and bake for 20 minutes. Reduce temperature to 350°F and bake an additional 20 minutes. Serve warm, room temperature, or chilled.

Sesame Cucumbers

YIELD: 4 servings

Ingredients:

2 tablespoons vinegar
2 tablespoons soy sauce
1 tablespoon sugar
1 teaspoon ginger, finely chopped
2 large cucumbers, peeled and thinly sliced
2 tablespoons sesame seed oil

Directions:

In a medium-sized bowl, mix vinegar, soy sauce, sugar, and ginger and blend until well combined. Peel and slice cucumbers paper thin and place in vinegar mixture. Cover and refrigerate for 2 hours, then add sesame oil, mix well, and serve.

Shallots Braised with Vermouth

YIELD: 8 servings

Ingredients:

2 pounds (16) large shallots
Kosher salt, to taste
4 tablespoons (½ stick) butter, cubed
pepper, to taste
1 cup dry vermouth
2 teaspoons white wine vinegar
¼ cup heavy cream

Directions:

Preheat oven to 325°F. Place shallots in a medium-sized saucepan, cover with water, and bring to a boil. Add a pinch of salt, reduce heat to low, and simmer for 10 minutes. Remove from heat, drain the shallots, and let cool a bit. Remove shallots from pan, and trim off the roots and tops until the skins easily slip off. Melt butter in a large skillet; add prepared shallots and season with salt and pepper. Cook over medium heat, stirring occasionally until shallots are browned, about 3 to 5 minutes. Add the vermouth and bring to a boil, reduce heat to medium, then cook until the liquid is reduced by half, about 3 to 4 minutes. Remove from heat, stir in vinegar, and transfer shallots with all the liquid into a 1½ quart baking dish. Cover dish with foil, place in oven, and bake for 30 minutes or until shallots are very tender. Transfer 3 tablespoons of the sauce in the baking dish to a small bowl, let cool a bit, then whisk in the heavy cream a little at a time, making sure that cream does not curdle. Stir the cream mixture back into the shallots, season with salt and pepper, and serve.

Spicy Indonesian Green Beans

YIELD: 4 servings

Ingredients:

4 tablespoons peanut oil
½ cup onions, minced
1 large clove garlic, peeled, sliced, and minced
2 tablespoons lemon rind, grated
¼–½ teaspoon red pepper flakes, to taste
1 bay leaf
1 pound green beans, washed and destemmed
1 teaspoon salt
pinch of sugar

Directions:

Heat oil in a large skillet and add onions, garlic, lemon rind, and red pepper flakes, and the bay leaf and sauté on medium-high for 3 minutes. Add prepared beans, mixing well, cover, and cook over low heat until beans are barely tender. Add more oil if necessary. Remove bay leaf and season with salt and sugar to taste.

Sweet Potato Casserole

YIELD: 4–6 servings

Ingredients:

2 large sweet potatoes
3 tablespoons butter plus ⅓ cup
2 tablespoons half-and-half
salt, to taste
½ cup brown sugar
¼ cup flour
1 cup pecans, chopped

Directions:

Preheat oven to 350°F. Poke sweet potatoes a few times with a fork, place on oven rack, and bake until they are tender. Remove from oven, peel, and mash them in a large bowl; you should have about 3 to 4 cups of mashed sweet potatoes. Add 3 tablespoons butter and continue to mash, then add half-and-half and salt and mix well. Scoop mashed sweet potatoes into a buttered or lightly greased large casserole dish. In a small bowl, mix the brown sugar, flour, remaining butter, and pecans together until crumbly and scatter mixture over top of casserole. Bake 20 minutes or until the edges are bubbling and the topping is lightly browned. Serve immediately.

CHAPTER 19
Herbed & Flavored Butters

Herbed & Flavored Butters

When you blend butter with other savory, sweet, or spicy ingredients they're called compound butters. I prefer herbed butters or flavored butters, as compound butters just sounds a little too pharmaceutical to me. These blended butters are just butter combined with various flavors, but they add convenience, flavor, and even a bit of showmanship if serving alongside a dish you've placed before your guests. If you find a sale on butter or an individual who is making fresh butter, stock up. Butter freezes nicely for many months and can also be canned for future use. Once you start blending butter with different herbs and spices, you'll start experimenting with all sorts of flavors as I have, and I've never put together any combination of flavors that weren't absolutely wonderful on the right dish. Flavored butters go well with many foods, whether they are grilled, steamed, barbecued, or baked. They are delicious on artichokes, asparagus, broccoli, carrots, corn bread, crackers, green beans, quick breads, rice, grilled cheese sandwiches, seafood, soups and stews, squash, steaks, and zucchini. Try them on corn on the cob, a baked potato or sweet potato, fries, mushrooms, and pasta. Put different types of flavored butter on your popcorn, make garlic bread from the blends with garlic, fry and scramble eggs, or make a frittata or omelet, and don't forget to use the sweet flavored butters on your pancakes, waffles, and breakfast breads.

The method for making flavored butter is very simple and basically the same regardless of the ingredients you use. Most often ingredients are rolled and frozen, then brought to room temperature 10 to 15 minutes before using, but they can also be formed in a jelly glass or ramekin. Make sure the butter you are starting with is at room temperature. Add the herbs, spices, or other ingredients and mix well until all ingredients are completely blended with a fork, spatula, mixer, or food processor. Once all ingredients are completely combined, scoop the butter mixture onto a sheet of plastic wrap, roll it evenly into a log shape, and wrap tightly around the butter log, making sure to seal the ends with the plastic wrap. The butter mixture is easily workable at room temperature, so make sure the log is rolled evenly whether you're making a short fatter log or a long thinner log, remembering that presentation of these round flavored butter slices will most often wow your guests. Some people prefer to make their logs on parchment paper, then seal in plastic wrap. Both methods work well. After your butter log is sealed, chill until firm in the refrigerator, where it will last for about five days, or in the freezer, where it should last for months. If you're planning on freezing, wrap the plastic covered butter log tightly in aluminum foil and then into a re-sealable plastic bag and don't forget to mark the blend on each log. To serve, dip a knife in hot water, which makes a cleaner cut, and slice the butter log into coins or round slices and bring to room temperature.

Anchovy Butter

YIELD: 1 butter log

Ingredients:

½ cup (1 stick) butter, softened
1 can (about 8 anchovy fillets) anchovies,
    drained and chopped
½ teaspoon hot paprika or cayenne
½ teaspoon fresh lemon juice
4 garlic cloves, minced
Kosher salt, to taste

Directions:

Combine all ingredients; mix well until all ingredients are blended. Roll into a cylinder per basic instructions above (pg. 373), and chill or freeze.

Garlic Chive Butter

YIELD: 4 butter logs

Ingredients:

1 pound (4 sticks) butter, softened
1 tablespoon fresh chives, finely chopped
1 tablespoon salt
2 garlic cloves, minced
1 tablespoon olive oil

Directions:

Combine all ingredients; mix well until all ingredients are blended. Roll into a cylinder per basic instructions above (pg. 373), and chill or freeze.

Cilantro Lime Butter

YIELD: 1 butter log

Ingredients:

½ cup (1 stick) butter, softened
2 tablespoons cilantro, minced
1 clove garlic, minced
zest of 1 small lime
½ tablespoon lime juice
salt and pepper, to taste (optional)

Directions:

Combine all ingredients; mix well until all ingredients are blended. Roll into a cylinder per basic instructions above (pg. 373), and chill or freeze.

Garlic with Herb Butter

YIELD: 2 butter logs

Ingredients:

1 cup (2 sticks) butter, softened
2 garlic cloves, finely minced
1 tablespoon rosemary, minced
1 tablespoon sage, minced
1 tablespoon thyme, minced
1 pinch each salt and pepper
1 tablespoon heavy cream

Directions:

Combine all ingredients; mix well until all ingredients are blended. Roll into a cylinder per basic instructions (pg. 373), and chill or freeze.

Blue Cheese with Herb Butter

YIELD: 2 butter logs

Ingredients:

1 cup (2 sticks) butter, softened
2 tablespoons chives, minced
4 tablespoons blue cheese
pinch salt
4 teaspoons walnuts, finely chopped

Directions:

Combine all ingredients; mix well until all ingredients are blended. Roll into a cylinder per basic instructions (pg. 373), and chill or freeze.

Blue Cheese & Sun-Dried Tomato Butter

YIELD: 1 butter log

Ingredients:

½ cup (1 stick) butter, softened
½ cup blue cheese, crumbled
1 tablespoon garlic, minced
¼ cup sun-dried tomatoes, minced
1 tablespoon basil, minced
1 tablespoon Worcestershire sauce
1 tablespoon lemon juice
1 teaspoon olive oil

Directions:

Combine all ingredients; mix well until all ingredients are blended. Roll into a cylinder per basic instructions (pg. 373), and chill or freeze.

Tarragon Butter

YIELD: 2 butter logs

Ingredients:

1 cup butter, softened (2 sticks of butter)
2 tablespoons parsley, minced
1 clove garlic, minced
1 teaspoon chives, minced
2 tablespoons fresh tarragon or 2 teaspoons dried tarragon
dash pepper

Directions:

Combine all ingredients; mix well until all ingredients are blended. Roll into a cylinder per basic instructions (pg. 373), and chill or freeze.

Bernaise Tarragon Butter

YIELD: 4 butter discs

Ingredients:

3 tablespoons butter, softened
2 teaspoons shallots, minced
2 teaspoons tarragon, minced
½ teaspoon fresh lemon juice or more to taste
⅛ teaspoon salt

Directions:

Combine all ingredients; mix well until all ingredients are blended. Roll into a cylinder per basic instructions (pg. 373), and chill or freeze.

Tarragon with Citrus Butter

YIELD: 2 butter logs

Ingredients:

1 cup (2 sticks) butter, softened
2 tablespoons tarragon, minced
zest from 1 large orange
juice from ½ orange
pinch salt (optional)

Directions:

Combine all ingredients; mix well until all ingredients are blended. Roll into a cylinder per basic instructions (pg. 373), and chill or freeze.

Jalapeño with Paprika Butter

YIELD: *2 butter logs*

Ingredients:

1 cup (2 sticks) butter, softened
2 jalapeños, deseeded and minced
2 tablespoons paprika (smoked or regular)
pinch salt (optional)

Directions:

Combine all ingredients; mix well until all ingredients are blended. Roll into a cylinder per basic instructions (pg. 373), and chill or freeze.

Lemon Butter

YIELD: *2 butter logs*

Ingredients:

1 cup (2 sticks) butter, softened
zest of 2 lemons
1–2 teaspoons lemon juice
1 tablespoon sugar
salt (optional)

Directions:

Combine all ingredients; mix well until all ingredients are blended. Roll into a cylinder per basic instructions (pg. 373), and chill or freeze.

Honey Butter

YIELD: 4 butter logs

Ingredients:

1 pound (4 sticks) butter, softened
½ teaspoon cinnamon
½ teaspoon vanilla extract
¼ cup honey

Directions:

Combine all ingredients; mix well until all ingredients are blended. Roll into a cylinder per basic instructions (pg. 373), and chill or freeze.

Basic Herb Butter

YIELD: 1 butter log

Ingredients:

½ cup (1 stick) butter, softened
1 tablespoon fresh flat-leaf parsley, chopped
1 tablespoon fresh chives, chopped
1 teaspoon lemon zest
2 teaspoons fresh lemon juice
salt and freshly ground pepper, to taste

Directions:

Combine all ingredients; mix well until all ingredients are blended. Roll into a cylinder per basic instructions (pg. 373), and chill or freeze.

Garlic & Horseradish Butter

YIELD: 1 butter log

Ingredients:

½ cup (1 stick) butter, softened
¼ cup horseradish, freshly grated
1 small garlic clove, minced
1½ tablespoons chives, minced
1½ tablespoons parsley, minced

Directions:

Combine all ingredients; mix well until all ingredients are blended. Roll into a cylinder per basic instructions (pg. 373), and chill or freeze.

Jam Butter

YIELD: 2 butter logs

Ingredients:

1 cup (2 sticks) butter, softened
1 cup jam, (strawberry, blackberry, raspberry, apricot, etc.)
1 tablespoon mint leaves, minced
1½ teaspoons salt (optional)

Directions:

Combine all ingredients; mix well until all ingredients are blended. Roll into a cylinder per basic instructions (pg. 373). Because of the fresh mint leaves, this is better served fresh and just chilled a bit.

Whipped Maple Butter

YIELD: 1 butter log

Ingredients:

½ cup unsalted butter, softened
3 tablespoons maple syrup
¼ teaspoon salt, or more to taste

Directions:

Combine all ingredients; mix well until all ingredients are blended. Roll into a cylinder per basic instructions (pg. 373), and chill or freeze.

Walnut, Brown Sugar & Raisin Butter

YIELD: 2 butter logs

Ingredients:

1 cup (2 sticks) butter, softened
¼ cup raisins
¼ cup walnuts, toasted and chopped
½ teaspoon cinnamon
½ teaspoon nutmeg
2½ tablespoons dark brown sugar
1 teaspoon pure vanilla extract

Directions:

Combine all ingredients; mix well until all ingredients are blended. Roll into a cylinder per basic instructions (pg. 373), and chill or freeze.

Jalapeño Butter

YIELD: 1 butter log

Ingredients:

½ cup (1 stick) butter, softened
2 small jalapeños, deseeded, and minced
1 clove garlic, minced
4 tablespoons cilantro with leaves and stems, minced
½ teaspoon salt (optional)

Directions:

Combine all ingredients; mix well until all ingredients are blended. Roll into a cylinder per basic instructions (pg. 373), and chill or freeze.

Roasted Garlic Butter

YIELD: 2 butter logs

Ingredients:

3 large heads of garlic (roasted with skins on)
3 teaspoons virgin olive oil
salt and pepper, to taste
1 cup (2 sticks) butter, softened

Directions:

Preheat oven to 375°F. Keep garlic intact with skins on, clip root ends so that garlic heads stand up straight, and cut just the top off of each head to expose garlic. Drizzle olive oil over each head and add salt and pepper to taste. Place garlic heads on parchment paper, then wrap in foil and place on middle rack of oven and roast for 30 minutes. Remove heads from oven, let cool on a plate, then gently squeeze the cloves of garlic into a bowl to remove them from the skins, mash, and combine with butter; mix well until all ingredients are blended. Roll into a cylinder per basic instructions (pg. 373), and chill or freeze.

Yum, Yum Texas Butter

YIELD: 1 butter log

Ingredients:

½ cup (1 stick) butter, softened
1 teaspoon cinnamon
1 tablespoon honey
¼ cup powdered sugar
pinch of salt (optional)

Directions:

Combine all ingredients; mix well until all ingredients are blended. Roll into a cylinder per basic instructions (pg. 373), and chill or freeze.

Maître d'Hôtel Butter

YIELD: 1 butter log

Ingredients:

½ cup (1 stick) butter, softened
2 tablespoons lemon juice
2 tablespoons chopped fresh parsley
⅛ teaspoon fine sea salt
⅛ teaspoon Dijon mustard
dash smoked paprika
dash pepper
dash hot sauce
lemon zest, to taste

Directions:

This is a little different than the traditional maître d'hôtel butter recipes, as it includes Dijon mustard, lemon zest, and a dash of hot sauce, but it's well worth trying and experimenting with these flavors. Combine all ingredients and mix well until all ingredients are blended. Roll into a cylinder per basic instructions (pg. 373), and chill or freeze.

Hidden Ranch Butter

YIELD: 1 butter log

Ingredients:

½ cup (1 stick) butter, softened
1 (1 ounce) packet Hidden Valley Ranch Salad Dressing & Seasoning Mix

Directions:

Combine all ingredients; mix well until all ingredients are blended. Roll into a cylinder per basic instructions (pg. 373), and chill or freeze.

Brandied Apricot Butter

YIELD: 1¼ cup

Ingredients:

¼ cup dried apricots, finely chopped
¼ cup cognac
2 tablespoons light brown sugar
1 cup (2 sticks) butter, softened
pinch of salt

Directions:

In a small saucepan, soak apricots and brandy for 10 minutes, then bring to a boil and carefully ignite. Reduce the heat to medium and when the flames have subsided, add the brown sugar and cook until sugar is dissolved. Transfer to a mixing bowl and let cool. With an electric mixer, add the butter and whip until ingredients are blended and smooth. Season with a pinch of salt, mix, then scrape the apricot butter into a large ramekin or serving bowl. Serve with popovers, pancakes, waffles, muffins, or on warm crusty bread.

CHAPTER 20
Make It Yourself

Bisquick Mix

YIELD: 2 cups

Ingredients:

2 cups all-purpose flour
3 teaspoons baking powder
1 teaspoon salt
2 tablespoons shortening or butter

Directions:

Mix all ingredients and blend until mixture resembles fine crumbs. Store in a tightly sealed container in a dry, cool place.

Bread Crumbs, Italian Style

YIELD: 1 cup

Ingredients:

1 cup plain bread crumbs
½ teaspoon salt
½ teaspoon parsley flakes
¼ teaspoon onion powder
¼ teaspoon garlic powder
¼ teaspoon sugar
dash oregano

Directions:

In a small bowl, mix all ingredients and blend well. Store in an airtight container. Use for frying or baking pork chops, seafood, chicken, and as a topping for asparagus and other veggies before roasting.

Corn Chips

YIELD: Medium-sized bowl

Ingredients:

½ cup white flour
½ cup cornmeal
½ teaspoon salt
¼ cup milk (more or less)
oil, for frying
salt, for topping

Directions:

Mix all the ingredients except the oil to form stiff dough. Adjust milk and flour as needed. Divide dough on floured board into golf ball–sized pieces and then roll until very thin. They should lift off easily with your fingers. Fry in very shallow oil until brown and bubbly, then drain thoroughly on paper towels. The corn chips should crisp as they start to cool. If they aren't crispy enough, they need longer frying. When cool, break into pieces and sprinkle with salt. Great with guacamole, salsa, or chili.

Greek Seasoning Mix

YIELD: 2 tablespoons

Ingredients:

1½ teaspoons dried oregano
½ teaspoon dried basil
1 teaspoon dried thyme
1 teaspoon dried mint
½ teaspoon dried marjoram
½ teaspoon dried onion
¼ teaspoon dried garlic

Directions:

Combine all ingredients in a small bowl. Store in an airtight container in a cool, dry place for up to 6 months.

Herb-Infused Honey

The following are herbs that make delicious herb-infused honey for cooking, teas, or even for a natural throat soothing cough suppressant. Try it in lemonade, marinades, salad dressings, or on the side of a cheese plate.

YIELD: 1 (4 ounce) container

Ingredient:

½ cup (4 ounces) good quality honey for each 4-ounce container you're making

Optional herb combinations:

Anise seeds, 2 teaspoons
Basil, 1 sprig per ½ cup (4 ounce) sterilized and dried jar
Basil and 1 teaspoon fennel seeds
Basil and 1 teaspoon anise seeds
Cardamom pods, 2 teaspoons
Ginger, peeled, 1 sprig per ½ cup (4 ounce) sterilized and dried jar
Lavender, dried blossoms, 1 sprig per ½ cup (4 ounce) sterilized and dried jar
Mint, 1 sprig per ½ cup (4 ounce) sterilized and dried jar
Oregano, 1 sprig per ½ cup (4 ounce) sterilized and dried jar
Rosemary, 1 sprig per ½ cup (4 ounce) sterilized and dried jar
Rosemary, 1 sprig and 1 strip orange peel, peeled with a hand vegetable peeler
Sage, 1 sprig per ½ cup (4 ounce) sterilized and dried jar
Sage, 1 sprig and 1 stick cinnamon per ½ cup (4 ounce) sterilized and dried jar
Tarragon, 1 sprig per ½ cup (4 ounce) sterilized and dried jar
Thyme, 4 sprigs per ½ cup (4 ounce) sterilized and dried jar
Thyme, 4 sprigs fresh and 1 strip lemon peel, peeled with a hand vegetable peeler

Directions:

For each ½ cup flavored honey, place one of the above-listed herb combinations into a ½ cup (4 ounce) sterilized and dried jar. Some sprigs will have to be bent to fit. Set aside. Place honey in a small saucepan and heat over medium heat until the honey becomes more liquefied or until candy thermometer reaches 180ºF. Honey must not come to a boil. Using a funnel (remember, this is very hot), pour hot honey into each jar, making sure the herbs are submerged by poking them down with a fork if necessary. Place honey jars on a cooling rack and cool to room temperature. When cooled, put a sterilized lid on the jar and tightly seal. Set jar in a cool dark place for at least 1 week before using. Herb-infused honey can be stored in a cool, dark place for up to one year.

Instant Onion Soup & Dip Mix

YIELD: 19 tablespoons

Ingredients:

¾ cup dry, instant onion
4 teaspoons onion powder
¼ cup celery seed, crushed
⅓ cup beef bouillon powder
¼ cup sugar

Directions:

In a small bowl, combine all ingredients and stir to blend. Store in an airtight container. A 1¼-ounce package of store-bought onion soup mix is equal to about 5 tablespoons of homemade mix. To serve as a dip, mix 5 tablespoons with 1 pint of sour cream, taste, and adjust.

Mediterranean Spice Mix

YIELD: ⅓ cup

Ingredients:

3 tablespoons dried rosemary
2 tablespoons ground cumin
2 tablespoons ground coriander
1 tablespoon dried oregano
2 teaspoons ground cinnamon
½ teaspoon salt

Directions:

Place all ingredients in a small bowl and mix well. Store in an airtight container. To use for 4 servings of lamb, beef, poultry, seafood, or for a satay or kabob, mix 2 tablespoons spice mix, 1 tablespoon oil, and 2 cloves of minced garlic and rub on lamb, beef, poultry, seafood, satay, or kabob ingredients and let marinate 30 minutes, then cook according to your recipe.

Red Hot Sauce

YIELD: 6 servings

Ingredients:

18 fresh or canned cayenne peppers, ends and
    stems removed
1½ cups white vinegar
2 teaspoons garlic, peeled, sliced, and minced
1 teaspoon salt
1 teaspoon garlic powder

Directions:

Remove the stems and ends from cayenne peppers and put into a small saucepan over medium heat. Add in all the other ingredients and bring to a boil. Reduce heat and let mixture continue to boil over a slow simmer 20 to 25 minutes. Remove from heat and carefully pour ingredients into a blender or food processor and purée until thick and smooth. Return blended sauce to the sauce pan and simmer for another 15 minutes. Transfer purée to a small saucepan, bring to a boil, and reduce heat and simmer 20 minutes. Refrigerate to age the sauce and incorporate the flavors overnight or longer.

Ricotta

YIELD: 2 cups

Ingredients:

4 cups whole milk
2 cups heavy cream
1 teaspoon Kosher salt
3 tablespoons white wine vinegar

Directions:

Dampen 2 to 3 layers of cheesecloth with water, line the large sieve, and set it over a deep bowl. In a stainless saucepan, combine milk and heavy cream, stir in salt to combine, and bring to a full boil over medium heat, stirring constantly. Remove pan from heat, add vinegar, and stir to combine. Let mixture stand for 1 minute until it curdles, which is called whey. Scoop out all ingredients into the sieve over the bowl and let it drain at room temperature for 20 to 30 minutes. Occasionally discard liquid that collects in the bowl during this time. The longer you let the mixture drain, the thicker your ricotta will be. When it's at your desired consistency, either thicker or moister, transfer ricotta mixture into a bowl, discarding cheesecloth and any remaining whey. Use immediately or tightly cover with plastic wrap or in a tightly sealed container and refrigerate for 4 to 5 days.

Snack Cake Mix

Use for assorted snack cakes. Banana Walnut and Gingerbread Snack Cakes to follow.

YIELD: 12–13 cups or 6 snack cakes

Ingredients for snack cake mix:
8½ cups all-purpose flour
2 tablespoons baking soda
1 tablespoon salt
5¼ cups white sugar

Directions:
Combine all ingredients in a large bowl and stir with a wire whisk until blended. Divide mixture evenly among 6 (2½ cup) containers with tight fitting lids. Each container should contain about 2¼ cups of mix. Makes enough for 6 cakes. Make sure you date the containers and use within 10 to 12 weeks.

Banana Walnut Snack Cake

YIELD: 1 cake

Ingredients:
1 package (2¼ cups) snack cake mix
1 egg
⅓ cup vegetable oil
½ cup ripe banana, mashed
½ cup milk
½ cup walnuts, chopped

Directions:
Preheat oven to 350°F. Pour 1 package (2¼ cups) snack cake mix into an ungreased 8 x 8-inch baking pan and set aside. In a small bowl, combine egg, oil, banana, milk, and walnuts. Beat with a fork until well blended, then stir into the snack cake mix in the pan until well blended. Bake 35 to 45 minutes until a knife or toothpick inserted into the middle comes out clean. Cool on a cooling rack. Makes 9 servings.

Gingerbread Snack Cake

YIELD: 1 cake

Ingredients:

1 package (2¼ cups) snack cake mix
¾ cup hot water
⅓ cup molasses
1 egg
⅓ cup vegetable oil
1 teaspoon cinnamon
1 teaspoon ginger
½ teaspoon ground cloves

Directions:

Preheat oven to 350°F. Pour 1 package (2¼ cups) snack cake mix into an ungreased 8 x 8-inch baking pan and set aside. In a medium bowl, combine hot water, molasses, egg, oil, cinnamon, ginger, and ground cloves. Beat with a fork until well blended, then stir into the snack cake mix in the pan until well blended. Bake 35 to 45 minutes until a knife or toothpick inserted into the middle comes out clean. Cool on a cooling rack. Makes 9 servings.

CHAPTER 21
Galley Hints

1. HOW TO MAKE BREAD CRUMBS

Dried bread crumbs:

1 slice dried bread = ¼ cup fine dry bread crumbs

4 slices dried bread = 1 cup fine dry bread crumbs

Dry bread crumbs are made from breads that have been baked or toasted to crisp them up. To dry bread, place on a baking sheet and put in a 300°F oven for twenty to thirty minutes until lightly golden brown. Be sure to allow the warm bread to cool before making the crumbs or your dry crumbs will become moist. Dry bread crumbs are most easily made in a food processor. Use a metal blade to make coarse crumbs or a grating blade to make finer crumbs. If you don't have a food processor, a standard hand grater will work. You can store dry bread crumbs in the freezer in an airtight container for up to three months.

Fresh bread crumbs:

1 slice fresh bread = ⅓ cup fresh bread crumbs

3 slices fresh bread = 1 cup fresh bread crumbs

Fresh bread crumbs are best when homemade and used immediately. The breads used to make soft or fresh bread crumbs are not quite as dry, so the crumbs are larger and produce a softer coating, crust, or stuffing. If you're making them by hand, cut the bread into small cubes or tear into small pieces. If you want finer bread crumbs, use a food processor on the small cubes or pieces.

Day-old or stale bread crumbs:

1 slice stale bread = ⅓ cup day-old bread crumbs.

3 slices stale bread = 1 cup day-old bread crumbs.

There is still too much moisture in day-old bread but it is not stale enough to make good bread crumbs, so I still put it in the oven to dry a bit more. Put the bread on a baking sheet and put in a 200°F oven for about 1 hour. Cool the bread on the counter before making your bread crumbs in a food processor or using a standard hand grater.

2. GELATIN

Always soften gelatin first in cold liquid, then dissolve in hot liquid. Don't boil as it will reduce its jelling power.

3. HOW TO SOUR MILK

To sour pasteurized milk when you need it for a recipe, add 1 tablespoon white vinegar or lemon juice to 1 cup of milk and let it stand at room temperature for ten to fifteen minutes, then stir gently.

4. YEAST

Yeast should be dissolved in warm (not hot) water and not more than 105°F degrees for cake yeast or 115°F for dry yeast.

5. BLANCHING & PEELING

Briefly blanching foods for one minute in boiling water will easily facilitate peeling or in some cases, the skins will just easily slip off.

6. TO FIX A CURDLED OR BROKEN HOLLANDAISE SAUCE:

To correct a sauce that has separated, whisk in a teaspoon or two of boiling water, one drop at a time. If that doesn't correct the sauce, put an egg yolk in a bowl and add the broken sauce slowly while beating with a whisk. It should make a nice creamy sauce in no time.

7. THICKENING GRAVIES OR SAUCES

When substituting cornstarch or arrowroot for flour as a thickener, use only half of the amount of flour called for in the recipe. Always cook your roux (the flour and butter mixture), a few minutes before adding the liquid. To prevent white sauce from lumping, it's best to have the milk hot when you add it to the roux.

8. CHECKING FOR SPOILED RAW OR HARD-BOILED EGGS

If you're not sure about the freshness of your raw eggs, gently lower them in a bowl of cool water. A stale or bad egg will float or tip upward in the bowl. When cracking eggs for use, crack only one egg at a time in a bowl, then transfer to another bowl. Too many times I've had the experience with eggs purchased in small villages or from a local islander and had to throw out all of my ingredients when I cracked the second or third egg into a bowl of ingredients and it was a bad egg. Not much more could be so offensive in a galley than throwing out perfectly good ingredients that were contaminated by bad. When a raw egg is cracked, if the white and yolk cling together, the egg is very fresh. The older the egg gets, the flatter the yolk becomes and the runnier the white.

It's happened to every cook I know that at one time or another they crack a raw egg, thinking it was a hardboiled egg. To check whether an egg is raw or hard-boiled, which seems like a no-brainer, but I promise you, it will come up, give the egg a gentle twirl on its side. A hard-boiled egg will spin nicely like a top, but a raw egg will make a sluggish uneven circle; it's the yolk inside bouncing from side to side and the raw white that causes it not to spin.

9. BEATING EGG WHITES & TEMPERING YOLKS

To successfully beat egg whites, always beat them at room temperature, not right out of the fridge. Use a clean, dry bowl and beaters. One egg white increases its volume to ½ cup when beaten and three egg whites will measure about 2⅔ cup or nine times their original volume.

Egg yolks should always be tempered by mixing them with a small amount of hot liquid before incorporating them into a hot sauce. Unless the sauce is bound by flour, don't let it boil again after the egg yolks have been added or they will curdle.

10. CANNING BUTTER

To can butter, use only the highest quality of butter like Land O'Lakes or equivalent. You'll need jelly jars with lids to equal the amount of butter you want to can. Wash jelly jars, rings, and seals and place on clean cloth to dry. Heat jelly jars in a 250°F oven for twenty minutes without the rings or seals. While jars are heating, melt butter slowly until it comes to a boil. Reduce the heat, cover, and simmer for five minutes. Pour melted butter carefully into heated jars. Do not get any butter on rim of jar. Add melted butter, put on the canning ring, and seal on each jar. They will seal as they cool. Shake jars a few times during cooling process to prevent separation. Put jars into refrigerator or other cool place until butter hardens. After it hardens, butter will store for three years.

11. BETTER PASTA

There are two great ways to enjoy tastier pasta, whether serving it alone as a side or dressing it with sauce. In a small saucepan, grate 1 large lemon with a fine grater and place in small saucepan. Cut the lemon in half, remove seeds, and squeeze juice and pulp out and add to the saucepan. Add 4 to 5 finely minced garlic cloves and 1 tablespoon olive oil. Stir well to blend and place on low heat. Cook pasta, preferably fettuccine, reserve ½ cup of pasta water, then drain pasta. Place drained pasta back into the pot, add ½ cup of reserved pasta cooking water, 1 tablespoon olive oil, then add the warm lemon and garlic mixture in the small saucepan and lightly toss to coat pasta. The second way to enjoy great pasta is to add a handful of Parmigiano-Reggiano cheese when pasta is cooked and drained; gently mix to coat pasta, then add your favorite sauce. Your pasta will be infused with a nice new layer of flavor.

12. POOR OLD IGNORED CELERY

When you have leftover celery, chop a few stalks along with their leaves, add some chopped onion, and gently cook until just barely soft. Add one can of tomatoes and serve as a side or as a slightly different pasta sauce. It's delicious.

13. USE YOUR SOCKS

If you're moving aboard full time or taking a short cruise, bring your socks; old and heavy are the best. Needless to say, glass containers are always a cause of concern aboard, but there are certain times and certain items, like a good bottle of wine, that comes in a glass container. If you put every bottle of wine into a thick sock, the chances of breakage are greatly reduced. We had a great bilge aboard *Native Sun* and found there were shallow areas which were always dry where we could store many bottles of wine—all in heavy old socks. We never had one bottle break, even in the heaviest of offshore sailing weather. We routinely stored pantry items that came in glass containers in socks, as well, but we found it necessary to write on the socks with a heavy marker to identify what was in each sock.

14. BARTER, BARTER, BARTER

The first time we cruised to Alaska, we were at anchor one afternoon when a large fishing vessel came into the harbor and anchored a short distance away. Almost immediately upon their anchoring, they called us on the VHF and said they would trade a nice salmon for some homemade chocolate chip cookies. What a barter that was! I got busy in the galley and made a few dozen cookies. When Stanley rowed over to give these fellows the cookies, they took one look at the cookies and selected a huge salmon for him to bring back. From that time on, we would call oystermen, shrimpers, and any type of vessel that looked like they might have a fresh catch aboard. We bartered many things, but chocolate chip cookies got us some of the sweetest and best seafood of every variety that we've ever had anywhere! We've also traded cans of mushroom soup for tomato soup or a loaf of bread for a dozen eggs. Once, when Stanley wasn't feeling up to par, we called on the VHF to any vessel in the anchorage who would trade something to help Stanley clean the bottom of *Native Sun*. This was probably our most unusual barter as the vessel that responded wanted to know if I could give the wife on board a perm. Though I'm nowhere near a hair dresser, we all agreed, and several hours later, the wife had a very pretty curly coif, *Native Sun* had a nice clean bottom, and everyone was pleased with the exchange. So again, consider bartering, especially if you find you've run out of a needed ingredient for your favorite recipe.

15. WATCH MENUS

On only one very long nineteen-day passage did we allow the watch crew to raid the refrigerator and pantry, but the results were that while we were off-watch, half a ham was eaten, as was a pound of cheese and many other items that had been inventoried and stored for future meals and recipes. After that, on the very few occasions that we had crew aboard, we compiled and printed up watch menus and very often prepared multiple meals to freeze and add to our watch menus.

16. STORING PAPER TOWELS AND TOILET PAPER

These big, round, bulky (but necessary) paper items can take up an inordinate amount of space, so we poked holes in the plastic wrappers to relieve the air, then we stood on them to flatten them out. We could store at least four times as many rolls of paper towels in the same cupboard with the flattened rolls than the off-the-shelf rolls.

17. LOOK, TASTE & ADJUST

All recipes do not come out the same each time you cook them. I've made hundreds of apple pies, for instance, and each is different in texture, moisture, sugar and spice content, and appearance. I have cooked all of the recipes within this book many times and I've seldom had the exact same outcome, even though I've followed the recipe as written. Using apple pie as an example, the differences comes from the variety of apples used, the size, freshness, and sugar content of the apples, and from subtle changes in spices used in the recipe. Sometimes I have fresh grated nutmeg to add and other times I only have bottled nutmeg. The dough can also be made exactly as written in the recipe, but can have different outcomes depending on something as simple as the temperature in your kitchen while you're rolling it out.

So again, I have to mention the necessity of tasting, watching, and adjusting flavors and sometimes even adding or subtracting from the primary ingredients such as adding more scallops to a dish if you're using bay scallops rather than sea scallops. While I am cooking, I always have a large pot or pan spoon set aside next to a smaller tasting spoon. I never dip my tasting spoon into a cooking dish as I don't want to contaminate it; care and cleanliness in my cooking is as important as the ingredients selected. I use the large pan spoon to transfer a small amount of the dish into the tasting spoon and then make my decisions as to adjusting flavors and ingredients as the dish progresses. I look at the food as it's cooking as well, whether it's on the BBQ, in the oven, or on the stove top. Times for cooking vary so much according to your stove. And what might take thirty minutes on my stove may well take twenty on your stove, so look, taste, adjust. Proper doneness is as important as the presentation of your wonderful meals.

CHAPTER 22
Freezing Foods

Many ingredients can be frozen and carried on board for months. In our freezer, we regularly had pestos, puff, phyllo and pie pastry dough, Philadelphia Cream Cheese, grated and hard cheeses, sour cream, butter, ricotta, crescent rolls, pearl onions and various other vegetables, lots of Kielbasa sausage, pork tenderloins, breakfast and bulk sausage, bulk hamburger, Cornish game hens, and lemon and lime juice. We packaged and froze just about anything that we didn't want to toss and still wanted to use in the months ahead such as opened canned tomato paste, as we seldom used a whole can in one recipe, so freezing was a great alternative to tossing. One of the things that we considered a real luxury was grapes. When we ate our fill of fresh grapes, on the few occasions we could find them anywhere other than the US, we put the remainder in re-sealable plastic bags. There is nothing more refreshing than popping a few frozen grapes in your mouth either on a hot day or for quick sweet treats while on watch. The red and purple grapes visually have the best results when frozen as the green grapes tend to change color a bit, but they are all taste-worthy. Some ingredients will lose consistency that might affect the visual appeal, but still will serve you well if mixed in recipes. Sour cream can be iffy as the texture will change so frozen sour cream is best used cooked in soups, stews, dips, and other dishes.

As you are cleaning veggies, chicken, or beef, keeping the meat and veggies separate of course, toss clean veggie pieces or peelings from such veggies as carrots, broccoli, etc. and bones and parts from cooked chicken or beef into a clearly marked re-sealable bag and store in the freezer. If you're cleaning raw meat and bones, such as when you're deboning a chicken breast or have pieces such as a neck from a whole chicken, boil those up quickly in just enough water to cover, cook, cool, and add to a re-sealable bag, saving the liquid in a tightly sealed container, and freeze. When a recipe calls for chicken or veggie stock or you simply want a flavorful broth for cooking, whether adding the water you're cooking potatoes in or even a ramen soup, boil up cooked parts and pieces of chicken with your saved veggies in enough water to cover and spices of your choice, or the same with cooked parts and pieces of meat and veggies.

If you have freezer room, it's such a shame to toss out healthy and useful ingredients, and once you begin using what so many people simply toss out, your freezer will quickly empty of these containers. As your freezer items are used, there is more air in your refrigerator, which causes more fridge charging time to keep things at your desired temperature, so it is most efficient to keep the freezer full. We carried an extra washable blanket plus a few pieces of closed foam material, such as Thinsulate (the same product that was used to insulate the hull of our boat), all of which we used to keep the freezer full. In both the fridge and freezer sections, we had small plastic coated wire baskets in several different sizes. This helped us with organization, which saves on cold air in your fridge/freezer. The less time you have the fridge or freezer area open, especially in the hot tropics, the better, so if you're looking for hard cheese, cream cheese, butter, chicken, meat, seafood, or re-sealable bags with various frozen items in them, you'll know that they're all in the same area and sorted by item. When we packed our freezer, or brought in new grocery items, we sorted everything on the countertop first and placed the items we would not be using for a while on the bottom and items we intended to use first on top.

CHAPTER 23
Basic Vegetable Cooking Methods & Suggested Times

VEGETABLE	MICROWAVE COOKING	STEAMED METHOD	BOILING
Asparagus	2–4 minutes	8–10 minutes	Not recommended
Beans	3–4 minutes	5–8 minutes	6–8 minutes
Beets	9–12 minutes	40–60 minutes	30–60 minutes
Bok Choy	2–4 minutes	Stalks: 6 minutes	Stalks: 3–4 minutes Leaves: 2–3 minutes Leaves: 1½ minutes
Broccoli florets	2–3 minutes	5–6 minutes	4–6 minutes
Brussels sprouts	4–6 minutes	8–10 minutes	5–7 minutes
Cabbage, cut	5–6 minutes	5–8 minutes	5–10 minutes
Carrots, sliced	4–5 minutes	4–5 minutes	5–10 minutes
Cauliflower	2–3 minutes	3–5 minutes	4–6 minutes

****

Corn on the cob (1)	1–2 minutes	4–7 minutes	5–8 minutes

****

Eggplant, sliced	2–4 minutes	5–6 minutes	Not recommended

****

Mushrooms	2–3 minutes	4–5 minutes	Not recommended

****

Peas	2–3 minutes	4–5 minutes	8–12 minutes

****

Peppers, sweet	2–3 minutes	2–4 minutes	Not recommended

****

Potatoes, sliced	6–8 minutes	10–12 minutes	15–20 minutes

****

Potatoes, whole (pierced)	8–10 minutes	Not recommended	Depends on size

****

Spinach	1–2 minutes	5–6 minutes	2–5 minutes

****

Zucchini, sliced	2–3 minutes	4–6 minutes	3–5 minutes

****

CHAPTER 24
Food Equivalents & Substitutions

Amount	Ingredients	Substitution
1 tsp.	Allspice	½ tsp. cinnamon, ¼ tsp. ginger, ¼ tsp. cloves, and 5 whole allspice berries
1 tsp.	Almond extract	2 tsp. vanilla extract or 1 tsp. almond flavored extract like Amaretto
2⅓ tbsp.	Apple pie spice	4 tsp. ground cinnamon, 2 tsp. ground nutmeg, 1 tsp. ground allspice
1 tsp.	Baking powder	¼ tsp. baking soda and ½ tsp. cream of tartar or ¼ tsp. baking soda and ½ cup buttermilk (decrease liquid in recipe by ½ cup)
1 tbsp.	Balsamic vinegar	Mix 1 tbsp. apple cider or red wine vinegar with ½ tsp. brown sugar or honey
1 cube	Bouillon cube	1 cup beef broth for beef or 1 cup chicken broth for chicken
1 cup	Bread crumbs	1 cup cracker crumbs or 1 cup Progresso crumbs
1 cup	Broth (beef or chicken)	1 bouillon cube and 1 cup boiling water or 1 tbsp. soy sauce and enough water to make 1 cup or 1 cup vegetable broth
1 cup	Butter (salted)	1 cup margarine or 1 cup shortening and ½ tsp. salt or $7/8$ cup vegetable oil and ½ tsp. salt or $7/8$ cup lard and ½ tsp. salt
1 cup	Butter (unsalted)	1 cup shortening or $7/8$ cup vegetable oil or $7/8$ cup lard
1 cup	Buttermilk	1 cup yogurt or 1 tbsp. lemon juice or vinegar and enough milk to make 1 cup

1 tbsp.	Cardamom	Mix together equal parts cinnamon and nutmeg to equal 1 tbsp. total
1 tbsp.	Celery salt	1 part celery seed, 2 parts salt, grind celery seed with a spice grinder, mortar and pestle, or food processor, combine with salt, and mix well
1 cup	Cheese (cream)	1 cup puréed cottage cheese or 1 cup plain yogurt, strained overnight in cheesecloth
8 ounces	Cheese (farmer's)	8 ounces dry cottage cheese or 8 ounces creamed cottage cheese, drained
½ cup, grated	Cheese (Parmesan)	½ cup grated Asiago cheese or ½ cup grated Romano cheese
1 cup	Cheese (ricotta)	1 cup dry cottage cheese or 1 cup silken tofu or 1 cup homemade ricotta (see recipe on pg. 391)
1 tbsp. chopped (fresh)	Chervil	1 tbsp. chopped fresh parsley
1 tbsp.	Chicken base	1 cup canned or homemade chicken broth or stock, reduce liquid in recipe by 1 cup
3 tbsp.	Chocolate (Dutch-processed)	Equal amount of unsweetened cocoa powder and ⅛ tsp. baking soda for every 3 tbsp. cocoa powder
1 ounce	Chocolate (unsweetened)	3 tbsp. unsweetened cocoa and 1 tbsp. shortening or vegetable oil
1 ounce	Chocolate (Mexican)	Equal amount semi-sweet chocolate or cocoa powder, then add ½ tsp. ground cinnamon and 1 drop almond extract for every ounce of chocolate
1 tsp.	Cloves	Use a 50-50 blend of cinnamon and nutmeg
1 tbsp.	Cornstarch	Replace cornstarch in your recipe with double the amount of all-purpose flour
1 cup	Corn syrup (light)	Substitute 1 cup sugar and ¼ cup water
1 cup	Corn syrup (dark)	Substitute 1 cup packed brown sugar and ¼ cup water

1 cup	Cream (half and half)	7/8 cup milk and 1 tbsp. butter
1 cup	Cream (heavy)	1 cup evaporated milk or ¾ cup milk and ⅓ cup butter
1 cup	Cream (light)	1 cup evaporated milk or ¾ cup milk and 3 tbsp. butter
1 cup	Cream (whipped)	1 cup frozen whipped topping, thawed
1 tsp.	Cream of tartar	2 tsp. lemon juice or vinegar
1 cup	Crème fraiche	Combine 1 cup heavy cream and 1 tbsp. plain yogurt and let stand for 6 hours at room temperature
3 tbsps. or 1.7 ounces	Egg, 1 whole	2½ tbsps. powdered egg substitute and 2½ tbsp. water or 3 tbsp. mayonnaise or half a banana mashed with ½ tsp. baking powder or ¼ cup liquid egg substitute
1 cup	Evaporated milk	1 cup light cream
1 cup	Fats (for baking)	1 cup applesauce or 1 cup fruit purée
1 cup	Flour (bread)	1 cup all-purpose flour and 1 tsp. wheat gluten (available health food stores)
1 cup	Flour (cake)	1 cup minus 2 tbsp. all-purpose flour
1 cup	Flour (pastry)	½ cup all-purpose flour and ½ cup cake flour or two tbsp. corn starch combined with enough all-purpose flour to make 1 cup
1 cup	Flour (self-rising)	7/8 cup all-purpose flour and 1½ tsp. baking powder and ½ tsp. salt
1 clove	Garlic	⅛ tsp. garlic powder or ½ tsp. granulated garlic or ½ tsp. garlic salt
1 tbsp.	Garlic (salt)	Mix three parts salt to one part garlic powder to equal 1 tbsp.
1 tbsp., granulated	Gelatin	2 tsp. agar agar
1 tsp.	Ginger (dry)	2 tsp. chopped fresh ginger

1 tsp., minced	Ginger (fresh)	½ tsp. ground dried ginger
½ cup, chopped	Green onion	½ cup chopped onion or ½ cup chopped leek or ½ cup chopped shallots
1 cup. whole	Hazelnuts	1 cup macadamia nuts or 1 cup almonds
1 tbsp. chopped (fresh)	Herbs (fresh)	1 tsp. (chopped or whole leaf) dried herbs
8 ounces	Herring	8 ounces sardines
1 cup	Honey	1¼ cups white sugar and ⅓ cup water or 1 cup corn syrup or 1 cup Karo syrup
1 tsp.	Hot pepper sauce	¾ tsp. cayenne pepper and 1 tsp. vinegar
1 cup	Ketchup	1 cup tomato sauce and 1 tsp. vinegar and 1 tbsp. sugar
1 cup	Lard	1 cup shortening or 7/8 cup vegetable oil or 1 cup butter
2 fresh stalks	Lemon grass	1 tbsp. lemon zest
1 tsp.	Lemon juice	½ tsp. vinegar or 1 tsp. white wine or 1 tsp. lime juice
1 tsp.	Lemon zest	½ tsp. lemon extract or 2 tbsp. lemon juice
1 tsp.	Lime juice	1 tsp. vinegar or 1 tsp. white wine or 1 tsp. lemon juice
1 tsp.	Lime zest	1 tsp. lemon zest
1 cup	Macadamia nuts	1 cup almonds or 1 cup hazelnuts
1 tsp.	Mace	1 tsp. nutmeg
1 cup	Margarine	1 cup shortening and ½ tsp. salt or 1 cup butter or 7/8 cup vegetable oil and ½ tsp. salt or 7/8 cup lard and ½ tsp. salt
1 tsp.	Marjoram	Closest substitute is 1 tsp. oregano
1 cup	Mayonnaise	1 cup sour cream or 1 cup plain yogurt
1 (12 ounce) can (1½ cups)	Milk (evaporated)	Mix 1 cup non-fat dry milk (powdered milk) and 1 ⅛ cup water until all powder has dissolved

1 cup	Milk (sour)	1 tbsp. vinegar or lemon juice mixed with enough milk to make 1 cup, let stand 5 minutes to thicken
1 (14 ounce) can	Milk (sweetened condensed)	¾ cup white sugar mixed with ½ cup water and 1 ⅛ cup dry powdered milk, bring to a boil and cook, stirring frequently until thickened, about 20 minutes
1 cup	Milk (whole)	1 cup soy milk or 1 cup rice milk or 1 cup water or juice or ¼ cup dry milk powder and 1 cup water or ⅔ cup evaporated milk and ⅓ cup water
¼ cup, chopped	Mint (fresh)	1 tbsp. dried mint leaves
1 cup	Molasses	Mix ¾ cup brown sugar and 1 tsp. cream of tartar
1 tbsp.	Mustard, prepared	Mix together 1 tbsp. dried mustard, 1 tsp. water, 1 tsp. vinegar, and 1 tsp. sugar
1 tsp.	Nutmeg	Replace the nutmeg in your recipe with an equal amount of mace
1 cup chopped	Onion	1 cup chopped green onions or 1 cup chopped shallots or 1 cup chopped leeks or ¼ cup dried minced onion or ¼ cup onion powder
1 tbsp.	Orange juice	1 tbsp. other citrus juice
1 tbsp.	Orange zest	½ tsp. orange extract or 1 tsp. lemon juice
1 tsp.	Oregano	1 tsp. marjoram
1 pint	Oysters	About 24 oysters
1 tbsp., chopped (fresh)	Parsley	1 tbsp. chopped fresh chervil or 1 tsp. dried parsley
1 tsp.	Peppercorns (black)	For every 8 peppercorns, use ⅛ tsp. ground pepper or if measuring peppercorns in a measuring spoon, replace peppercorns measure for measure with ground black pepper
1 ounce	Pepperoni	1 ounce salami

1 tsp.	Pumpkin pie spice	Mix ½ tsp. ground cinnamon, ¼ tsp. ginger, ⅛ tsp. nutmeg, and ⅛ tsp. ground cloves
1 cup	Raisin	1 cup dried currants or 1 cup dried cranberries or 1 cup chopped pitted prunes
1 cup, cooked	Rice (white)	1 cup cooked barley or 1 cup cooked bulgur or 1 cup cooked brown or wild rice
1 tbsp.	Rum	½ tsp. rum extract and enough water to make 1 tbsp.
¼ tsp.	Saffron	¼ tsp. turmeric
2 tbsp.	Sake	2 tbsp. rice wine vinegar or dry sherry or vermouth or dry white wine
1 ounce	Salami	1 ounce pepperoni
½ cup	Shallots (chopped)	½ cup chopped onion or ½ cup chopped leek or ½ cup chopped green onion
1 cup	Shortening	1 cup butter or 1 cup margarine minus ½ tsp. salt from recipe
½ cup	Soy sauce	¼ cup Worcestershire sauce mixed with 1 tbsp. water
1 cup	Stock, beef or chicken	1 cube beef or chicken bouillon dissolved in 1 cup water
1 cup, packed	Sugar (brown)	1 cup white sugar and ¼ cup molasses and decrease the liquid in recipe by ¼ cup or 1 cup white sugar or 1¼ cups confectioner's sugar
1 tbsp.	Sugar (castor or super fine)	In a food processor or blender, pulse 1 tbsp. granulated sugar until it reaches a super-fine consistency but not powdery
1 cup	Tapioca (instant)	1 cup arrowroot, cornstarch or wheat flour can be substituted
1 cup	Vegetable oil (for frying)	1 cup lard or 1 cup vegetable shortening
1 tsp.	Vinegar	1 tsp. lemon or lime juice or 2 tsp. white wine

1 cup	White sugar	1 cup brown sugar or 1¼ cups confectioner's sugar or ¾ cup honey or ¾ cup corn syrup
1 cup	Wine (red)	1 cup beef broth or unsweetened cranberry juice or red grape juice
1 cup	Wine (white)	1 cup chicken broth or apple juice or white grape juice
1¼-ounce package	Yeast, active, dry	1 cup compressed yeast or 2½ tsp. active dry yeast or 2½ tsp. rapid rise yeast
1 cup	Yogurt	1 cup sour cream or 1 cup buttermilk or 1 cup sour milk

CHAPTER 25
Cooking Conversions, Equivalents, Volumes & Temperatures

Dry Volume Measurements (US Equivalents)

$1/16$ teaspoon	= dash
Less than ⅛ teaspoon	= a pinch
1 teaspoon	= ⅓ tablespoon
1 tablespoon	= 3 teaspoons
2 tablespoons	= ⅛ cup or 1 standard coffee scoop or 1 ounce
4 tablespoons	= ¼ cup
5 tablespoons +1 teaspoon	= ⅓ cup
8 tablespoons	= ½ cup or 4 ounces
10 tablespoons + 2 teaspoons	= ⅔ cup
12 tablespoons	= ¾ cup
16 tablespoons	= 1 cup
4 pecks	= 1 bushel
1 pound	= 16 ounces
8 quarts	= 1 peck or 7¼ kilograms

Liquid Volume Measurements (US):

1 cup	= 8 fluid ounces. or ½ pint or 16 tablespoons
2 cups	= 1 pint or 16 fluid ounces
4 cups	= 2 pints or 1 quart
16 cups	= 1 gallon or 4 quarts or 32 ounces
1 dash	= 3 to 6 drops
1 jigger	= 3 tablespoons or 1½ ounces
4 quarts	=1 gallon or 3¼ liters
1 tablespoon	= ½ fluid ounce
2 tablespoons	= 1 fluid ounce
1 teaspoon	= ⅓ tablespoon

US to Metric Conversions:

$1/5$ teaspoon	= 1 ml
1 teaspoon	= 5 ml
1 tablespoon	= 15 ml
1 fluid ounce	= 29.5 ml
$1/5$ cup	= 47 ml
1 cup	= 236.5 ml
2 cups (or 1 pint)	= 470 ml
4 cups (or 1 quart)	= .95 liter
4 quarts (or 1 gallon)	= 3.8 liters
1 ounce	= 28 grams
1 pound	= 454 grams

Metric to US Conversions:

1 milliliter	= $^1/_5$ teaspoon
5 ml	= 1 teaspoon
15 ml	= 1 tablespoon
30 ml	= 1 fluid ounce
100 ml	= 3.4 fluid ounces
240 ml	= 1 cup
1 liter	= 34 fluid ounces
1 liter	= 4.2 cups
1 liter	= 2.1 pints
1 liter	= 1.06 quarts
1 liter	= .26 gallon
1 gram	= .035 ounce
100 grams	= 3.5 ounces
500 grams	= 1.10 ounces
1 kilogram	= 35 ounces

Pan Size Equivalents:

9 x 13-inch baking dish	= 22 x 33-centimeter baking dish
8 x 8-inch baking dish	= 20 x 20-centimeter baking dish
9 x 5-inch loaf pan	= 23 x 12-centimeter loaf pan (8 cups or 2 liters in capacity)
10-inch tart or cake pan	= 25-centimeter tart or cake pan
9-inch cake pan	= 22-centimeter cake pan

Oven Temperature Conversions:

275°F	=140°C
300°F	=150°C
325°F	=165°C
350°F	=180°C
375°F	=190°C
400°F	=200°C
425°F	=220°C
450°F	=230°C
475°F	=240°C

Stovetop Temperature Definitions:

180ºF	(85ºC)	= simmering point of water
212ºF	(100ºC)	= boiling point of water
234ºF–240ºF	(115ºC)	= soft-ball stage for syrups
290ºF–310ºF	(143º–155ºC)	= hard-crack stage for syrups
320ºF	(160ºC)	= caramel stage for syrups
220ºF	(180ºC)	= jellying point for jams and jellies

Oven Temperature Definitions:

250ºF	(120ºC)	= very low, slow cooking temperature
300ºF	(150ºC)	= low, slow cooking temperature
325ºF	(165ºC)	= moderately slow cooking temperature
350ºF	(180ºC)	= moderate cooking temperature
375ºF	(190ºC)	= moderately hot cooking temperature
400ºF	(205ºC)	= hot cooking temperature
450ºF–500ºF	(230ºC– 260ºC)	= very hot cooking temperature

Oven Roasting Temperatures:

Beef: Thermometer in the center, do not touch the bone

130ºF	(54ºC)	= rare
160ºF	(71ºC)	= medium
180ºF	(82ºC)	= well done

Lamb: Thermometer in the center, do not touch the bone

140ºF	(60ºC)	= pink
145ºF	(63ºC)	= medium-rare
165ºF	(74ºC)	= well done

Pork: Thermometer in the center, do not touch the bone
160ºF (74ºC)

Poultry: Thermometer in the center, do not touch the bone
170ºF (77ºC) - chicken in the breast
185ºF (85ºC) - chicken in the thigh
180ºF (82ºC) - duck in the thigh

Veal: Thermometer in the center, do not touch the bone
160ºF (74ºC)

Equivalents:

¾ cup bread crumbs (dry)	= 4 sandwich slices
2 cup bread crumbs (fresh)	= 4 sandwich slices
1 stick butter	= ½ cup or 8 tablespoons or 4 ounces
2 sticks butter	= 1 cup or ½ pound or 8 ounces
6 carrots (sliced)	= 3 cups or 1 pound
6 carrots (puréed)	= 1 ⅓ cups or 1 pound
8 ounces cheese, cream	= 1 cup
¼ pound cheese, grated	= 1 cup
1 chocolate square	= 1 ounce
1 (3½ ounce) coconut (canned, shredded)	= 1⅓ cup
4 cups confectioner's sugar	= 1 pound
1 cup cornmeal (polenta)	= 4½ ounces
1 pound crabmeat	= 2 cups
1 pint cream, heavy	= 4 cup whipped
1 egg, large	= ¼ cup or 4 tablespoons or 2 ounces
1 egg, white	= 2 tablespoons plus 2 teaspoons
1 egg, yolk	= 1 tablespoons plus 1 teaspoon
1 cup flour	= 5 ounces
1 pound flour	= 4 cups sifted flour
⅛ teaspoon garlic powder	= 1 small clove
¼ –½ teaspoon herbs, dried	= 1 tablespoon fresh
1 lemon	= 2 to 3 tablespoons juice and 2 teaspoons rind
½ pound mushrooms (sliced, fresh)	= 2½ cups
1 pound mushrooms (sliced, fresh)	= 8 ounces, canned
4 ounces nuts (chopped)	= ¾ cup
4 ounces nuts (ground)	= 1 cup loosely packed
3 onions, medium (sliced or chopped)	= 3 cups or 1 pound
1 orange	= ½ cup juice and 2–3 teaspoons rind
3 potatoes (raw, sliced, or chopped)	= small to medium, 3 cups or 1 pound
1 cup sugar (brown)	= 6 ounces
⅔ cup sugar (brown)	= 1 pound
1 pound sugar (granulated)	= 2 cups or 16 ounces
1 cup sugar (powdered)	= 4½ ounces
1 pound walnuts	= 3½ cups

Canned Bean to Cooked Bean Equivalents:

14–16 ounce can	= 1.5 cup cooked beans
19 ounce can	= 2.25 cup cooked beans
28 ounce can	= 3–3¼ cup cooked beans

Dry Bean & Lentil Equivalents:

½ pound dry beans (most kinds) or lentils	= 3 cups fully cooked and drained chickpeas
1 pound dry beans (most kinds) or lentils	= 6–7 cups cooked beans, drained
1 pound dry beans (most kinds) or lentils	= about 2 cups dry beans
1 cup dry beans (most kinds) or lentils	= 3 cups cooked beans
⅔ cup dry beans (most kinds) or lentils	= 2 cups cooked beans
½ cup dry beans (most kinds) or lentils	= 1½ cups cooked beans
⅓ cup dry beans (most kinds) or lentils	= 1 cup cooked beans

Can Size Equivalents:

Can Size	Can Ounces	CUP Measurement
8 ounces	8 ounces	1 cup
12-ounce vacuum	12 ounces	1½ cups
Baby food jar	3½ to 8 ounces	depends on size
Condensed milk	15 ounces	1⅓ cups
Evaporated milk	6 ounces	⅔ cup
Frozen juice concentrate	6 ounces	¾ cup

Shortening, Butter, Cheese & Other Solid Fats Conversion Measurements:

Spoons & Cups	Stick	Ounces	Grams:
1 tablespoon	⅛ stick	½ ounce	15 grams
2 tablespoons	¼ stick	1 ounce	30 grams
4 tablespoons (¼ cup)	½ stick	2 ounces	60 grams
8 tablespoons (½ cup)	1 stick (¼ pound)	4 ounces	115 grams
16 tablespoons (1 cup)	2 sticks (½ pound)	8 ounces	225 grams
32 tablespoons (2 cups)	4 sticks (1 pound)	16 ounces	500 grams (½ kilogram)

Flour (Un-sifted) Measurements:

Spoons & Cups	Ounces	Grams
1 tablespoon	¼ ounce	8.75 grams
4 tablespoons (¼ cup)	1¼ ounces	35 grams
5 tablespoons (⅓ cup)	1½ ounces	45 grams
½ cup	2½ ounces	70 grams
⅔ cup	3¼ ounces	90 grams
¾ cup	3½ ounces	105 grams
1 cup	5 ounces	140 grams
1½ cups	7½ ounces	210 grams
2 cups	10 ounces	280 grams
3½ cups (1 pound)	16 ounces	490 grams

Granulated Sugar Measurements:

Spoons & Cups	Ounces	Grams
1 teaspoon	$^1/_6$ ounce	5 grams
1 tablespoon	½ ounce	15 grams
4 tablespoons (¼ cup)	1¾ ounces	60 grams
5 tablespoons (⅓ cup)	2¼ ounces	75 grams
½ cup	3½ ounces	100 grams
⅔ cup	4½ ounces	130 grams
¾ cup	5 ounces	150 grams
1 cup	7 ounces	200 grams
1½ cups	9½ ounces	300 grams
2 cups	13½ ounces	400 grams

About The Author

Sylvia Williams Dabney, with her husband Stanley, sailed some sixty thousand offshore miles during their fifteen years living aboard. She holds a 100 Ton United States Coast Guard Masters License and has been a charter captain in the Caribbean for over six years, entertaining and cooking for the thousands of guests who sailed aboard their *Valiant 40, Native Sun*. She piloted the Water Island Ferry as well as *The Saint*, a large commercial ferry taking US navy sailors to and from shore leave while anchored in St. Thomas Harbor.

Having spent several years in the corporate world after graduating from university, her eclectic background over the past thirty years has included food service and hospitality management. She has contributed to and helped edit and market several cookbooks and has managed an historic resort inn and restaurant on Lake Superior where she directed the staff in all departments, managed the kitchen, created menus, and catered special events. Her love of cooking and culinary experimenting came from a childhood filled with moms who collected and tried new recipes every day, and who shared and guided her in the pleasure and art of cooking and entertaining.

Sylvia has been a member of Boating Writers International for thirty years and has written articles, reviews, newsletters, and gazettes for sailing industry publications including *Valiant World* and *Cedar Mills & Pelicans' Landing* newspaper in Texas.

About The Illustrator

Roger H. Newell, AIA, the sketch artist for this book, was Stanley's roommate and fraternity brother at the University of Washington. He is a renowned architect and, in fact, designed our home in Chelan, Washington. We all have been friends for forty-five-plus years and he's my best guy "girlfriend." (Kind of an odd term, but we can't think of anything else to call each other.) We've just been such good friends since we met when I was nineteen that we've always told each other everything, shared our secrets, laughed when no one else thought something was funny, and cried together through marriages, births, deaths, and everything in between. You can Google Roger H. Newell, AIA and see the many beautiful homes and buildings he has designed.

Roger's hobby is sketching, and when I officiated at his son's wedding, he created four large colored sketches for me of the places he's seen in Europe; they are beautiful and hang in the main hallway of our home. He often sends calendars and packs of notecards of his sketches as little gifts to us and each is such a pleasure to look at that after years and years, I can't bear to toss out one of his calendars. His other hobby is sailing, having had a classic *Blanchard 40* for many years. He first sailed with us, bought a smaller Blanchard within months of that first sail as many of our friends have done, and now sails with his wife and teenage grandchildren on board their classic wooden sailboat *Arroyo*. Every year he sails his beautiful boat to the Port Townsend Wooden Sailboat Show where people just stand and stare at this gorgeous, professionally kept, classic sailboat. Roger spares no expense in keeping his *Blanchard 40* in nearly museum quality condition.

He cooks, he makes and flies model planes (the kind that really have motors and you can fly), and he fishes for salmon with great success. He's always supported anything that either Stanley or I have done with such love and passion, and a friend like Roger is a once in a lifetime relationship. Roger asked if I'd like his sketches for this cookbook, so I am proud to include his beautiful sketches throughout these pages and I hope you enjoy the talent of Roger H. Newell as much as I do.

Acknowledgments

Many thanks to all the boating friends who shared meals, recipes, stories, and many wonderful days during our cruising years. We have loved every moment of these magical times with magical people who traveled from all over the world and who somehow crossed our path. Each has been a blessing in our lives.

Huge thanks to our dear friend and Stanley's fraternity brother, Roger H. Newell (AIA), who spent many hours creating the beautiful sketches for this book and who has supported me throughout this process.

Special thanks to Steve Stresau who, along with his lovely wife, Karen, has taken beautiful photos on their sailing journey and who immediately said yes when asked if I could use his gorgeous photo of Orchid Bay in the book.

My greatest appreciation to my editor Nicole Mele at Skyhorse Publishing for the many hours of reading *every* word, making suggestions, guiding me, and bringing my words together to create a real book. I am very grateful to her and for her patience through this long process.

And lastly, the greatest thanks, appreciation, and love to my husband, Stanley, who loves and encourages me through all things and who has willingly been my "test kitchen" for so many years!

Recipe Index